IF BORROWED AT DUBBO, PLEASE
REFER TO PRINTED RECEIPT FOR
DATE DUE.

FRANK HARDY

and the making of
Power Without Glory

FRANK HARDY

and the making of
Power Without Glory

Macquarie
Regional Library

PAULINE ARMSTRONG

MELBOURNE UNIVERSITY PRESS

MELBOURNE UNIVERSITY PRESS
PO Box 278, Carlton South, Victoria 3053, Australia
info@mup.unimelb.edu.au
www.mup.com.au

First published 2000
Text © Pauline Armstrong 2000
Design and typography © Melbourne University Press 2000

Designed by Sandra Nobes
Printed in Australia by Brown Prior Anderson

National Library of Australia Cataloguing-in-Publication entry

Armstrong, Pauline.
    Frank Hardy and the making of Power Without Glory.
    Bibliography.
    Includes index.
    ISBN 0 522 84888 5.
    1. Hardy, Frank (Francis Joseph), 1917–1994. Power without glory.
    2. Hardy, Frank (Francis Joseph), 1917–1994—Biography.
    3. Authors, Australian—20th century—Biography. I. Title.
A 823.3

Publication of this book was assisted by a special publications grant from the University of Melbourne Publications Sub-Committee.

In loving memory of Liri Armstrong, 1973–1987,
Deborah Lloyd, 1957–1994,
and Julie Peaslee, 1953–1999.

CONTENTS

ILLUSTRATIONS

Studley Hall, former residence of the late John Wren and family.
Photo by Bruce Armstrong.

A young Paul Mortier, *c.* 1935.
Photo courtesy of the late Tom Kavanagh.

Staff of the Australian Army Education Service magazine, *Salt*, Melbourne,
c. late 1944–45.
Photo courtesy of Vane Lindesay.

'The young revolutionaries'. Eureka Youth League gathering, Kelvin Hall,
winter 1944.
Photo courtesy of Michael Marmach.

The young John Wren.
Photo courtesy of Niall Brennan and the Hill of Content Publishing
Co. Pty Ltd.

Ticket-sellers at John Wren's Tote were disguised against police informers.
Drawing courtesy of Niall Brennan and the Hill of Content Publishing
Co. Pty Ltd.

Police raid on John Wren's Tote.
Drawing courtesy of Niall Brennan and the Hill of Content Publishing
Co. Pty Ltd.

Ralph Gibson, Victorian Executive, CPA, *c.* 1940.
Photo courtesy of John Sendy.

Ted Hill, Victorian Executive, CPA.
Photo courtesy of Hugh Anderson.

Cedric Ralph, solicitor for the CPA.
Photo courtesy of Cedric Ralph.

Deirdre Moore (née Cable), 1945, early member of the Realist Writers' Group.
Photo courtesy of Deirdre Moore.

255 Bridge Road, Richmond, location of Frank Hardy's rented room.
Photo by Bruce Armstrong.

Entrance to Frank Hardy's rented room (upstairs), 255A Bridge Road,
Richmond.
Photo by Bruce Armstrong.

George Seelaf, Secretary of the Butchers' Union and close associate of Frank
Hardy.
Photo courtesy of Hugh Anderson.

Frank Hardy talks with Eureka Youth League members at Camp Eureka, Yarra
Junction, *c.* 1949.
Photo courtesy of Michael Marmach.

Les Barnes and Vic Little.
Photo by Bruce Armstrong.

J. B. Miles, National Secretary of the CPA.
Photo courtesy of Hugh Anderson.

Richard (Dick) Dixon, National President of the CPA.
Photo courtesy of Hugh Anderson.

Ted Hill (left) and Rick Oke with Mao Tse-Tung, *c.* 1964.
Photo supplied by Bruce Armstrong.

The Frank Hardy Defence Committee.
Photo from the *Guardian*, 23 November 1950.

Melbourne writers entertain visiting delegation of Eastern European writers, *c.* 1956–57.
Photo courtesy of the University of Melbourne Archives.

Alvie Booth, organiser for the Frank Hardy Defence Committee.
Photo by Bruce Armstrong.

Yevgeny Yevtushenko, poet.
Photo courtesy of Hugh Anderson.

A night at Dirty Dick's Elizabethan Rooms, Sydney, *c.* 1972.
Photo courtesy of Eva Jago.

Eva Jago dining with Frank Hardy, *c.* 1972.
Photo courtesy of Eva Jago.

George Kirkland, a central character in Frank Hardy's novel *Who Shot George Kirkland?*
Photo in *Police Gazette*, 26 July 1924, courtesy of the Victoria Police Historical Unit.

Frank Hardy speaking at the Centenary Celebrations of St Bernard's School, Bacchus Marsh, 5–6 May 1990.
Photo courtesy of the late Laurie Wheelahan, curator of the Blessed Mary McKillop Museum, Bacchus Marsh.

ACKNOWLEDGEMENTS

IN WRITING THIS biography, I was greatly assisted by the many people who shared their experiences and opinions with me. To each I extend my sincere thanks.

Paul Adams, Phillip Adams, Dawn Anderson, Hugh Anderson, Shirley Andrews, Bruce Armstrong, Karl Armstrong, the late John Arrowsmith, the late Bill Barnes, the late Les Barnes, Thelma Barnes, Jack Blake, Alex Boag, the late Beryl Boag, Alvie Booth, Mick Bourke, Mona Brand, Niall Brennan, the late Ted Bull, Jim Cairns, Geoffrey Camm, Sue Camm, Carlo Canteri, Eileen Capocchi, Clem Christesen, Betty Collins, Nadine Dalgarno, Zelda D'Aprano, Ralph de Boissiere, Vera Deacon, Vance Dickie, the late Hume Dow, the late Frances Driscoll (née Hardy), the late Fred Farrall, the late Mervyn Feehan, Mary Fiorini-Lowell, Len Fox, John Fraser, Len Gale, Ann Godden, the late Sam Goldbloom, Malcolm Good, the late Maclaren Gordon, Jim Griffin, Alan Hardy, Jim Hardy, Shirley Hardy-Rix, June Hearn, Albie Heintz, Joan Hendry, Dorothy Hewett, Margaret Hutton, Bill Irving, the late Nancy Irving, Eva Jago, Walter Kaufmann, Cedric King, John Lamp, Merv Lilley, Vane Lindesay, Vic Little, Wendy Lowenstein, the late Ian Mair, the late Kath McFarland, the late Bruce McKissack, Ruby McKissack, Jack McPhillips, the late Peter Miller, Deirdre Moore, the late John Morrison, Dulcie Mortier, Nikki Mortier, Ron Neave, Sharon Nicholson, Bert Nolan, Alan Oliver, Nick Pagonis, Shirley Pinnell, Graham Pitts, Cedric Ralph, the late B. A. Santamaria, Frank Scully, Carmel Shea, Carmel Shute, the late Ted Seedsman, W. G. (Bill) Smith, Eric Stark, June Stephens, Rose Stone, Beverley Symons, Bernie Taft, Dot Thompson, Fred Thompson, Ted Thompson, Don Tonkin, the late Ali Verrills, the late Ray Verrills, Alf Walton, Bill Wannan, the late Joseph Waters, Vic Williams, Colin Yarsley, Joan Younger.

I wish to thank the librarians and staffs of the Australian Broadcasting Corporation Archives, Sydney; City of Whitehorse Library (Box Hill); City of Boroondara Library (Camberwell); Carringbush Regional Library (Collingwood); Footscray Municipal Library; Baillieu Library, University of Melbourne; Australian Special Research Collection, University College, the University of New South Wales, Australian Defence Force Academy; Mitchell Library, State

Library of New South Wales; City of Monash Library; Monash University Library; Manuscript Library, Australian Collections and Services, Newspaper Collection and Oral History Collection, National Library of Australia; Arts Library and La Trobe Newspaper Collection, State Library of Victoria; Victorian State Parliamentary Library; Sydney University Library; the Literature Board of the Australia Council; City of Townsville Library.

My special thanks to those people and organisations who gave permission for the reproduction of photographs and illustrations, and to those who gave or loaned newspapers, books, documents, audio and video cassettes, or leaflets for photocopying, and to those who sent replies to questionnaires and requests for information. Allansford and District Primary School History Sub-Committee (Marie Ziebell); Lyle Allan; the late Gough Armstrong; Gerry Barretto, Student Administration, University of Melbourne; Marie Boyce, Beverley Brennan, archivist, St Brendan's Catholic Church, Kilmore; Michael Cannon; Council of Adult Education; Phillip Deery; Fawkner Crematorium and Memorial Park; Grace Gale; Brother Gerard of the Treacy Centre, Christian Brothers College, Parkville; Hill of Content Publishing Company Pty Ltd; Father Michael Linehan, church of the Infant Jesus, Koroit; Margaret Love, St Bernard's Catholic Church, Bacchus Marsh; the late Laurie McCalman; John McLaren; Carmel Moore; Dave Nadel; Alan Oliver; Helen Price, archivist, St Joseph's Catholic Church, Warrnambool; Royal Park Hospital Archives; Sandra Salmon, archivist, Anglican Parish of Kilmore; Moira Shepherd, archivist, Mentone Girls' Grammar School; Ian Syson; University of Melbourne Archives; Victoria Police Historical Unit; Tom Watkin; Laurie Wheelahan, curator, the Mary McKillop Museum, Bacchus Marsh; Bill Wigley; Nancy Wills.

My grateful thanks to the *Age* newspaper for permission to quote the reports of the Hardy committal and trial proceedings that were published in the now defunct *Argus* newspaper.

My thanks to the Estate of the late Frank Hardy for permission to publish Frank Hardy's 'Caricatures of the Bacchus Marsh RSL Committee 1937'.

My sincere thanks to Leon Arrowsmith, the executor of the estate of the late John Arrowsmith; Thelma Barnes, the executor of the estate of the late Bill Barnes, Geoff Driscoll, the executor of the estate of the late Frances Driscoll (née Hardy); Roy James, the stepson of the late Les Barnes; John Morrison, junior, the son of the late John Morrison; Joseph Santamaria and the executors of the estate of the late B. A. Santamaria; Jennie Seedsman, the daughter of the late Ted Seedsman; Marjorie Waters, the executor of the estate of the late Joseph Waters. They each granted permission for extracts from interviews with the deceased to be included in this book. Dulcie Mortier gave permission to publish Paul Mortier's letter to Frank Hardy.

I wish to thank Hugh Anderson for permission to quote from Ralph Gibson, *The People Stand Up*, Red Rooster Press, Ascot Vale, 1988; Michael Cannon for permission to quote from *The Human Face of the Great Depression*, self-published, Mornington, Victoria, 1996, and *That disreputable firm . . . the inside story of Slater and Gordon*, Melbourne University Press, Carlton South, Victoria, 1988; and Oxford University Press for the extract from *Santamaria: A*

Memoir by B. A. Santamaria (*Reproduced by permission of Oxford University Press Australia from Santamaria: A Memoir by B. A. Santamaria, OUP, 1996 © Oxford University Press*).

I extend my sincere thanks to Chris Wallace-Crabbe for his encouragement and interest throughout the years of my research. Thanks also to Garry Kinnane, who read some of the early chapters in their original form.

Finally, my sincere thanks to my husband, Bruce, who has never wavered in his support and belief in my project. He also provided many of the photographs which appear in this book.

ABBREVIATIONS

AAES	Australian Army Education Service
ABS	Australasian Book Society
ABC	Australian Broadcasting Commission
ABV2	Australian Broadcasting Television Channel 2
ACP	Australian Communist Party [a name adopted by the CPA for some of its life]
ADFA	Australian Defence Force Academy
AES	Army Education Service
AIF	Australian Imperial Force
ALP	Australian Labor Party
ASIO	Australian Security Intelligence Organisation
BWIU	Building Workers Industrial Union
CIB	Criminal Investigation Branch
CPA	Communist Party of Australia
CPA (M–L)	Communist Party of Australia (Marxist–Leninist)
EYL	Eureka Youth League
KC	King's Counsel
MLA	Member of the Legislative Assembly
MLC	Member of the Legislative Council
NLA	National Library of Australia
PA	Pauline Armstrong
QC	Queen's Counsel
RSL	Returned Services League
SBS	Special Broadcasting Service
SM	Special Magistrate
SP	Starting price (bookmaker)

PREFACE

IN 1991 I conceived the idea of writing a biography of the Australian writer and public figure Frank Hardy. It was difficult to locate him. If people knew where he lived, or knew his telephone number, they were reluctant to pass on the information. Finally, I saw an advertisement in the press for a writers' function at the Caulfield Arts Centre, with Hardy listed as one of the speakers.

This was the first occasion I had seen Frank Hardy in performance mode. He was a superb story-teller; it was impossible not to get caught up in the atmosphere he created, and he was a hard act to follow. I had prepared a letter stating my mission; at the conclusion of the evening I handed it to him. He read the letter, and it was arranged that I telephone him and make an appointment.

At the appointed time, 11.45 a.m. on 16 July 1991, I knocked on the door of his Carlton home. I waited. There was someone peeping through the window. The figure disappeared, and a voice came through the door, 'Who is it?'. I replied, 'It's Pauline, Frank'. The voice replied, 'Go away, you've got the wrong house'. I made another attempt, but the voice through the door insisted that I had the wrong house. The scene could have been taken from Hardy's book *The Obsession of Oscar Oswald*, which I had only recently read. A sketch on the front cover of the novel shows a figure peeping through a blind; on the back there is a photograph of Hardy peeping through a blind. I had travelled across the city for this failed appointment, and I departed in a state of extreme irritation: hardly a propitious beginning. It was only my husband's calming words that made me decide not to abandon the project.

Another telephone call, another appointment; Hardy grumbled that he hadn't been feeling well, and that he had just been to the doctor when I had called earlier that day. It was with some trepidation that I knocked on the door at 2 p.m., two days later. The door was opened by a young man called Phil, who informed me that Frank would be back soon. I was given a chair near the 'kitty litter'; the cat prowled around my feet. Within a quarter of an hour Hardy did arrive, accompanied by his secretary and companion Jennie Barrington.

I had prepared a letter for Hardy's approval which stated that he was willing to co-operate with me, and give me access to his papers for the proposed work. He read it, and a discussion followed regarding my political background and family connections. Hardy had become friends with my mother's half-brother Paul Mortier in the Northern Territory during the war. When the Hardy family moved to Sydney in 1954 the relationship was renewed. Mortier, a communist journalist and theoretician, and Hardy were to remain close until Mortier's death in 1965.

At this point Hardy displayed signs of irritability and rudeness. I decided that I had had enough! As I started to gather up my papers, there was an amazing change of mood. Frank told me to sit down and asked me if I wanted a cup of tea. He put the kettle on, and peace was restored. Jennie re-typed the letter to Frank's satisfaction. After a petulant display regarding the whereabouts of his pen, Frank signed the letter, saying that I would probably be the best person to do the work. He inquired about Mortier's widow, Dulcie, and their two daughters. After further discussion about the reading I would need to do, I departed.

I did not see Hardy again until some time in December 1991 at a left-wing book sale in the Collingwood Town Hall. Frank was selling his own books. When I spoke to him, he displayed extreme hostility to me. Moments later he warmly embraced Alvie Booth, who had been the organiser of the Frank Hardy Defence Committee in 1950–51.

By now however I had become engrossed in plans for my research. I was intrigued. I wanted to learn more of the man who had seldom been out of the news since *Power Without Glory* was published in 1950. What was behind the public face of Frank Hardy?

During November–December 1992 I returned for a second visit to the National Library of Australia to continue my study of those Hardy papers which were then open to researchers. I spent a considerable time examining Hardy's correspondence, both inward and outward, dating from 1943 until 1971, and other miscellaneous documents. This material proved to be invaluable, as it covered a particularly significant part of Hardy's life. In the third week of my visit Frank Hardy and Jennie Barrington were in the Library when I arrived one morning. We sat at tables facing each other. Frank's greeting was barely civil, although Jennie was cordial. She told me that Frank was working on his autobiography, tentatively titled *An Unexamined Life*. She said that he became upset when going through his personal papers. I continued with my work; they returned on several occasions. Apart from a brief greeting each day, there was no exchange between us. Frank eventually became more friendly; just before their departure he, Jennie, my husband and I talked, at the top of the steps outside the Library. It was then Hardy said to me, 'Keep up the good work'. This was the last occasion that I met him.

In late 1993 Hardy suffered a stroke, and he died in January 1994. So I was unable to interview him.

In response to my inquiries to the Australian Defence Force Academy (ADFA) regarding access to the Frank Hardy Papers, I received a letter dated 25 January 1995, from Marie-Louise Ayres, Supervisor, Australian Special Research Collection, ADFA, that read in part:

Jennie [Barrington, Hardy's literary executor] . . . updated me on the conditions Frank himself imposed on his papers. She notes that Frank wrote a letter on July 18, 1991, supporting your research project and giving you access to his papers. However, she also notes that before Frank's death, he wrote to the National Library stating that he wanted access 'to the Frank Hardy papers forbidden (refused) . . . and this to apply to those people who had access to certain papers before . . . They should be informed that any right they believed they had to access some of the papers is withdrawn forthwith.' These conditions also apply to our own holdings. She [Barrington] repeats that the only way in which researchers can access the papers is by seeking permission directly from her . . .[1]

It was difficult to negotiate even restricted access because of the conditions which would have been imposed upon me. That is, Barrington had informed me that she would have to read everything I wrote. Because of the retrospective nature of Hardy's restrictions, I decided not to use the material already gathered; I have relied on other sources. However, I had already gained considerable understanding of my subject. I have since been informed that some of Hardy's papers are closed until fifty years after his death. I have also been unable to quote directly from Hardy's work.

I have endeavoured to construct an accurate record of Hardy's life, based on his family background, religion, education, employment, army service, marriage, membership of the Communist Party and the events which preceded the publication of his first novel, *Power Without Glory*, and the years that followed. I have tried to relate my findings to Hardy's fiction and autobiographical fiction.

My research led me to the Western District of Victoria, the area where Hardy's Irish and English ancestors settled. I learned not only of his parents' background, but also that of his grandparents and great-grandparents. Bacchus Marsh residents proved to be a valuable resource. Some still lived in Lerderderg Street where the family had rented a house; the current owner went to school and grew up with Hardy. Jim Hardy, Frank's eldest brother, was able to make a significant contribution to the task of establishing a profile of the Hardy family, and of Frank in particular. Frank's children, the late Frances Driscoll, Alan Hardy and Shirley Hardy-Rix, consented to be interviewed; they gave permission for access to their father's Army records. Photographs and documents were exchanged.

In constructing a biographical narrative, I have chosen to highlight those aspects of Hardy's boyhood and youth which had shaped Hardy, the man. The personae that Hardy presented to the world—the dedicated, serious, theoretical, Marxist, socialist realist writer, or the beer-drinking gambler, pipe-smoking *habitué* of pubs, clubs and casinos that he presented to another audience, or the charming 'ladies' man'—were a minefield for the biographer. One needed to be wary of reading as 'fact' certain aspects of Hardy's autobiographical fiction or autobiographical journalism. I believe that, in most instances, I have been able to evaluate and select fact from fiction.

In search of a variety of sources, I travelled to Canberra, country New South Wales, Sydney and Townsville, and within Victoria. I have engaged in correspondence and discussions with people known to Hardy. I have relied on the testimony of former Communist Party and Eureka Youth League members, family, friends, former lovers, associates, detractors and others, who were closely associated with Hardy, both during the war and after. More than one hundred people were interviewed, and I have spoken informally to many others. Particular attention was given to those who had been involved in the gathering of information and the physical production of *Power Without Glory*. The current crop of autobiographies of former communists and theses on the CPA were consulted; these shed more light on the genesis, gestation and publishing of Hardy's novel.

I was aware that a biographer needs to present and understand the period in which the subject lived. M. H. Ellis has succinctly described what is required of the biographer:

> Familiarity with the age in which your victim lived, with its conventions, with its mode of thinking, with the limitations of its thought, with the stage of its civilisation, with its sumptuary conditions and with its social climate—all this is vital to the biographer.[2]

I believe I fit this profile. My Irish-born Catholic mother came from a politically aware family, some of whom abandoned the Labor Party in the 1930s and embraced the Communist Party of Australia. When I was a child, my mother's half-brother Paul Mortier had introduced me to the New Theatre and the Australian Labor League of Youth when I visited my relatives in Sydney. In 1943, when I was fifteen, Mortier came to Melbourne on leave from the Northern Territory; and at my request he accompanied me to the Eureka Youth League headquarters in 317 Collins Street, Melbourne, when I became a member. Two years later I joined the Communist Party of Australia.

This biography is peopled by those who knew and mixed with Frank Hardy; they were also my people. The 1940s and the 1950s were tumultuous and exciting years. During 1949 I worked for short periods in several communist-led trade union offices. I then became secretary to solicitor Cedric Ralph, who represented the Communist Party of Australia during the Royal Commission into Communism (June 1949–March 1950). I continued in this position during the *Power Without Glory* trial. I believe these factors have enabled me, a lapsed Catholic and a lapsed Communist, to understand the times and the pressures, and have assisted me in constructing a reliable outline of Hardy's life.

The main emphasis of this biography will encompass his life up to and including his acquittal on a charge of criminal libel. For Hardy, unlike many authors, his first major work was his *magnum opus*. He was aged thirty-three when *Power Without Glory* was published. A substantial body of Hardy's work was autobiographical fiction. It is not however suggested that Hardy's creative imagination transformed some of the events of his own life into *Power Without Glory*; rather that his life's experiences enabled him to write the novel. Hardy had many friends and many enemies; indeed in the intervening years and after his death, assertions were made that Hardy did not write the novel. This biography will investigate these claims.

From a literary point of view the novel received sharp criticism: it was a work of fact or reportage; it was clumsily constructed; it was not literature. However, it also received wide acclaim and attracted a diverse readership. Its admirers far outnumbered its critics. It has seldom been out of print for fifty years, and it has been published in many countries in many languages. This says much for its enduring appeal.

Hardy lived for nearly seventy-seven years; for more than half of those years he was a public figure. No biographer can chronicle a whole life. For this reason Hardy's later years, after his acquittal on a charge of criminal libel, are treated in less detail.

This biography, whatever its limitations, will cast more light on the life of Frank Hardy, and on the lives of the many thousands of people who were profoundly affected by World War I, the Great Depression and World War II, who, like Hardy, either joined or supported the Communist Party of Australia and the Eureka Youth League, in search of a better world. They were among the many who assisted Frank Hardy in the making of *Power Without Glory*. Like Martin Luther King they had a dream. That their dreams were not fulfilled, for a multitude of reasons, was one of the great disappointments of the era.

Chapter One

CHILDHOOD AND YOUTH

FRANK HARDY'S proud boast was that he was born in 1917, the year of the Russian Revolution—a coincidence which was of great significance to him. The event took place at Southern Cross, near Warrnambool, on 21 March. His birth certificate shows his date of birth as 22 March; his father registered his birth on 22 April at Koroit.[1] Tom Hardy may have failed to register the birth within the prescribed one-month period and moved Hardy's birth forward by one day, or it may have been a genuine error. The confusion was, perhaps, a portent. As a story-teller, Frank was always inclined to blur fact with fiction to make the most of a tale.

Hardy's mother, Winifred, was born in 1887, the youngest of seven children. Her parents, Michael Bourke and Margaret Fogarty,[2] were from Irish farming families,[3] and they were married in St Patrick's Catholic Church, Belfast, now Port Fairy, in 1876.[4] Michael Bourke, like many Irish immigrants, abandoned farming; he became the proprietor of the Railway Hotel, Timor Street, Warrnambool. He died there on 3 June 1889, aged forty years. He had been in Australia for about eighteen years at the time of his death. His widow, Margaret, died at the hotel on 30 June the following year, aged thirty-three.[5]

One of Winifred's older brothers, Eddie, was to describe to his son, Mick Bourke, the desolate scene following his mother's funeral at the Tower Hill Cemetery, Warrnambool. The women were dressed in black, and the six surviving Bourke children were separated and taken by different relatives. The memory of the bleak winter setting of sea and lonely landscape was to remain with the older Bourke children forever.[6] Winifred was three years old at the time.

Frank Hardy's father, Thomas Hardy, was born at Mailor's Flat in 1881. His father James, like Winifred's parents, was from an Irish family, and was probably born in Ireland; but his mother, Sarah Jane Surkit, was born in Warrnambool, the fifth child of English migrants.[7] They were married in 1879 at Christ Church, Warrnambool, according to the rites of the United Church of England.[8] Frank's eldest brother, Jim, recalls being told that his grandfather took his sons to the Catholic Church, and his grandmother and her daughters attended the Church of England.[9]

1

The British writer Malcolm Muggeridge once called Frank Hardy 'the most Australian of Australians'.[10] Hardy was delighted to accept this mantle, although he continued to mention his Irish background. Hardy's first cousin, Mick Bourke, was the owner of the Koroit Hotel, and maintained the local Irish tradition with song and entertainment in the bar and boisterous Saturday evenings. His tourist brochures referred to the 'delightful little Irish settlement of 1500 people'.[11] Bourke's father Eddie, Frank's maternal uncle, was a jockey who rode in the 1904 Melbourne Cup, later becoming a successful horse-trainer and publican.[12] These influences were to play a significant part in the shaping of the young Frank Hardy.

Tom Hardy and Winifred Bourke were married on 25 April 1911, at St Joseph's Roman Catholic Church, Warrnambool, where they had both been baptised. The bride's occupation was shown on the marriage certificate as a 'lady', a term frequently used for women who remained at home.[13] She had, however, been trained as a costumier/dressmaker.[14] Tom Hardy was described as a 'labourer'.

Following their marriage, the couple lived in Dennington. In 1913 their first child, James, was born in Warrnambool at Sister Ingpen's Private Hospital.[15] They then moved to a modest cottage at Southern Cross, just a few feet back from the Warrnambool–Penshurst Road, which intersects with the road west to Mailor's Flat and east to the township of Koroit.[16] Seven more children were added to the family between 1915 and 1931. Gerald, Francis, Margaret and Raymond were born in Southern Cross; Dorothy and William were born in Bacchus Marsh; and Winifred returned to Warrnambool for the birth of Mary.[17] Francis Joseph Hardy was baptised at the Infant Jesus Church, Koroit, on 1 April 1917 by Father J. H. Hyland. His sponsors were Bridget and Patrick Murphy. His birth date was shown as 21 March 1917.[18]

Despite firm evidence to the contrary, Hardy maintained that his mother was a Catholic and his father was a non-practising convert.[19] Jim Hardy said his father was a Catholic; he frequently accompanied them to Mass, and although his political views were tending towards socialism, he did not display hostility towards the Catholic Church.[20] Hardy's play *Mary Lives!* (1992) claimed to be a celebration of the life of his late sister. In the play, Mary's father indicated that he and his wife had been married in the church vestry.[21] It is unlikely that two Catholics, baptised in the same church, would be denied marriage before the altar. Winifred Bourke's brothers did oppose her marriage, not because of religious differences, but because Tom Hardy was 'a hard man on the farmers'.[22] This comment did not necessarily reflect on his character. It is likely that he was only enforcing procedures to ensure that unadulterated milk reached the factory.

Tom Hardy worked for the Nestlé Company in the milk factory in Dennington; he later moved to their depot at Southern Cross, where the family lived until around 1919, when they were obliged to move to a nearby house which was owned by the factory.[23] In 1920 he was transferred to Bacchus Marsh to take up employment with the Nestlé Company in Maddingley. For a time he lived at the Merrimu Coffee Palace, which accommodated forty or fifty boarders.[24] Winifred spent a short time in Bacchus Marsh with her husband locating a suitable house; and for a brief period their children were left in the care of various relations.[25]

This separation from his family apparently left an indelible impression on the young Frank. Fifty years later, his creative imagination was able to transfer the anxiety and fear engendered in the child to the character Jack in his novel *But The Dead Are Many*, when he wrote of his feelings as he waited for his parents to arrive. He had stayed with an Aunt Guinea.[26] Jim Hardy recalled that Aunty Guinea was the family name for Winifred Hardy's maternal aunt, Winifred Guiney. Hardy's belief that his parents had left him had apparently caused him ongoing anxiety until he was an adult.[27]

The Hardy family was reunited when they rented a cottage in Sydney Street, Bacchus Marsh.[28] Frank started school at St Bernard's Catholic Primary School, Bacchus Marsh, in 1922.[29]

Tom Hardy's job as farm inspector—a position of some standing in the community—and his interest in sport, particularly football, soon made him an identity in the town. Although he was nearly forty at the time of the move, he played in the Bacchus Marsh Football Team on at least one occasion, and in 1924 he was Vice-President when they defeated the Darley team. He appears in a photograph taken to commemorate the win: a tall man with very bushy overhung eyebrows and dark hair parted in the middle, dressed in a three-piece suit and bow tie. He cut quite a figure as he strode through the town, or rode his motorbike to the outlying farms.[30] Billiards was a favourite pastime for many Bacchus Marsh residents, and Tom was no exception. He was also a good cricketer and played in local teams. During this period Winifred was occupied with the care of the children and the birth of her sixth child, Dorothy.

In 1925 the Hardy family was uprooted once again when Tom was transferred back to the Warrnambool district. For a short time they stayed with relatives in Raglan Parade.[31] On 23 November 1925, Jim, Gerald and Frank were enrolled by their father at the Christian Brothers College, Warrnambool. Their sister Margaret attended St Brigid's Catholic School. But their education was interrupted once more when Tom was transferred to Allansford. He enrolled the four children at the Allansford State School No. 3 in February 1926.[32] Although Winifred Hardy would have preferred her children to remain in Catholic schools, she was concerned about the length of the train trip to Warrnambool.[33]

The family spent less than a year in the area. During this time, Tom Hardy acted as a betting agent for the farmers in the Koroit district, purchasing Tattersall's lottery tickets from Hobart and selling them to the farmers. It was illegal for these tickets to be sold in Victoria, but Tattersall's had 'undercover' agents in the state, and some people ordered tickets by mail. The Hardy family shared a private joke about their father's 'girlfriend', Dorothy, a hairdresser who lived in Hobart. Whenever Tom wrote to Dorothy for further supplies of tickets, they would tease him. On one occasion, the police came to their home near Koroit, but Winifred had the tickets hidden away.[34] These activities were part of country and city life; the many people who invested in race cards and bought lottery tickets did not consider the misdemeanour to be a crime. Certain wowser elements protested, but working people believed they had the right to indulge themselves in a little 'flutter', as wealthier sections of the community had access to gambling facilities via exclusive clubs and the Stock Exchange.

Frank's memories of his early years are somewhat hazy; he mentioned that he had started at Allansford State School when he was six or seven, whereas he had been admitted to grade four, the earlier years at St Bernard's in Bacchus Marsh having been forgotten.[35]

Late in the winter of 1926, Tom Hardy was confined to bed with influenza. Walter Hoadley and Charles Dickie, partners in the Federal Milk Company at Bacchus Marsh, arrived at the Hardy home in Allansford in a big Buick car, as Jim Hardy was to remember in his old age. They proposed that Tom return to Bacchus Marsh and work for them as a farm inspector, and he agreed.[36]

Allansford State School records show that the four Hardy children 'Left for Bacchus Marsh' in August 1926. The family rented No. 48 Lerderderg Street from a widow, Mrs Platt, Tom Hardy's former landlady. She was reputed to be a very shrewd businesswoman and owned houses all around the town.[37] It is impossible to determine if Mrs Platt was a harsh landlord, or whether the rumbustious young family were ideal tenants. But the view is widely held that she was unflatteringly portrayed in Hardy's acclaimed *Legends from Benson's Valley*.[38]

The children were re-enrolled at St Bernard's Catholic Primary School, which forms the dead-end of Lerderderg Street to the west. The house is just a few doors to the west of the Bacchus Marsh State School, and the substantial buildings of St Bernard's Catholic Church and Presbytery are across the road. On the corner diagonally across from the family home were the saleyards, now a playground. This house was to remain their home for more than twenty years.

A number of prominent and prosperous citizens had their homes in Lerderderg Street, but No. 48 was a small four-room house with a skillion at the rear; later a bungalow was built in the backyard.[39] During the 1930s the front verandah was enclosed to provide additional bedrooms. The street was a hive of activity, with the bustle and traffic of two schools, the rhythms of services at the church, and the clamour, dust and excitement of the saleyards on market days. The lively Hardy family playing football and cricket would have added to the colour and sounds of the street.

The Hardy family quickly re-established themselves in Bacchus Marsh. Tom worked from the factory in Bennett Street close to his home, and travelled to the farms in the district. He would walk home from the factory swinging his billy-can of milk. On other occasions, neighbours remember Tom balancing a large bag of hot pies on his arm, and he was often called 'Pies'

Hardy.[40] Others recall him zooming up to St Bernard's School, where he would sit two or three of his smaller children on the Douglas motorcycle for a thrilling ride home for lunch. School friends remember calling in to No. 48 after Mass on Sundays; there was always a pot of sausages cooking, and the Hardy children would take a piece of bread and wrap up a sausage for lunch.[41]

Vance (Pat) Dickie, son of Tom's employer, Charles Dickie, remembered the Hardy family very clearly, sixty years on. He believed his father had a paternalistic attitude to his married employees, and that Tom Hardy was well treated by the Federal Milk Company. They got free milk and, upon request, cream too. He resented Frank Hardy's claims that his father was frequently out of work, as there was a policy that married men were not put off during the lean times. However, it would have been difficult for the owner's son, from a privileged background, to comprehend the reality of life for a family of ten living in a rented house on a small income. When Vance left boarding school, he joined Federal Milk and worked with Tom Hardy, who had very definite political views; 'he was a bit of a radical'. When the situation in Europe worsened in the 1930s, Tom was outspoken about the stupidity of getting into another war, while Vance was contemplating enlisting.[42]

Tom and Winifred Hardy, like many Catholics, had supported the anti-conscription campaigns against the 1916–17 referenda.[43] In discussions with old residents it was clear that Tom was not a man to be forgotten. A number of his children inherited his extrovert qualities, whereas Winifred is remembered as a quiet, hard-working woman, who helped with activities at St Bernard's Church. With a young family, she found little time for other social commitments.[44]

In his later years Frank often reminisced about the six or seven schools he attended, and about his memory, which was so good that he could remember sitting on a milk can when he was sixteen months old, or even back to the day he was born.[45] His memory played tricks, as it is almost certain that he spent all his school years at St Bernard's, with the exception of a few weeks at the Christian Brothers College and a few months at Allansford State School.

St Bernard's School was founded by the now Blessed Mary McKillop. The Josephite nuns in their brown habits, who were affectionately called 'the Brown Joeys', were responsible for much of the education of the eight Hardy children.[46]

The St Bernard's Grade VI roll shows Gerald and Frank Hardy as students. Gerald was more than a year senior to his brother, and his results were outstanding; he received the top mark of ten for grammar, spelling, written and oral. Frank scored ten for spelling, and eight for written and oral.[47] Jim Hardy recollects that Frank was such a bright student that he advanced rapidly and was promoted to the same grade as Gerald. He described his younger brother as a profound thinker. One of Frank's teachers, Sister Lambert, recognised his talents and told him he could write.[48] Despite these results, Hardy claimed that he had learned little at school.[49] However, his schoolfriend, Alf Walton, said that Frank was a good student. His school days seemed to be untroubled. He was to say, sixty years on, that the nuns were fine women, but they had trouble controlling the boys. He played a lot of cricket and represented the town in the Country Week at the Melbourne Cricket Ground while at the convent; Gerald was also an outstanding cricketer. The Hardy boys also served on the altar at St Bernard's, and if ever there was an absentee, Frank or one of his brothers would be hastily summoned from No. 48.[50]

The local children went on swimming picnics, rabbiting expeditions and fishing trips. Some of the schoolboys had their own football team, known as the Lerderderg Wanderers; and the Condons, Pattersons, Waltons, Kyles and Hardys were players in scratch matches in the Showgrounds and around the town. They were known as a tough team, and there were often fights during and after the matches.[51] Mary Hardy joined in the street matches when she was a small child; she was a feisty footballer. The children would gather at the saleyards and get up to mischief; Frank once broke his collar-bone there.

Despite the harsh economic conditions during the late 1920s and 1930s, Bacchus Marsh had many attractions for its children, one of which was an open-air picture theatre at the rear of the Landsberg Hall. The children would sneak in there to see the programme. 'We also had pictures at the Mechanics' Hall, with thunder and lightning music.'[52] Each month a vaudeville show was held in the Public Hall:

> They were good nights and whole families went along. In between acts, there was community singing, and we sang along to words on the slides. Singers, dancers, comedians and magicians were brought up from Melbourne. We also had our own acts with local talent. Bill Cook, Valda Jones, Sylvia and Norma Farrow, the Barry boys and the Vallence boys were all good singers . . . Frank Hardy recited poems once in a while.[53]

Much of their entertainment was self-generated, and on one occasion Frank Hardy invited Alf Walton to come to a concert he was staging in the backyard of Number 48. Frank said it was threepence to get in. After a prolonged wait, nothing happened, and Frank announced to the hopeful audience that 'the concert is off'. No refund was offered. The paddock on the corner and No. 48 were the sites of many noisy and exciting games of cricket initiated by the Hardy brothers. Frank was a good cricketer and a great stonewaller, and always managed to bat first; it was almost impossible to get him out.[54]

After more than fifty years, contemporaries of the Hardy family recall that not only was Tom Hardy a good storyteller with a keen sense of humour, but that some of his children were 'talented comedians' who could turn the most solemn situation into an hilarious event. Margaret (Peg) Hardy studied the piano at the convent; she qualified at the Conservatorium with very good results. Later, she had her own band, which played at dances in the district.[55] Six-year-old Mary Hardy made her stage debut at the school concert and fancy dress ball. Jim Hardy was well-known as a comedian, singer and dancer. He wrote songs about local characters and performed at concerts, dances and balls. Frank claimed that he wrote Jim's songs which he later sang in Hollywood.[56] Jim said he wrote his own songs, and although he worked for a time as a professional entertainer after the war, he never went to Hollywood. But he was a member of an AIF entertainment unit during World War II, and his talents were appreciated by troops in the Middle East and elsewhere. Winifred Hardy welcomed visitors of all ages to No. 48, and great times were had around the piano.[57]

Frank acknowledged that his father was renowned as a story-teller, but Tom Hardy never wrote his stories down. He just polished and re-told them.[58] What is certain is that some of his children inherited Tom's extrovert manner. It is evident that their Irish background from both the Bourke and Hardy families contributed to their interest in dancing, music, story-telling, writing and poetry.

Several members of the Hardy family showed a certain disregard or irreverence towards authority, and an unwillingness to be intimidated that may be attributed to their Irishness. As has been well documented elsewhere, discrimination and bigotry towards Irish Catholics in Australia was widespread in the first half of the twentieth century. Among the older Catholic residents of Bacchus Marsh, there remains a protectiveness towards the Hardy family that probably stems from their own experiences.

There were a number of billiards clubs at the Royal, the Bridge Inn, the Railway and the Courthouse Hotels. Two cafes in Bacchus Marsh had billiards tables, and there were three tables in the RSL Hall. The Australian Natives' Association also had four tables, and their billiards club was to figure prominently in Frank Hardy's *Legends from Benson's Valley*. Tom Hardy and his sons were skilled in the art of billiards. How was Tom Hardy remembered? The overall picture, gleaned from discussions with old Bacchus Marsh residents and members of the Hardy family, is of a typical man of his generation, one who was loyal to his wife and family, who liked to participate fully in the life of the community.

Jim Hardy said that although his father was interested in horse-racing and bet on racehorses, he never ran an illegal book. However, in the 1930s his brother Gerald conducted a large SP (Starting Price) bookmaking business. He also had a lucrative sideline selling Three-Place Cards, while Jim sold Doubles Cards. These illegal betting cards were very popular at that time, the names of two or three horses were printed on cheap card and then machined at the edges. These operations were tolerated by the local police until a campaign was initiated by headquarters for a clean-up. Jim recalled one occasion when he was 'dragged off the dance floor' in nearby Coimadai by the local policeman, who questioned him about the Doubles Cards. Jim said offenders would, most often, be given a warning and sent on their way.[59]

So, this was the atmosphere in which the young Hardy grew up; where cricket, football, billiards, horse-racing and betting were a way of life. The

Australian culture has a long established tradition which embraces sport and gambling. While most people confine their gambling to a modest bet, the foundations were already in place for Frank's lifetime addiction to gambling. In his novel *The Four-Legged Lottery*, Hardy wrote with great clarity of the addiction which besets one of the main protagonists: the craving, the excitement, the urge to gamble.[60]

Hardy was to bring with him into manhood not only an addiction to gambling, but a very real sense of the deprivations and suffering of working people during the Great Depression. When he left school at the age of fourteen, his first job was as a messenger/bottle washer at the local chemist's shop. He later worked in the grocery store: serving, collecting orders, delivering groceries, packing shelves, painting signs on the windows and ticket-writing.

He had earlier displayed a talent with pen, pencil and brush; his mother had taken him to Melbourne to be enrolled in an Art Training Institute correspondence course, with the aim of gaining competency in commercial art; his drawing of a black and white dog was to be displayed in the Institute's foyer. His talent for caricature was well known, and he frequently drew cartoons which the publishers of the local newspaper, the *Bacchus Marsh Express*, were happy to print; although this enhanced Frank's reputation in the town, he seldom received a fee. Jim Hardy said his brother was very fond of drawing hands, and he or his sisters and brothers were often dragooned into holding a stick or spear while Frank tried to perfect the difficult art of drawing the human hand. He did sketches of local residents for five or ten shillings. One of his early works shows the office-bearers of the Bacchus Marsh Returned Services' League, signed 'Frank Hardy, Oct. 1937', for which he was paid a few pounds.[61]

Later Frank also worked in and around Bacchus Marsh in the milk factory, digging potatoes, picking tomatoes and fruit; for a short time he managed the store where apples were packed. He was to claim that he had no ambitions to be anything else because of his interest in billiards, cricket, gambling and girls.[62] This retrospective claim by Frank Hardy in his autobiographical novel, *The Hard Way*, might well be dismissed. Family members and friends throw some light onto the young Frank Hardy. There was always a serious and introspective side to the child and the adolescent. His mother noticed how he could travel in a jinker with other children who were all chattering, and he could remain silent for upwards of half an hour. When he did speak, it was generally to ask a serious question, or make a thoughtful observation.[63]

When his brother, Jim, went 'on the track' for six months with the thousands of unemployed men carrying their swags, this made an indelible impression on Frank. In a newspaper interview many years later, his creative imagination was to transfer Jim's experience to himself, when he claimed that he had to leave home because his father could not claim the dole while Frank lived in the family home.[64] However, Jim was more irritated by the fabrication than the transference of his experience. In reply, he wrote:

THE NOT-SO-BAD OLD DAYS.

On October 7, an article appeared accredited to Frank Hardy: 'Hardy declares war on poverty'.

As the eldest of the Hardy family I'd like to clear up a couple of points. We were never evicted from any house we lived in. My brother did not leave home so my father could get the dole. There was no reason to.

Our father never lost a day's work in his working life. He worked for only two companies, Nestlés [sic] at Dennington and Federal Milk Co-op, Bacchus Marsh, over a period of 34 years.

Father retired in 1942 due to illness. He died of cancer in 1943, in his 50s. Jim Hardy, Dandenong.[65]

Frank and Jim's differing views on their father's employment are of interest. When Frank was born in Southern Cross, the midwife who attended Winifred Hardy was assisted by 13-year-old Annie Bowman, daughter of share-farmer Daniel Bowman. In later years Annie recounted to her son, James Griffin, that she had been present at Frank Hardy's birth. To the eyes of the young girl, from a family of eleven children, the Hardy household appeared to be prosperous. She knew that Tom Hardy was a farm inspector which was a position of some importance.[66]

Hardy may have regretted that he had not spent at least some time 'on the track', because he was to further embroider the myth when he claimed to have grown a moustache like Henry Lawson and carried his swag for three years.[67]

Although Frank was cushioned to some extent by his father's employment, he, too, was a victim of the times. As a teenage lad, he was able to listen to the stories told by those 'on the road' who passed through Bacchus Marsh, and who were typical of the men described by Michael Cannon:

Australia's legion of the lost poured out of all the Depression-racked cities, heading for what they imagined would be a better life tramping country roads, and finding occasional odd jobs to earn their keep. Never was there such a pathetic illusion or sad awakening . . . The early optimism of travellers quickly faded in the face of everyday hardship.[68]

The worst of all fates for the poorly-nourished swagman was to fall seriously ill in the loneliness of the bush . . . Swagmen who died on the track often could not be identified, and were buried in anonymous graves where they lay. Mick Masson helped to inter three such men on his travels, simply wrapping the emaciated bodies in their blankets and burying them as deep as possible.[69]

Although Hardy may have considered taking up his swag and going on the track, his observations of these men and the tales he had heard were probably the factors which deterred him.

Frank's first-hand experiences of casual labour, his brothers' efforts to find permanent employment, the shortage of money within his family and the sufferings of the unemployed were enough to impress upon his consciousness the struggles and tragedies of working people denied the right to work, and their subsequent loss of dignity. As with many of his generation, Frank grew up with an understanding of poverty and oppression in all its guises. Later on, as a means of enhancing his stories, Hardy fantasised that he had gone 'on the road'. When fame and fortune came to Hardy he never quite lost his self-image of 'a battler from the bush'.

Tom and Winifred Hardy, like most country people with large families, faced the drift of their children to the cities where prospects for employment were better. There is no doubt that Frank Hardy was looking for an avenue to escape from the poverty and constraints of small-town life. His skill with pen, pencil and brush became his passport to the world beyond the green valley.

Chapter Two

RITES OF PASSAGE

ON 25 SEPTEMBER 1937 the *Radio Times* published a cartoon titled *The Man They'd Like To Kick*, which had been submitted 'with apologies to *The Herald*, by Frank Hardy of Lerder-berg [sic] Street, Bacchus Marsh'.[1] Hardy was to recall the events preceding its publication, when he had waited at the local newsagent's shop to look at the *Radio Times*.[2] The *Radio Times* published several *Man They'd Like to Kick* and other cartoons. These events provided the catalyst for Hardy to make his rite of passage.

Hardy described his feelings about leaving Bacchus Marsh, the town that he immortalised, when he wrote *Legends from Benson's Valley* in 1963. He believed that if he did not move on, he would be caught in an aimless existence, until he no longer wanted to leave.[3]

In 1938, Hardy left the lush green valley and went to Melbourne. Whether he travelled on the Ballarat Brewery wagon to interview Harry Drysdale Bett, as he claimed, is not known.[4] The references to the *Radio Times* and the brewery wagon were, of course, written by Hardy about Ross Franklyn, his *alter ego*, the pseudonym he adopted at the beginning of his writing career, an amalgam of his and his wife's names. But Hardy's cartoon was published, he did travel to Melbourne for an interview, and Bett did give him a job on the *Radio Times* as a cartoonist and advertising salesman.

Frank first lived with his paternal great-aunt Hardy and her adult children in Stewart Street, Brunswick, travelling back every second weekend to Bacchus Marsh.[5] His cartoons appeared regularly in the *Radio Times* from 25 September 1937 until 5 March 1939.[6] They covered a wide range of topics, many referring to proprietor Bett ('a very remarkable individual who had successfully defied a *Herald* ban on his *Radio Times* by selling it through all kinds of channels other than newsagents'[7]) and his battle with Sir Keith Murdoch's press.

Some of Hardy's cartoons were of a political nature and showed Murdoch, Hitler, Mussolini and Stalin as dictators. It is unlikely that Hardy had communist sympathies at that time, as Stalin was revered by most Australian communists. His cartoons reveal that he was able to tell a story in just a few words, concluding with an ironic twist so typical of much Australian humour.[8] Hardy was to say, many years later, that he had only a small talent for drawing. When he discovered literature, he greatly admired the American writer William Sydney Porter, better known as O. Henry, who also had talents as an illustrator. Like Hardy, O. Henry had left school early and worked in a number of jobs, and his stories often featured the unfortunate and showed life's ironies.[9] O. Henry and Henry Lawson became role models for the aspiring writer, and in later years Hardy frequently discussed their work with his friend, printer and fellow communist Vic Little.

Hardy remained with his relatives for some months, and then moved into a boarding house with a friend. It is likely that he went to 92 Canterbury Road, Middle Park, one of a group of two-storey terraces which are still standing; many of these were used as boarding or rooming houses in the 1930s and 1940s. Frank would have been at ease in this location, as Middle Park had a village-like atmosphere and character reminiscent of Bacchus Marsh. The Middle Park Hotel remains a favourite watering hole for local people, as it was for dads in 1938, who stopped for a quick pot on the way home. In the 1930s the Middle Park Cinema, also known as the Bug House, in Armstrong Street, attracted crowds of adults and children on Saturday nights. Upstairs was a billiards saloon. Just across the way there is still a short cobblestoned laneway behind the newsagency. This was once Pope's Newsagency, and the local SP bookmaker found the laneway a good place to make his book on Saturday afternoons. 'Cockatoos' were strategically placed to give a whistle when the local police came into sight. It was a handy spot, just across from the pub. The punters could dash over, put a couple of bob each way on their nags, and rush back in time to listen to the race on the radio and polish off their pots. The many cricket ovals and other sporting facilities were an added attraction for the young Hardy, together with the area's proximity to beach and city.

Late in 1939 Frank Hardy joined the Cavalcade Radio Company as a salesman, following some casual employment after he left the *Radio Times*. His employer, Mr Petch, had inherited money and was involved in the racing game, which surely interested Hardy. Not only did Frank have a new job, but it was there that he met Rosslyn Couper, the office stenographer. Their acquaintance quickly blossomed into romance, and Frank was very jealous of Rosslyn. Jim Hardy called at the office to see Frank; when he mentioned to Rosslyn that he was going ice-skating later in the day, she expressed an interest, and he offered to come back later and take her to the rink. Jim became aware that young brother Frank was glowering in the background, and decided to forget his offer. Earlier, Frank had announced to his family that he was bringing someone called Ross to stay for the weekend. His sisters and brothers wondered about his friend, and Winifred Hardy suggested that the visitor may be a girl. Ross as she became known was, indeed, a girl, and she was quickly accepted by the Hardy family. Jim said, 'She would visit Bacchus Marsh and talk about Catholicism with Mum'. Ross became a convert to Catholicism, and they married within six months.

The wedding took place in St Patrick's Cathedral, Melbourne, on Monday, 27 May 1940. Frank, an advertising manager and salesman, was twenty-three, and his bride, a stenographer, was twenty. Ross was living with her parents at 515 Main Street, Mordialloc, and Hardy was boarding at 92 Canterbury Road, Middle Park. The witnesses to the marriage were Thomas Hardy, factory manager, and Alfred Couper, butcher, the fathers of the bridal couple. Permission for Ross to marry was given by her parents, as she was under age.[10] Hardy's eldest brother, Jim, attended the wedding, which was held in one of the side-chapels. A photograph taken in front of the Cathedral shows a smiling Hardy and his bride dressed in street clothes.[11] Considering the events which were shortly to occur, it is ironic that the celebrant was Father Arthur F. Fox, later auxiliary bishop to Archbishop Mannix and ultimately, the Bishop of Sale. Fox was one of the most prominent clerical opponents of communism in Victoria.[12]

The bride and groom came from disparate backgrounds. Rosslyn Phyllis Couper was born in Wonga Street, Canterbury, a suburb of Sydney, on 5 November 1919. Her parents, Alfred Edward Couper, a butcher, and Jessie Noble, had married on 31 October 1917 in St Peter's, Sydney.[13] Jessie was the daughter of the manager of the Long Tunnel Extended Gold Mine at Walhalla.[14] Alfred Couper had been divorced, and there were two children from the earlier marriage. Rosslyn may not have been aware of this until she was an adult, when she met her half-sister, who had been living in South Africa.[15] Because of the social attitudes of the times, it is likely that her parents had left Victoria temporarily until their matrimonial affairs were resolved.

Rosslyn was their only child. She had a comfortable childhood. She was a student at the Mentone Girls' Grammar School. Given the economic climate of the 1930s, Rosslyn was, unlike many of her peers, able to have more than a basic education. Her dancing classes were one facet of this; her name appears in the 1934 School Prize Giving Programme as part of a tap dancing group.[16] Hardy occasionally mentioned that his wife was a talented ballroom dancer, and up to the time of her death she loved to dance. She also received training in secretarial skills, and became an excellent stenographer and office secretary. Prior to her move to Cavalcade Radio, she had been employed by Homecrafts, a large radio company. Following their marriage, the couple rented a flat in an inner suburb, but not long after they moved to a maisonette at 17 Hillard Street, East Malvern. Jim Hardy, who had enlisted in the AIF, was stationed at the nearby Caulfield Racecourse Induction Centre prior to his embarkation for the Middle East. He frequently visited Frank and Ross, and he enjoyed an excellent rapport with his sister-in-law. The quiet Ross readily embraced her husband's family and enjoyed their convivial get-togethers.[17]

On 15 June 1940, just nineteen days after Hardy was married, the Communist Party of Australia was declared illegal by the Menzies United Australia Party Government. Later that year Hardy joined the Communist Party. The lean years of the 1930s had influenced his decision. Before long he was attending meetings and performing other tasks. He believed that, with his help, the revolution was close at hand.[18] These views were an accurate reflection of how Frank Hardy and many recruits felt when they joined the Communist Party of Australia (hereafter CPA). When Frank was a boy of ten or eleven he would sit on the floor and listen to his father discussing and arguing politics for hours on end with his friend Mr Connolly and Uncle Paddy Murphy—a great Labor man who fought for Jim Scullin (who had been best man at Murphy's wedding). As a result of these discussions, Hardy became a regular visitor to the Mechanics' Library, where he read widely on a range of subjects. But at that time, his real ambition was to become an artist.[19]

Fifty years on, Hardy could remember buying a copy of the CPA newspaper, *Workers' Voice*, from a stranger who was working at Alkemade's Lime Kilns in Bacchus Marsh.[20] He was to appear again in Hardy's story *The Stranger from Melbourne*.

An important influence on Hardy's development was the Campion Society. On 28 January 1931, eight Catholic intellectual men met in Melbourne. They applied to Archbishop Mannix for permission to constitute a Catholic Young Men's Society under the name of Edmund Campion, a Jesuit who had been executed in 1581 during the reign of Elizabeth I for his allegiance to his ancient religion. At a meeting on 13 May 1931 the group was informed that permission had been granted. The Campion Society had begun.[21]

The Catholic newspaper, the *Advocate*, published the aims of the Society:

1. To give young Catholic men a true picture of the function assigned to them by the Pope as lay apostles.
2. To increase their knowledge of Catholic principles so that they may be able to answer for the faith that is in them.
3. To train them effectively, and to put their ideas clearly in ordinary conversation.
4. To make them realise the importance of the crisis facing modern society and the necessity of applying its principles of justice and charity lest it perish.[22]

As the Campion Society became established, it extended its sphere of influence to major provincial cities, and 'Other Campion circles appeared at Ararat, Bacchus Marsh, Benalla, Daylesford, Horsham, and Iona'.[23] These country groups were not affiliated with the Melbourne Society, but visits were paid to the country centres, and on 27 June 1937 the first of a series of addresses in various centres 'were given on the Campion Idea and on Spain, and study groups formed. Shortly after, a talk was given to a newly formed group at Bacchus Marsh'.[24]

Hardy became a member of the Bacchus Marsh group, and claimed that in 1937 he took part in a debate on the Spanish Civil War with Father Rovira, a curate at St Bernard's Catholic Church from 1936 to 1937.[25] He had supplied Hardy with pamphlets supporting the Republicans. Rovira also lent him other left wing books and pamphlets. Hardy and Rovira argued the Republican case, but the adjudicator, a Mr Santamaria who came up from Melbourne, awarded the anti-Republican team the winners.[26] 'B. A. Santamaria, member of the Campion Society and founding editor of the *Catholic Worker* . . . gained his early identity in public life by his part in a debate at Melbourne University over the Spanish war.'[27] On that occasion the motion was 'That the Spanish Government is for the ruination of Spain'. The debate on 22 March 1937 at the

University precipitated heated controversy on the issue, and there was extensive newspaper coverage.[28]

B. A. Santamaria had no recollection of attending a debate at Bacchus Marsh, but he had known a Father Rovira.[29] It has been impossible to verify if such a debate took place, but there was an address on the Campion Idea and Spain held in Bacchus Marsh.[30] Fifty years later Hardy was to recall that although they had lost the debate, his political education was under way. He also recalled that within a year or eighteen months he had joined the Communist Party, mainly because of Father Rovira's influence.[31] This address or debate took place at least three years prior to Hardy joining the CPA; as evidenced, Frank's recall is open to question, and his political education had begun much earlier. The advent of Rovira in Hardy's life was in the transition stage to early manhood, a period when rejection of parental values is not unusual, and it may well be that he wanted to explore avenues of political thought other than those of Tom Hardy and his friends. Jim Hardy said that Frank was in a very religious phase of his life at that time. Father Rovira was an enthusiastic curate, and he participated very fully in the life of the parish:

> We also had a group called 'The St Bernard Players'. During the 1930s, we put on a number of three-act plays . . . Father Rovira, a young curate, used to direct them. At one performance he fell out on stage with a kero tin and got his pants caught in the curtain as it went up. Everybody laughed and roared.[32]

In later years in Melbourne, Rovira was known as a lovable but slightly eccentric parish priest. Such a character would have appealed to Frank Hardy. It is doubtful that Rovira had communist sympathies, but it is likely that he stimulated Hardy's keen intellect and steered him into more selective reading, and encouraged his interest in politics. Whatever Rovira's intentions, his words fell on fertile soil. In his later years, Hardy enjoyed the piquancy of blaming a Catholic priest for his recruitment to the CPA.[33]

During his employment with the *Radio Times* and after, Hardy met and mixed with other journalists in Melbourne, many of whom were communists, or fellow travellers. The wife of a prominent journalist recalled that although they had a very large sitting room with many chairs, it was necessary to hire extra seating to accommodate communist journalists who attended a meeting in their home in the 1940s.[34] The CPA Victorian weekly, the *Guardian*, had lost all but one of its journalists to the armed services. 'Quite a few professional journalists from the dailies gave much valuable help at different periods.'[35]

Hardy's employer, Bett, was interested in communism and in his newspaper, *Mid-day Times*, 'he re-interpreted Marx and Lenin at great length. (We [the CPA] had to dissent from some of his interpretations)'.[36] Hardy was aware that among the ranks of the CPA were 'a number of militant Australian Catholic trade unionists [who] left the Church at this time over its attitude to Spain—and what they saw as the Church's moral failure during the Great Depression and joined the Communist Party of Australia (CPA)'.[37]

So, there were diverse influences at work on Hardy, coupled with his own experience of a society which, in those lean and seemingly hopeless years between wars, offered little future to a whole generation. When war was declared, he was aware of the thousands of other young men who had never had continuous employment; among the first to enlist at the outbreak of World War II were many who had never had a job. Another factor that may have contributed to Hardy joining the CPA was the event that took place on 15 June 1940. Les Barnes, an autodidactic historian and CPA member, wrote: 'At 9.30 p.m. on Saturday night the Menzies Government declared the Communist party an illegal body. The police, secretly mobilised beforehand were sent out in swift cars to carry out raids on the homes of reputed Communists. Books, papers, documents, were seized. Communist headquarters and printing plants were occupied'.[38]

As there are no membership lists of the CPA available, it is impossible to verify who were members at that time. Oral history can be unreliable; however, some surviving former CPA members, who claim to have joined during the illegal period, are willing to discuss who, or what reasons, determined their decision. Hardy's children believe that he did not become a member of the CPA until after his marriage. Their mother had no interest in politics, but when she became involved in her husband's activities she joined the CPA.[39] There is no clear evidence to establish how or when Hardy was recruited, and his own recollections changed from time to time.

Some time after their marriage, Ross gave birth to a stillborn daughter.[40] Hardy continued to work as an advertising and sales manager prior to being called up for the Army on 26 March 1942. He attended at Area 39C, Maben Place, Armadale. The Mobilization Attestation Form, bearing the flowing signature 'Frank J. Hardy' that was to become famous on thousands of copies of *Power Without Glory* and many of his later works, gives an insight into his aspirations at that time. To questions '5(a) What is your normal trade or occupation?' Hardy replied 'Commercial Artist', and '5(b) Present occupation? Advertising and Sales Manager'. He had attained entry to secondary school, but claimed no diplomas. He gave his date of marriage as 24 May instead of 27 May 1940. He was inducted into the army despite being classified as Class II because of a chest deformity, poor physique, and tachycardia (abnormally rapid heart action). He underwent one medical examination on 26 March and another on 22 April when both doctors made a similar diagnosis. Private Hardy, Army Number V281357, was marched to Caulfield Receiving Camp (the Racecourse) on 22 April 1942.[41]

Hardy wrote of Ross Franklyn that he joined the Army in 1942. But Hardy, a CPA member, did not enlist; he waited to be called up for army service. Prior to Germany's attack on the Soviet Union on 22 June 1941, he would have been following the party line, because when war was declared in 1939 'the CPA opposed the war as an "imperialist war" akin to the 1914–1918 war, and before it switched to supporting the war against fascism, following Germany's attack on the Soviet Union on 22 June 1941'.[42]

It was not only the CPA members who were affected:

> For communists world-wide, Hitler's attack on the Soviet Union and its entry into the war decisively transformed the 'imperialist war' into a 'people's war' to defeat fascism. As the party president, L. L. Sharkey, later stated, this 'changed the character of the war into a war of independence on the part of the democratic peoples against fascist imperialist aggression . . . The central committee called for the fullest support for the war . . . The greatest battle of all history has been joined! The battle of darkness against light, night against day, death against life . . . To achieve this victory [of the Soviet Union and Red Army] *every nerve must be strained, all else must be subordinated . . .*'[43]

If Hardy suffered some confusion about the CPA line, it is hardly surprising. He had grown up with parents who had supported the anti-conscription struggles of the 1916–17 referenda, and Tom Hardy was outspoken about the futility of getting involved in another British 'imperialist' war. Perhaps Hardy's tardiness to enlist, despite the new CPA policy, can be explained. In 1958 when he wrote *The Four-Legged Lottery,* he mentioned the protagonist, Jim, had not volunteered, because of the influences at work on him during his childhood.[44]

The change in CPA policy after June 1941 resulted in some members, disgusted by the turn-around, resigning from the CPA. It was left to the leadership to mollify and rally those who remained. 'It was one thing for the CPA leadership to switch party policy but quite another thing to gain the kind of acceptance needed from members to carry through the necessary measures for waging an all-out war effort.'[45]

Following the formation of the Curtin Labor Government in 1941, the bombing of Pearl Harbor and the Japanese successes as they pushed south, the war gained acceptance among the Australian people, and the focus was on victory. 'Communists concentrated their considerable organisational abilities over the next four years on two major fronts—the fighting forces and production —involving full support for the armed forces, including conscription for overseas service and civil defence organisations, and for ensuring maximum war materiel production and minimum industrial disruption.'[46] Hardy, like other communists in the services, accepted the new CPA policy. Even during the illegal period, communists were prominent in the war effort.[47]

Possibly due to his Class II medical classification, Hardy spent the first fifteen months of his war service in Melbourne, where he was variously employed as a clerk or draughtsman at the Victoria Barracks, Melbourne, and other army offices in the city area.[48] Hardy had shown no enthusiasm to become a soldier; however, once inducted, there is nothing to suggest that he was unhappy. As a 'base wallah', a contemptuous term used by other servicemen for those who spent their service in safe havens, he was able to live at home and continue with his CPA work. Hardy the pragmatist adapted to the army; he learned how to make a comfortable life for himself.[49] Hardy had never broken his connections with Harry Drysdale Bett, his first employer at

the *Radio Times* and *Mid-day Times*, and he was able to intermittently supplement his meagre army pay by drawing cartoons from 1942 onwards.[50]

On 17 July 1942, Ross gave birth to a daughter, Frances Rosslyn, who was
baptised in the Catholic Church. Her uncle, Gerald, and his wife were the god-
parents.[51] As Hardy was by now a member of the CPA, the baptism may have
been performed to please the Hardy and Couper families. However, when completing his Army form just a few months before the baptism, he had left the
optional question of religion blank. Did Hardy still retain some allegiance to
Catholicism, despite his CPA membership?

On 10 May 1943 Hardy enlisted in the AIF, and this Attestation Form
shows some interesting changes from his original call-up sheet. His answer to
the question of religious denomination was 'agnostic', his usual trade or occupation is shown as 'cartoonist and journalist', and his educational qualification
is now shown as Sub-Intermediate, an advancement of one year. There is the
addition of a Diploma—A.T.I. Commercial Art. Hardy may have completed his
training course at the Institute; his army service would not have necessarily
interrupted his studies. What the AIF enlistment form does suggest is that
Frank Hardy had resolved the question of religion, and although his claim to
be a journalist was yet to be realised, he was certainly not without ambition![52]

In the early autumn of 1943, Hardy was appointed campaign director to
the Communist candidate for the State seat of Prahran, Corporal Malcolm
Good, a member of the Victorian State Committee of the CPA. Good was
serving in New Guinea, and armed services candidates were initially denied
leave to conduct their campaigns. When this policy changed, Good, like all
other candidates, was given leave.[53]

The Prahran–South Yarra–Malvern branches of the CPA rented a shop in
Commercial Road, Prahran, which was set up as campaign headquarters for
Good. A former CPA member, Bruce Armstrong, recalled meeting Hardy for the
first time:

> I went into this nearly empty shop which had a few posters on the
> windows; sitting at a table, hunched over a pile of leaflets, was a very thin
> dark-haired young man in army uniform. He was almost skeletal; I won-
> dered how he had been accepted into the services. He introduced himself
> as Frank Hardy and welcomed me. He was very enthusiastic about the
> campaign.[54]

The election result for the State seat of Prahran came as a complete surprise to the Labor candidate, J. J. Ryder, who lost to the United Australia Party
(Liberal) candidate, T. D. McD. Ellis, because he had not been prepared to
exchange second preference votes with the CPA candidate. Bett's *Mid-day
Times* gave the front page to the election and the events which preceded it:

> Private Hardy who acted as campaign director for Corporal Malcolm
> Goode [sic], together with another member of the committee, visited
> Ryder's rooms and held out the hand of friendship. They suggested that

irrespective of any differences the parties or candidates may have had on other matters, unity was most essential so far as the election was concerned.

At least that was what they intended to convey . . . Roaring like an enraged bull, he [Ryder] slammed the door with such force that a large plate-glass window was almost shattered.[55]

This was Hardy's first experience of being a campaign director, and candidate Good said that 'Frank did an extremely good job. But I believe that he was penalised for this, because shortly after he was transferred to Mataranka in the Northern Territory'.[56] As a consequence of Hardy's work in these elections, together with his enthusiastic participation in CPA activities, his standing with the CPA leadership and the rank and file was greatly enhanced. He became a prominent and trusted CPA cadre.

In 1943, Tom Hardy was admitted to the Caritas Christi Hospice in Kew; he was suffering from carcinoma of the face. Hardy visited his father at the Hospice when he was campaign director for Good. Frank Hardy wrote in *The Hard Way* that 'the father of Ross Franklyn' believed that the Labor Party was owned by John Wren, millionaire financier and sportsman, and it was no longer the workers' party. These comments may have come from Hardy's creative imagination, but Wren's notoriety and connections with the Victorian Labor Party were common knowledge, and it is likely that Tom Hardy could have made such a statement many times over the preceding years. As events transpired, in 1950 Frank Hardy's name was to become sensationally linked with John Wren and Daniel Mannix. Tom Hardy died on 11 June 1943; his funeral took place at the Fawkner Cemetery on election day, 12 June.[57]

The Caritis Christi Hospice was a large, though modest version of the existing Hospice today, and opened in 1938. The Irish-founded Sisters of Charity, who gave care to the sick and dying, had few funds when they proposed to open the Hospice. The effects of the Great Depression and the threat of another war made it difficult to raise money. But they put their trust in the 'Bank of Divine Providence'. When they had collected five hundred pounds, a very desirable property in Studley Park Road, Kew, became available. 'A deposit of five hundred pounds was offered . . . This was quickly supplemented by a further two thousand pounds.'[58] The unnamed benefactor was almost certainly John Wren, who became a major contributor to the Hospice. He also played a significant role in encouraging other Catholics and interested people to help the Sisters of Charity enlarge the Hospice and give succour and comfort to many more in need.

It is certain that the Hardy family discussed Archbishop Mannix's residence, Raheen, with its gracious gardens and splendid trees, located next door to the Hospice. Despite its grandeur, the mansion presented a gloomy and forbidding visage with its dark red bricks, balconies and tower. It had been widely rumoured that John Wren had bought the property for the Archbishop. But it seems more likely that it was purchased by the Diocesan Council, who were probably funded by donations from wealthy Catholic patrons, one of whom would most certainly have been John Wren.[59] Hardy later wrote that Wren's own home, Studley Hall, was opposite Raheen; in fact, it is situated on a minor road, a few minutes walk to the west. When members of the Hardy family visited Tom Hardy at the Hospice, they may well have detoured to look at the Wren home.

John Wren had brought his wife, Ellen, to the two-storey white house following their marriage in 1906. Studley Hall is reminiscent of the white colonnaded and balconied mansions favoured by Southern cotton plantation owners, as romantically depicted in American films. The Wren home was extensively enlarged and renovated in 1917, and its opulence inspired some critics to refer to it cynically as the Wedding Cake House. Its rear section overlooks the suburb of Collingwood that John and Ellen had left behind; its main entrance faces east to the Dandenong Ranges. When Hardy wrote *Power Without Glory* in 1950, the description of the home of the main protagonist, John West, was readily identifiable to Melburnians as the home of John Wren. The building has changed little since the 1917 alterations, although the surroundings have altered. It now belongs to Xavier College and is known as the White House.

On 14 July 1943, Hardy was transferred to Camp Pell (Royal Park, Melbourne) prior to his departure for Darwin on 25 July.[60] He was to claim that he started the *Troppo Tribune*, the unit newspaper, but issue No. 45 shows the *new* editor as Pte F. J. Hardy.[61] Hardy's own recollections varied; he was to claim that he started the *Troppo Tribune*, and on other occasions he mentions that Ross Franklyn took over the editor's job.[62] Frank Hardy launched his career with a three-paragraph editorial.

This edition of the *Troppo Tribune* shows an unsigned humorous cartoon that is typical of Hardy's style. The contents are what might be expected of an army newsletter, but the distinctly Australian humour that was to become Hardy's trademark is clear.[63]

Some time later Hardy became acquainted with Sergeant Frank Ryland, a professional writer and journalist. Ryland considered Frank had a natural talent; he told him to write down some of his stories. After encouragement and coaching in literary forms from Ryland, Hardy wrote and polished an oft-told tale and called the story *A Stranger in the Camp*. Ryland entered it in a School of Modern Writers Competition when he went on leave to Sydney. The story gained first place in the competition, and Hardy had found his vocation.[64]

Other influences were at work on the emerging writer; Sergeant Paul Mortier came to Mataranka from Adelaide River. Hardy and Mortier had Irish Catholic backgrounds; although Mortier's mother was Irish, his father was a Belgian. An ex-seminarian, Mortier had joined the CPA just prior to the outbreak of war, and he was already a seasoned political activist. Mortier, too, encouraged Hardy to write; he tutored him on literary forms, syntax and grammar.[65] They were also bound by their membership in the local CPA branch and played their roles as communist servicemen:

Wherever practicable, communists endeavoured to initiate wallboard bulletins, unit newspapers and discussion sessions about social and political issues and developments in the war . . . they fully supported the activities of the official Australian Army Education Service and a number of communists became AES lecturers or assisted it in other capacities. Of course, large numbers of soldiers never saw front-line action but spent the entire war in various camps around the country, often in isolated locations. In those situations boredom became a big problem, together with a drop in morale and any sense of involvement in the war effort, and communists endeavoured to alleviate these problems by organising discussion groups, sporting events, concerts and plays, unit newsletters and so on.[66]

Hardy and Mortier, together with other CPA members in the camp and adjoining areas, would have considered their activities as part of their political work.

In June 1944 a new issue of the *Troppo Tribune* had undergone changes to its content, if not format. Hardy had by now been promoted to the rank of corporal. This issue reports on the activities of the Welfare Committee, and there is an apology for the irregular appearance of the paper due to paper shortages. A sardonic cartoon reveals the bureaucratic problems experienced by soldiers who were trying to get leave.

Also present in Mataranka was Private Sumner Locke Elliott, an established actor and writer for radio and a member of the Independent Theatre, Sydney. He later wrote *Rusty Bugles*, a play based on the six months he spent at Mataranka. It was 'the most popular production with Australian audiences since *On Our Selection* (1912). A mirror of the unspectacular daily life of the ordinary soldier, it represents the deprivation, boredom, irritations, loneliness, disappointments, loves and griefs of wartime, familiar to many of its first audiences'.[67] Hardy's wide use of the vernacular would have interested Elliott, and it is likely he used some of it in *Rusty Bugles*. Unlike Hardy, Elliott's future career was already determined. Mataranka was a significant turning point for Hardy; had he not met Ryland, Mortier and Elliott, his life might have taken another path.

Hardy's army service in the Northern Territory was probably very close to the life 'of the ordinary soldier' as depicted in *Rusty Bugles*. His larrikin sense of humour, irreverence and contempt for petty bureaucracy irritated some officers, and he was occasionally disciplined. It is certain that Hardy's membership in the CPA, with its obligations and restraints, curbed some of his behaviour. Without this discipline, he may have been a less compliant soldier.

In November 1944, according to Hardy, Ross Franklyn, was transferred back to Melbourne to work as an an artist on the Army Education Service (AES) journal *Salt* (an acronym for Sea Air Land Transport). The circumstances surrounding Hardy's transfer to the Australian Army Education Services Publishing Branch in Melbourne are unclear. Hardy's later recollection, when discussing the matter with historian Beverley Symons, was that he got the job because most of the staff were CPA members. The *Salt* CPA branch had a meeting and decided that, as Hardy was a communist, they would give him the job.[68] Hume Dow, editor of *Salt*, believed that this was doubtful, as Major Mungo MacCallum, the managing editor, was the least likely person to tolerate interference. Dow believed that *Salt* had a vacancy for an illustrator, and Hardy was given the job.[69]

The assistant editor of *Salt*, Maclaren Gordon, was of the view that Hardy's claim was inaccurate. His recollection was that there were possibly three communists among a staff of thirteen. He had had a lot to do with Hardy during this period; he had found him agreeable to work with, and he was well liked by the other members of the team. He always had a fund of humorous stories. Gordon thought that he spent a lot of time on his political activities, apart from his work in the Unit.[70]

Historian Ian Turner was a member of the AES in Queensland. His recollections on the composition of the AES vary considerably from those of Dow and Gordon:

> The head of A.E.S. was Colonel Bob Madgwick (later Sir Robert of New England University and the A.B.C.). He was an uneasy buffer between the army brass, who thought that A.E.S. was riddled with commos, and the officers and men under his command. The suspicions of the brass were pretty right. Army education was an obvious point of communist concentration, and comrades all round the army tried to transfer in. Besides, the times were radical; the Russians were popular, and the dreams of post-war reconstruction were grand. From the editorial offices of *Salt* in La Trobe Street, Melbourne, where there worked among others, Vane Lindesay, Frank Hardy, Amby Dyson, and my future father-in-law Itzhak Gust, to the lecturers and librarians in the field, the A.E.S. personnel were overwhelmingly on the left. (Just where was not so important in those days: the relations between communists and Labor men, other than those dominated by Bob Santamaria, were good.)[71]

Beverley Symons shares Turner's views: 'An important area of activity for CPA members, as we have seen, was the Australian Army Education Service'. Certainly, many communists were actively involved, not only the rank and file soldiers, but also officers like Elliott Johnston, who was an AES lecturer in Port Moresby.[72] Johnston later became a Queen's Counsel in South Australia.

After a time lag of fifty years, it is impossible to establish the means by which Hardy became a member of the *Salt* team. Given the influence of the CPA and the number of communists in positions of authority, it is likely that, unknown to AES officers, Hardy did receive preferential treatment when a vacancy occurred. How he arrived at *Salt* is unimportant; but the transfer played a vital part in his development.

Artist Vane Lindesay describes his first meeting with Hardy in the back room of the *Salt* offices:

It must have been some time during 1944 when the lean, dark-haired, ebullient (with perhaps a shade more than the usual male vulgarity) Private Frank Hardy, an aspiring writer who had already won the School of Modern Writers Competition with his story 'A Stranger in the Camp', joined our unit, surprisingly not as a writer, but as an artist, a general penman for the journal and producer of dinkus and map illustrations.

Frank worked earnestly in his spare hours on his writing, and, we suspected, on his talking. It seemed in those days when he was not doing one, he was certainly doing the other.

And so, myself, Ambrose Dyson, nephew of the famous Will and *Salt's* editorial cartoonist . . . and Frank Hardy, formed the 'art department' and, for the remainder of the war years, an inseparable trio of mates endlessly discussing the political and aesthetic responsibility of the artist in society.[73]

Lindesay became a warm friend of Hardy, but not a mate in the Lawson meaning, as was Dyson. The relationship between Amby and Frank had that special quality of the much talked about 'mateship', and it continued after the war. Lindesay believes that Dyson was probably Hardy's one true mate in that sense, and he was extremely upset when Amby died prematurely in 1952. In *The Hard Way* Ross Franklyn related the exploits of the trio; Lindesay said there was an element of truth in one or two instances, some never happened, but a good story is a good story and should be left alone.[74]

The storemen in the *Salt* offices were mostly Jewish refugees from Hitler, who had been wrongly interned in Britain as enemy aliens. They were shipped to Australia, together with Nazi prisoners of war, on HMT *Dunera* and placed in holding camps. When the British Government acknowledged its error, many went into the Eighth Australian Employment Company of the Australian Military Forces, where they loaded stores and munitions onto trains and transports, and performed tasks which released regular army personnel for other duties. Britain's loss was to be Australia's gain, for many of the 'Dunera Boys' as they became known enriched our cultural, sporting and business life. Lindesay remembers that the three *Salt* storemen were Bruno Simon, a talented sculptor, Erwin Fabian, a painter and graphic artist of distinction and Frank Schonbach whom Lindesay described as being 'an enviously talented cartoonist for one so young'; they were regular contributors to *Salt*.[75] It was the first time that Hardy, the working-class battler from the bush, rubbed shoulders with cultured, artistic, European Jews. These years were vitally important to Hardy, and fifty years on he was fond of harking back to highlights such as the *Salt* article he worked on with Manning Clark, then a lecturer at the University of Melbourne. Maclaren Gordon said Manning Clark wrote the article, and Hardy supplied the illustrations. Hardy was on a sharp learning curve; through his work on *Salt* and *Mid-day Times* and his CPA membership he had access to artists, university lecturers, intellectuals, journalists, trade union leaders, New Theatre actors and importantly, he had long since come under the eyes of the leadership of the Victorian CPA who were watchful for rising young cadres.

Wendy Lowenstein was employed during 1944 and 1945 by Harry Drysdale Bett as a cadet journalist on the *Radio Times* and *Mid-day Times*. It was then that Lowenstein first saw the soldier, Frank Hardy. Each week he would hurry in and deliver copy for his racing column.[76] Both newspapers had horse-racing guides and tipping information. Despite all his activities, Frank was still able to supplement his army pay. The *Salt* editorial office was a short walk away.

Hardy's posting to *Salt* also enabled him to have an agreeable social life. Dyson and Hardy regularly had morning tea at the nearby Catholic Women's Association hut behind St Francis's Church. Then lunch at the Australia–Soviet House Canteen and afternoon beers at a pub in La Trobe Street.[77] The Canteen in Flinders Lane was just a short tram ride down Elizabeth Street. It was a favourite meeting place for communists and members of the Eureka Youth League (EYL), a communist youth organisation that had been formed in late 1941, trade unionists, New Theatre actors and those of left-wing persuasion, and one was assured of interesting company.[78] Hardy was well known there, as he had organised slide nights and lectures for the Australia–Soviet Friendship League.[79] Similarly, at the close of the working day, there were many favoured watering holes. It was in the mid-1930s that

> ... the Swanston Family Hotel began to enter upon its full bohemian glory. If you were a writer, artist, political radical, musician, academic in search of a different audience, or an actor, it became the place to drink. Here Melbourne's intelligentsia came to air its opinions, intrigues and prejudices, to plan campaigns for this or that cause, and as often as not drank themselves into alcoholic stupors that they would talk about with pride for the rest of their days.[80]

During the war years the hotel still had a devoted following of bohemians; on occasions it offered unique opportunities for Hardy, the beginning writer, to mingle with them.[81] The CPA's membership had had a phenomenal increase since the entry of the Soviet Union into the war in 1941; some members were referred to as 'Red Army Communists'. In these years, many male communists and left-wingers could be found at other favoured hostelries: the Mitre Tavern, the Phoenix, John Connell's, the Duke of Wellington, Phair's, the International, the Dover and the London Hotels. Each had its drinking schools, that peculiarly Australian male domain from which women were excluded, where the post-war and political future of Australia was hotly debated. Hardy's gregarious manner, fund of stories and political input added zest to the sessions. Some CPA and left-wing women, whose work or studies were centred in and around the city, were sometimes part of the scene. But on these occasions the men were restricted to the ladies' lounges in the hotels, where the drinks were more expensive; besides, they probably felt more comfortable in the protected male environment of the public bars, which were out of bounds for women.

When the hotels closed at six o'clock, Hardy was able to continue with his CPA activities. The word *activities* might conjure up a sombre image, but CPA members fell into a number of categories according to their depth of commitment and personalities. What was expected of them? Most CPA members were the foot-soldiers, hard at work on the tasks of pasting up political posters, or standing in suburban and city shopping centres trying to sell the CPA weekly *Guardian* to reluctant and, sometimes abusive, passers-by. Others knocked on suburban doors and proselytised to interested or suspicious occupants, and walked miles in browned-out wartime streets putting leaflets into hard-to-find letterboxes. Members painted and chalked the latest CPA slogan on walls and bridges, attended cadres' meetings in rooms behind the Savoy Theatre in Russell Street, in suburban halls, in sparse living-rooms of workers' suburban homes, or the comfortably furnished studies of middle-class CPA members and sympathisers. They listened to political reports by the leadership, participated in classes on the works of Marx, Engels, Lenin and Stalin; they handed out how-to-vote cards for municipal, state and federal elections for CPA candidates, and they arranged fund-raising cottage lectures and house-parties. Most attended trade union meetings in the austere rooms of the Trades Hall and other venues. The tireless and unselfish dedication of thousands of people of all ages was the central core of the CPA and the EYL. They made friendships and shared the mutual inspiration and camaraderie of people united in their purpose of winning the war, as a precursor to the overthrow of capitalism and the establishment of a socialist Australia.[82]

The foregoing highlights the dedication, discipline, fervour and mode of operation of the CPA and its members. These were the significant factors that assisted Frank Hardy to publish *Power Without Glory*. Similarly, when he was committed for trial on a charge of criminal libel, these same forces swept into action. The CPA leadership was able to rapidly mobilise the required financial, physical and moral support.

In 1940 the new recruit, Frank Hardy, had been an eager respondent for the many tasks assigned to Party acolytes. However, following his return to Melbourne in 1944, Hardy was by now an experienced CPA member, and he became more focused on his writing ambitions and interests, although still firmly attached to the CPA. There were a wide range of cultural organisations that had emerged in the 1930s and 1940s, many of them instigated and promoted by the CPA. Their purpose was not only to encourage the arts and promote their members' work, but to increase the CPA's influence in diverse areas. These organisations attracted CPA members who were interested in cultural pursuits, and they were often directed by the leadership to fulfil their commitment to the CPA by working within this or that organisation. It was a method by which the CPA retained members who might otherwise have drifted away when confronted with the more mundane activities.

Historian and former CPA activist Ian Turner recalled those years:

> If you were interested in theatre or film, music or painting or writing, there was an appropriate party group. If you wanted to study there was Marx School. It was an ideal world within the real; we were 'forming the structure of the new society within the shell of the old'; and we lived and socialised and married—and expected to die—within it.[83]

However, the CPA did not always plan effectively when setting up 'front' organisations, as there was often a paucity of resources. Les Barnes was a member of the Artists' Branch in 1940 which was 'a kind of underground', and later, although he was neither an artist nor a scientist, he was given responsibility for the Arts and Sciences Branch of the CPA, because the party 'decided there was a cultural conscience in Australia'. In 1944 the CPA had decided that he should organise the writers, probably because he had conducted the 'Historical Corner' in the *Communist Review* and also wrote articles for the party papers. He joined the newly formed Realist Writers' Group; among the early members were Jack Coffey, Deirdre Moore (née Cable), John Morrison, Helen Palmer, Nellie Stewart and Margaret Sutherland.[84] The Group studied realism and socialist realism in literature and the technique of writing, and held workshops where they read and discussed their work.

Some time during 1945, the khaki-uniformed young soldier, Frank Hardy, joined the Realist Writers' Group; he had found his 'appropriate party group'. On 5 October 1945 Ross Franklyn's story *The Man From Clinkapella* won the *Guardian* Short Story Competition, and the by-line above the story mentioned that the author had been writing for only two years, and he contributed regularly to the *New Theatre Review*. Ralph Gibson, the CPA Victorian State President, spoke on 'Marxism and Literature' at a Marx School literary night on 14 October. On that occasion Frank Dalby Davison, 'one of Australia's foremost writers' reviewed the competition and the prize was presented to 'Mr. Ross Franklyn' (Hardy).[85]

Despite his successes, Hardy was aware of deficiencies in his education and writing skills, and he enrolled at the University of Melbourne for Single Subject Modern English. He never attended a lecture or presented for an examination.[86] But the experience was not wasted; Hardy used it to humorous advantage when speaking to a large audience at the University prior to his trial in 1951, when he dealt with libel, censorship and many other contentious issues.[87]

Considering the political climate while he was on bail awaiting trial in 1951, this and other speeches made at the time could be viewed as either extremely brave, or extremely foolhardy. But his skill in holding an audience had been finely honed in the preceding years in the CPA and the Army, and he revelled in the role of an actor.

During 1945 Hardy continued his work on *Salt*. Amby Dyson regularly visited his wife, Phyl, and daughter, Janie, who were in a sanatorium suffering from tuberculosis. On their discharge from hospital, Amby was unable to find accommodation. Hardy suggested that they should come to live with his family, and the Dysons stayed with the Hardy family in Hillard Street for six months. It says much for Ross's tolerance and generosity of spirit to take the family into the small five-room maisonette, but she may have welcomed the company. Although there were visits from her parents, members of the Hardy family, and those who attended CPA functions at the house when Frank was in the Northern Territory, Ross must have experienced many lonely and anxious times with a small child her only company. Frank's return to Melbourne to *Salt* proved to be a doubtful blessing; on the one hand he was able to live at home, on the other he had found many more new diversions. Despite his ambition to improve his writing, Hardy continued to gamble.

When Frank was transferred to the Northern Territory in July 1943, Frances was a year old. Some insight into the state of the marriage and the personalities of the couple, at the time of their separation, can be gained from Hardy's novel *The Four-Legged Lottery*, much of which appears to be semi-autobiographical. The wife is described as being sentimental, as is the husband, but he soon adjusts to the new life, with its gambling and new experiences and new companions. It is the wife who keeps up the regular correspondence, as her husband's letters become shorter and more infrequent. When he wins money playing two-up, he sends her some, but just as quickly wants it returned when his winning streak is over.[88]

It would be unjust to conclude that Ross was always compliant with Hardy, but her role as a wife, and the marriage, itself need to be viewed in the context of the times. She was of medium height, very slender build, quietly spoken and pleasant mannered. It is fair to assume that the twenty-year-old Ross was deeply and passionately in love at the time of her marriage, and almost certainly sexually inexperienced when the courtship began. One of Hardy's relatives believes that Ross was his first serious girlfriend. Frank did have an earlier admirer, a shy young girl who lived up the line from Bacchus Marsh. She had requested a friend to deliver a book of poetry to Frank for his birthday. The choice of gift may have stemmed from Frank occasionally reciting poetry at the monthly concerts, but the tentative approach was unsuccessful. Eva Jago, a close friend of Hardy's in later years, believes that the seduction of the young man delivering groceries to a married woman, as described in *The Four-Legged Lottery*, was a description of his first sexual encounter.[89] From a distance of sixty years, it is impossible to establish if Frank was involved with any other women after he came to Melbourne in 1938, but he may have formed some attachment before meeting Ross at Cavalcade Radio late in 1939.

Her children have indicated that Ross was not interested in politics when she was first married, but their home became a centre for CPA branch meetings, classes and parties, and Ross formed new and stimulating friendships. The house was often filled with interesting people. Within the confines of her domestic life, Ross became involved in party classes and endeavoured to come to grips with the theoretical aspects of Marxism and Leninism. One of her CPA comrades, Rose Stone, recalled that when the couple had parties, Ross was hospitable; she liked to dance, and she enjoyed a glass of beer. When the occasion was a fund-raising one and tickets for drinks were sold, Ross was adamant that if Frank ran out of tickets she would not let him have hers.[90] Her involvement with the CPA was certainly more than superficial, and Hardy was fortunate, unlike some CPA members, that he did not have a politically hostile wife.

After Hardy determined to become a writer, Ross became his secretary. Her meticulous typing, carbon copies of which are in the National Library of Australia, gives some indication of her literacy and skills, and the vast amount of time devoted to her husband's work and correspondence. The picture of Ross, given by family, friends and CPA members, was that she was a loyal, loving wife and mother, a devoted daughter and a woman who enjoyed social activities and welcomed those who came to Hillard Street.

On 15 August 1945 the Pacific War ended, and Frank Hardy joined the joyful thousands who crowded Melbourne's streets. In his exhilaration, he threw his AIF slouch hat up in the air, and it disappeared into the crowd. The *Salt* staff carried on while awaiting discharge. Meanwhile, Hardy continued to write for the *Guardian*, became more involved with the Realist Writers' Group, New Theatre, and the CPA and its offshoots, and generally pursued a bachelor's life. After almost six turbulent years of marriage, Ross awaited the birth of their child, perhaps with some trepidation for herself and her children.

In the beginning Hardy had not been an eager soldier, and it may be said he shared the views of Jaroslav Hašek's *The Good Soldier Švejk*. However, unlike Švejk, Hardy had managed, with relatively few exceptions, a comfortable and exciting war. The broad range of experiences, opportunities and vistas which had opened up to Hardy had given him new worlds to conquer.

Chapter Three

THE GENESIS OF
POWER WITHOUT GLORY

WHEN FRANK HARDY was discharged, return to civilian life was an easy transition for him; he was not concerned with the question of returning to his former occupation, or taking whatever employment was open to him. Months before his discharge from the army, there is little doubt that Frank had accepted and was working on a secret assignment from the CPA to write a book. Not just a book, but a book about his city, his Alma Mater, and the main protagonist was to be based on the powerful Melbourne businessman, John Wren, a name both admired and feared.

John Wren was born in Gold Street, Collingwood, on 3 April 1871, the son of illiterate Irish immigrants, John, a labourer, and Margaret (née Nester). They were not without some modest financial resources. The family later moved to a double-fronted house in Ballarat Street. John was their third son. When Wren was born, Melbourne was a busy frontier town. By the time he had entered his adolescent years Melbourne had changed. Niall Brennan, Wren's biographer, has described that colourful period in *John Wren: Gambler*:

> Melbourne had graduated from the role of a bustling cow-town to a gorgeous, vulgar, noisy cheap imitation of London. As the pioneers moved out, the money-lenders moved in. The canvas and shanties, and their attendant stores, were pulled down and rebuilt elsewhere, further out; and in their place arose banks, emporiums, insurance offices and railway stations, theatres and pleasure domes of staggering obscenity. John Wren was able, in his youth, to witness the phenomenon of 'progress' taking place before his eyes. If his taste in art was never refined, it is not surprising.[1]

Wren started work in a wood-yard when he was twelve years old. For a time he was swallowed up by the voracious octopus that was the boot industry. He became a boot-clicker, and he was paid 7s 6d per week. The slums and the bustling city influenced the lad; he soon ventured into distributing small-time betting cards, taking wagers and lending money. Like many slum youths he was able to defend himself; he was handy with his fists. He played cricket and football, despite his bandy legs.[2]

He soon adopted a rather 'natty style of dress', and he neither drank nor smoked. He had long since realised that money was the road to freedom. One morning in November 1890, the young Wren wended his way to the Flemington Racecourse to see the Melbourne Cup. He had withdrawn all his savings from a tea-tin, with the intention of backing the heavily weighted Carbine. The horse had a sensational victory, and Wren brought home £180— a substantial amount of money at that time—which, according to Melbourne folklore, was the foundation on which he was to build his fortune.[3]

The shrewd Wren carefully planned his future. He obtained work in the illegal betting shops where two-up was played, and he became familiar with the procedures required to run such establishments. By 1891 the whole economy, that had been built on greed, began to collapse. The economic crash of the 1890s brought many to the conclusion that steps should be taken to ensure that such a catastrophe would never happen again. John Wren had certainly determined that it would never happen to him. 'The Irish had a deep-seated and ancient contempt for the law', and Wren had seen many people in high places protected by the same laws which dealt with the underprivileged and kept them in poverty and bondage. 'John Wren had many capable teachers. During the 1880s, he probably watched the fantastic land speculations of Thomas Bent, Cabinet Minister, municipal councillor and land shark of the first magnitude . . . Bent was the outstanding example of a man using his political position for personal profit', writes Michael Cannon in *The Land Boomers*, 'and degrading the standards of public life.'[4]

In 1893 Melbourne had many wowsers . . . 'the real wowser is a Protestant of limited spirituality, deeply concerned with the sins of others . . . a killjoy, a sombre long-faced puritan, often a hypocrite'. The Irish Catholics had their share of wowsers too, but they were likely to close ranks with their co-religionists in 'the face of Protestant wowserism'. John Wren and the wowsers became foes when the Wren Tote opened at 136 Johnston Street, Collingwood, during 1893. Wren became an object for their spleen, even though he had not introduced the gambling mania to Melbourne, as there had been widespread gambling venues and two-up schools all over the city long before. 'It was in such a golden age of humbug that the Collingwood Tote accepted the first shillings of those who yearned for a bet', wrote Hugh Buggy nostalgically.[5]

The Tote was to become a Melbourne legend. The clerks wore Klan-type hoods, the premises were highly fortified and heavily guarded, and the police found it impossible to gain entry. The money and the betting slips were passed through small openings, where only hands could be seen. 'Anyone who passed in a fake ticket had his knuckles rapped by a cane kept for the purpose. The whole thing was obviously delicious fun, as well as being very profitable.'[6] There were many attempts to close Wren down; in 1898 the Attorney-General, Isaac Isaacs, attempted to introduce a Bill, which was humorously described as 'the Wren Suppression Bill'. Faction fighting occurred, and the Bill was lost by twenty-three votes to twenty-two. By then, Wren had many friends in high places.[7]

Wren later opened a number of betting shops in different parts of Melbourne. Thomas Bent's Lotteries, Gaming and Betting Act (1906) was passed in an effort to destroy Wren's betting empire. Wren had by then achieved millionaire status; he was having success as a sports promoter, and he was involved with three private racecourses. He had set his sights on different goals. The Wren Tote was closed in early 1907.[8] Wren had long since realised the importance of having influential friends. It was reputed that there was a 'Wren man' on the Richmond Political Council when it was formed in 1901. In 1910 Wren was the subject of a scurrilous attack in an article in *The Lone Hand* magazine. Wren, as was his wont, ignored the article.

After Wren closed the Tote, he never relinquished his business interests in legitimate racing, boxing, cycling and other sporting ventures. His empire was also to embrace almost every aspect of business life: goldmines, grazing properties, theatres, newspapers, collieries, restaurants, real estate, oilfields, distilleries, clothing shops, cosmetics, suburban cinemas and hotels. His businesses spread over thirty-one companies . . . Politician Jack Lang, 'no friend of Wren (or of his associate Theodore), called him a champion wire-puller . . . there is no doubt that Wren was co-broker in forming the Labor-supported Dunstan government of 1935'.[9]

Stories abounded of Wren's generosity to those in need. He was a substantial donor to many charities, not necessarily Catholic, and good causes; quite often these were made anonymously. Just as these stories circulated, so, too, did the exploits of Wren's associates and his influence on inner suburban politics. It was claimed that Wren had been implicated in murders and bombings. There were rumours of rigged ballots, branch stacking and the like. Wren 'obviously enjoyed political fixing, as he did his popularity with sections of the working-class. An eight-hour day procession gave "Three Cheers for Jack Wren" as it passed City Tattersalls. He was often generous to strikers and gave one thousand pounds to the waterside workers in 1928'.[10]

John Wren was a dominant, controversial and influential figure; he had many friends and many enemies. For more than fifty years Wren was a prominent, if mysterious, figure in Melbourne. He was also a Catholic. As time would reveal, whatever his sins of commission or omission, he had been firmly fixed in the sights of the CPA leadership, and more latterly, Frank Hardy.

Hardy was a trusted CPA member, a Realist Writer and a regular contributor to the *New Theatre Review*. He was writing book reviews and feature articles for the CPA weekly *Guardian* under the pseudonym of Ross Franklyn; he was also associated with other cultural groups promoted by the CPA. Some time earlier Frank Hardy had rented a room above a shop at 255A Bridge Road, Richmond; access was gained via a short carriageway to a steel door on the right. The door to the room faced down the staircase.[11] It was the right setting for the working-class writer to continue work on his *magnum opus*.

What was the precise nature of his assignment, and who initiated it? A pre-requisite of understanding the circumstances surrounding the genesis of *Power Without Glory* requires some further insight into the operational style of the CPA and the political climate during and after the war. Cedric Ralph was a prominent CPA member and later, instructing solicitor for the Party during the Royal Commission into Communism in 1949 and the challenge in the High Court to the Communist Party Dissolution Act in 1952. He recalls that during the war years Ted Hill, lawyer and member of the Victorian State Executive of the CPA, became deeply concerned with what he perceived as attacks by Catholic Action on the CPA and the communist leadership of some unions. Hill also believed that B. A. (Bob) Santamaria was directing, or deeply influencing, Catholic Action tactics within several unions and in many Labor Party branches.[12] Ralph said:

> . . . it was Ted's idea from the very beginning; Ted wanted to put a dent into the activities of Catholic Action, and he thought that an attack upon Wren was really hitting at the core of the whole thing. He believed Wren was responsible for much of the Movement's finances . . . but at what point Frank was brought into it I don't know. But the early conception I do know.[13]
>
> Two or three people I know who saw Ted Hill in action used almost exactly the same phrase—he was master of the offensive—and his mastery of the offensive was such that he could see a way around a problem which nobody else had thought of, and I think that applies to *Power Without Glory*, you see nobody had ever thought of attacking Wren through a novel, but Ted did.[14]

What was the cause of their concern? A retrospective view of the ALP discloses that by 1930 most religious denominations were represented in its membership, but the Catholics were the largest and most cohesive group. There is no evidence that a decision had been taken that Catholics should become an organisational force in the ALP at that time; but if they exerted some power to achieve their own interests, so be it. It was inevitable that religion and politics were discussed at the various locations where they met: after Mass, at Holy Name Society and Knights of the Southern Cross meetings. The National Secretariat of Catholic Action for Australia and New Zealand, that functioned as a body for direction, expansion and co-ordination, was formed in 1937 as a result of a suggestion made by senior members of the Campion Society to Archbishop Mannix and the bishops.[15]

The first meeting of a selected group of Catholics was held during 1941. From this group the organisation to become known as 'The Movement' was born. In 1943 groups of anti-communist trade unionists were formed in some trade unions and the larger workplaces. Whereas the struggle against the communists had previously been on an individual basis, these groups were able to develop cohesion and considerable industrial muscle.[16]

The CPA published a pamphlet titled *Catholic Action at Work* [c. 1945] which carried what purported to be excerpts from a confidential report [written by Santamaria[17]] for the Catholic bishops for an Extraordinary meeting held in Sydney in September 1945. One bishop [Archbishop James Duhig of

Brisbane[18]], en route by rail to the meeting, had left the document under the pillow in his sleeping compartment.[19] How it ended up in CPA hands can only be guessed.

Another excerpt from Santamaria's report quoted in the CPA pamphlet noted that: 'It was only towards the end of 1944 that a satisfactory national organisation and centrally guided policy was developed . . . The first full Central Committee meeting [of the National Secretariat of Catholic Action] was held on March 26th 1945'.[20]

'With the formation of the Industrial Groups [at the Victorian ALP conference in 1946] it became one of organisation, of getting the numbers to win and maintain positions in the labour movement. In the course of this struggle the two machines [the CPA and the Industrial Groups] fought each other with the single determination to win at almost any cost to principle.' Many Catholics in the Industrial Groups were members of 'The Movement', a separate body that 'had mounted a massive organisation in the trade unions and Labor Party to resist communists and those they chose to believe were as bad as communists'. The Movement was 'a specifically Catholic organisation: the Industrial Groups were not, although it was the Movement which provided the drive and the numbers within the Groups. The Movement was secret: the Industrial Groups were not, being official formations of the ALP'. The Industrial Groups were unique to Australia which was 'the only country where for a time . . . the political party which had grown out of the trade unions, and whose organisation continued to be based on them, attempted to influence the policy and the controllers of the unions'.[21]

An article on the front page of the *Guardian* newspaper of 10 November 1944, read 'Scandal on Church Rates—By-Election Deal' and under the secondary heading 'John Wren Mentioned' the article continued, 'It is freely rumoured in Parliamentary circles that Mr. John Wren—the power behind Dunstan and the Labor Right Wing—took a leading part in the Dunstan–Right Wing negotiations'.[22] This was the beginning of the offensive against Wren, and ultimately the ALP Industrial Groups in the unions.

Late in 1944 Jim Coull, Secretary of the Liquor Trades Union, and Les Barnes, CPA member in charge of the Realist Writers' Group, organised the Tom Mann Society to investigate the Labour Movement in Victoria. Barnes said:

> We drew together all the old people like J. B. Scott and various others, because we believed that the earlier history was too much about New South Wales and not enough about Victoria, and people knew too little. As a result of this, the name of John Wren came up and he was supposed to be running the government behind the scenes. Now, I have always had my doubts about this, but Ralph Gibson was obsessed that Premier Albie Dunstan, who was in at the time, was carrying out his orders from John Wren . . . Gibson proposed that we should write a book based on historical material which would expose John Wren and all these activities, but it should not be an ordinary straight book because that would be open to libel charges and court cases.

He suggested the book should be written on the lines of Upton Sinclair, an American writer; it should tell the truth, but use names close to the people. The truth should be such that the people would not be game to take court action. Well, it did not appeal to me at all; I said, 'No, I wasn't a novelist, I was a writer, whatever I wrote was history, and it was factual. It was either factual, or it was propagandist, but it was not a distortion of the truth. But, I tell you what I will do, I will research the material for you and while I'm researching the material, I'll get others to do it, and when you find a bloke to do the job, we will turn the material over to him'.[23]

So, Barnes commenced his research in a voluntary capacity at the Public Library; he was aware that another man, Otto Gruber, who worked at the then Melbourne Technical College, was also collecting material. Although they were engaged on the same project, the two men never met, nor did Barnes ever see Gruber's name on paper.[24] While this may appear unusual, it is consistent with the secrecy which surrounded much of the CPA activities. Prior to the CPA being declared illegal on 15 June 1941, membership lists were kept. But, following that event, it was claimed that this practice was discontinued. The CPA, like the EYL, was never an incorporated body, which meant that it could not own real estate and was not required to keep a list or register of members. Nor were balance sheets or statements of accounts presented to members.[25] Former CPA solicitor Cedric Ralph said:

To my knowledge no list or register of party members was ever in existence excepting such prepared by ASIO or its predecessors ... To make a list would have been entirely against Party policy. In illustration of this policy I do know that at Annual Meetings at which office holders were elected by ballot papers, no record even of those who stood or of those who were elected survived the end of the meeting. And Party Members [sic] who may have had occasion to make notes during such meetings were expected to destroy them promptly.[26]

These practices could only have occurred in an unincorporated body. The CPA loftily espoused the concept of democratic centralism as in Rule 9 of its constitution:

The essential features of democratic centralism are—
(1) The election of all leading Party organs.
(2) The responsibility of leading Party organs to submit reports at regular intervals to the Party organs that elected them.
(3) The adherence to majority decisions.
(4) The decisions of higher committees to be binding on lower Party organisations.[27]

According to former CPA functionary Bernie Taft, 'Theoretically the party operated on the principle of "democratic centralism". In practice, the party was directed from the top'.[28]

During the illegal period of June 1940 to December 1942, CPA members found it necessary to act in a clandestine way. The habits formed during this time were not discarded, and members exerted pressure on each other to be security conscious. If, as the CPA leadership believed, Wren had power in many quarters, it is certain that a decision was made to throw a veil of secrecy over the production of the novel. Any party member or sympathiser who was enlisted to help on the project would be well aware of the nature of the operation, and their discretion and loyalty would be assured. It is also certain that each person so recruited would be told only as much as they needed to know. Such was the nature of the organisation during those years.

Soon after the formation of the Realist Writers' Group in 1944, it was not long before the CPA envisaged a different role for Les Barnes. In 1945 he was sent to the Carlton area to work as an organiser, a job for which he believed he had little talent and less inclination.[29] This is an illustration of the ad hoc way the CPA allotted tasks to its members. This style of operation was not always successful, but on many occasions it was highly effective, as resources and people-power could be diverted to deal with some immediate political problem. CPA members' responsibilities were switched with little or no demurral, and illustrates the unquestioning loyalty afforded by many to the leadership. For example, Barnes related, in his self-deprecating manner, how he was amused by a report that when Sydney-based J. B. Miles, the General Secretary of the CPA, was asked, 'Why is Barnes in charge of the Arts and Sciences in Melbourne?', he replied 'He's got more gramophone records than anyone else'.[30]

Meanwhile, in his leisure time, Barnes continued to gather material on Wren. He said:

> Soon after the war finished in August 1945, Gibson came to me and said, 'I've found the bloke,' and he introduced me to this Frank Hardy. Well, Frank was then a soldier, digger hat on and all that. He was an easy bloke to get on with. So, down to the pub we went, got full and went home and drank more beer and all that sort of thing. We got on very well together. So, as a result, we made arrangements, and the arrangements were made with the party [CPA] that I was to be put on an open job; a job that was open, but I was to spend my time in researching this.[31]

Barnes's statement on these events differ from those of Frank Hardy. When the first edition of *The Hard Way* was published, the dust jacket stated that it was the story behind the publication of *Power Without Glory,* Hardy's early years, his political education, the years gathering material, his supporters and the battle in the courts.[32]

What might the reader have expected from this statement—an autobiography, a factual work, reportage or a story? The confusion deepened with the introduction of the character Ross Franklyn (the pseudonym previously used by Hardy), who became Hardy's *alter ego* and is woven into the text. This device enabled Hardy to add an almost heroic dimension to his own character. It also ensured that the events surrounding the genesis, writing and publication of *Power Without Glory* are difficult to verify. The line between fact and fiction is blurred. Hardy/Franklyn claimed that the first discussion about writing the book—to be centred on a fictitious character based on John Wren—took place in February 1946 with Ambrose Dyson. Hardy/Franklyn later visited Ralph Gibson at the *Guardian* office, and they discussed the proposed book. It was mentioned that Gibson said the party was considering offering Hardy/Franklyn a full-time organising job when he left the Army. Gibson mentioned sources that Hardy/Franklyn could use; he made various other helpful suggestions. Hardy/Franklyn's idea had crystallised into a definite project.[33]

Hardy's account of the genesis of *Power Without Glory* is at variance with those of Les Barnes, Ted Hill, Cedric Ralph and Vane Lindesay. The latter described his time with Hardy on *Salt* from late 1944 to 1 February 1946:

> During this period in Melbourne, Frank was planning his *Power Without Glory* and I recall this title was settled before the first paragraph was written. Most of the book was later completed over a Dry Cleaning shop on Richmond Hill close to the corner of Bridge Road and Lennox Street.[34]

Lindesay's article was published in 1986, and there is no evidence that Hardy ever refuted this statement.

It was also in 1986 that Mungo MacCallum recalled 'that many well known names made their debut in *Salt*, among them . . . Frank Hardy who even then nurtured the seeds of his notorious novel of exposure, *Power Without Glory'*.[35]

Nor do the recollections of Deirdre Moore (née Cable) of that period accord with those of Hardy. She was an Honours graduate from Sydney University; in 1943 she came to Melbourne to carry out research work for her employer. Moore had been one of the seven members of the CPA branch at the Sydney University. Following the usual practice she was given a letter of introduction to the CPA branch at Melbourne University. She was agreeably surprised to learn that the branch had forty-eight members. She also discovered that the CPA in Melbourne had a far greater proportion of academics and middle-class members than in New South Wales. Moore was also a member of the Council for Encouragement of Music and the Arts (CEMA), which later became the Arts Council. She joined the Realist Writers' Group from its inception. She believes her first encounter with Frank Hardy, who was in army uniform, was during 1945; this was at an informal meeting of *Salt* personnel and Realist Writers at the Collins Street flat of New Theatre member Bob Mathews.[36]

Early in 1946 at a similar gathering, Frank approached her after the meeting to ask if she knew anything about research. She explained that that was what she did. He asked for her help, and suggested they have a cup of coffee. She accepted the invitation, and during this meeting he told her he was writing this very 'hush hush' book, and his life was in danger. Moore remembered how conspiratorial Frank was. He asked, 'Would you be able to help me?'. He dropped the name of Ralph Gibson, and said Ralph had given him the idea for the Wren book. Moore agreed to assist him. As Gibson was very highly respected, his involvement in the project would have ensured her favourable response.[37]

So, where did the concept for *Power Without Glory* originate? Cedric Ralph, a close political ally and personal friend of Ted Hill, is sure it came from Hill. Les Barnes knew that Ralph Gibson was obsessed with such a project in 1944; Gibson suggested that Barnes should write the book, and although he declined, with the blessing of the CPA he started research in anticipation of a suitable person being found. Hardy/Franklyn in *The Hard Way* states that he had the idea in February 1946, and he first mentioned the theme to Ambrose Dyson. Some time later, he saw Gibson at the *Guardian* office, and was told the party was thinking of offering him a job as a full-time functionary when he left the Army. (Hardy had, in fact, already been discharged.) In early 1946 Moore said Hardy had told her the idea for the book had come from Ralph Gibson.

If Hardy was yet to discuss the project with Gibson, it might be asked how could his life have been in danger (as mentioned to Moore early in 1946), presumably from Wren's associates, when the idea for the book was yet to be conceived? Vane Lindesay, his fellow staff member on *Salt*, was aware that the title for the book had been chosen and work was under way before Hardy was discharged from the Army on 1 February 1946. Major Mungo MacCallum was also aware of the proposed novel when Hardy worked on *Salt*. In August 1945 Gibson had introduced Les Barnes to Hardy as the person who was going to write the book.

There is strong evidence to suggest that *Power Without Glory* was the brainchild of some members of the executive of the Victorian branch of the CPA. The most likely scenario is that Ted Hill conceived the idea and discussed it with Ralph Gibson, who was enthusiastic about the project. Possibly one or more other members of the State Committee may have been involved but, given the need for secrecy and the *modus operandi* of the CPA, it is more likely that Hill and Gibson planned the project and were seeking a suitable author. 'Gibson would never have proceeded unless he had the full blessing of Hill.'[38] Once Hardy's credentials were established, and he had undertaken the assignment, Gibson was appointed to oversee his work. Gibson was admirably suited to such a task; he had taken his Master of Arts degree at Manchester University; he was a formidable researcher, 'and an absolutely loyal and incorruptible CPA member'.[39]

In 1945 Bernie Taft 'was appointed director of Marx School (the CPA's educational wing). He worked as a full-time functionary of the CPA from 1945 until 1982'.[40] When questioned on the origin of *Power Without Glory* and Hill and Gibson's involvement, Taft replied:

> I know that Ted Hill was quite interested, I know that but I was not closely connected . . . but I remember in the office that Ted was quite keen on the idea . . . my impressions are that Ted pushed it. I think without the CPA's help he [Hardy] couldn't have possibly done it. Ted would have been behind the scene as always.[41]

For approximately two years Barnes worked at the Public Library each morning, and in the afternoons he would return to the CPA headquarters at 49 Elizabeth Street to work on other tasks allotted to him. Beryl Boag (née

Thompson) worked with Dave Barter, the CPA accountant; it was her responsibility to make up the wages. She recalled that Barnes was on the payroll.[42] At this time, Alex Boag, a CPA member and an organiser for the Musicians' Union, regularly called at 49 Elizabeth Street to see Beryl. He often encountered Les Barnes, and he was interested why he was frequenting the office. He was told that Barnes worked in the mornings at the Library, and sometimes into the afternoons, doing research for Hardy's book.[43]

Ross Hardy also spent a long period working with Barnes at the Library. Barnes said she was a very nice woman and worked diligently. They were doing extensive searches on old newspapers, and later looked into the Irish question. Barnes, with hindsight, felt some of his research was not very good, as he took much of it from the *Argus* 'which was particularly vicious to the Labour Movement, and not always too close to the truth. You see, all I did was get to the papers and copy out, and Ross did too'. He said they attracted the interest of a number of people, who were curious as to what they were doing. Barnes gave all this material, together with information gleaned during his earlier research, to Hardy.[44]

Deirdre Moore also honoured her promise to help. After Hardy had decided what information he required, she spent a period of about eight weeks on research. In the beginning she did not know he was married. During this period Frank mentioned the birth of his first child, Frances. Frances was, in fact, then nearly four years old. Years later, Moore learnt that his second child, Alan, was born on 16 March 1946, which pinpointed the time of her research.[45]

Moore would go, during her lunch hour, to the Titles Office to search out the interlocking directorates of companies and directors. She recalled one of the names, Cody of the Young and Jackson's Codys, a Catholic mate of Wren from the early Collingwood days, whom she believed was a 'front' for Wren. Moore was greatly assisted by John Lloyd who worked at the Titles Office.[46] Lloyd had left-wing connections, and it must be presumed that prior arrangements had been made to facilitate her research. Moore did not indicate who she was; she would put in her request, and Lloyd would have it ready the next day; he was always very discreet and never gave himself away. Cedric Ralph, his life-time friend, would have been surprised if Lloyd had acted in any other manner.[47] The fee was 2s 6d, which was quite a sum in those days, as Moore was only earning £250 a year. Lloyd was of great help to her. She transcribed the work meticulously; Frank never offered to pay for the outgoings.[48]

As the research progressed, Frank would say, 'It's the Tunnecliffe slush fund, Deirdre, you can look up Tom Tunnecliffe, this is going to be big'. Moore said Frank was so enthusiastic in those days, and that was a long time before the book came out. He had a huge number of five- by three-inch cards, quite a few of them already with entries. His small table was cramped. She recalled:

> There was my work at the Titles Office, and then I would have to bring the stuff to this awful little dump/hideout he had in Richmond. I went up some very rickety stairs with my notes, and he would be sitting there with

his cards. He would file the stuff onto the cards. It was winter, and to keep his fire going he would twist *The Sporting Globe* or any paper like a bolt, so it was quite thick, and it became a sort of log although it was newspaper; it would last for ages.

Yes, he was probably the first member of the working-class I had ever met. I came from a private school and then I went up to the Women's College . . . my parents were wholesale manufacturers . . . We talked about the worker in theory [at University], and then actually I met this guy, he was lean and cadaverous looking . . . [as though] suffering from malnutrition . . . Being Frank he cashed in and made a great deal of his working-class background . . . He was alienated from his wife; he said he had been forced to marry, and the child was stillborn, and he was a victim of fate, kicked around, and I thought, 'My God, this is the proletariat that I dedicated my life to'.

I helped him enormously with a radio thing on the ABC called 'To Arms, To Arms'. It was for the French Revolution Bastille Day, and I heard it [on the radio]. It had to be submitted to the ABC months before . . . I had done Honours, and I had read *The French Revolution* by Carlyle, all three volumes. Frank wanted to get himself known as a writer, and obviously Bastille Day was down his alley. I got all my notes from Carlyle and culled them, things like 'To Arms, To Arms' . . . all my best phrases, needless to say Frank used them. That's how things were. That would have been about March or April [1946].[49]

Frank had an all-consuming enthusiasm and drive for his project. But, Moore said, he still had time for his two obsessions, that he never had more than eight drinks on any one day, and that he went to the races twice a week. She said she completed the research for Hardy during the winter of 1946, and later that year she left Melbourne.[50]

Moore's contribution to Hardy's research was incumbent on her CPA membership. Since 1943 the CPA had enjoyed an impressive upsurge in its numbers and a degree of popularity undreamed of just a few years earlier. The victory of the Soviet Union over the Nazis had given impetus to the belief that 'a Socialist Australia was not far away'. CPA members believed that Socialism must be an effective system if victory could be won in the face of such overwhelming odds. They were imbued with the belief that no project or task presented to them, that might 'put a nail in the coffin of capitalism', was too arduous or too big. Moore's help was consistent with the loyalty and intellectual, physical and financial contributions made by many communists to campaigns initiated by the CPA leadership. Those members recruited to assist in the *Power Without Glory* project were similarly motivated.

Years later when Hardy wrote *The Hard Way* he overlooked many people's contributions, mentioning only those made by Ross and two or three other people. He acknowledged that he did have occasional help when they copied material he had already located.[51]

There is strong evidence to support the assumption that Hardy was approached by the CPA leadership to apply his skills to the writing of a political novel which would bring Wren, Catholic Action and some members of the State Labor Party into disrepute. Under directions from his mentor, facilitator and supervisor, Ralph Gibson, it would have been arranged that the novel be seen as a completely independent work from the pen and mind of Frank Hardy. Most importantly, it was to be presented as a work of fiction. The CPA, like all political parties, was skilled in orchestrating campaigns and projects for which they neither claimed, nor indeed wanted, recognition.

Given the CPA style of operation, and Hardy being a man of his times and a party member, it is unlikely that Ross, the person who was to be most affected by her husband's decision to write *Power Without Glory*, was privy to the early discussions between Frank and Ralph Gibson. Wives of CPA members, even if party members themselves, were frequently not involved in decisions about extended trips overseas, changes of occupation and other matters which were vital to the welfare of the family.

Certainly, the CPA advocated equality for men and women in all spheres of activity, but in practice women were relegated to their traditional roles. There were, of course, a few women, mostly childless, who held positions of some power; but, with notable exceptions, they were responsible for issues relating to women, and they were not the decision makers. Several former CPA women members' autobiographies reveal hurt and anger at their treatment, both as wives and party members. Nancy Wills, former CPA member and Realist Writer, was two months pregnant and had a fourteen-month-old child, when it was raised that her husband would go abroad to study. She wrote:

> On the question of money, we were told some small sacrifices would be called for, I'd have a small income, a subsistence allowance, the same as the Party functionaries were receiving. I thought if they could manage so could I, so I again urged Geoff to accept. 'Go, love, go . . . you are the right person . . . I'll be O.K.' And I meant what I said then.
>
> Overnight things changed . . . he had been told, but he wasn't to tell me, where they were going. And he wouldn't. I resented this being shut-out, bitterly resented it. I was the one who urged him to go; I was the one who'd be making the sacrifices, and I was not to be trusted.
>
> There was more to come: we were to write one letter every two months through an intermediary—evidently **someone** was trusted . . . I protested . . . what if your mother dies, what if I die or the baby dies?
>
> 'The Party will look after any arrangements,' I was solemnly told.
>
> 'You and your fucking Party!' I was crying again . . . 'You mean you won't tell me!', I spat [the words] at him. We didn't part good friends, not a kiss, not even a handshake, not a smile . . . John Rockwell Wills ('Rocky') was ten months old before he and his father first met.[52]

The CPA wife was in an even worse position than the non-political wife, because she was fettered by her loyalty to the CPA, and her frustration at being overlooked or discounted. An illustration of how many men viewed women in those years may be gleaned from former Realist Writer Walter Kaufmann's recollections of Ross Hardy nearly fifty years later:

> Compared to Frank a rather pale figure. One of those pale Australian women, who fade into the background as their men become more famous, but she was very stalwart at the period of his trial. Extremely stalwart. And a fine mate and companion for him and kept his spirit up through that time . . . and kept the house together too, and she must have had a bitter and hard time afterwards . . . A hard life.[53]

In the prevailing climate of 1945/46, CPA member Ross Hardy would have been expected, and she probably felt duty bound, to support her husband with his important project. It is impossible to establish the precise time that she was acquainted with the plans for the proposed novel, but she was quickly recruited to work with Les Barnes at the Public Library. As Hardy had decided to become a full-time writer after his discharge, there was no question of him enrolling under the Commonwealth Rehabilitation Training Scheme for ex-service personnel to further his career prospects. His wartime literary experiences had been seductive, and he had no intention of becoming a weekly wage-earner. His assignment from the CPA further fuelled his ambition to become a writer. When Hardy wrote *The Hard Way* in 1961, he recalled that he had his deferred army pay, and he earned a little from freelance writing. He said that he had written a few plays for the Australian Broadcasting Commission, and he continued to write short stories.[54] Whatever concerns Ross had, Frank clearly had her co-operation and assistance.

Hardy was almost certainly in an elated state at the prospect of becoming a fully-fledged writer. He was also immersed in his political life, and he had his private life. He believed that his activities were creating complexities in his personality.[55] In the beginning Hardy had adopted the pseudonym of Ross Franklyn. Later, Franklyn was to become like the ventriloquist's doll; he wrote things that Hardy could not have written about himself. Whatever Hardy's personal insecurities, he was not a modest man. What prompted him to conceal himself behind this facade?

In *The Hard Way* Hardy revealed that he had not only adopted Ross Franklyn as a pseudonym, but he had assumed another name, Frank Rice, when he had a room in Richmond during 1947 and 1948.[56] No mention was made of the room Hardy rented in 1946, as disclosed by researcher Deirdre Moore. It is unlikely that Hardy's wife was aware of this 1946 tenancy. There is a possibility that the CPA and Hardy may have decided it was desirable for him to have quarters in Richmond, Wren's territory, where much of the research would be centred. In this event, the CPA may have paid the rent. Otherwise, considering the parlous state of the family's finances, separate accommodation was a luxury they could ill afford. However, Frank's association with members of the New Theatre, the Realist Writers' Group and others who lived in and around the inner city, may have sparked the idea of a 'room of one's own', away from the scrutiny of family, friends and even CPA members and functionaries. It is likely that he kept this, or another room, until he departed for Sydney in 1954.

Ross had learned to cope with unexplained absences during their marriage, but now her husband had a political reason to absent himself, because he was engaged on a secret and possibly dangerous mission. For a gambler and drinker like Hardy, Melbourne had its share of sly-grog shops, and Henry Stokes's baccarat and two-up school on the top floor of an old building on the north-west corner of Elizabeth and Little Bourke Streets, close to the *Salt* offices, was not the only one that operated all night. A communist could always claim some protracted meeting or covert activity which kept him from home. If Ross had cherished any notions of a family life after the war, these were soon dispelled.

Not only did Frank pursue his research for his novel, but he continued to become more involved with CPA work. Bernie Taft, the director of Marx School, recalls Frank was the tutor for a class for CPA members who wished to be efficient branch secretaries. His recollection is that he was a very able member of the team.[57] It was in early 1946 that Bill Smith, a recently discharged soldier, attended Marx School for his first class:

> Hardy arrived late; he held up a paper and said, 'There's going to be another war'. This surprised me because the *Guardian* had been writing about peaceful co-existence.
>
> I liked Frank; I'm a bit of a larrikin myself, and I like that sort of person. I met him at quite a few party functions and socials later on, and we became quite friendly. But I was taken aback at his so selfish attitudes, as to how he would hop into the crayfish or some particular dish that didn't go very far. He would say 'You should never get left'. I thought this was a little bit of a contradiction for a communist. Mind you, I was a bit like that myself; I'm not just rubbishing Frank about that. But it still got to me a bit, I wondered about this. He borrowed money from people. I got to know him a bit better, and then I went to the country; I didn't see him much till later on.[58]

Although Smith felt a certain uneasiness about some aspects of Frank's character, he was charmed by his easy-going manner, his interest in left-wing politics and, of course, he was extremely good company.

Marx School classes were just one of the myriad activities in which Hardy was involved in 1946. He continued to write short stories, to read widely and acquaint himself with the great literary figures of the past, and to delve deeply into Australian literature. He also became president of the Realist Writers' Group. Members had serious difficulties in having their work published. Hardy suggested that if the establishment publishers refused to publish their work, why not try the unions?[59] Such was Hardy's enthusiasm and his ability to sell an idea that the unions agreed. By now Hardy had become acquainted with George Seelaf, the secretary of the Butchers' Union, who gave him the job of editing the *Butchers' Union Journal*. This did not attract a salary, but the advertising was profitable. The Realist Writers' stories began to appear in trade union journals, and they were paid modest fees for their work.[60]

Towards the end of 1946 Frank received further affirmation that he was on the right career path. His story *The Load of Wood* was chosen by Flora Eldershaw to appear in Angus and Robertson's anthology of the best Australian stories, *Coast to Coast*. This was a propitious sign for the budding young writer.[61]

It has been impossible to precisely determine all the sources from which Hardy gathered his material before his discharge from the Army in 1946, and the printing of *Power Without Glory* which commenced in late 1949. Dot Thompson (née Kellett) was secretary to Ralph Gibson. She has very clear recollections of the part Gibson played in assisting Hardy during those years:

> I always got the impression, when I worked for Ralph Gibson, that the one who did a hell of a lot of work and arranged for Hardy to meet people at certain corners and certain times was Ralph. I remember hearing it being arranged. In actual fact Ralph did do an enormous amount of the work. I don't know whether you were able to get stuff from Ralph. He arranged meetings with people for him [Hardy] to see, and of course, Ralph himself was an extraordinary researcher, absolutely fantastic and detailed. He made all these preparations for anything he wrote. I always felt that Hardy would never have written it without Ralph's assistance . . . *but Hardy wrote it himself.*[62]

Thompson also discussed the number of party sympathisers, journalists and writers who contributed a substantial amount of information. 'There is no doubt about that, there were a number of very good writers around at that time, journalists, particularly journalists; they were together in the Army Unit [*Salt?*]. I had a lot to do with all that group.'[63]

The CPA continued to exert a strong influence in the Realist Writers' Group and monitored its progress. Ralph Gibson, then editor of the *Guardian*, later wrote:

> In touch with the group later were two of Australia's best known writers—the late Judah Waten and the master short story teller John Morrison—also David Martin, Ian Turner and Stephen Murray-Smith.
>
> I was personally closer to some than to others. With Frank I was in touch during his four years of writing *Power Without Glory*. I read many chapters in draft form. From time to time I gave advice. It was not always taken. But I was close enough to Frank to appreciate the great sweep of his book and his enormous persistence in reading, interviewing, writing and re-writing, and his daring dives into the underworld and his utter determination to finish the book despite all the difficulties. I have disagreed with Frank about some things rather basically over the years, but nothing would lessen my appreciation of this bold initial enterprise. Nor would I agree with some critics that Frank had an excellent subject but ruined it

by faults of style. I note that the British Communist Palme Dutt, himself a master of style, writing in praise of the book in 1952, notes *'its creative literary and artistic value, its lively narrative, its close and individual portraiture of character and human understanding and sympathy which raise it to a level of an outstanding work of present-day literature'*. I agree with Palme Dutt's estimate.[64]

In *The Hard Way* Hardy/Franklyn described the hand-to-mouth existence during 1946; he mentioned the frayed cuffs on his only suit; but he was rescued, because he had a win on a trotter and bought a new suit with the proceeds. He had the gambler's belief that he could have made good money if he had had a bank.[65]

Franklyn acknowledged that he was constantly harassed by debt, and it was a worrying time for him, and for his wife.[66] During the period from 1946 to 2 December 1949, Hardy wrote for the *Guardian* under the pseudonym of Ross Franklyn; some items were special features in the Magazine section, others in the Book Review column, or in the general news columns. He also contributed racing tips for the newspaper. Amirah Inglis worked at the *Guardian* and recalled that 'Frank himself exploded upstairs one day a week with his regular racing tips for *Guardian* readers, after he had finished editing the pink trotting paper the *Beam* which was printed downstairs'.[67]

Given that Hardy was under the wing of the CPA and writing for the *Guardian*, it is unlikely that he was not in receipt of some income from his journalism; it is certain that payment of a retainer was also arranged to enable Hardy to continue his research, just as Les Barnes had been paid for an 'open job' during his involvement with the Wren project. One former CPA member has clear memories of being approached by Ralph Gibson for a donation to help Frank Hardy and his family during the writing of *Power Without Glory*. She did not like Hardy, but because of her respect for Gibson, she felt compelled to accede to his request.[68] Hardy also had other sources of income; he received commission for managing the advertising in the *Butchers' Union Journal* and for the publication of his short stories which were being 'syndicated in trade union journals'. He was the manager for the *Beam*, and operated out of 534 Waverley Road, East Malvern, just a short distance from his home in Hillard Street.[69] His involvement with trotting may not, of course, have improved his finances, as the temptation to bet on a 'good thing' or on a 'whisper' was great. Some people gamble modestly, others not at all, but Frank Hardy was as addicted to gambling as others to alcohol or drugs, and it would not have mattered how much money he had, the result would have been the same— 'turkey today and feathers tomorrow'. In left-wing circles those who knew Hardy were aware that he was always broke, and he was forever trying to borrow money.

Although it was never acknowledged by either the CPA or Hardy, the financial input from the party cannot be underestimated. For example, Jack Blake, Victorian State Secretary of the CPA, wrote:

Margaret Bourke (née Fogarty), Frank Hardy's maternal grandmother.

Eddie Bourke, maternal uncle of Frank Hardy and father of Mick Bourke.

Tower Hill Cemetery,
Warrnambool.
The Bourke family grave.

Frank Hardy's birthplace at Southern Cross (near Koroit), Victoria.

Jim Hardy, Frank's elder brother, 1998.

The former home of the Hardy family, 48 Lerderderg Street, Bacchus Marsh.

Bacchus Marsh Football Team, 1924. Frank Hardy's father, Vice-President Thomas Hardy, standing at far left.

Frank Hardy's sister, Mary Hardy. St Bernard's School, Bacchus Marsh. Fancy dress concert and ball, c. 1937–38.

Caricatures of Bacchus Marsh R.S.L. personalities by Frank Hardy, October 1937.

Wedding day of Frank Hardy and Rosslyn Couper. St Patrick's Cathedral, Melbourne, 27 May 1940.

Frank and Rosslyn Hardy's home, 17 Hillard Street, East Malvern.

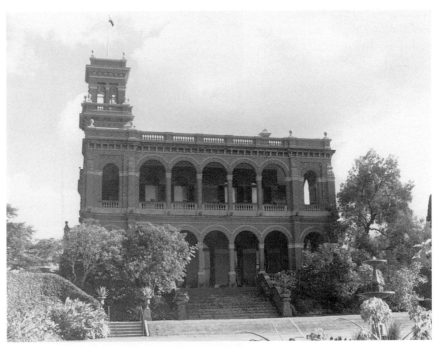

Raheen, former home of the late Archbishop Mannix.

Studley Hall, former residence of the late John Wren and family.

*A young Paul Mortier,
c. 1935.*

Staff of the Australian Army Education Service magazine, Salt, *Melbourne,
c. late 1944–45. Back row: Frank Hardy (ten from left), Ambrose Dyson (twelve
from left), Vane Lindesay (fifteen from left), Jock Hector (sixteen from left).
Front row: Mungo McCallum (five from left), Hume Dow (seven from left).*

*'The young revolutionaries'.
Eureka Youth League
gathering, Kelvin Hall,
winter 1944. Right front
row: John and Lorna Spink
and Heinz Altshul (in
uniform), a 'Dunera Boy',
a member of the 8th
Employment Company.
Third row, far right: the
author, Pauline Armstrong
(née Watkin).*

The young John Wren.

Police raid on John Wren's Tote.

Ralph Gibson,
Victorian Executive, CPA.

Ted Hill, Victorian Executive, CPA.

Cedric Ralph, solicitor for the CPA.

Deirdre Moore (née Cable), 1945, early
member of the Realist Writers' Group.

255 Bridge Road, Richmond, location of Frank Hardy's rented room.

Entrance to Frank Hardy's rented room (upstairs), 255A Bridge Road, Richmond.

George Seelaf, Secretary of the Butchers' Union and close associate of Frank Hardy.

Frank Hardy talks with Eureka Youth League members at Camp Eureka, Yarra Junction, c. 1949.

Les Barnes, compositor (left), and Vic Little, and printer/letterpress machinist, both engaged in the production of the first edition of Power Without Glory, 1949–50.

J. B. Miles, National Secretary of the CPA.

Richard (Dick) Dixon, National President of the CPA.

Ted Hill (left) and Rick Oke with Mao Tse-Tung, c. 1964.

Defend Hardy Committee sign in support of author

MEMBERS of the Defend Hardy Committee signing the petition in support of the author of Power Without Glory. Front row, left to right: Mr. J. O'Connor (Democratic Rights Council); Mr. E. Platz, journalist; Mr. Alan Marshall, author; Miss J. Campbell, secretary, Fellowship of Australian Writers; Mr. "Doc" Doyle, secretary, Ship Painters' and Dockers' Union.

The Frank Hardy Defence Committee.

Melbourne writers entertain visiting delegation of Eastern European writers, c. 1956–57. From left: Alan Marshall, unknown, Vance Palmer, Judah Waten, unknown, Bulgarian writer, unknown, Frank Hardy.

Alvie Booth, organiser for the Frank Hardy Defence Committee.

Yevgeny Yevtushenko, poet.

A night at Dirty Dick's Elizabethan Rooms, Sydney, c. 1972. Clockwise: Eva Jago, Frank Hardy, Shirley Hardy, Garry Argate, Galia and Alan Hardy, 'serving wench' Nikki Mortier.

Eva Jago dining with Frank Hardy, c. 1972.

George Kirkland, a central character in Frank Hardy's novel
Who Shot George Kirkland?

Frank Hardy speaking at the Centenary Celebrations of St Bernard's School, Bacchus Marsh, 5–6 May 1990.

Ralph Gibson gave me the rough drafts of *Power Without Glory* to read, and suggested the Party might consider giving Frank Hardy some financial assistance to enable him to finish the book. I proposed to the Victorian State Executive of the CPA that we give Frank Hardy £100. The Executive agreed to my proposal.[70]

In 1950 £100 was equivalent to approximately ten weeks' pay for a trades-man; in 2000 this would be equivalent to approximately $6500.

How much money Hardy earned, or was given during those years is im-possible to determine, but what is certain is that his wife was in a constant state of anxiety as to how she was to keep the family afloat. A gambler's wife is unable to budget as she never knows how much her spouse spends or gambles; Ross Hardy would have been no exception, and it is doubtful if she had any idea of Frank's true income. In retrospect, her daughter Frances had much admiration for her mother, 'I really don't know how she kept clothes on our backs, and food in our mouths. She did everything, the typing . . . everything'.[71]

The CPA had a puritanical attitude towards sexual morality, alcohol and gambling that was enforced by a Control Commission, the vigilante system modelled on the Communist Party of the Soviet Union. The members of the Commission were usually two or three party 'trusties', but they were not necessarily the most intelligent, if Bernie Taft's description of one member is accurate. 'O'Sullivan was a semi-literate shady figure, slightly built, with an expressionless face, who shuffled around in a furtive manner.'[72] The Com-mission issued stern warnings and imposed penalties on those members who strayed from the paths of party righteousness. Hardy's addiction to gambling made him an unlikely candidate to be entrusted with a major project. How-ever, as was usual with a CPA protégé, if some criticism of his behaviour had arisen it would have been quickly stifled. For example, *Guardian* journalist, Duncan Clarke, was 'notorious for his drinking and womanising . . . Ted Hill used to say that he received more complaints about Duncan Clarke than about the rest of the twenty odd functionaries put together'.[73] But Clarke's behaviour was tolerated by the puritanical Hill, and in 1963 he was to join Hill in the breakaway Maoist party, the CPA (M–L).

Once Hardy accepted the commission to write a novel on John Wren, he was in a very privileged position within the CPA. The substantial resources of the CPA were at his disposal for the completion of his work. The groundwork was already in place. In the years preceding the publication of *Power Without Glory*, the *Guardian* periodically printed articles attacking John Wren. The 16 August 1946 edition featured an article decrying the influence of John Wren in the Parliamentary Labor Party—the issue being the acquisition of the Ascot Racecourse for public housing—this trotting track was owned by Wren. The article was written 'By a Special Correspondent'. In gambling terms, there is an even money chance that Hardy was the contributor. So, too, with another article without a by-line bearing the headline 'John Wren's Grip on Trotting to End—

Pantomine [sic] in House Over Bill' published in the *Guardian* of 20 December 1946. If gambling, trotting and racing were taken out of the hands of Wren it would make little difference to Hardy, the gambler. But for Hardy, the man engaged on research to write a book about Wren, it became expedient for both Hardy and the CPA newspaper to continue to wage a campaign against him. Hardy, and the CPA members involved, may have believed that these articles would also elicit information about John Wren from their readers.

In the *Guardian* of 17 January 1947 an article, 'First Shot from Wren's Industrial Fund Group Fails', claimed that Wren gave £50 000 to Catholic Action Industrial Groups to fight communists in the trade unions. The article also claimed that £100 of Wren's anti-communist fund 'was used up in a futile attempt to dislodge left wingers from executive positions in the Building Workers' Industrial Union during recent annual elections'.

The *Guardian* of 18 April 1947 contained an item under the heading of 'RAHEEN' [Archbishop Mannix's residence]:

> 'What prospects are there if wages are too high and working hours too few?' Archbishop Mannix asked 400 tramworkers last Sunday morning.
>
> Pretty dismal prospects—people like John Wren could not present pretty palaces to Archbishops and there would be no £50 000 for ALP Industrial Catholic Action Groups and pimping groups like the Young Christian Workers' leaders, whose course in spying on their workmates received the imprimatur of the Archbishop.

Next to the column is a large cartoon drawn by Noel Counihan that depicts two well-fed business tycoons dining and wining on the proverbial fat of the land. One with twinkling diamond cuff-link, and the other saying: 'Well, it's going to need more than £50,000 to make those Industrial Groups work'.

The political accuracy or otherwise of these articles is of little significance here; what is significant is that the *Guardian*, in its issue of 10 November 1944, had published an article attacking Wren. That was the same year that Ralph Gibson suggested to Les Barnes that he should write a book of fiction based on Wren. That article was the first step taken to discredit John Wren.

A close examination of the facts and chronology, as detailed in the preceding pages, leads to the conclusion that the genesis of the novel, *Power Without Glory*, must be attributed to Ted Hill and Ralph Gibson and other members of the Victorian Executive of the CPA. Les Barnes had been Ralph Gibson's first choice to write the novel in 1944, but Barnes declined. Later, Frank Hardy agreed to undertake the project. Hardy and the CPA leadership were aware of the explosive nature of the novel, but not even they could have foreseen the events that followed the publication of *Power Without Glory*.

Chapter Four

THE GESTATION OF
POWER WITHOUT GLORY

WHEN RALPH GIBSON introduced Frank Hardy to Les Barnes in August 1945 as the person who was going to write a novel about John Wren, the wheels were set in motion for the gestation of *Power Without Glory*. On 5 October Hardy applied for discharge from the army, but it was not until 1 February 1946 that he returned to civilian life.[1]

Ross gave birth to a son, Alan, on 15 March 1946. Six days later Frank celebrated his twenty-ninth birthday, and he was, undoubtedly, in a state of excitement over his writing project. There is no way of knowing how much Alan's birth impinged on Hardy's consciousness, apart from wetting the baby's head with his mates in the pub. When Hardy published *The Hard Way*, more than ten years after his trial, he discussed his doubts and his fears at that time. He was, of course, writing about his *alter ego* Ross Franklyn, and with the benefit of hindsight. He bestows upon Franklyn all the virtues, qualities and minor faults he believed he possessed when he first started his research for *Power Without Glory*.[2] Did Hardy perceive, or was he concerned about the fragmentation of his personality at that time? Or did he reach this conclusion during the writing of *The Hard Way* in an effort to understand, and perhaps excuse, some of his behaviour in those early years?

Because of the secret nature of Frank's project and the elusive nature of memory, many of the events surrounding the research for *Power Without Glory* have faded into history. Although a number of people claimed to know a lot about where Hardy got his information, they were unable to recall exact details; but they were adamant that 'many party members helped Hardy enormously'. Ralph Gibson, CPA executive member closest to Hardy, was aware of Frank's drive and his determination to finish the novel, whatever the cost. Dot Thompson, Gibson's secretary, knew of Gibson's contribution in directing and introducing Hardy to those people who could help him with one or another line of enquiry. Because of the esteem and respect accorded Gibson by CPA members, trade unionists, sympathisers and others, his support and fostering of Hardy cannot be underestimated. Gibson had a vast collection of information on all aspects of Australian and, more particularly, Victorian political life. If Gibson was unable to answer Hardy's questions, he would know who to ask, or where to go.

With the passage of time, Les Barnes was not satisfied with his research at the Public Library, but this does not detract from his contribution, as Hardy also had access to Barnes's remarkable recall, and the extensive records he had collected on the history of the Victorian labour movement. But Hardy himself developed increasing skills as a researcher as he studied documents and papers in public libraries. He learnt how Melbourne had developed with its land booms and subsequent busts, and the coming of Federation. He was able to acquaint himself with reports on raids on the Collingwood Tote and Wren's ongoing battle with the police and wowsers. As a former Catholic he also learned much that was previously unknown to him about the structure and politics of the Catholic Church hierarchy, and the events surrounding the formation of 'The Movement' and a host of other subjects.

For a man of Hardy's temperament these years were both exhausting and exhilarating. Friend and fellow CPA member, Amirah Inglis, remembered that when she lived at 393 Church Street, Richmond, Frank Hardy would frequently call to see her and her husband, Ian Turner, when he was returning from a dive into the Richmond underworld; 'dizzy with success' he would relate some of the 'dirty doings of the Richmond councillors' or other line of investigation. He would entertain them with a multitude of hilarious stories; 'Frank was an inspired story teller and bull-shit artist'.[3]

In the early period of his research Frank Hardy met R. J. Mortimore, a linotype operator at the *Herald* and *Sun News Pictorial* newspapers. Mortimore was the owner of several trotting horses, and the trotting paper the *Beam* that was produced at the CPA printing press.[4] There is no evidence to link Mortimore with the CPA, other than the fact that they printed his paper. He may have been a CPA member or a party sympathiser, or he may have just wanted an editor for the *Beam* and gave the job to Frank Hardy. Certainly, there were a number of communist journalists and tradesmen working at the *Herald-Sun* at that time.[5] The Phoenix Hotel in Flinders Street was a favourite watering-hole for many of them. So, too, for members of the New Theatre which was just a couple of doors away, and it is possible that is where Hardy met Mortimore. He appointed Frank Hardy to the post of editor of the *Beam*, which was advantageous for Frank, not only in a pecuniary sense, but in a political way. The CPA had already published articles on John Wren's alleged control of trotting, and Hardy was engaged on research for *Power Without Glory*.

Les Barnes described the conflict in the trotting world at that time concerning the system of automatic handicapping versus discretional handicapping:

> In discretional handicapping if your horse won, you went back ten yards, and every time you won you kept going back ten yards. But, if you started to lose, the handicappers would say you have lost form and they'd take you back to one. That, in a simple form, explains what used to take place. According to Mortimore, Wren used to run his horses dead, and they

would get discretionary handicapping and bring them to five yards instead or ten yards, and then they would win. He'd bring off a coup and the *Beam* became the advocate of non-discretionary handicapping.[6]

When asked how Hardy lived during this period, Barnes replied:

> He was also a qualified bum. He'd go to Mortimore and say, 'Give me fifty quid, I'm broke'. Mortimore would give him fifty quid and a few tips, and he'd go out to the trots. Sometimes he came home with two hundred and fifty quid, and he'd live on that until he was broke again.[7]

Mortimore's role as a benefactor with his loans and contributions to keep Hardy solvent, to at least some degree, has been overlooked in *The Hard Way*. It must be taken into account that when the book was published Mortimore may have wished to remain anonymous. Frank did, however, mention that at that time he owed a lot of money to people.[8]

Hardy became involved with the fight of the trotting men who wanted to wrest control of trotting from Wren, and get night trotting legislation carried. He made valuable contacts when he was editor for the *Beam* that were to prove invaluable in meeting people who supported or opposed Wren. Clyde Palmer, who was the sporting writer for *Truth* newspaper, was a source of information about Wren's control of boxing and wrestling. He was unaware of Hardy's interest until *Power Without Glory* was published.[9]

The friendship that Frank Hardy and George Seelaf had formed in 1946 was to have significant effects in the years to come. The events surrounding the printing, publishing and distribution of *Power Without Glory* may have taken quite a different direction without this powerful alliance. Seelaf and Hardy, both CPA members, shared a widely held belief that a socialist Australia was just around the corner. Hardy claimed that only Ross, Dyson, Gibson and Seelaf knew of his project at that time.[10] But Deirdre Moore was already engaged on research in early 1946, and Les Barnes was gathering material for the CPA's project much earlier, even before Hardy was discharged from the army.

Hardy had a number of people in his confidence who were committed to secrecy. On his own admission, he acknowledged that he liked to 'big-note' himself by telling his informants that he was writing a book, without necessarily telling who or what the book was about. He gathered quite a lot of his material in pubs around the Collingwood–Richmond–Fitzroy areas; sometimes he would break his own rule and mention Wren when the atmosphere was convivial, and his tongue loosened under the effects of a few beers. On one occasion he formed a drinking school at the Duke of Wellington Hotel with an old man who said he knew a lot about the Wren family. Under the mellowing influence of a few drinks caution departed, and Hardy/Franklyn told him he was writing a book about John Wren. This encounter led to a mysterious meeting in an old home in one of the bayside suburbs, but the three occupants became suspicious and Hardy/Franklyn left soon after. He realised that he needed to be more careful in future enquiries.[11]

Wherever Frank Hardy travelled, he struck up conversations with people, especially old people, who were willing to discuss John Wren; a man of mystery.[12] Wren controlled a large empire, and people had many tales to tell if they considered there was no risk of reprisal. There were many 'inside' stories.

This is how Ted Seedsman described his connections with the Wren family. Eileen Murphy was the cook and general housekeeper to the Wren family for several years before her marriage in 1937, and again in 1940–41. John Wren knew that Eileen's boyfriend, Ted Seedsman, was prominent in the Victorian Athletic League. Wren asked Ted to come to his office above the Lucas Café in Swanston Street, and discuss some matters. Wren wanted the Victorian Athletic League to waive/bend the rules to enable footrunning to be held at the Motordrome (now Olympic Park) where he conducted motor-cycle races. Arrangements were made, but the joint meets lasted for only about one season.

Prior to the meeting between Seedsman and Wren, Billy Darcy, who had been a footrunner back in the heyday of athletics, was also involved with Wren at his Ascot, Fitzroy and Richmond racecourses. They raced unregistered ponies, trotters and horses. Darcy gave Seedsman a folder of cuttings from an early (around 1917) Sydney *Bulletin* which contained a series of most libellous material on Wren, about which no action had ever been taken. Darcy thought Seedsman should know the sort of person Wren was *before* he met him. Seedsman recalled that around 1928 Wren had organised a big athletic race called 'The Melbourne Thousand', a sprint race for which the prize money was one thousand pounds (a huge sum in those day). Wren had set Jack Donaldson up to win, but a drunken footballer/athlete from Brunswick called Henry Chase took off the prize much to Wren's chagrin.[13]

Seedsman, a Catholic, later joined the CPA when it was made illegal during 1940–42, when there was an influx of new members. Ted believed, with hindsight, that the main attraction for him was the illegal aspect. Wren's daughter, Elinor, was friendly with a CPA identity called Sammy White; Seedsman and another daughter, Mary Wren, were members of the Council Against War and Fascism. Mary Wren was a member of the Kew branch of the CPA. Seedsman's and similar stories about John Wren and his family were widespread.[14]

Certainly Hardy had plenty of fertile soil in which to dig; he had already discovered that many old people were familiar with the Collingwood totalisator in the early days, and some were willing to share their recollections.[15]

When Hardy was doing his research, Wren's totalisator at 136 Johnston Street, Collingwood, had changed little. The site had an attraction for Hardy, and he mentioned that on more than one occasion, he went to the rear of the premises and drew a map of the location.[16]

In *The Hard Way* Hardy has blurred the activities of his *alter ego* Ross Franklyn with his own. For clarity, it must be assumed that they are one and the same. After Frank had started to write, he encountered problems with the large volume of material he had collected. He discussed this with Ralph Gibson who explained the card system perfected by English socialist writers, Sidney and Beatrice Webb. Frank and Ross spent many worthwhile hours putting thousands of details onto filing cards.[17] Frank's recall must again be questioned as Deirdre Moore had observed that, early in 1946, he was already recording her research data onto cards in his room in Richmond. The most likely scenario is that Gibson had recommended the Webb system to Hardy when he started his research. With his temperament, Hardy had probably tired of the monotonous task; but later on, when it became impossible to retrieve facts and figures, he recruited his wife to assist him in setting up a comprehensive reference system.

In 1948, Hardy/Franklyn obtained an introduction to Miss Harriet Middlecoat of Brunswick.[18] It was reputed that she had been the lover of Frank Anstey, Labor member of Parliament. Hardy did not disclose the name of the person who gave 'Franklyn' the introduction. Les Barnes was friendly with Frank Anstey and his family and Miss Middlecoat; he may have been the contact. When Hardy's novel *Who Shot George Kirkland?* was published in 1981, he then claimed that it was the mysterious character in the novel, Alan Hall, who had gone with 'Franklyn' by tram to Brunswick, and introduced him to Middlecoat.[19]

'Franklyn' was alleged to have received some of Anstey's papers from Middlecoat, but they did not relate to his public life or about John Wren. It was claimed that Anstey had burned the papers following a visit from Ted Theodore, Queensland Premier and later Federal Treasurer.[20] But, 'According to Ted Hill, Ralph Gibson had Frank Anstey's papers, on which much of the middle part of the novel seems to be based, but Hardy was the author'.[21] However, what Hardy wrote 'corresponds with the account in the novel, although the character Frank Ashton, based on Anstey, leaves a memoir after his death'.[22]

Hardy had many such disappointments; he undertook journeys interstate that sometimes led to nothing, and interviewed those who claimed to know all about John Wren and his machine, but offered little that was of value. Other leads enabled him to make new discoveries that were vital links in the chain. What does emerge is Hardy's tireless quest for information that would enable him to reconstruct, with some accuracy, the life and times of John Wren, albeit with a hidden agenda for the contemporary political scene, more particularly in Melbourne. The assertion that the CPA was behind the genesis of *Power Without Glory* may be strengthened by Hardy's own words; he mentioned that he was apprehensive that his secret work might be uncovered.[23] CPA members commonly referred to their political activities as 'party work'. The use of the word *work* reinforces the thesis that the novel was part of a carefully conceived plan by the CPA to bring discredit to John Wren and some sections of the Victorian Labor Party. There may have been good reasons why Frank Hardy was concerned for his safety. It had been widely known that Wren had exerted power in inner eastern suburban politics for more than half a century.

In the beginning Frank Hardy had realised that he must penetrate the ranks of those who had been, or still were, part of the Richmond–Collingwood–Fitzroy political machines. He described how he had established contacts. He was introduced as Frank Rice to Cornelius, a former Mayor in the area allegedly controlled by Wren. An all-night drinking session followed, first in the Town Hall's banquet room, and later in a sleazy boarding-house.[24]

If the fear and tensions of the evening were accurately depicted in *The Hard Way*, it is little wonder that Hardy/Franklyn became ever more nervous of a crashing noise in the middle of the night, or a tall window rattling in the wind. He maintained contact with Cornelius for several weeks, during which time he introduced him to many people from all walks of life.[25] The physical and behavioural descriptions attributed to Cornelius closely resemble Cornelius Anthony (Con) Loughnan, prominent Richmond identity, Councillor and former Mayor of Richmond during some of its most turbulent years. He had been known to carry a gun, and in May 1925 he had assisted police when he fired several shots at a man who was attempting a robbery; in May 1942 Loughnan had been given a suspended three-year sentence for wounding a pensioner with a rapier in his walking-stick.[26]

When Vic Little, CPA member and friend of Frank Hardy, was printing the first edition of *Power Without Glory* in early 1950, he would read sections of the book as it came off the press. He quizzed Hardy about how he got the stories. Frank told him a slightly different version of his meeting with Con Loughnan:

> Hardy said it was a bit dicey because he was on the Council, he, Con, sort of ran the Council, and he was pretty close to a lot of shady characters of the times. He used to pack a gun; he had it in his drawer, and he showed it to Hardy. Hardy knew he had a gun. When he went to see him to try and get some stuff, particularly about Squizzy Taylor, he took a front line —a few bottles of beer—and anyway he just pumped him all night, and got him drunk. While Hardy, who said there was a pot plant or something close by, was siphoning off the beer. I can't imagine Hardy not drinking the bloody stuff if it was available.
>
> Yes, he said, so he could keep his wits about him; he needed to with this bloke with the gun in the drawer; Frank was siphoning off the beer into the pot plant, trying to keep sober while he quizzed this Loughnan, and get those stories. That is how he got that story. I would say that a whole lot of those stories were done in the same sort of manner.[27]

Little was a professional bike-rider, and he was intrigued when he read the chapter on the 1901 Austral Wheel Race. He described his conversation with Hardy thus:

> I said to Frank that is a bloody good story you have got about the Austral Wheel Race; it is just written like a bike rider. 'It ought to be', Hardy said, 'because I used to go out and see A. A. Middleton'. Now Middleton rode in that race. He was an old bike rider; he was pretty old, but still getting around in those days. I used to see him. I was riding on the board track, and he used to back me a bit. I was on talking terms with A.A., he provided all the language of that bike riding event, and Hardy must have made notes, or mental notes. For me, it was just like someone who was a top bike rider detailing a race. You know the language was there, it was all authentic. He did this in a lot of ways. He would see someone, just like Middleton, who was involved in the thing, and was able to describe it.[28]

Hardy's literary style was to receive strong criticism from some, while others were intrigued by his ability to create a world with which readers could identify. This was certainly the case with *Power Without Glory*. He had a talent which enabled him to sift his research material and present a convincing visual and verbal picture.

Hardy's forays into the shadowy world of criminals, gamblers, petty thieves, and political henchmen were not without cost. He became increasingly anxious that if word was leaked to certain people he might be in danger. It was at this time that he obtained the loan of a repeating rifle which he kept by his bed.[29] His daughter, Frances, clearly remembered that as a small child there was always a gun in the house. Her early memories of life at Hillard Street were of constantly being told to be quiet as 'Father is working'. The impact of those years on Ross was something that she would not like to go through again. She believed in her husband's right to write, and she took part in it, but it was very difficult. Ross said that the children had to be shielded as much as possible.[30]

Ross's domestic and maternal duties, secretarial tasks and her substantial contributions to the research project were not ameliorated by the camaraderie that Frank experienced during these years. He was a trusted CPA member with an important commission. He was also president of the Realist Writers' Group, where he was able to mix with other writers and hone his writing skills. He was involved with the New Theatre in Flinders Street, just a short tram-ride from his room in Richmond. There was usually a rehearsal taking place, or a review or play being staged. New Theatre was the training ground for many as yet unknown actors, writers, artists, singers, film-makers and set designers. It was also the venue for the Realist Film Unit that showed films on Sunday evenings, a rare treat in staid old Melbourne. Frank was well suited to the bohemian lifestyle, and there is little doubt that by this time he had discovered he was attractive to the opposite sex. There were any number of unattached women in these organisations who might have welcomed advances from Hardy, or, indeed, made advances to him.

In a photograph taken outside St Patrick's Cathedral following his marriage to Rosslyn, the twenty-three-year-old Hardy's cheeks still have the roundness of youth, and he has a boyish grin, perhaps even looking a little self-conscious. He is conventionally dressed in a three-piece suit with his dark hair neatly parted and smoothly combed. Hardy's photograph on the fly-leaf of the first edition of *Power Without Glory* shows that the intervening ten years have narrowed his face, and the first of the vertical lines that were to multiply as he aged are visible. His eyes have a quizzical, penetrating look, perhaps associated with his loss of innocence. Many years later, writer Dorothy Hewett described her first encounter with Hardy:

> Once we went to a party in Collingwood to raise money for the defence of Frank Hardy in the libel case brought against him for his novel *Power Without Glory*. Frank was riding high. *Power Without Glory* was a bestseller, and he was an Australian celebrity. He came into that crowded, drunken

gathering of his fans, a slim, dark, Irish larrikin with a bit of a swagger befitting the hero of the hour. Frank's charm was always infectious. But suddenly I found myself arguing with him about his novel.[31]

Later, during an interview, Hewett described Hardy as having 'that narrow, sexy, Irish face'. When she became a member of the Realist Writers' Group in Sydney, she said that Hardy had encouraged her to concentrate on her writing.[32]

Although women were always to play a significant part in Hardy's life, he was a man's man. During his time as editor of the *Beam* while he was working on his research project, and his long association with bookmakers, gamblers, trainers and punters, he would have observed the role played by the women who were the wives, girlfriends or mistresses of the bookmakers, trainers, pencillers and their hangers-on. While the important male business of the day or evening was taking place, the women had to amuse themselves. These women, had they been aware of the circumstances of CPA wives married to gamblers, may have felt they were better off. Their roles were clear; they were fashionably dressed, dined in the best restaurants at the tracks and were given money to gamble if they so wished. At day's end they were part of the evening's festivities and were financially well rewarded if their partners had had a good day. If they were not beset by qualms regarding their inferior position on the scale, they would, indeed, have felt better off than women like Ross Hardy. Hardy was an apt pupil, and it is certain that he absorbed not only the philosophy of the racetracks, but further expertise in how to handle and charm women. Hardy did not always confine his interest in women to those connected with the CPA and its fringe organisations. One of his CPA associates believed that much of *The Four-Legged Lottery* was based on Hardy's own life.[33] In the novel when one protagonist reflects on the other, mention is made of his friend's companion, a hard case, and again, his dubious women acquaintances, and an affair is referred to as sordid.[34]

The description of one woman being a 'hard case', the other with whom the protagonist had an affair as being 'dubious', and the use of the word 'sordid' in relation to a sexual relationship reveals Hardy's puritanical streak. Similar examples are to be found peppered throughout his writing. When he abandoned the strict morality of the Catholic Church, he embraced the puritanical male double-standard that was often applied within the CPA ranks.

Meanwhile, as Hardy pursued his research he continued to have Ross's assistance. She was looking after the family, working at the Public Library, typing her husband's short stories and drafts, and keeping the family in food and clothing on an income that could only be described as variable. It is certain that Ross loved and believed in her husband at that time, and even when she had doubts about some of his projects she was caught up in his waves of enthusiasm. She was also genuinely concerned that he be given a chance to write. Their daughter, Frances, believed that her mother was ill-used not only by her father, but by some CPA members too. She said she was never given due recognition for the part she played in the production of *Power Without Glory*.[35]

Frank was in a very strong position; not only did he have Ross's support, but also the invisible patronage of the CPA executive to pursue his research in whatever manner and whenever he chose. Given that he suffered some anxiety and felt threatened at times, there is little doubt that he was a 'free spirit'. The nature of his project was such that it was not expected that he account for his time or his whereabouts. He had freedom to follow any leads or contacts that might contribute to his novel, and the opportunity to enjoy an exciting and interesting personal life.

He made a number of interstate journeys. For a peripatetic character like Hardy, it is likely that some of his trips were undertaken on a whim. But there is little doubt that as he gained more and more insight into the politics of earlier years, he was able to piece together the material for his as yet unwritten novel. He could retreat to the room in Richmond where he lived under the name of Frank Rice and enjoy the convivial atmosphere in the pubs he frequented. When he chose, he returned to the family hearth in East Malvern, where he was, as one frequent and perceptive woman visitor recalled, 'the master of the house. He did all the talking, and his wife was obliged to conform'.[36] During these years, Hardy was also writing political articles for the *Guardian*, as well as its racing and tipping column. Members of the CPA could participate in many enjoyable social and cultural gatherings, in addition to the more serious tasks allocated to them. Frank's personality, storytelling and wit made him a welcome addition at these functions. Just as Amirah and Ian Turner were filled with admiration for his enthusiasm and fearlessness in pursuing information and amused by his tales, so, too, were those who were party to his project. Hardy had long since discovered his talent as an entertainer and storyteller, and he knew how to keep an audience enthralled.

Just how successful was Frank Hardy's research? This question was still being debated as late as December 1976 when the Council of Adult Education conducted a day-long seminar at Monash University on 'The historical significance of *Power Without Glory*'. The speakers were author Niall Brennan, academics June Hearn and Lloyd Robson, and author Frank Hardy. A range of viewpoints emerged as to the veracity of characters, politics and events as depicted in *Power Without Glory*. Brennan believed that 'the novel rings funny all the way through. It is written by someone who wanted to write about a cause, and who didn't bother ever finding out anything like that sympathy and understanding which makes a novel a great work'.[37] Whereas Hearn, a former fourth-generation Collingwood resident, affirmed that much of the life as depicted in the novel was accurate. For example, her father, Bill Mackinnon, was aware of the political implications of belonging to the so-called Wren machine. When Mackinnon became president of the local ALP branch, he received a message that John Wren was interested in him. By this time, Mackinnon was disillusioned with the reformist policies of the party; he had decided he wanted to be his own man.[38]

Hearn gave a detailed account of life in Collingwood. The spectre of the footwear industry hovered over the mean cottages and streets, and as the main employer it dominated the lives of the residents. There were the pushes, the betting shops, the gambling, the fights and the sporting prowess of its young men; life was hard, and they needed to be able to defend themselves. There was general contempt for the police; they were known to accept bribes. The ethos of the district precluded implicating the police regardless of whether an offence was a misdemeanour or a felony, and this rule applied even when homicide was involved. The hostility between the Catholics and the Protestants was not based on a philosophical understanding of their respective religions, but was a case of 'them' against 'us'. From Hearn's own personal experience and knowledge and the information and stories told to her by her parents and other local identities, she considered that Frank Hardy had accurately portrayed the life and times of Collingwood, Richmond and Fitzroy, as described in *Power Without Glory*.[39]

The opposing views expressed by Brennan and Hearn in 1976 were echoes of the spirited discussions which took place when *Power Without Glory* was first launched in 1950. These echoes can still be heard. There are those who remain hostile to Hardy and claim his research was inaccurate, faulty and a farrago of lies and half-truths; while others applaud Hardy for his vivid and accurate representation of the people and the times as depicted in his novel.

Frank Hardy had a great deal of help with his research, but the assistance he received from the sources available to him in no way diminishes the scope of his own research, nor minimises the risks taken. History has shown that, given the dubious activities of some of the characters involved and the political climate at that time, his life may have been in jeopardy. Once Frank Hardy had the material within his grasp, he then faced the formidable task of writing and publishing *Power Without Glory*, at a time when 'the class struggle was reaching its height in Australia [and] the Cold War was beginning between Russia and the west'.[40]

Chapter Five

THE WRITING OF
POWER WITHOUT GLORY

IF THE COLLECTION of the material had been a mammoth task, the writing of the novel appeared to be insurmountable. In the beginning Hardy, like many inexperienced writers, wanted to put everything in. Later, when he tried to reduce the chapters he had written, he made no progress. By February 1948 he came to the conclusion that he did not have the skill to construct a novel. When he faced this defeat, he decided instead to write about his own life and experiences. Again he realised his inadequacies, as he became increasingly aware that constructing a novel was quite another matter to short story writing. He undertook a study of Elizabeth Bowen's essay *Notes on Writing a Novel*, in which she stressed the importance of relevance. This text left an indelible impression on the young writer, and he was to mention it frequently over the years.[1]

Then he started his novel afresh. Hardy later wrote that he heard a story in a pub about an illegal bookmaker who spun a golden sovereign in front of the new policeman in a country town; then he spun it again in the direction of the policeman, who caught it and put it in his pocket. This tale gave Hardy inspiration; he knew how to incorporate it at the beginning of the first chapter.[2]

The task of refining, pruning and restructuring the novel absorbed Hardy. He was later to claim that after attending a school on Marxist philosophy, he worked out a theme that the accumulation of great power will corrupt a man and destroy personal relationships.[3] Hardy did not gain power in the accepted sense, but had he, in his later years, substituted the word 'fame' for 'power' in applying this theme to his own life he might have found parallels.

Some time before, Guido and Jean Canteri had leased Gibson's Farm at Moondarra, about one and a half miles south of Erica in the Great Dividing Range in Victoria. Guido had been a prominent activist in the Italian community in Melbourne, and was well known to Ralph Gibson. When Hardy wanted to escape the distractions of city life to work on his novel,[4] Ralph arranged with the Canteris that they accommodate him. Guido's son, Carlo, has retained strong images of Hardy's arrival with Gibson:

Ralph and Frank were walking, engaged in serious conversation, along a ridge; without warning, they took off their shoes and with arms akimbo they ran joyously, like two kids, down the slope through the mature wavering grasses shimmering in the late afternoon breeze.

Before Ralph returned to Melbourne, the two men packed sandwiches into a rucksack and trekked up Mt Erica. Each night Frank would sit with my sister and me on his knees and sing songs—lots of songs—but especially 'Old McDonald had a farm' which he sang so fast we would become hysterical with laughter and collapse. We reckoned it was impossible for anyone to talk or sing that fast. Later, I remember the glee expressed by my parents when my uncle brought them a copy of the 'wharfie-bound' edition of *Power Without Glory*. They listened with intense interest to the reports of the criminal trial on our six-volt battery-driven Golden Voice radio.[5]

The images of Ralph and Frank running down the grassy slope and their trek up Mt Erica were, perhaps, an indication of the relief they had felt during this brief respite from the tense political situation they had left behind in Melbourne.

Frank stayed with the family for about two months. He later wrote that one evening as he sat working at the table, the words 'power without glory' appeared on the paper. This was the title for his book![6] In 1986, however, Vane Lindsay wrote that the title *Power Without Glory* had been chosen before Hardy left the army in 1946.[7] So, when was the title chosen, before February 1946 or in autumn 1948? This discrepancy raises the problematic nature of autobiographical recollection:

> a teleological theory of autobiography . . . argues that generally speaking, autobiographers primarily document those incidents that they see as contributing to the overall pattern of their lives—a pattern they impose in the present onto the past. One of the central problems of memory is that people tend to remember their past in a way that accords with their present. This has obvious implications for the reliability of autobiographical memory.[8]

Frank Hardy, by introducing his *alter ego* Ross Franklyn in *The Hard Way*, has added yet another dimension to the minefield of memory and truth in autobiography. Many of the people, events and places mentioned are easily verified, but in the absence of original documents and without unrestricted access to Hardy's papers, there must be a degree of acceptance or conjecture. When William Butler Yeats introduced his first autobiography he wrote, 'I have changed nothing to my knowledge; and yet it must be that I have changed many things without my knowledge; for I am writing after many years and have consulted neither friend, nor letter, nor old newspaper, and describe what comes oftenest first, into my memory'.[9]

Hardy, were he alive to defend *The Hard Way*, would concur with Yeats's view, and he might consider it reasonable to ask why Lindsay's recall was more reliable than his. Hardy would also claim that he had written an autobiographical novel, a work of fiction, even though the cover described it as 'The story behind *Power Without Glory'*. Whatever the facts regarding the choice of a title, it was not long before Hardy returned to Melbourne. He worked throughout that winter of 1948, often into the early hours, wearing the thick, polo-neck jumper his wife had knitted him, to combat the intense cold.[10]

The new year of 1949 had many unpleasant surprises in store for CPA members, and Frank Hardy was not to be exempt. John Sendy noted that 'It is difficult for those who did not experience Party work in 1949 and the following years to appreciate the extent and the fury of the attacks on the CPA, the constant barrage in the daily papers and in parliaments, the violence at Party public meetings'.[11]

Ralph Gibson described that year as a 'Year of Battles'. By 1949 the 23 000 CPA membership of the war years had halved.[12] Since the beginning of the Cold War the hostility towards the communists had intensified. In the first weeks of the New Year, the CPA organised a party-school at the home of CPA member and party benefactress Molly Inge in Tintern Avenue, Toorak. The main participants were party functionaries; but there was an absentee, Cecil Sharpley, who was in charge of trade union work and a member of the Victorian Executive of the CPA. When he was eventually found by party members, it was announced that his membership was under a cloud.[13]

In April 1949 the *Herald* published a series of seven articles written by Cecil Sharpley bearing the captions 'I Was a Communist Leader'. Stories about Sharpley's heavy drinking and gambling had long abounded among party members. Their silence had been assured by their loyalty to the party, but his defection unleashed bitter criticism, and there was no epithet harsh enough to describe Sharpley and his sell-out to the press. A cartoon by Ambrose Dyson appeared in the *Guardian* titled 'Hark the Herald Angel Sings' that depicted Sharpley as a rat standing in the witness box, while all around held their noses.

In these articles Sharpley claimed that the communists were involved in disrupting industry, rigging trade-union ballots, receiving money and instructions from Moscow, instigating violence, and other clandestine activities aimed at overthrowing the elected government. In tune with the anticommunist hysteria prevalent at that time, the Victorian Liberal Government established 'The Victorian Royal Commission on Communism—1949–1950'. The Commission sat from June 1949 until March 1950, some 159 witnesses were called, and communists, sympathisers and fellow-travellers read the newspaper reports with trepidation to see if they, or someone they knew, had been named in the proceedings. People stood in queues to listen to the evidence presented to Justice Sir Charles Lowe. 'Communism on trial was a box-office success and the customers got their money's worth.'[14] The findings of the Royal Commission proved disappointing not only to the Liberal Government, but to the anticommunists in the community, as Lowe could find no reason to bring charges against the CPA or any of its members. Sharpley was discredited as an unreliable witness.[15]

When Frank Hardy had read Sharpley's first article in the *Herald*, his main concern was that if Sharpley knew about *Power Without Glory*, he would inform the security police. Frank hid his notes, cards and manuscripts, and became involved in the fight against the Royal Commission. He came to the conclusion that he should finish the novel as soon as possible, and decided to go to the country again to write. The CPA had been informed that a frame-up might be attempted to shore up Sharpley's evidence. What form that might take was not known, but the permanent Eureka Youth League Camp at Yarra Junction, near Warburton, was vulnerable if someone were to plant arms and ammunition there. A party official suggested that Frank and another writer could live there for a time. Each day they checked the camp and guarded it, but they spent most of their time writing.[16]

The other writer, whom Hardy did not identify in *The Hard Way*, was Eric Lambert. As Zoë O'Leary disclosed in her biography of Lambert, *A Desolate Market*, 'he made one of the most significant contacts of his life: he met Frank Hardy. They were at a cottage lecture . . . it was Hardy who joined him up in the Australian Communist Party (CPA) in 1947'.[17]

Lambert had stayed with the Hardys after a disagreement with his mother:

> The 'mateship' they both wrote about, the great 'Australian ethic' was a living, developing thing in their personal lives . . . both men liked long drinking sessions, and the resulting hectic discussions; both were becoming increasingly involved in the political scene . . . Physically, they resembled each other slightly; there were points of contact in their personalities; both were splendid raconteurs and both had a highly developed sense of humour . . . When Hardy and Lambert were approached by the CPA to guard Camp Eureka and work on their writing, it was an extension of the close relationship they already enjoyed. They lived in the dilapidated old homestead near the camp gates. When their patrol duties were over, they worked on their writing: Lambert on *The Twenty Thousand Thieves* and Hardy on *Power Without Glory*.[18]

The two men were not alone at the camp, as they had the company of an elderly couple, Stella and Sid Rawlinson, who had become permanent caretakers. Sid Rawlinson was an uncle to Jean Canteri, Frank's hostess at the farm in the Great Dividing Range. Former EYL member Eric Stark recalled how Rawlinson considered himself to be a working-class philosopher. He believed that there were only four true Marxists in Australia—J. B. Miles, Lance Sharkey, Jack Blake and himself—but not necessarily in that order![19] Hardy's cameo in *The Hard Way* of this eccentric character is a gem, confirming Vic Little's opinion of Hardy's skill in recording the language of those he encountered.

On occasions Hardy and Lambert also had the company of the EYL members, trade unionists, CPA members and other volunteers who worked some weekends to maintain and extend the camp buildings and facilities. It was on one such weekend, according to Wendy Lowenstein, that Hardy and Lambert came down from the old house and joined the workers around the camp-fire. Hardy sang 'The Overlanders'; it was her first exposure to an Australian folk song. Lowenstein said that although Frank's voice left much to be desired, the experience kindled her interest in Australian songs and folklore. Some years later, Ian Turner discussed with Lowenstein the possibility of forming a folklore society; they held a meeting, and the Folk Lore Society of Victoria was born. Lowenstein was to become the driving force behind the FLSV and the editor of the journal *Australian Tradition*.[20] Perhaps the folk lore and folk music revival owes a small debt to Hardy for his song around the camp-fire.

The weekend campers provided some respite for Hardy and Lambert from their writing. They could eat at the mess-hut, and on one occasion they were able to go to Melbourne for a short break when CPA member Ron Neave and a friend, who had been working at the camp, drove them back to the city. On the way the two writers developed a great thirst; they needed a beer. The four men called into the Woori Yallock Pub where they spent a convivial hour or two, but, as usual, Hardy and Lambert couldn't pay for their beer as they were flat broke.[21]

It is of historic interest that one weekend in the winter of 1949, Camp Eureka was host to three young writers who later became well known for their work: Frank Hardy (*Power Without Glory*), Eric Lambert (*The Twenty Thousand Thieves*), and Wendy Lowenstein (*Weevils in the Flour* and *Under the Hook*). The CPA and the Realist Writers' Group had been prominent in promoting the socialist realist school of writing from the mid-1940s.

Hardy made progress with the novel while he was at the camp, but after some weeks he went back to town where he continued to work on the novel and helped in organising the campaign against the anticommunist Royal Commission. It was during this period that Ambrose Dyson made a decision that the powerful scraperboard drawings which later enhanced the first edition of *Power Without Glory* would be suitable for Frank's novel.[22]

Hardy was convinced that the expected frame-up of the CPA had arrived when Ken Miller, a CPA functionary, was arraigned on a charge of carnal knowledge of an eleven-year-old girl in the suburb of Richmond. Hardy wrote several articles on the subject, including one in the *Guardian* about the Haymarket Martyrs of Chicago, the anarchist labour leaders convicted of murder in 1886, after a bomb was thrown at police at a mass meeting by someone unknown. When Miller came before the court, the magistrate declared that he had no case to answer. The *Herald* reported the acquittal, without comment, on an inside page.[23]

During 1949 the political climate in Australia was becoming even more anticommunist. On 17 October 1949, Lance Sharkey, the General Secretary of the CPA, was gaoled for three years after it was claimed that he had made a seditious statement. In June, during the national coal strike, the Chifley government set in place emergency legislation that ultimately resulted in troops being used to produce the coal. The miners' leaders were isolated, and the workers became antagonistic to the strike. Eventually the strikers voted to return to work. Consequently the CPA was further weakened, and its influence in the trade unions declined. Conversely, the anticommunist ALP Industrial Groups gained further support.

Hardy made another determined effort to finish his work, and by the spring of 1949 the novel was almost completed. Communists received another crushing political defeat following the coal strike debacle when, in a pre-election speech on 16 November, Robert Menzies promised to outlaw the CPA if elected. His success at the polls on 10 December was a great disappointment to the forces of the left. The disappointment would have been greater had they realised that twenty-three unbroken years of conservative government had been ushered in. The CPA's influence in the trade unions had waned, and it is clear that any counter-attack that could be used against the anticommunist ALP Industrial Groups, the right wing of the Labor Party and the conservative forces in general, might give a much-needed respite to the besieged CPA. It was fortuitous for the CPA that Hardy's novel was virtually completed.

Frank Hardy asked Hume Dow, the former editor of *Salt*, to read the *Power Without Glory* manuscript. The following text is an excerpt from an interview with Dow in June 1994:

> PA: Do you believe that Hardy wrote *Power Without Glory*?
> Dow: I do, I read the manuscript circa 1949 and it was clear in my discussions with Hardy that he was the author. No one else could have written the manuscript. I made a few suggestions about the manuscript, but they were not too far-reaching.
> PA: Did you think it was publishable?
> Dow: Yes. I told Frank that I believed it was publishable, but I felt he would have trouble getting a publisher. He said that if that happened he would publish it himself.
> PA: Did you think it might be libellous, and if so, did you mention this to Frank Hardy?
> Dow: It did occur to me, but I did not discuss this with him.[24]

Frank Hardy had spent much of the last four years researching, writing and rewriting the novel; now he faced the task of having it published. His wife, Ross, had helped with some of the research, and the transference of information onto cards. She had typed all the original early drafts, then the first thousand-page manuscript which was later abandoned; finally, she had had the daunting task of typing the revised and final manuscript. Ross apparently did not demur when her husband brought, at different times, the Dyson family and Eric Lambert to live in their small maisonette. In addition there were the CPA members and delegates to conferences who were occasionally billeted with them. The Hardy family life had been dominated by the characters and events of the shadowy world of *Power Without Glory*, but the tyranny of the novel was not yet over.

In 1944 when Ralph Gibson had a discussion with Les Barnes about the desirability of writing a novel based on the life of John Wren, the prime purpose was to bring discredit to the right wing of the Labor Party and the anticommunist groups. This purpose was unchanged when Hardy commenced his research in 1945. At that time the CPA was exerting unprecedented influence in the trade union movement; the novel was to be used by the CPA as a counter-attack to expose these bodies before they had developed too much industrial muscle. However, by the end of 1949, when Hardy was finishing *Power Without Glory*, the CPA faced a more immediate threat from the Menzies Government. The original purpose of the novel had been overshadowed by the events which were taking place. It was apparent to Hardy and the CPA that the challenges being mounted against the forces of the left required decisive action; *Power Without Glory* could now be used as a powerful diversionary defence against the political assaults which were in train.

Hume Dow's opinion that it might be difficult to get a publisher may have influenced Hardy's decision to self-publish. However, Hardy and the CPA knew it was essential to retain control over the potentially explosive novel. It would have been considered a political risk to place it with a commercial publisher could one be found; and the CPA had its own substantial printing facilities. Both Hardy and the CPA were highly motivated to get the novel into the public arena as quickly as possible. The printing, publishing and distribution of *Power Without Glory* was to become the most remarkable saga in Australia's literary history.

Chapter Six

PRINTING, BINDING AND PUBLISHING

THERE ARE A NUMBER of versions of how the *Power Without Glory* manuscript moved onto the printed pages of the first edition, which is dated April 1950. Once the novel was almost finished, Frank Hardy and the CPA were anxious to get the printing under way. After several discussions with Ralph Gibson, it was decided that Frank should organise the printing.[1] It is certain that the CPA was anxious to disassociate itself from the novel.

When Hardy wrote *The Hard Way* he devoted much of chapter four to the events surrounding the printing, but there is evidence to suggest that while his exciting story is close to the truth, it is not the exact truth. This may have been because at the time of writing, during 1960–61, anticommunist feelings were again powerful.

Frank's fictionalised version was colourful. He acknowledged that several people had lent him money during the crucial period of the printing of the first edition, but he concealed the fact that he had had the organisational and financial backing of the Victorian State Executive of the CPA throughout the entire period from the project's inception.[2] Both Hardy and the CPA still wanted to conceal the CPA's involvement.

Hardy was fortunate that he had Ralph Gibson as his mentor. Gibson was well known to prosperous CPA members and sympathisers, and could be very persuasive when raising funds for an important project. Hardy also had an ally in businessman Itzhak Gust, a prominent member of the Jewish community who had worked in the *Salt* office; he, too, helped in raising funds.

Three CPA members played vital roles in the printing of the first edition of *Power Without Glory*: Les Barnes, a compositor, and Vic Little, a printing machinist, who were both employed by the CPA's Federal Press, and George Seelaf, the secretary of the Butchers' Union. According to Hardy, he had discussed with Vic Little, and possibly one or two others, the virtues of various printing machines. The conclusion was reached that the best type of machine to buy was probably a Double Royal Wharfedale, an English machine. Little told Hardy that it was very solid and reliable, and although it was not fast, it produced good quality work.[3]

Hardy claimed that he was fortunate that, once having decided to print the book himself, he had a substantial win at the races. Even the most ingenuous reader would doubt Hardy's version of some of the events described in *The Hard Way*. Gamblers are known to believe in fanciful omens as to what might or might not bring them luck; but it is unlikely that even an addicted gambler like Hardy would invest his winnings in setting the type before he had arranged for a printer to undertake the work. His doubts about the risks attached to seeking credit for the metal were valid. It is probable that he did hire metal for the type-setting on a rotating basis, and his fears about getting the metal type-set were well grounded. The head of any firm engaged could have raised queries about the contents of the book. His reference to finding a 'comping' firm was incorrect.[4] Les Barnes was adamant that, as the compositor at the party's printing press, he had set the metal type into sixteen-page formes for the entire first edition of *Power Without Glory*; Vic Little has confirmed Barnes's statement. This work was completed at the press, and Barnes was paid his normal wages during the process.[5] His brother, Bill Barnes, who worked as a machinist at the press, also confirmed that Les did the composing for *Power Without Glory*. Bill said that the party press had the facilities to produce the papier mâché stereotypes used to make metal printing formes for rotary presses; these were stored in 'safe' premises until further editions were required, avoiding the risk of losing all the typesetting in the event of a police raid.[6]

It has been acknowledged that the CPA could be imprudent, even reckless, and wasted resources by engaging in campaigns and plans that were doomed to failure; but the CPA also had many spectacular political successes. Because of the hopes pinned on the publication of *Power Without Glory*, there is no doubt that Hardy was given as much assistance as possible, despite the mounting political crisis which faced the CPA. In addition, Hardy had been contributing to the *Guardian* as a journalist and a tipster for some years, and he had also been closely involved with the production of the *Beam*. He was friendly with all the staff at the party press, and he was part of the team. It is certain that Gibson had been briefed by Ted Hill as to the extent of the CPA's support; one important financial contribution was that Barnes and Little continued to be paid by the party press for the duration of their work on the novel. This was the method used when Barnes was paid by the CPA during the period he was doing research for Frank.

Hardy had told Little that when he discussed the purchase of the printing machine with the owner of Batten's Printery, who had advertised the Double Royal Wharfedale machine for sale for £1000, he had explained that he was writing a trilogy of novels. As he had nowhere to house the machine, Frank explained to the owners that he was having a factory built in the suburbs, but it would not be finished for some time. He wanted to start printing the first novel immediately, and he would like to use the machine in Batten's premises until his factory was completed; then he would transfer the machine. This suited the owner, and Hardy arranged to use the machine for four days each week, with Batten's printing auction posters each Friday. He had paid £100 deposit, and the balance was to be made in monthly payments.[7]

However, in *The Hard Way* Hardy wrote that the owner of the machine wanted payment for the machine, but it could not be removed until his new machine arrived from overseas in about six months time. Hardy agreed to the proposal, provided he could use the machine on site.[8]

He also wrote that the machine cost £1800; a friend loaned him £500, and the next day he paid £400 deposit on the machine, and £100 on further type-setting. His bank manager agreed to finance the balance on monthly payments.[9]

Little, as far as Batten's Printery knew, was an employee of Hardy. He said that when he started work soon after Christmas 1949, he was approached by the shop steward, who asked him, 'Have you got your ticket?'. He gave him his union ticket which showed that he was paid up well in advance. Little was, in fact, the shop steward at the CPA press, and he was on the Board of Management of the Printing and Kindred Industries Union.[10] Little's account that the machine was used to print Batten's auction posters each Friday bears little resemblance to Hardy's version in *The Hard Way*; he said he had discovered that Batten's printed Liberal Party propaganda. However, Hardy's reference to the Liberal Party certainly added a nice touch of colour.

Les Barnes said that it was possible that Frank Hardy had hired the use of the printing press from Batten's Printery. This was a frequent practice among printers, who would hire time at another press if their own machines were busy. However, because of the covert nature of the operation, Barnes could only be sure of what he himself had contributed.[11] The most likely scenario is that Hardy hired printing time only. Little had no knowledge of any hiring arrangement; his impression was that Hardy had paid a deposit, and when the printing was completed, he had just left the machine behind.[12] Eventually Hardy was to write in *The Hard Way* that Ross Franklyn was £2000 in debt when the printing was completed. The book was written as an autobiographical novel/reportage, and while some of the statements can be verified, others cannot be confirmed. In chapter four Hardy appears to have changed many of the events associated with the printing and binding of the first few editions of *Power Without Glory*.

Hardy wrote that he had worked with a printer during the Christmas vacation in 1949 when the printery was closed down.[13] It was unlikely, however, that the management would have given two strangers access to their premises during the vacation period.

When Little started work after Christmas 1949, he was aware that Hardy and Ernie Bowles, an experienced printer who worked at the party press, did work for two or three weeks during December 1949—*before* and not *during* the vacation. His recollection was that Hardy and Bowles had printed the first thirty-two pages.[14]

Batten's Printery was situated in the veritable maze that was the old Rialto building in Collins Street, Melbourne. The Wharfedale machine was in a basement serviced by a lift which had to be pulled up and down by a hand-cord— the only means by which goods could be transported to and from the basement. It was at this time that George Seelaf became a 'mover and shaker' to get the printing under way. Either he and Frank Hardy, or sometimes just one of them, would collect the used metal formes and deliver the new sixteen-page formes which had been made up at the party press. They used a trolley to cart the formes from the truck to the rickety old lift. The linotype was being set at one of the trade houses; Little believed the firm was Trade Composition. He thought that another firm, possibly Dudley King & Sons, may also have been employed.[15]

Who made the payments for the metal used in the typesetting cannot be established, but in *The Hard Way* Hardy said that he had paid £200 in advance for the metal, which had to be continually recycled during the printing of the book. Until the first thirty-two pages were printed, it was impossible to return the type. Therefore, it seems that he had required three quantities of metal to keep up a continuous supply for the two sixteen-page formes needed to produce each sheet of thirty-two pages. As one set was being printed, the other was being typeset, and the third had to be melted down ready for the next type-setting.[16] It is possible that Hardy had to rely on loans from friends, advances from the CPA or an occasional win at the races, to maintain the rotation of the metal. But, it is more likely that there was a firm arrangement with the CPA to provide Hardy with the funds to pay for the metal. There was every reason to avoid any interruption to the production of the novel, given the political crisis in which the party was embroiled.

The source of the printing paper remains a mystery, but it is reasonable to assume that it was donated by the party press. As the Victorian Executive of the CPA had arranged that Barnes and Little were to be paid from the party press offices, they were unlikely 'to spoil the ship for a halfpennyworth of tar'. It would have been an easy matter to supply Hardy, or Seelaf, with official order forms to the paper merchants, where arrangements could then be made to collect the large bundles of pre-cut paper. In the absence of any firm evidence, and given the fact that Hardy did not mention either the cost or the difficulties of buying the paper for this edition, it is probable that this was another and logical contribution by the CPA.

The description of a typical day as described in *The Hard Way* coincides with Little's recollections of that summer of 1949–50, although Hardy does not mention Seelaf's tremendous contribution, perhaps once again because of the political situation at the time of writing. The handling of the heavy metal type in all its stages required a huge physical effort. The typesetters were up a steep flight of stairs, and the lift at the CPA's Federal Press was even more primitive than the one at Batten's; it worked by means of a hand-wound cable pulley. Taxi trucks were used to transport the metal and the chases of type.[17] This pattern of pick-ups and deliveries was maintained all through the hot summer of 1950.

Before the printing had started, Hardy had emphasised that Little must keep all the 'spoils', because if any were returned in the waste-paper collections to the Australian Paper Mills in Fairfield, someone might just read them. Perhaps Wren would get wind of it! The cloak-and-dagger nature of the printing placed a heavy burden on Little; he had to be ever on guard. Some of the workers from Batten's occasionally wandered over during their morning-tea break to where Little was printing; they would pick up sheets and read a page or two. They would ask Little questions:

Worker: This is interesting, a bit of politics in it?
Little: Yes, a bit of politics—there is a bit of gang stuff in it—a bit of romance.
Worker: What sort of a book is it?
Little: It is a bit of everything.

Little said that although the men were mildly intrigued by the book, they never 'woke up' to what it was about. Each day he collected the 'spoils', and he took them home to South Melbourne, where he burned them. He, too, was very concerned that Wren might find out. While he was still printing, Batten's foreman asked Frank if Little wanted a job when he was finished working for Hardy, because he was so impressed with his tidy workmanship.[18]

Little suffered anxiety that the nature of his work might be discovered. He was unwilling to ask the help of other printers working nearby in lifting up the sixteen pages of solid linotype metal formes onto the Wharfedale, which was up on a platform, and he sustained a back injury that was to prove permanent. Normally, this job would be done by two men. Little, as a shop steward, would never have tolerated other union members working under such conditions, but as a communist he was prepared to risk his personal safety for the sake of the CPA. He toiled all through the hot summer and into the autumn of 1950 until the 10 000 copies were completed.[19] Given the clandestine nature and isolation of his work, it was a monumental effort, and is a further illustration of the dedication that some CPA members gave to tasks allotted to them by the leadership.

The deliveries made by Seelaf and Hardy would have been welcome interludes in an otherwise lonely day. On occasions Hardy remained after making a delivery, and Little remembered him helping by standing by the shaker preventing the sheets from falling crookedly and becoming damaged, then lifting them down when they piled up.[20] While he stood on the high platform, Hardy would be mulling over the proof corrections and working out how to integrate the material for the last three chapters that were being rewritten as printing continued.[21]

Little was aware that while he was printing the early sections of *Power Without Glory*, Hardy was still working on the final chapters. Towards the end of the printing, Hardy was writing about the ALP Industrial Groups. Little believed that these chapters were not as well formulated as the earlier ones, because they had not been spruced up. At one stage, the writing was only one chapter ahead of the printing. Earlier, when Little was working at the party press, he knew that brown-paper parcels were sent from Sydney to Hardy, who eagerly examined the contents. These contained sections of the manuscript that had been read and vetted by R. (Dick) Dixon, who was then National President of the CPA. On occasions Hardy would show Little letters which accompanied the revised copy; some were ten or twelve pages long. This continued up until the last chapter was revised. Little knew that Hardy was being given political guidance by Dixon, who was in close contact with him until the novel was finished.[22]

It was not only the National and Victorian leadership who sometimes disagreed with the contents of the novel. Les Barnes said that he had had two conflicts with Hardy and the CPA during that time. He lost one, and he won one. The first was over the love affair Nellie West/Wren was alleged to have had with the bricklayer, Bill Evans/Egan. Barnes told Hardy that it was her own private business, and he had no right to introduce her into the book. Frank told him that it was a part of the book, and it showed the character of Wren. Barnes felt that he was dealing with it in the old-fashioned way. He told Hardy that he didn't know if it was true, but Frank claimed that it was 'pretty' authentic. Barnes asked him if the 'bloke' who told him would stand up in court. Barnes had a discussion with others at the party press; it was agreed that it should not be included. Then it was referred to Sydney, and J. B. Miles, the General Secretary of the CPA, said, 'It's a damn good book and don't alter it for anyone'. Barnes commented, 'To hear the words of J. B. Miles was to hear the words of "His Holiness"'. Hardy was jubilant that he had received Miles's approval. Soon after, in a rather nasty and petulant display, Hardy told Barnes, 'You've got too much Australian fair go, it's boots and all, you know. They did it to us'. Barnes's recollection is that he replied, 'Why do it to them?'. However, Barnes yielded to party authority, and no deletions or alterations were made.[23]

Vic Little did not believe that the love affair, as depicted in *Power Without Glory*, was based on a true happening; he thought that it had arisen out of Hardy's reading of D. H. Lawrence's *Lady Chatterley's Lover*. When Little had questioned Frank about some of the incidents in his stories and in *Power Without Glory*, he was fond of saying 'that was not what happened, but it was what should have happened'.[24]

The second conflict arose when Barnes started to compose a chapter which, in his opinion, slandered Pat Kennelly who had always been a Labor man. Hardy claimed in the manuscript that Kennelly had been a scab, but Barnes was well acquainted with his history and knew this to be untrue. Barnes pointed out to Hardy that Kennelly had been elected as organising secretary of the Victorian ALP in January 1932. The feeling at that time against scabs, following the bitter waterside strike, was such that Kennelly would never have been elected to that post had that been the case. Barnes was adamant that he would have no part of such a slander. He told Hardy that he had got away with the story about the wife, but he was not going to put that in about Kennelly. He told Hardy that he would go on strike. Hardy defended his position by claiming that Kennelly was on the side of the Groupers (ALP Industrial Groups). Barnes said that Hardy 'kicked up a bloody fuss'; he went down to the party headquarters at 49 Elizabeth Street. Vic Bird, also known as Vin Bourke, a party functionary, was sent by the CPA leaders to settle the matter; Bourke called Barnes aside and said 'It's his book'.[25] In reply Barnes told Bourke:

Normally, we've got nothing to do with the printing of a book, I'd take that stand. He's paying for it and he's entitled to say it should be printed, but in this case it involves us and me. I said this book is going to be distributed by us and handled by us and it is going to be an expression of us. We are not going to criminally libel a leading member of the Labor Party. Finally, they took it out. Now, I consider it would have been a major tragedy; it wouldn't have been right. From then on the relations with Hardy and me were never cordial.[26]

Despite his growing irritation with Hardy, Barnes continued to compose the type into formes. He believed that the book was worthwhile, but he was not prepared to sacrifice his labour principles, although he had, in the first conflict, bowed to CPA pressure. Barnes had been completely supportive of Hardy since 1945, when he was introduced to him by Gibson as the man who was going to write the book. Their association had spanned the entire research and writing period. Barnes had been entrusted with reading some of the manuscript which Hardy would bring to his home in East Melbourne. They would discuss aspects of the novel, and particularly what names Hardy had chosen. On one occasion Barnes's step-daughter, Helen James, had mentioned to Frank that she had read some of the manuscript, and she thought it was going to be a good book. Frank was very disturbed that she had seen it, but Barnes assured him that he had warned her not to discuss it with anyone else.[27]

Ralph Gibson of the Victorian Executive of the CPA had also been closely associated with Hardy during the four years of its writing, and had 'read many chapters in draft form'.[28] Despite Gibson's standing in the party, the national leadership continued to oversee the writing of the novel. It is apparent that both the Victorian and the National CPA leadership believed that the novel would be a strong political weapon, as 'By 1950 the Industrial Groups were a powerful force in the unions and in the Labor Party'.[29] The National leadership was clearly unwilling to allow the Victorian Executive to be the final arbiter of what did or did not go into the novel, although the idea for the project had originated in Melbourne! Like all political parties the CPA had its inner rivalries and tensions, particularly between the State Executives and the National leadership, despite a public image of unity.

Ambrose Dyson's father-in-law, Jack Alexander Ross, was also reading the work. He was a solicitor who occupied a senior position in the Victorian Titles Office.[30] His granddaughter, Janie Dyson, has a copy of *Power Without Glory*, together with a statement by Ross advising Hardy which sections were libellous.[31] There is nothing to suggest that Ross was anything other than conservative in his politics; so it must be assumed that his reading of the novel was undertaken at the request of his daughter, Phyl Dyson.

While this struggle between the Victorian Executive and the national leadership quietly continued, the Wharfedale machine in the old Rialto building churned on day after day. Hardy and Seelaf had a joke they shared; they had always greeted each other as 'fella slave', and during that summer it did, indeed, apply.[32] The physical strain of transporting the metal printing formes, the collection and delivery of paper for the printing, and finally, as each thirty-two page section was completed, it had to be transported to 'safe' houses in the suburbs. Stan Johns, a long-time CPA member, owned an engineering works, and he used the company truck to ferry the printed sheets for storage. George Seelaf worked on the deliveries with Johns. Nancy and Bill Irving offered storage space in their house in Marco Polo Street, Essendon; and Nancy, along with many others, helped with the hand-folding and collating of the printed sheets.[33]

Following the publication of *Power Without Glory* there was some criticism that the final part of the novel dropped away in form and content. Were this criticism justified, consideration must be given to the increasing pressures affecting Hardy. He was under the constant supervision of the CPA leadership. As a CPA member and first-time novelist, he may have welcomed Dixon's political guidance and suggestions. But any writer would acknowledge the difficulty of producing a work of fact or fiction, under those circumstances.

Hardy's first commitment was to finish the novel, the second to the printing, and the third to the binding and distribution. On 2 April 1950 Menzies acted on his election undertaking to outlaw the Communist Party of Australia. The CPA was very unpopular with a large section of the Australian public, but the Parliamentary Bill, by reason of its loose definition of just who was a 'communist', caused Ben Chifley, the leader of the Labor Party, to announce 'that the Bill could be used just as effectively to crush the Labor Party as the Communist Party of Australia'. Frank Hardy, like all communists at that time, was immersed in the struggle against the legislation.

The supportive role that Ross Hardy played during those years cannot be overlooked. As Hardy was writing and revising the final chapters, Ross was typing and re-typing those sections of the manuscript. Frances, who was then seven years old, had clear memories of her father either writing or sleeping.[34] For years Ross had been living with the presence of Frank's novel; she had made an outstanding contribution. She also had the full responsibility of caring for the children, running the home and of stretching £1 to do the work of £3 or £4. As the political climate worsened, and the hard work and tension mounted regarding the printing of the novel, it is certain that, on the occasions that Frank was at home, he became increasingly nervous and difficult to please.

Joseph Waters, a former member of the Communist Party of Great Britain and then a member of the CPA, was a book distributor who had arrived in Melbourne in the postwar years. He became the sole distributor for *Power Without Glory*. His name appears on the dust jacket of the first edition. He was closely associated with Hardy, and his comments on the pressures that Hardy was under at that crucial time are of interest:

> In addition you've got to remember that *Power Without Glory* was a novel, so there was a certain amount of creativeness. Frank dumped on Mrs Wren, but personal relationships weren't well done. Frank was so intent on the politics of the thing, that was the side part of it you see, therefore it lacked a bit of balance, nevertheless he worked a lot of time on it, and

he worked very hard on it. It had a greater effect on him than Frank, even now, is prepared to admit, because there were threats on his life, a whole series . . . and Frank Hardy described it very well in *Power Without Glory*.[35]

Hardy was to look back on that critical period; he had realised that he was too close to the material and in the third part of the novel, there were incidents and characters included that should have been omitted.[36]

The printing of the first edition of *Power Without Glory* had its fair share of mystery and intrigue, but the folding and binding was an even more extraordinary operation. The CPA rallied trusted party members, pensioners, trade unionists and other volunteers to collate and fold by hand each thirty-two-page section of the ten thousand copies of the 672-page novel. CPA member Fred Farrall recalled how the Reverend Victor James taught the volunteers how to do the bookbinding by hand. The binding was done on a small, simple wooden frame; it consisted of four pieces of timber, the base being twelve inches wide by eight inches across, with three pieces of three by one, sixteen inches high screwed onto the base.[37]

The logistics of transporting the printed sheets to 'safe' houses throughout Melbourne and country districts, the organisation and training of the volunteers, and the co-ordination of assembling all the sections into book form prior to binding and stitching demonstrated further great enterprise. When this was completed each book had to be trimmed by guillotine on three sides. Discussions with many old CPA members revealed the covert nature of the handling, and no one person seemed to be acquainted with how the overall work was completed. Volunteers were only aware of their specific tasks; this method of operation was not new to CPA members, and it was the means by which security was maintained.

Some of the binding of the 'illegal' second edition was done in the best (never used) bedroom of Marie Kaiser's family home in Ivanhoe. The completed copies were stored in a wardrobe. Kaiser's favourite recollection of Frank Hardy was not a political one. Occasionally, he would ring her for a lift home on her motor-bike when he was 'under the weather'. Due to his state, whenever they hit a corner, he would lean against the turn, trying to stay upright. Any motorcyclist would know just how difficult it would be to cope with this![38]

The printing on the spine of the red cloth covers was a feat of endurance. Vic Little was again recruited for the final task of printing, in black ink, the legend on the spine of the novel: POWER WITHOUT GLORY—Frank J. Hardy —'Ross Franklyn'. This operation took place at the premises of Thos Urquhart & Sons, Printers. Urquhart was a party sympathiser, and his daughter, Irene Ellis, was a member of the CPA. The individual printing of many thousands of covers on the ancient machine was extremely slow. Volunteers then glued the completed books into the printed covers. As before, Little had remained on the party press payroll.[39]

After the completion of the first edition, Hardy had become increasingly anxious that there might be a police raid on his home. In May 1950 he asked a friend, Nick Pagonis, if he would store two suitcases containing all his research material. Pagonis took the suitcases to his mother's home, where they remained until Frank required them. It was in late June or early July that Hardy asked him to drive Ross, Frances and Alan to a farm in Gippsland. Some wharfies then moved into the Hardy home. 'Hardy was a very worried man.'[40]

In *The Hard Way* the only reference to the contribution made by so many CPA members, sympathisers and others was that 'Volunteers folded the remainder of the sheets inexpertly by hand'. When 'Ross Franklyn' was looking through the first completed copy of *Power Without Glory* early in August 1950, he commented that it was a roughly produced book, but it seemed to be the best in the world.[41]

Examination of the first edition of Frank Hardy's novel, dated April 1950, does disclose the faults attributed by booksellers and others; nevertheless, even detractors must admit that the remarkable story of the genesis, gestation, writing, printing and binding of *Power Without Glory* has no parallel in the history of the Australian novel.

Hardy's reference to August 1950 as the time of completion of the first copy does not coincide with the recollections of CPA members. Prior to this, copies of the book were being sold, as they were completed, to people in an underground operation. The purchasers, in turn, sold copies to other reliable people. The CPA had a network of bookshops in the city, suburbs and country towns as sales points. Each CPA branch had a literature secretary referred to as the 'agit prop' (agitation and propaganda work based on the Soviet Union model), who was responsible for selling *Power Without Glory* to the members.[42] These methods of distribution used for the 'First edition: April 1950'[43] were confirmed by John Sendy:

> But in August 1950, Frank Hardy's *Power Without Glory* stirred political and literary circles and recorded huge sales. Within a year four editions had appeared, but this was only the beginning. The subsequent court case sent its popularity soaring as did the television series much later. But in those early days when *Power Without Glory* sold from under the counter, the [CPA's] International Bookshop played an important part in its distribution.[44]

Hardy's claim that the first edition was published in August 1950 accords with the official book launch on 3 August. But, in reality, it was the *second* first edition. It is significant that Hardy chose to record in *The Hard Way* that the first copy of the first edition came into his hands in August 1950. On the original and subsequent editions published in 1950 and early 1951, there were no addresses cited for the publishers, nor did the April 1950 edition bear a GPO registration. This would have been in accord with the CPA policy of keeping few, if any, records, particularly at that time as the party knew it could be outlawed by the Menzies Government.

In April/May 1950 another edition had been ordered from Fraser & Jenkinson, Printers, who had long been associated with the Labor Party. During the protracted absence of the managing director, Arthur ('Chook') Elmslie Fraser, in Queensland, his manager had accepted the order. Dudley King & Sons had undertaken the typesetting. When Fraser returned to Melbourne for a short visit, he was greatly disturbed when he became aware of the subject of the novel, and stopped production. Fraser returned to Queensland, where he died on 30 September 1950. When his widow later found a copy of *Power Without Glory* in signature form, she realised it was of historic significance. It appears to be identical, both in typeface and paper, to the April 1950 first edition. However, on examination, there are slight variations in the length of lines and odd variations in spacing. This copy is now in the possession of their son, John Fraser, who had always believed that it was an early 'underground' copy of the novel.[45]

It is clear that the CPA, Frank Hardy and others associated with the production of the early editions of *Power Without Glory*, were aware that secrecy was a vital ingredient to protect not only the actual printed material, but also the participants who were working on the project. For these reasons, it is impossible to establish just how many copies and how many editions were printed during that stressful period from December 1949 until Hardy's acquittal, on the charge of criminal libel, on 18 June 1951. It is unlikely that any one person, including the author himself, was aware of every link in the chain of events that brought the novel into being.

Hardy had claimed that *Power Without Glory* was launched at a Realist Writers' Group Function when many copies were sold.[46] But, on 3 August 1950 a small item appeared in the *Sun News-Pictorial* newspaper; this was the public precursor of a major upheaval in Australian literary and legal history:

NOVEL TO BE 'LAUNCHED'

An Australian novel will be launched tomorrow night at a public reading by the Arts Council of Australia. This ceremony is new to Australia. The novel—Power Without Glory, by Frank Hardy—will be launched at the Athenaeum Gallery, 188 Collins-st., at 8.p.m.[47]

It is possible that the Arts Council of Australia became involved with the promotion of the novel because some CPA members were on the Council's committee responsible for promoting cultural functions.

The response to the novel's publication was slow; on 16 August 1950, two weeks after the launch of *Power Without Glory*, the CPA's national paper *Tribune* made its first reference to the novel; on 21 August the Brisbane *Courier Mail* announced the publication, as did the *West Australian* on 26 August. On 9 September, however, *Smith's Weekly* reported that 'This book rocked Australia'.[48] The Melbourne press failed to mention the launch until 12 September, when the *Argus* reported:

Politicians in Melbourne no longer ask, on meeting one another, the prospects for the next session or the progress of seat nominations. They ask, simply: 'Have you read THE BOOK?' We have not found one who gives an answer in the negative. 'The Book' is 'Power Without Glory', a novel on the Australian political scene by youthful author Frank Hardy of Malvern.

Hardy seems to have achieved the rare distinction of writing an Australian novel which immediately became a best-seller in his own land.

'Power Without Glory' has been Melbourne's most consistent bar-room topic ever since it appeared four weeks ago and despite minor publicity has completely sold out its first edition of 7,800 copies. Publishers are rushing through a second edition of 10,000 copies of which 4,000 are already ordered.

Publishers in Britain, the United States, France, Italy, and Poland are considering bringing out editions of the novel. First copies appeared in New Zealand bookshops this week.

Hardy, a 34-year-old ex-serviceman, has been writing professionally since the end of the war, but mainly short stories. This is his first novel. His short stories have been published in 'Coast to Coast' and he has won short story contests. 'Power Without Glory' represents four years' research and writing, but it is clearly paying dividends.

He is now writing another novel—less controversial—he says, based on life in the Victorian town of Bacchus Marsh [Southern Cross], where he was born. He expects to have his new novel with the publishers before June next.[49]

On 14 September *Australasian Post* published a book review, 'Social Indictment'. The CPA Victorian weekly *Guardian* waited until 15 September to make its first reference to *Power Without Glory*, and in this article Frank Hardy told why he wrote the novel. *Smith's Weekly* of 23 September advised that overseas rights were being negotiated for *Power Without Glory*. The *Bulletin* reviewed 'the muckraking novel' on 27 September, and in the Spring 1950 edition of *Meanjin*, Flora S. Eldershaw damned the novel with faint praise in a review titled, 'Bastardry, Bastardry, Bastardry'.[50]

On 28 October 1950 the *Age* published an advertisement for this issue of *Meanjin* which had a prominent heading: *Power Without Glory*; but otherwise the novel appeared to have been ignored or deliberately overlooked by the editorial department.

However, a review was submitted to the *Age* by Ian Mair, freelance critic and journalist. He had been close to the CPA during the 1930s, had joined the party early in the war years, and had remained a member for some time after the war. He had read *Power Without Glory*, but had found 'it hard to get through. Frank was so illiterate; his writing was so shallow, bloody awful, and he was an unreliable writer'. Mair's personal relationship with Frank was agreeable, 'as he was a pleasant fellow, and he was very able'; but his main observation was that Hardy was 'country Irish, that is, he had not been brought up near any great school or university, nor was he brought up for that purpose; his father had a rural job'. Frank did not understand 'the world of literature'. Mair believed that an uneducated working man like Hardy was unlikely to produce a work of literary merit, although he was, like Hardy, a devoted admirer of the work of Charles Dickens, who had left school at the age of eleven. He was also critical of Frank's addiction to backing racehorses: 'that's very Irish'.[51] Mair, as late as 1992, reflected the class distinctions and sectarian hangovers that members brought with them into the CPA, despite its much proclaimed egalitarianism. Hardy had to contend not only with the detractors from without, but also from within the ranks of his own party.

When Hardy asked Mair to review *Power Without Glory* and submit it to the *Age*, Mair agreed because he was, at that time, still 'rabidly left', and it was a case of 'God bless our side, and Frank was on our side'. As a reviewer he was critical, but as a friend he praised him. However, the review was never published in the *Age*, and it was the only time in Mair's career that he was paid for a review which was not used.[52]

Just how many copies and how many editions were printed from April 1950 until June 1951, and how many launchings, official and unofficial, that *Power Without Glory* had, cannot be established, but suffice to say that the Arts Council function on 4 August 1950 was the one which brought the novel to the attention of the newspapers and, in turn, to the general public.

Chapter Seven

CRIMINAL LIBEL

ONCE *POWER WITHOUT GLORY* had entered the consciousness of Melburnians, the demand for copies of the novel grew from a trickle to an avalanche. Joseph Waters, Frank Hardy's book distributor, arranged to have the next edition produced by Wilke, the biggest printers and binders in Victoria.[1] Meanwhile, orders came from booksellers all over the country.

Hardy and Seelaf held a meeting at Angliss's Meat Works at which copies were sold to individual union members at 16s 6d, and twenty-four copies were given to the Shop Committee to lend at two shillings a time.[2] Members of other trade unions became involved with selling and lending copies of the novel, and Hardy was actively publicising his work. At the large Vickers-Ruwolt plant in Richmond, a worker would borrow a copy for a few shillings a week. It was common practice for the workers to cover the absence of a workmate while he retreated into the lavatory to read. Lists identifying the characters in the book with actual people were being sold for almost as much as the book itself. Such was the demand for the book and 'the list' that those in the queues in work-places and offices around Melbourne grew restless.[3]

On 29 September 1950 the Arts Council, in conjunction with the Realist Writers' Group, organised a meeting at which Frank Hardy gave an address entitled 'Why I Wrote *Power Without Glory*'. The *Age* reported the event on 30 September:

> Mr. Hardy said the man on whom he had based the main character, John West, was to him a very colourful and interesting figure. He had not set out to do him any injustice, but to hang on him a big social novel.
>
> Mr. Hardy explained that his main reason in writing the novel was to give a complete or reasonably complete picture of a self-made man who came up the hard way and played the game hard when he got there.
>
> 'Our man John West was ready made,' said Mr. Hardy. 'I could not have invented him. I have never invented a character in my life.'
>
> 'I am told there is now a glossary in circulation which purports to show what characters approximate mostly closely to living people. I did not prepare that glossary.'

'A man asked me recently who the characters actually were. He did not believe me when I replied that they all came out of my head, and I don't believe anyone here does, either.' (Laughter.)

'You all know whom the book is about, or have worked it out to your own satisfaction.'

Discussing the law of libel, Mr. Hardy said that this law had probably stopped many good writers from producing 'Power Without Glory' in the last 20 years.

Discussing a suggestion that he had been anti-Catholic in his book, Mr. Hardy said his mother and several brothers and sisters would be the first to deny that he was anti-Catholic. They were all Catholics.[4]

Hardy's reasons for writing the novel, and the comments made about the central figure, John West, could only be described as provocative. Was Hardy taking this risky initiative to promote the sales, and thus enhance his reputation as a novelist? As a gambler he had already shown a willingness to play a wild card; was his address yet another manifestation of this? Had he hoped that John Wren would sue him for libel? Was it part of the CPA's far-reaching plan, first formulated in 1944, to undermine the anti-communist groups in the unions?

When the Victorian ALP Conference in 1946 voted to establish the ALP Industrial Groups in the unions to fight elections against the communists, there is little doubt that this decision gave further support to the CPA's earlier plan to enlist Frank Hardy to write a novel that would expose John Wren and his alleged links with the Labor Party and the Industrial Groups. In January 1947 the CPA had claimed in the *Guardian* that Wren had given £50 000 to the Industrial Groups to fight communism in the trade unions.

On 18 April 1947 another report appeared in the party press affirming that Wren had given £50 000 to the Groups.[5] The second report quoted from the first article.

There is some evidence that Wren had given money, but nothing to support the CPA's assertions. Historian James Griffin wrote:

In the early 1940s Wren was persuaded to make an initial contribution to the Catholic Social Studies Movement, organized by B. A. Santamaria, but withdrew support when he feared sectarianism would 'wreck the Labor Party he knew'. In 1948 the Catholic industrial grouper S. M. Keon excoriated Wren in the Victorian parliament . . . Wren's Labor sympathies finally soured.[6]

A hindsight view of the events surrounding Wren and his alleged close relationship with the Industrial Groups tends to lead to the conclusion that the CPA might have 'got it wrong'! In 1948 Standish Michael Keon, a prominent Catholic and MLA for Richmond, attacked Wren under parliamentary privilege, claiming that Wren had financed the Country Party to bring down the Labor Government which had denied him the right to conduct night trotting.[7] It seems unlikely that Wren would have switched his allegiance to the Country Party had he been so deeply financially involved with the Groups. During an interview B. A. Santamaria outlined the events that had taken place prior to Keon's attack on Wren:

> The Movement that I was responsible for, didn't pick a fight with Wren, it was Stan [Keon]. Stan lived in Richmond all his life, and he and a number of people in the Richmond CYMS [Catholic Young Men's Society] decided to get rid of the Wren control of the Labor Party [Richmond Council], and we helped them, but the initiative was a local initiative, it wasn't a Movement thing at all.
>
> Wren was nobody's hero. He was quite a ruthless political operator; he was of a totally different generation from mine. He had no time for me or anything that I was doing, he detested us, basically because of the Richmond thing.
>
> I had this view of him, I thought that however sinister, call it what you like, he was, the establishment determined to kick him as a Catholic, and I thought that all he was doing was trying to climb the scale, climb the ladder in a different way.[8]

Santamaria was aware that Wren had both supporters and detractors. He said:

> I have no reason for defending him; his understanding of politics was about money, if you wanted to be effective politically, you bought members of parliament, whether you bought them for the right reasons or the wrong reasons was another question I don't know, but that was his [Wren's] understanding of politics.
>
> I remember Frank Scully [Labor MLA for Richmond] for instance. Frank hadn't been in Parliament a month, and there was a fellow there, I think his name was Becker [Beckett]. He was in the Upper House; Frank was just a young boy [man], and he took him to lunch. In the parliamentary lunch room, he said, 'Frank, you're in a safe seat, but you are going to find political life very expensive, much more than you think, perhaps this will help you'. And he threw £200 on the table, and Frank told him to take it back, to keep it, but that's how I think a lot of them [did it] . . . £200 was a lot of money.[9]

In 1998 Frank Scully confirmed Santamaria's statement.[10] William James Beckett served several terms in Parliament; he was a Labor member of the Legislative Council from June 1940 until June 1952. He was heavily involved in the racing and trotting industry; he served on their official bodies for many years. He was a Freemason. He served as a Fitzroy city councillor for twenty-two years during which time he served two terms as mayor. He associated with John Wren.[11] Wren's involvement with Beckett, a Freemason, tends to support Santamaria's recollections of how Wren operated, and the sequence of events that had taken place in those years. They do not accord with the CPA's published views that Wren was hand-in-glove with Santamaria's Movement, and that he was financing the ALP Industrial Groups within the trade unions.

In Chapter 14, pages 633–41, of *Power Without Glory*, John West/Wren receives a visit from Archbishop Malone, Mr Cregan and Mr Parelli, the secretary of Catholic Action. As the discussion proceeds, the reader is privy to the thoughts of John West/Wren. He is uneasy that Michael Kiely [Keon] had won a pre-selection ballot from one of his men. As the discussion continues, West is determined that they would not get any money from him. Then he has a reverie; if he gives money to the Church, it will enhance his chances of getting into heaven. He then agrees to donate the money on the condition that the Catholic Action members would not oppose his men, who were not 'communistic', in the pre-selection ballots in future.[12]

Hardy's fictionalised version that John West was bitterly opposed to the Movement concurs with that of Santamaria, but differs from the CPA's reports in earlier editions of the *Guardian*, which had indicated that Wren was a fervent supporter of the Movement. The CPA's assertion that John Wren had donated £50 000 to the Movement can neither be proved nor disproved. It must be assumed that Wren, being a well-known Catholic of doubtful business ethics, was made the 'fall guy' on one premise in the *Guardian*, and on another in *Power Without Glory*. Were the CPA and Frank Hardy, by politically aligning Wren with the Movement and by including the alleged love affair between Nellie West/Wren and the bricklayer, hoping to provoke Wren into taking action against Hardy? Perhaps Frank had had one beer too many before addressing the Arts Council and the Realist Writers' Group, or had he been carried away with his own oratory? Or did the Victorian Executive and the national leadership of the CPA, unknown to Hardy, have a separate agenda? Did they intend to exploit the weaknesses in Hardy's flamboyant character and his love of playing to the gallery, thus allowing him to become vulnerable to the forces of the law?

This was a period of great tension for the party and its members. The time was certainly ripe for the CPA to remove itself from the spotlight by pulling a rabbit out of the hat. Both the CPA and Hardy were well aware of the role that political martyrs could play in certain campaigns. If the CPA had a martyr, it could build an even more effective national campaign against the Communist Party Dissolution Act, which was to become law on 20 October. Apart from the possibility that Hardy had overplayed his address on 30 September, due to alcohol or excitement, there were three likely scenarios: the address was a carefully conceived plan by the CPA and Hardy to force the Wren family to take legal action; Hardy had made a private decision to become a working-class writer/martyr; or the CPA had, for its own purposes, encouraged Hardy to be provocative without warning him of the possible consequences. If this were the case, it would not have been the first occasion that a political party was prepared to sacrifice a member for the sake of expediency.

The following weeks proved to be the lull before the storm. Hardy and Seelaf continued to hold lunch-time meetings at work-sites. Orders flowed in from all parts of Australia; Joseph Waters, the distributor, was awaiting the completion of a new edition by Wilke Printers. Then Wilke's manager rang to say that the police had warned him against finishing the job. Wilke's had printed all the sheets and the covers; everything was ready for binding; but the job could not go ahead. The manager told Waters, 'You know, we can't do it'. Waters then arranged to take all the material to a small printer in Port Melbourne.[13]

Two days after the Communist Party Dissolution Act became law, on Sunday, 22 October, Detective-Sergeant Currer and Detective Mooney visited Hardy at his home in Malvern. They disclosed that an anonymous phone caller had said that there was a corpse in the house. Hardy assured them that that was not the case. They then asked Frank if he was the author of *that* book and questioned him about the characters in the novel. Were they real people, and were they still alive? Some discussion followed, and half an hour later they departed. Hardy decided to consult Ralph Gibson and Fred Paterson, a solicitor and former communist member for the Queensland State seat of Bowen, who was staying with Gibson. Paterson believed that there was some prosecution pending over *Power Without Glory*, and felt it was imperative that such a matter should be made public. He suggested that Hardy should approach a Labor member to ask a question in Parliament. The next day Hardy visited Parliament House and discussed the matter with Charles Mutton, the Independent Labor member for Coburg. Mutton was apprehensive, but two days later he acceded to Hardy's request and asked the Chief Secretary why the detectives had called at Hardy's house. The Chief Commissioner of Police replied that the phone call received at Russell Street Headquarters was apparently a hoax.[14]

On the same day the *Age* reported that Frank Hardy had claimed that a campaign of intimidation had been launched against him; two of five printers involved in producing 16 000 copies of a second edition had refused to carry out the work.[15]

Meanwhile, Hardy and Seelaf also had an order under way at the *Argus* and the Industrial Printing and Publishing Company. Frank McManus, the assistant secretary of the Victorian ALP, and the party secretary, Denis Lovegrove, had attended the *Argus* office for an interview on another matter, when McManus noticed a trolley heavily laden with printed pages of a book. As he read them, he realised that 'the book purported to be an account of corruption inside the Labor Party inspired largely by a financier called John West'. McManus knew one of the printers, who told him that the rest of the book was being printed at the Industrial Printing and Publishing Company, a co-operative owned by the ALP and the unions. When he told Lovegrove 'he exploded' and went to J. V. Stout, secretary of the Trades Hall Council and chairman of the Board of Management of the Industrial Printing and Publishing Company, and 'demanded that the printing of the book be stopped and it be confiscated'. Stout complied with the demand, but soon after 'the book was spirited away. It was *Power Without Glory*'.[16] A raid or robbery did take place early on the morning of 23 October 1950 when the printing, finished and unfinished, and substantial quantities of paper were removed. The 'spirits' had taken the forms of burly wharfies, seamen, other trade unionists, Frank Hardy and George Seelaf.[17]

When Albie Heintz, later the general manager of the Industrial Printing and Publishing Company, started his apprenticeship with the company in 1953, it was almost taboo for the apprentices to mention the book. But Heintz and the other apprentices used to ask questions, and his recollections are based on what they were told. Jackie Cahill, Owen O'Neill and other tradesmen provided some of the information. Cahill had worked for many years as a labourer; he was employed to open the printery at least an hour or so before the men started work. His main tasks were to heat up the metal pots so that the type-metal would be hot for the linotype operators to work, and he also cleaned the space bands. Heintz's understanding is that the Board of Directors had stopped the printing. Bob Brodney, a senior partner in the legal firm of Maurice Blackburn and Company, was also involved in the negotiations to guard the building; but, the Industrial Printing and Publishing Company had arranged for the services of a policeman because they had heard that Wren might intervene. When Cahill was called before the Board, he was asked why he had let the raiding party into the building. He reported that Seelaf had said they were just going to take away the *Power Without Glory* job. Cahill told him they should wait until the boss came in. When he saw three big wharfies in the lane, he thought, 'Who am I to stop them?'. Many years later Heintz was told that someone had given the policeman fifty shillings to go for a walk around St Anne's Mission building on the corner, so that he would not be able to see what was going on.[18]

In *The Hard Way* Hardy's report of the raid varied somewhat from that of Heintz, but some of the details are similar. He did not mention that the *Argus* was involved with the so-called second edition, which corresponds with McManus's account. But in an earlier chapter Hardy had referred to an occasion when the *Argus* was folding sections of the first edition. When they declined to carry on with the work, he gave a detailed description of how 'Ross Franklyn' loaded the material onto a truck, and thousands of sheets slipped off and blew into the gutters, road and footpaths. Many sheets were soggy and stained, and eventually eight hundred copies of the novel could not be completed because of the accident. Vic Little did not believe this story, because he is sure that, as the printer, he would have heard about it.[19] This version may have been based on a much earlier event, when Hardy and a friend had been drinking one evening in the basement bar at Phair's Hotel in Collins Street, a favourite meeting place for left-wingers. As six o'clock closing time approached, Hardy's inebriated crony wanted to buy some bottles of beer, which were then in short supply. The manager and barman refused, and a fracas developed as Frank and his mate were leaving by the rear entrance. The brawl spilled over into the laneway. EYL member Eric Stark and a friend managed to calm the situation, but in the scuffle Hardy dropped a brown paper parcel and sheets of typed paper scattered over the cobblestones. Hardy yelled for help to pick up the sheets; he indicated they were his precious manuscript.[20] Was there a blurring between fact and fiction? It is possible that the *Argus* was never involved in folding the original edition of April 1950, but that Hardy had linked the manuscript incident to the period in October 1950 when the *Argus* was printing one section of the novel, and the Industrial Printing and Publishing Company was printing another.

Hardy claimed a moral justification for the robbery at the printery because if the next edition was not published, a great deal of other people's money would be lost. The truckload of printing and stolen paper was taken to a hiding-place. Later that day—Monday, 23 October—Hardy contacted his wife by phone and discovered that another two detectives had been looking for him.[21]

CPA solicitor Cedric Ralph's understanding was that payment, in cash in full payment of the agreed price, was delivered to the Industrial Printing and Publishing Company the same day.[22]

The events which took place during the raid, and the days that followed, are fictionalised in Hardy's *The Hard Way*. 'Ross Franklyn' had displayed guts, determination and selflessness that would have impressed a *Boy's Own Annual* reader.

So, too, would an entertaining article, 'The Fella Slave', in the *Australian Literary Quarterly 3*, written by Hardy in 1987 about his relationship with George Seelaf. There are not only variations regarding the robbery, but of many other aspects of the publication of the novel. The claim was also made that the Industrial Printing and Publishing Company was owned by John Wren, and that the company employees had worked an unofficial night shift to print and fold the copies which were later stolen.[23] Albie Heintz said that, as far as he was aware, there had never been a night-shift worked at the Industrial Printing and Publishing Company, either official or unofficial.[24]

Hardy's article referred to events which had taken place nearly forty years earlier. Was the seventy-year-old writer revealing facts not previously released in the public arena, or was he suffering lapses of memory or some confusion, or did the article stand somewhere between fact and fiction? Hardy was on his own admission, first and foremost, a storyteller; he polished and re-polished his tall stories. His contribution to the *Australian* Literary Quarterly 3 was lively and enjoyable; but was it yet another embellishment of the many stories surrounding the publication of *Power Without Glory*, or was it a piece of factual writing? It is impossible to determine just what demarcation lines, if any, Hardy drew in his writing. With Frank Hardy, the wary reader needs to know that nothing is certain! The events that had preceded the raid on the printery, and the events that had followed, were quite remarkable without need of added colour or spice.

The sequence of events which took place at that time is of interest:

Friday, 20 October 1950—The Communist Party Dissolution Bill (passed on 15 June 1950) became law.[25]

Writs are issued in the High Court questioning the validity of the Communist Party Dissolution Act.[26]

Sunday, 22 October 1950—Detective-Sergeant Currer and Detective Mooney visited the Hardy home in East Malvern.[27]

Monday, 23 October 1950—Frank Hardy, George Seelaf and others raided the Industrial Printing and Publishing Company. The material was taken to a safe hiding place.[28]

Security police swooped on the CPA premises at 49 Elizabeth Street, Melbourne, as part of synchronised raids on CPA headquarters in the various states.[29]

Hardy visited Charles Mutton, MLA, at Parliament House with a request that he ask a question about the reason for the detectives' visit to Hardy's home.[30]

Two other detectives visited Hardy's home in East Malvern and questioned Rosslyn Hardy. Hardy went into hiding.[31]

Tuesday, 24 October 1950—The detectives had again visited Hardy's home. Hardy returned with two seamen bodyguards. Hardy contacted CPA lawyer, and he was advised to stay away from home overnight.[32]

Wednesday, 25 October 1950—a.m. Hardy consulted Thomas Dall, Solicitor, who arranged an appointment at his office for Hardy to meet detectives from the Criminal Investigation Branch.[33]

p.m. Hardy was arrested at Thomas Dall's office. He was taken to the Melbourne City Watchhouse in Russell Street. Hardy was granted bail of £100 with a similar surety to appear in the City Court the following day.[34]

Charles Mutton, Independent Labour [sic] MLA for Coburg, asked a question in Parliament about detectives visiting Hardy's home.[35]

Thursday, 26 October 1950—Hardy was remanded until November 27 on £500 bail by Mr Jackson, SM, in the City Court. Mrs Alice Mary [Molly] Inge of Tintern Avenue, Toorak, provided the £500 surety.[36]

Dr H. V. Evatt appeared in the High Court to challenge the validity of the Communist Party Dissolution Act.[37]

Whether Hardy's arrest was timed to coincide with the Communist Party Dissolution Act being made law cannot be determined. But the campaigns that were to be waged around Hardy, the Communist Party Dissolution Act and the 1951 Referendum, certainly became inextricably interwoven as part of the defence against attacks on academic and literary freedom and the democratic rights of Australian citizens.

It was little wonder that Hardy felt threatened following the early-morning raid on the Industrial Printing and Publishing Company, the knowledge that CPA headquarters had received a visit from the police, and that detectives had visited his home all on the same day. Hardy's exciting fictionalised account in *The Hard Way* of 'Ross Franklyn's' reactions at that time bears some resemblance to the facts. Cedric Ralph has clear memories of Hardy arriving at his home in Wrixon Street, Kew, on Tuesday evening, 24 October. Ralph was the instructing solicitor for the CPA in the High Court challenge to the Communist Party Dissolution Act. His wife, Rhea, set another place at the table; when the meal was finished, Ralph and Hardy had a discussion about the detectives' visit that day. It seemed likely that he was about to be arrested. Ralph was unable to become involved because of the pressure of work, and the small number of people employed in his office. It is probable that when Hardy had contacted Ralph Gibson and Fred Paterson on the previous Sunday evening, they had suggested that he should consult Cedric Ralph about his predicament. Ralph was aware that Thomas Dall, a solicitor, had a reputation for accepting unusual cases. Ralph contacted Dall and made an appointment for the following morning. He invited Hardy to spend the night in his living room; early the next morning he drove him to the city to keep the appointment.[38] Late in the afternoon Hardy was interviewed by Detectives O'Connor and Downie at Dall's office. He was then arrested on a charge of criminal libel on a warrant issued by a justice of the peace, on the information of Mrs Ellen Wren. He was taken to the Melbourne City Watchhouse in Russell Street. Hardy was granted bail of £100 with a similar surety to appear in the City Court the following day.[39]

Australians, and Melburnians in particular, were greeted by front-page banner headlines in their morning newspapers of Thursday, 26 October 1950:

'Power Without Glory' sensation
AUTHOR ARRESTED IN LAWYER'S OFFICE
Charge by Mrs. Wren

A photograph of a pensive Hardy reading a copy of *Power Without Glory* bore a caption 'To defend libel suit'. An *Argus* journalist forecast that the case promised to become a *cause célèbre*.[40]

Hardy appeared before Mr Jackson SM in the City Court that day. He was remanded until 27 November on £500 bail. The court was overflowing during the seventeen minutes of the proceedings. Mr John Galbally, who was acting for Mrs Wren, had dramatically objected to bail being granted. He claimed that Mrs Wren had been foully libelled by the book which said 'that her ninth child was not her husband's'. He further claimed that 16 000 copies of a second edition would be a repetition of the offence. However, Mr Jackson said that keeping Hardy in gaol would not prevent circulation of the book. Galbally believed that if Hardy was guilty, so, too, was every bookseller. Mrs Alice Mary [Molly] Inge, a wealthy, prominent communist, provided the £500 surety. After Hardy acknowledged bail with her they left the court, arm in arm, and posed for photographers.[41] Hardy's face became familiar to many thousands of Australians in the ensuing months. The young, unknown writer had been catapulted from obscurity into public fame.

Almost before the ink had dried on the bail documents, plans were afoot to launch what was to become a remarkable campaign in support of Hardy. In the month before he was to answer bail, 'The Frank Hardy Defence Committee' was organised. The CPA was the driving force and called on its many resources, but other groups and individuals worked separately, or together. A photograph showing some members of the Defence Committee signing a petition in support of Hardy disclosed an interesting assembly: Jim O'Connor, solicitor and president of the Democratic Rights Council; Ernst Platz, journalist and member of the Jewish Council Against Fascism and Anti-Semitism;

Alan Marshall, author; Jean Campbell, Fellowship of Australian Writers; and 'Doc' Doyle, Secretary of the Ship Painters' and Dockers' Union.[42] Author Judah Waten played a prominent role in the founding of the Committee. C. B. Christesen became the chairman, and Ross Hardy and Alan Marshall were the joint secretaries. The honorary treasurers were Jack Coffey, Realist Writers' Group, and John Morrison, author.[43]

Ted Hill, CPA State Executive member, made an impassioned plea on Hardy's behalf at a meeting held in mid-November 1950. He claimed that Hardy's work would live when his enemies were on the scrap-heap. Everyone knew that what Hardy had said was a portrait of what had gone on in real life: everyone knew that bribes had passed. Hardy had the support of every decent, honest person, and he would never be left defenceless. 'They can try to jail him, to frighten him, to defame his character, but his book will live long beyond these pygmies: their plans are doomed to failure.'[44] It might be said that Hill had a degree of prescience when he made this statement. Fifty years later, Frank Hardy, *Power Without Glory*, and the events surrounding the celebrated trial are now the subject of research and recollection.

The charge of criminal libel was seldom used except for political purposes, and a conviction could lead to a long gaol sentence. The law went back to the days of the Star Chamber, a British court of civil and criminal jurisdiction primarily used in cases concerned with offences affecting Crown interests; this arbitrary and oppressive tribunal had been abolished in 1640.[45] As the charge laid by Ellen Wren in no way related to Crown interests, it could be presumed that the wealthy and powerful who identified themselves in *Power Without Glory* were not prepared to be exposed to public scrutiny. They were, however, prepared to skulk behind a woman's outraged modesty and reputation. Although it was widely believed that the 75-year-old Mrs Wren had been unfairly treated and libelled, there was grave concern over the charge of criminal libel. Such a charge had not been used in Victoria for over thirty years; why had it been resurrected against Frank Hardy?[46] Financial retribution was not sought; therefore it can only be concluded that the motive for the action was to wreak vengeance on Hardy in the form of a heavy gaol sentence. If Hardy was convicted, it would be a deterrent to others who were contemplating writing similar works exposing the struggle for power and the corruption within Australian society. So the charge was seen as a serious attack on the freedom of expression for all writers and on the democratic rights of individuals. Accordingly, the Frank Hardy Defence Committee was to become something of a paradigm for future campaigns, in which people of all creeds, politically aligned or non-aligned, were able to work together to protect their democratic freedoms.

Chapter Eight

THE FRANK HARDY DEFENCE COMMITTEE

THE FRANK HARDY Defence Committee set up its headquarters in Arlington Chambers, Room 1, fourth floor, 229 Collins Street, Melbourne.[1] The Committee had members of different political persuasions, who were prepared to work together to oppose what they perceived to be an attack on democratic freedoms and civil liberties. The CPA played an important, if often unseen, role in the conduct of the campaign. Although the CPA's membership had declined from its war-time peak, and its power within the trade unions was waning, it was still able to orchestrate successful campaigns and mobilise its members. Some participants in the Defence Committee's activities were probably unaware of the CPA's significant input, by way of personnel, resources and organisational skills.

Prior to the formation of the Defence Committee, Nancy Wills, a member of the CPA and the Realist Writers' Group, had been asked by Ross and Frank Hardy if she would be prepared to accept nomination as secretary, when the Committee was set up. She agreed. A meeting was arranged; Wills, Frank and author, Alan Marshall, had dinner at Phair's Hotel, when they discussed procedures. Later, in the meeting hall, Hardy sat on the platform with Marshall, who was in the Chair; Wills sat, by herself, in the front row. She said:

> The meeting had been going for about fifteen minutes when Alvie Booth . . . whispered to me 'You're not to stand for Secretary.' Astounded, I said 'What?' She repeated the dictum. I don't remember whether I was stunned or angry or both . . . some time later I know I was definitely shamed . . . nominations were called for secretary, and Roz [Ross] nominated me.
>
> After the longest few seconds of my life I murmured, 'I can't do it.' No one heard me. 'I'm sorry,' I said. 'I must decline.' I wasn't game to look at Roz [Ross], or Frank, or Alan. I got up and had to walk the length of the hall.[2]

The demand for Wills's compliance with the instruction was typical of the obedience that was expected by the CPA leadership. Alvie Booth was a reliable CPA member and activist of proven performance, who had been employed by the CPA for some years; she was a trusted and loyal worker. Booth has stated that Ross Hardy did not nominate Wills for the position of secretary.[3]

Some time before this meeting, Wills had become aware that she had fallen out of favour with the Central Committee of the CPA when a letter, in which she had quoted a comment from a trade union secretary that 'in the opinion of a lot of us, Comrade . . . (one of the top boyos in the Party) is not worth two bob', had been stolen and sent on to the Central Committee. With hindsight, Wills said, 'The astonishing thing is that nobody then, thought it was a dishonourable thing to do. It was protecting the Party'.[4]

Soon after, the Realist Writers' Group changed its meeting night and place. Wills failed to receive any notification. 'But I got the message. The Control Commission still had their feelers out. It was hurtful.' Wills was very disappointed that her writer comrades had not given her the opportunity to discuss the matter. When she demanded a confrontation with the Realist Writers' Group, she was somewhat reluctantly allowed to attend meetings again. Later, she suffered further censure when she was dismissed from her secretarial job by her boss John Rodgers, the director of Australia–Soviet House. Rodgers was regretful, but he had received the instruction from the party. He told her, 'Nancy, I am sorry. I nearly threw my hand in . . . You've been doing a great job. The bastard [Ted Hill?] told me to sack you . . . He said you'd know'. That Wills suffered these indignities, if not gladly, at least with resignation, was borne out when she was again treated shabbily by the CPA, when her husband was sent to China in June 1955. Why did she accept this treatment? Because she believed that 'It's as much my Party as theirs, damn them'.[5]

It was more than forty years later when the author read Wills's account of her dismissal that she realised she had almost become unwittingly implicated. In about 1952, John Rodgers, who was known to her by sight and reputation, had telephoned her and requested that she meet him at the New Treasury Hotel in Spring Street, as there was a matter that needed to be discussed. Rodgers offered her a job as his secretary in Australia-Soviet House. She declined quite firmly, stating that she was well established in her present employment, which was very well paid. Rodgers made a second attempt, and insisted on a further meeting at the same venue. She made excuses that she had housing troubles and a small child; her real reason was that she was no longer interested in working within CPA circles. Rodgers told her that if she took the job she could get the party to buy her a house, as they had done for him! She remained firm, but was shocked that these sorts of deals were made.

In *The Hard Way*, Hardy did not mention the CPA's directive to Wills. He did mention that the Frank Hardy Defence Committee's headquarters was a dreary room in a building in Collins Street, with Alvie Booth as organiser. When Booth became ill, Nadine Dalgarno took over her role for a short period. Hardy's use of the term 'organiser' in *The Hard Way* is of particular interest, as within CPA circles this meant a paid party position. Booth gave the CPA its desired voice on the Defence Committee.

Another CPA member, Vic Williams, had also been co-opted to work for the Committee. His main tasks were to ask prominent people to sign a petition on behalf of Hardy, to give financial support to the Committee, and to seek their active participation on the Committee. One of his assignments was to visit the University of Melbourne and approach lecturer Kathleen Fitzpatrick. His mission proved to be disastrous, as Fitzpatrick was hostile to Hardy, and she 'almost threw him out of the office'. Williams was compelled to make a hasty retreat. When Williams told Hardy, he was loudly abused. Although shocked by Frank's verbal assault, he accepted it, as he knew that Hardy was under considerable pressure. Williams commented that by the time Frank wrote *The Hard Way*, his [Williams's] role on the Committee was not acknowledged, as he had fallen out of favour with the CPA leadership.[6] Some members of the Defence Committee would have been unaware that Booth and Williams were CPA members.

Ross Hardy immediately became a hard-working joint secretary. She had, in the months prior to the publication of the novel, been compelled on more than one occasion to take the children and go to the country. Hardy believed that there could also be risks, now that the book had been published. Ross was reluctant to leave home; Frank insisted, but she soon returned.[7] In the court hearings that followed, evidence given by Wren family members and associates revealed the rage that had been generated by the publication of *Power Without Glory*. Certainly Hardy was the prime target for their spleen. Whether this might have been extended to his wife and children cannot be known.

Perhaps Hardy liked the absolute freedom such absences afforded him. One member of the Realist Writers' Group was friendly with Ross; she recalled that she had rejected Hardy's sexual advances, when Ross was away with the children.[8]

For four years Ross's life had been dominated by the production of *Power Without Glory*. She was already emotionally and physically exhausted by the time Frank was charged. Pictures taken at the time of the court hearing reveal the strain that she was under. The rounded, smooth cheeks of the hopeful, young Rosslyn in her wedding snapshot a decade before had been replaced by a smiling, tired, thin-faced young woman. Frank, too, showed the pressure of the court proceedings. The prospect of her husband being sentenced to a long gaol term was a heavy burden to carry. Nadine Dalgarno, who worked for a short time at the Defence Committee office, was conscious of Ross's concerns and felt sorry for her. She recalled that Ross was obliged, on occasions, to bring her small children, Frances and Alan, with her when she came to work in the office.[9]

By the time Hardy answered his bail on 27 November 1950 for the first day's hearing of the criminal libel charge, the Defence Committee had made significant progress in planning its campaign. Mr Thomas Dall was the instructing solicitor, and Mr Don Campbell, KC, with his junior, Mr John Starke, was to appear on behalf of Hardy.[10] In 1964 Mr Starke (later Sir John) was appointed a judge of the Victorian Supreme Court. Forty years on, Sir John recalled his association with Hardy's trial, when he was interviewed by ABC presenter Jon Faine, who asked him about Campbell:

> Starke: He was one of the leaders of the common law Bar. A very fine advocate. He was a touchy old bugger. He developed polio when he was 13 and had both legs in irons, which he used to his own advantage in court when he wanted to, and he was a first class barrister.
> Faine: Why did Frank go to that solicitor [barrister]? Was he someone who had a particular reputation?
> Starke: Oh well, Don and Ted Hill were friends. Ted, of course, would have done the junior job, but he didn't think it was wise, because he was a well-known communist, and he was sure that some of the jury would know that and there would be an anti-communist thing in the jury, and he thought it would be undesirable that he be junior. He would have been first pick as junior, there's no question of that.[11]

Faine then arranged a meeting between Hardy and Sir John; it was their first since the trial in 1951. On this occasion Hardy claimed that George Seelaf had recommended Dall as a good, honest solicitor. Hardy said that Hill was willing to appear as junior, but Fred Paterson had felt it politically unwise.[12] Cedric Ralph, CPA solicitor, and Frank differ in their accounts as to how Hardy engaged Dall. According to Ralph, he had made all the arrangements.[13] Despite the close relationship between Seelaf and Hardy, it seems unlikely that Hardy would have sought his opinion as to a suitable legal representative, when he had ready access to CPA members of the legal profession. Hardy and Seelaf, no doubt, discussed the legal position, but Seelaf, following the raid on the printery, had his hands full making arrangements for the completion of the new edition. Would Seelaf have considered that any solicitor, other than those in the CPA, was good or honest? It also conflicts with what Hardy had written in *The Hard Way* about the days prior to his arrest, when he was in constant contact with Gibson and Paterson.

On 27 November 1950, the first day of the preliminary hearing of the criminal libel charge, Mr Campbell made a three-and-three-quarter-hour address to the Court, during which he challenged that Mr Jackson SM, who constituted a legal tribunal, had no jurisdiction to hear the charge. He was assisted by Mr Starke, who selected authorities from the fifty books on the Bar table. Frank and Ross Hardy sat in the crowded courtroom close to John Wren, Sr. Campbell's address was marked by fiery clashes with Mr John Galbally, the prosecuting barrister.[14] Many years later Sir John Starke said:

> We had a pretty weak magistrate at the committal, and we were front page news all over Australia. Campbell got in, one way or other, every piece of roguery we could lay our hands on, and there was plenty of it, against old man Wren, and it was all published in the papers. Now we knew that this wouldn't be let in, or probably wouldn't be let in at the trial, but the jury had read all this and Wren had become rich by this

time, and a lot of younger people either didn't know or had forgotten about his criminal background, and we reminded them in a big way. And that's how it worked, that's how he [Hardy] got off.[15]

Sir John's comments were made with the benefit of hindsight, but on that first day passions were high, as Mr Galbally and Mr Campbell bitterly attacked and counter-attacked each other. Following the luncheon adjournment, Mr John Wren, Sr, was allowed to leave the court, as he would not be called that afternoon. Galbally said that Mr and Mrs Wren could, if required, be brought to the court within twenty minutes. Mr William Barry, Labor MLA for Carlton, was in court in answer to a subpoena, and he, too, was allowed to leave.[16]

Mr Galbally argued forcefully that while proceedings were pending against Hardy, he should not be allowed to go on selling his book, and trying to enlist sympathy for his 'filthy book'. When Mr Campbell called to Mr Galbally to restrain himself, he then clenched his fist and in a loud voice said: 'Anybody who has read this book agrees that there is no defence for this charge'. After further heated exchanges, Mr Jackson closed the court to hear the evidence put in support of the submission to refuse Hardy bail.[17]

The bail hearing was held *in camera*. James Martin, a private inquiry agent, gave evidence that on 24 November he had heard Hardy talk to about 130 people in a reserve outside the Newport railway station. He claimed that Hardy had said he was proud he had written *Power Without Glory*, and that if 'coppers are here tonight I will probably be charged with Contempt of Court, as I should not be discussing a case that is pending. If I should be imprisoned . . . I shall write another book, in fact, several books'. Martin continued his evidence; he stated that he had attended a meeting at the Yarra Bank on the previous Sunday when Hardy had addressed about 1000 people, and copies of his book had been sold. He had bought a copy for 19s 6d.[18]

Detective Henry Murfett of Russell Street Police Station also gave evidence that, on 12 November at a Communist Party meeting on the Yarra Bank, Hardy said, 'I am charged with criminal libel, and have been granted £500 bail. A leading solicitor told me £1 was plenty for this type of crime'. According to Murfett, Hardy had said:

The Crown promised me every assistance in this case, but now it ignores me.

Mr. Oldham [Trevor Oldham, former Victorian Attorney-General] is supposed to be a solicitor. He has probably had one or two cases in the country. That is, he is a bush lawyer.

I will answer their attack. It has been alleged certain things were said about Sir Thomas Blamey. Mr. Barry, who was Minister for Housing in the Cain Government, claims he is Brady in the book.

I challenge him to prove he is Brady, and I will challenge him in court, although I know it will be ganged up against me. Some say the 'Argus' published this book, but they did not.

The Press will not print my statements, apart from a little bit in the 'Age'.

I will challenge Mrs. Wren to prove she is Mrs. West in the book. It is all an attempt to intimidate me, to put me in gaol to stop the second edition . . . he would write the second edition of the book in Pentridge if he could get a pencil.[19]

Murfett said to Mr Campbell that he had not been sent to the Yarra Bank by Mr Galbally, Mr Wren, or any of these people, but in the course of his police duty. Nor had he been tailing Hardy. He did admit that Hardy was replying to attacks made on him by Mr Oldham and Mr Barry in Parliament . . . Hardy believed that the attacks made on him in Parliament were prejudicial to him.[20]

Mr Jackson SM said he would refuse bail because of Martin's evidence that Hardy had been addressing meetings to justify his conduct; he had 9000 copies of his books ready for sale, and he had given twenty-four copies to the men at Angliss's Meat Works to start a library. Mr Jackson said it was obvious that Hardy had done this with the intention or possibility of affecting the trial. If he had the power to impose conditions of bail, he would have released Hardy. Hardy then went into the witness box. He told Mr Campbell that he had not, in any of his speeches, suggested he should be acquitted of the charge. He said that when he had referred to Parliamentarians, he had been replying to their attacks on him in Parliament, which he felt had badly prejudiced him.[21]

Mr Jackson adjourned the hearing of the preliminary examination until 2.15 p.m. the following day. Mr Dall said outside the court that an urgent application to release Hardy on bail would be made in chambers to the Supreme Court of Victoria after 10 a.m. the following morning.[22]

There was one event that was not reported in the newspapers after the first day of the committal hearing. Hardy had, after discussion with Mr Campbell, arranged to bring an elderly woman to the Court lobby. Mr Campbell spoke to her. Soon afterwards she left the Court building.[23]

On the afternoon of Monday, 27 November 1950, Frank Hardy was taken into custody. That was the *only* night that Hardy spent in the City Watchhouse throughout the entire committal and trial proceedings of the *Power Without Glory* case. In *The Hard Way* there is some obfuscation that makes it difficult for the reader to establish that fact.

Nothing escaped the keen-eyed Hardy as the warder led him to the exercise yard. A decade later, in *The Hard Way*, the pages devoted to his overnight incarceration in the Watchhouse, and his observations of his fellow-prisoners, detailed a wide range of human frailties and emotions. These cameos rank as some of Hardy's best writing. They were written with compassion and humour, and Hardy, the political activist, also made penetrating comments on the nature of imprisonment. Despite his own vulnerable position, he had ingested the atmosphere and captured not only the physical environment but its effects on those who were imprisoned.[24]

Was Hardy influenced by the work of an earlier political activist, [James] Vance Marshall? Marshall, the son of a Presbyterian minister, was the first organiser for the Miscellaneous Workers' Union in New South Wales, and a member of the Social Democratic League. He was imprisoned for making what were considered subversive speeches during World War I, and again after the publication of *Jail from Within* in 1918.

He was arrested in the Domain in Sydney, just before he was to chair the weekly open-air gathering one Sunday afternoon in October 1917. Marshall had previously criticised the conscription of Australian youth to serve in the trenches in World War I.[25] He had publicly stated that 'so far as the working class is concerned, the colour of a flag matters not, so long as that class gets a share of the good things of life'.

Marshall was charged in 1919 with having unlawfully incited persons to riotously assemble to disturb the peace. 'A public outcry this time prevented another injustice being dealt out and thereafter the young socialist was left in peace.'[26] When he was released after his first sentence, he wrote *Jail From Within*, a text which did not please officialdom:

> The first edition was set to print when, as Vance stated, 'in furtherance of their efforts to silence me, the Billy Hughes Federal (Nationalist) Government confiscated all the metal under the authority of the War Precautions Act. It was not the first time I was silenced and, indeed, as it turned out, it was not the last either . . . Undaunted, the metal for a second "clandestine" edition was hastily prepared. The printing press churned out 48 000 copies, all of which were sold immediately'. 'Jail From Within' naturally created a political sensation and was instrumental in Marshall again being arrested, charged and sentenced to another term of hard labour in a vain effort to silence him.
>
> The sequel to this second term of imprisonment was another exposure of the injustices, ill-treatment and brutality graphically portrayed in 'The World of the Living Dead', a book which a leading Sydney publisher declined to handle with the comment—'It's good, but, in places, too raw —too creepy—too real. From a business point of view the sordid truth is not always the most acceptable'.
>
> The working class press and the Trade Union Movement assisted in publishing and distributing both these works. These were factors contributing to their scarcity in later years, notwithstanding the fact that over 40 000 copies of 'The World of the Living Dead' were sold as they came off the press.[27]

Marshall's experiences, and the involvement of the working-class press and the trade union movement in printing his books, were a precedent for the travails that Hardy was to endure in 1950–51 when *Power Without Glory* was published. Marshall was a personal friend and admirer of Henry Lawson, who wrote the preface to *The World of the Living Dead*.[28] Hardy, too, was a great admirer of Lawson. There are some similarities in the descriptions of life in the cells, as portrayed by Marshall and Hardy. In *The Hard Way*, Hardy described an incident in the Watchhouse when the discussion soon turned to women. There was laughter about the bawdy message chalked on the wall.[29]

In *Jail From Within*, Marshall recorded what he had observed in Long Bay Gaol:

A pencilled inscription scrawled across the opposite wall attracted my attention. It was evidently the work of an underworld professional who believed whole-heartedly in the theory that, irrespective of when or where, it pays at all times to advertise. 'Boys, when you get out go to Miss Lottie Beach's, 46 — Street, Paddington, for a good time,' so it read.[30]

Hardy wrote about the unshaven and physical appearance of some of his fellow inmates on the morning they had to face the magistrate.[31]

Marshall, too, was aware how the prisoners were disadvantaged by lack of washing facilities. 'The whole atmosphere was nauseating and revolting . . . "If yer wasn't a dorg they'd give yer a chanst ter clean up. It stands to reason a bloke ain't got no show in the court with three days' whiskers an' jail dirt on 'im"'.[32]

Marshall's two books describing a prisoner's life in 1917 and 1918 were damning indictments of the penal system. Whether Marshall was a role model for Hardy cannot be established. But there are parallels in the Marshall and Hardy legal proceedings. Marshall, the socialist, had asserted his right to free speech, and he was gaoled. Then he wrote about his experiences and uncovered the horrific conditions in the gaols, and he again fell foul of the law. Hardy, the communist, had written of the corruption in governments and high places, and he was brought before the courts. Although Hardy had spent only one night in the Melbourne Watchhouse, and some hours in daytime custody, he, too, had shown an awareness of the disastrous effects on those who were imprisoned. Just how much this short time had affected Hardy may be judged by the number of pages he devoted to his experience in *The Hard Way*.[33]

However, when Hardy continued to write of his time in the Watchhouse, the quality of his prose was marred when he lapsed into political rhetoric.[34] And again, when he penned an obsequious passage, a Magnificat to Ted Hill. Was Hardy sincere, or had experiences in Australia, the Soviet Union and Eastern Europe taught him the value of the protection and patronage of a mentor? Hill was still a powerful figure in the CPA at the time of writing, ten years after the trial. Hardy had written of his feelings on the occasion that his solicitor, Tom Dall, and Hill had visited him at the Watchhouse.[35] When Dall and Hill visited Hardy that afternoon in the Watchhouse, did Hardy really believe that Hill had all the qualities that he attributed to him a decade later? Whatever his private thoughts, Hardy certainly needed Hill's support and guidance at that time.

In 1999 Paul Adams, Hardy's literary biographer, revealed that Frank had a long-standing mistrust of Ted Hill, and had described him in the blackest of terms. His feelings towards Hill pre-dated the writing of *The Hard Way*.[36]

In *The Hard Way* Hardy related how Dall and Hill prevailed on him to accept a bail condition that he give an assurance that he would not sell the book. Hill had pointed out that the mass campaign would be difficult to conduct were he in gaol. Hardy saw the tactical soundness of Hill's advice and lapsed into rhetoric again.[37]

Later that day, 28 November 1950, Hardy was taken from the Watchhouse to appear before Mr Justice Hudson of the Supreme Court in the Practice

Court, when he gave his undertaking that copies of his book would not be distributed. He was granted bail of £500 and one surety of £500. Soon after he was released.[38]

The third day of the case was devoted to the legal argument surrounding the defence claim that Mr Jackson SM had no jurisdiction to deal with the matter, while the prosecution argued that he had the right. Mr Jackson adjourned the hearing until the following day.[39]

On the fourth day Mr Jackson mentioned to the court that he had received ten telegrams on the previous evening, including one which read, 'Emphatic protest refusal grant bail. Demand you refuse to continue with case. Williams, Frank Hardy Defence Committee'. 'It is a grave matter that any outside person is ready to try to influence the course of justice like that,' said Mr Jackson. Hardy denied that the Defence Committee had anything to do with the telegrams. Mr Jackson defended his jurisdiction to hear the case. Mr Campbell sought a week's adjournment so that the ruling could be tested in the Supreme Court. Mr Galbally objected to the adjournment as Hardy had already been granted a 28-day adjournment. He said that there was every reason to dispose of the matter of criminal libel at once. Mr Galbally opposed bail for Hardy, but Mr Jackson released him on £500; he adjourned the tribunal until 10 a.m. on 7 December. Mr Campbell and Mr Starke then proceeded to the Practice Court where the first step was taken in the application for a prohibition order. Late in the afternoon Justice Hudson reserved his judgment after hearing argument, and on the following day he rejected the application. Mr Campbell then approached the State Full Court, which adjourned on 5 December to a date to be fixed, to consider Mr Campbell's application for an order nisi to prohibit Mr Jackson continuing to hear the case.[40]

Pending a decision by the State Full Court, the City Court resumed on 7 December; Mr Jackson listened to Mr Galbally's arguments that Hardy should not be granted bail, because he was carrying on with his public activities. Mr Galbally believed that the purpose of applying for adjournments was to frustrate the course of justice. 'Hardy is a Communist, and is employing the well-known methods of the Communist when he is brought to justice. He puts everyone on trial except himself.'[41]

Hardy's counsel, Mr Campbell, was unsuccessful in his appeal to the State Full Court, and the preliminary hearing in the City Court was not resumed until 15 January 1951.

Meanwhile the Defence Committee had not been idle. The CPA Victorian Executive was also rallying its forces. Despite Hardy having given an undertaking to the court that he would not distribute copies of *Power Without Glory* while on bail, he was aware that his supporters were forging ahead with the completion and distribution of another edition. In many private homes around Melbourne, volunteers folded, stitched, cheese-clothed, rounded and backed around 16 000 copies of the 672-page book.[42]

Fred and Dot Farrall were CPA members whose home was in Fawkner Street, South Yarra. Their home became one of the centres where *Power Without Glory* was collated and bound. Farrall's first intimation of the project occurred one evening on his way home from work. He was hailed by Rick Oke, one of the CPA Control Commissioners, who was sitting in a parked car. Oke informed Fred that it had been arranged with Dot that voluntary workers would use their house as a base. Mountains of printed pages were secretly delivered and, just as secretly, carefully chosen volunteers bound many thousands of copies of *Power Without Glory*. After some time Farrall was again contacted by Oke, who informed him that there was doubt about one of the volunteers whose lifestyle was irregular, and might prove a risk. The whole operation was transferred to another location. Farrall expressed his admiration for the way that Frank Hardy had written the book, but he had no doubt that the CPA leadership's political judgment and expertise was the driving force that brought the book to the public.[43]

The success of the operation further indicates the loyalty given to the CPA by its highly disciplined members and sympathisers. People had worked not only in teams, but also in isolation. Zelda D'Aprano hand-sewed the signatures together for long, tedious hours. She remembers a meeting at which Hardy spoke to members of the West Heidelberg CPA branch; he displayed a lack of interest in his audience and soon departed. 'He was extremely off-hand, and his demeanour was one of enduring the experience. It was as if he was doing us a great favour.'[44] D'Aprano was irritated, but she dismissed her doubts, as she did not wish to be disloyal. Hardy's disdainful attitude to his supporters remained in her memory.

D'Aprano was only one among many who became disenchanted with Hardy's behaviour during those crucial times. Ted Thompson, a New Theatre activist and printer who then worked at the CPA press, had been recruited to meet Hardy and drive him to a meeting in Footscray. One Saturday evening he arrived at Hosie's Hotel on the corner of Elizabeth and Flinders Streets and waited. 'When Hardy arrived he was very drunk; he was rocking on his feet; he had spent the afternoon at the races.' Thompson said Frank had little respect for those who were trying 'to save [him] from the gallows'. He drove him to Footscray, where he delivered a long and rambling address to the assembled workers, who thought 'he was God'. The audience appeared to be happy, and 'at least Frank saw the night out for a change, which was something'. But Thompson was disgusted with Hardy's performance, and he refused to support him on further speaking engagements.[45]

When Frank Hardy was arraigned on the charge of criminal libel, some CPA members elevated his status to that of a working-class hero. However, this status was not accepted by all CPA members and supporters. In the lead-up to his trial Hardy had been invited by the Glen Iris Branch of the CPA to address their members, and, more particularly, people who were residents of the new Housing Commission estates in Ashburton and Alamein. Members made great efforts to ensure a good attendance, including personal visits to householders who lived in muddy, unmade streets, and letterbox drops of leaflets advising of the function. Despite the early winter rain and cold, a large audience attended on the Saturday evening at the home of CPA member Harry Cleveland, in Somerset Road, Glen Iris. When an hour had elapsed and there had been no telephone call to advise of a delay, much to the discomfiture of party members present, it became clear that Hardy was not going to appear. Apologies were made. Cleveland, a talented photographer, decided to entertain the gathering by showing a selection of his slides, and the guests were served supper. When one of the members called at CPA headquarters and complained of Hardy's non-attendance and the embarrassment that it had caused, she was reprimanded, and told that 'Comrade Hardy was a very busy man'.[46] Accountability within CPA circles was clearly selective. Given Hardy's gambling proclivities, the choice of a Saturday evening (a race day) was unwise.

Hardy's addiction to gambling was such that, even while he was on bail facing a serious charge, race-days were still sacred. Most serious gamblers keep away from the bar until the racing programme is finished, but not Frank Hardy. The combination of alcohol and gambling is a poor mix. Hardy was also a bad loser, and he did not mellow with the years. Graham Pitts, a member of the Libertarian group in Sydney, first met Hardy when he attended their drinking sessions. Later, when he came to Melbourne he would go to the races with Hardy. If Frank was on a winning streak, the afternoon would be successful; but if he had a losing bet, Frank would throw a public tantrum, and he would blame everyone from the jockeys, the horses, the trainers, the owners, the bookmakers—no one escaped his highly emotional outbursts. Whereas the normal gambler might only betray, by a twitch of the lips, that he has lost, Hardy was so different. It was embarrassing to be with him.[47]

When Hardy attended a fund-raising function at the home of Atida and David Levine, Sam Goldbloom, a prominent member of the Jewish community, was present. Hardy became progressively more drunk and made very anti-Semitic remarks. Goldbloom was shocked at Hardy's behaviour, and subsequently tried to avoid him. On another occasion Joseph Waters was present at an evening organised by 'progressive Jewish people' in Camberwell. Hardy was a guest, and after he had a few drinks, he felt 'he had to say something, and lo and behold, he told an anti-Semitic joke'. He went to Waters's office the following morning and said 'What did I do last night?'. Waters replied, 'My God, Frank, you made a mess of it'. 'Why did I do it?', he said. Waters said, 'The point was that he had done it, and there were complaints made'. Later, Frank apologised to his hosts.[48]

Hardy, as a Catholic, had been subjected to sectarianism and as a communist had suffered the fate of belonging to an unpopular minority. He had grown up at a time when some sections of the community were opposed to the arrival of the Jewish refugees from Nazism. Historically it is true that one persecuted group of refugees does not necessarily welcome the later arrival of another group. But Hardy belonged to a party that had a declared policy against racism, and given that 'In response to Nazism and the Holocaust, most [some?] Jews supported the political left in the immediate post-war decade. Many Jews, both in Australia and internationally, joined socialist and communist movements'.[49]

The Victorian CPA was no exception, and some members and supporters were Jewish. What motivated Hardy, under the influence of alcohol, to make anti-Semitic remarks? Hardy was not in unfamiliar surroundings, as he was used to addressing middle-class audiences in middle-class homes; the CPA had a large number of academics, doctors, lawyers, clergymen and successful business men and women in its ranks. The question of what attracted these groups to a revolutionary working-class movement did exercise the minds of most worker members of the CPA. Was Hardy envious of the status these groups occupied within the CPA? Were this the case, why should he single out the Jewish members? No explanation can be offered for his outbursts.

Whatever his weaknesses, Hardy could not have been accused of cowardice in the months following his arrest. Private enquiry agent James Martin disclosed at the bail hearing that Hardy had spoken at a meeting in Newport three days earlier. John Arrowsmith, CPA organiser, who had arranged the meeting, recalled the electrically charged atmosphere that had prevailed on that warm November evening. Sid Rawlinson, by now the caretaker of the EYL building in North Melbourne, with his wife, Stella, had driven Hardy to the small public park near the Newport railway gates. Rawlinson was reassured that Bill Ipsen, a very large man, was chairing the meeting. Writer Alan Marshall, the joint secretary of the Frank Hardy Defence Committee, hobbled towards the small group. A loudspeaker had been erected in the trees; Marshall rested on his crutches, shuffled his papers and began his address to the gathering of about fifty people. A crowd of burly men, some in shirt-sleeves and others in athletic singlets, including Tom Healy, a leader of the ALP Industrial Group on the waterfront, pushed through the crowd. Arrowsmith said that Marshall continued to address the crowd. Meanwhile, the vigilant Bill Ipsen had moved closer to Marshall. Rawlinson struggled with the group, who had by then disconnected the battery from the microphone. Alan Marshall bravely continued with his speech. The crowd had grown to more than a hundred by now. Despite Marshall's protests, Arrowsmith insisted that he should leave; apart from the danger, he was to speak at another meeting at nine o'clock. As he was driven away in a friend's car, Marshall saw some men leaving the pub nearby. Fortunately, they were Hardy supporters.

Hardy started to address the meeting. The aggressors were intent on attacking him; Rawlinson brandished the crank handle of his car. One of Healy's men sang out, 'I'll kill the commo bastard'. An old woman hit someone over the head with an umbrella. Arrowsmith shouted, 'Ring out those who want to hear Frank Hardy. Form a circle. Ring out! Ring out!'.

Hardy's few supporters and a hundred or so members of the public did form a circle around him. By then, the microphone had been reconnected. As the crowd grew to around several hundred people, Hardy continued to talk on a multitude of subjects. Healy finally asked Hardy how old he was. When Hardy replied that he was thirty-three, Healy asked how he could have written about things that happened before he was born. After further interchanges, Healy was asked by Hardy if he had read *Power Without Glory*. He replied, 'I wouldn't read the filthy commo thing!'. The Healy mob then dispersed, and Hardy continued to speak until ten o'clock. John Arrowsmith's précis of the events of that evening corroborate Hardy's written account in *The Hard Way*.[50]

The campaign outside the courts continued to grow. Hardy addressed meetings all over Melbourne and in country areas. He also travelled to Sydney and Brisbane to enlist support for his cause, and Defence Committees were established in those states. Many successful meetings were held. Ross Hardy joined the growing band of speakers who went out to the people to plead Hardy's cause. Author Judah Waten was closely involved with the writing of the tens of thousands of leaflets which were distributed all over the country. The Defence Committee sent members to speak to groups, large and small, in houses, halls and workplaces.

In 1951 Don Tonkin, a graduate in his early twenties, worked in a research and development laboratory in Melbourne. He had obtained a copy of *Power Without Glory* before the injunction was placed on Hardy that the novel not be distributed. He was quite surprised to find that another staff member was discreetly circulating duplicated copies of the list of characters in the novel alleging who they were in real life. This person was a staunch Freemason and, certainly, strongly anti-Catholic; there were others there who were sympathetic to Hardy and the Left. Tonkin had contacted the Defence Committee to arrange a meeting; Judah Waten was the speaker. Tonkin mustered as many as possible from among his colleagues. These are his recollections of that meeting in early 1951:

I think that no more than three people came, plus my wife, Miriam, and me, and Judah made six altogether. We had a tiny flat in Parkville—it consisted of one room (a bed-sitter)—and a kitchenette in the main passageway through which most of the other tenants had to pass to reach their flats.

I set up my amplifier and record-player (quite an operation in those circumstances) and played a recording made by Frank Hardy about his book and the reasons why it was banned, and why he was being sued for criminal libel. Sitting there, we must have looked (and probably felt) like a war-time Resistance group listening to the BBC, expecting at any moment a knock on the door or a brick through the window.

Judah Waten was then introduced as 'Mr Smith' (or some such nom-de-plume)—probably because it was illegal to sell the book, or to promote it in any way—I can't remember a word he said, but he would certainly have dealt with the situation of Hardy in particular, and the Left in general.

We took up a collection for Hardy's defence, gave everyone a cup of tea and a piece of cake, had a bit of a yarn, and then the others went home.

We followed the case like bloodhounds when it went to court, and laughed our socks off at the wriggling of the prosecution witnesses denying that they had done any of the deeds detailed in the book, but still claiming that they were clearly identifiable.

We were astounded and overjoyed when Hardy was found not guilty.[51]

Tonkin's recollections encapsulate the strong emotions of that period. Support for Hardy often came from unexpected quarters. Kenneth Wallace-Crabbe was a journalist on the *Herald* when Hardy's novel was first published. His son has recounted how his father 'hated Catholics, he did not care for Communists, but he loved *Power Without Glory*'.[52] George Seelaf said that 'the Masons, motivated by their anti-Catholicism, assisted with the collection of evidence'.[53]

The recording of Hardy's speech, played at Tonkin's meeting, had been made after private enquiry agent Martin and Detective Murfett had given evidence in the bail hearing. It was believed that if Hardy were to be misquoted, this could lead to contempt of court charges. Who conceived the clever idea that the record be cut, or who was involved in its production is not known, but the Defence Committee had many talented members who would have had the technical expertise for such a project. A number of copies were made, and some were sent interstate. When Hardy had several meetings in Melbourne on the same night, the recording was also used.[54]

It was fortunate for Hardy, the CPA and the Defence Committee that the preliminary hearing was adjourned on 5 December until 15 January 1951. This breathing space enabled them to rally their forces, plan effective strategies, hold more public and private meetings, collect money, print and distribute leaflets, enlist new supporters, and embrace other organisations and groups who felt threatened by the criminal libel charge brought against a writer. As the campaign broadened, 'Free Hardy—Jail Wren' slogans appeared mysteriously on walls, bridges and fences. The campaign to free Hardy was coupled with the struggle against the Communist Party Dissolution Act, the gaoling of union leaders and other attacks on the labour movement.[55]

What was the effect on Frank Hardy of those early days in court? Behind the facade of the experienced communist public speaker with the ready quip and the funny story, was there a man who masked his own feelings of inadequacy by brashness and vulgarity? His recollection of how he reacted when he was taken to the enclosure yard at the Watchhouse is significant; he mentioned the slight swagger he adopted when he wanted to show that he could look after himself.[56] Underneath the brash exterior did he still believe he was just 'a battler from the bush'? Ten years later he wrote of his feelings at that time. He was aware that there were changes taking place, but whether for better or for worse, he did not know.[57]

When Hardy left Bacchus Marsh and went to Melbourne, it was not long before the CPA beckoned, and he was soon tilting at windmills. But, by the time he had written *Power Without Glory*, he had become involved in a real battle. If he was defeated, he would be deprived of his freedom. If he was successful, there would be no limits to his horizons. As 1950 drew to a close, and the New Year of 1951 dawned, the Defence Committee quickened its campaign. As day followed day, Hardy moved inexorably closer to the committal hearing in the City Court, that had been set down for 15 January 1951 before Mr Jackson SM.

Chapter Nine

CONCLUDING THE PRELIMINARY HEARING

ON MONDAY, 15 January 1951, Frank and Ross Hardy travelled into Melbourne. The following is a précis of the *Argus* newspaper report of the adjourned preliminary hearing.

The City Court was crowded. It was not long before Mr Jackson, SM, reprimanded counsel, he said 'he would not have the hearing turned into a "dog-fight" or a "circus"'. Newspaper reporters' credentials were checked before they were allowed to sit at the Press tables. Witnesses were cleared from the court on the application of Hardy's counsel, Mr D. M. Campbell KC.[1]

Mr Campbell submitted that Mrs Ellen Wren had not voluntarily laid the charge against Hardy, that she was under duress from her husband, and that Mr Wren was hiding behind his wife's skirts, statements described as 'outrageous' and 'cowardly' by Mr J. Galbally, counsel for Mrs Wren. Mr Campbell insisted that, according to law, once there was any doubt that the informant had acted under pressure, it then had to be proved. Mr Jackson ruled that Mrs Wren did not need to come to the court. Mr Galbally read from *Power Without Glory*; he submitted that anyone reading the book would know that the character Nellie West was the wife of John Wren. He maintained that a reader would be able to locate Wren's home from the description in the book; and he submitted that what Hardy had written in his author's notes published at the back of *Power Without Glory* left little doubt that the characters were not fictional. He went on to discuss how Hardy had mentioned Marx, capitalism and Communism in Russia. At that point Mr Campbell objected: 'I take strong objection to Hardy's political beliefs being mentioned in connection with this case. If he is a Communist he is entitled to the same fair trial under British justice as a Conservative or a Liberal'.[2]

Mr Jackson agreed that it was not proper to refer to the political or religious beliefs of a defendant; 'he is just a citizen before the law'. He said that it would be of benefit to those involved if Mr Galbally refrained from referring to Hardy's political beliefs. Mr Galbally continued his address at length about the alleged adultery between Ellen West and the bricklayer. He said:

It is true that adultery is not, in criminal law, a criminal offence, but it was always punished by ecclesiastical courts, and they viewed it very gravely.

Adultery is forbidden by one of God's commandments, and to say of a woman that she has committed adultery is one of the worst things you can say of a good and virtuous woman.

The argument may be raised that no case has been produced to the Court where a criminal information has been laid by a woman who has been libelled . . .[3]

Mr Campbell immediately indicated that it soon would be raised. Mr Galbally claimed:

Libel has been compared to murder. In one case you murder a man's body, in the other his reputation. If a man invented a new and diabolical means of murder, just because there had been no case like that before would you say he was not guilty of murder?

Only once in 500 years would you get a case as bad as this one.

There is evidence that Mrs Wren is a woman of outstanding virtue. She will be described by those near and dear to her as a woman of saintly disposition.[4]

After a long legal argument, the tone of the committal hearing had been established. Mr Campbell and Mr Galbally clearly intended to continue with the tactics which had been employed in the earlier preliminary court hearings.

John Francis Wren, the eldest son of John and Ellen Wren, was called. Under questioning from Mr Galbally, Wren, Jr, gave evidence that he had purchased seven or eight copies of *Power Without Glory*. He had read the book and believed that the character Nellie West referred to his mother, Ellen Wren. When asked why, he said his mother had had nine children, five of whom were named in the book. Mr Campbell objected; he said that Wren, Jr, did not know how many children his mother had had. He might know how many children there were in the family, but he might not know if a child had been adopted. Wren, Jr, acknowledged that the reference to Marjorie West studying the violin for three years was partially correct as regards his sister. One of the exhibits in the court was a fine print of Beethoven which had been mentioned in the book; this had hung in the music room at the Wren family home. He also confirmed that he had had a brother, Xavier, who, he understood, had died from pneumonia. The book had referred to the death of Xavier, the illegitimate son of Mrs West. He also gave evidence that Hardy had described 'more or less accurately' the relationship that existed between Mrs Mahon and her daughter, Ellen Wren. In the book Mrs Mahon was known as Mrs Moran. He further detailed that Hardy's description of John Wren's home was substantially correct. He said that he accepted that Carringbush, the suburb named in the book, was, in fact, Collingwood because of the boot factories and the black and white colours of the local football club.[5]

John Wren, Jr, agreed that additions had been carried out to his father's house, and these were described in the book. He identified Mr Tunnecliffe, MLA, as the 'Tom Trumbleward' referred to by Hardy. He identified that the character Ted Thurgood was Mr E. G. Theodore, who had formed a gold mining company in Fiji with his father, John Wren, as the principal shareholder. When he was asked if his father was worth £2 000 000, he said he could not say. Mr Galbally asked him how he felt when he read the book. Wren, Jr, said, 'My reaction was to smash up Hardy'.[6]

Clashes between Mr Campbell and Mr Galbally marked the day's proceedings, and Wren, Jr, denied repeatedly that a group of lawyers had given advice to the Wren family; he claimed there was only one, Mr Galbally. After persistent questioning from Mr Campbell, Wren, Jr, then disclosed the truth. His family had consulted Mr Gillard, Mr Shillitoe and Mr McInerney. He admitted that he had had a number of discussions with his mother about who should take the action. At first he had denied that he had attended conferences with his father and the lawyers. Later he agreed that he had been in attendance, and that the question was raised as to who was the best person to take the action. It was agreed that Wren, Sr, would not bring an action. At the conference it was decided that his mother should bring the information. Why this decision might have been reached was revealed in the following exchange between Mr Campbell and John Wren, Jr:

> Mr Campbell: And that was on the basis that if your mother brought the information the defence of truth and public benefit could not be used?
> Wren, Jr: No, the information was brought because of the grossest libel.
> Mr Campbell: At this conference was the question raised of the defence of truth and public benefit?
> Wren, Jr: I don't think so.
> Mr Campbell: Will you pledge your oath that at none of these discussions was the defence of truth and public benefit discussed?
> Wren, Jr: Not to the best of my recollection.
> Mr Campbell: Was it not suggested by the legal advisers, 'If Mr John Wren brings the information for libel, the defence of truth and public benefit can be raised?'.
> Wren, Jr: Not to the best of my recollection.
> Mr Campbell: Was it ever said at one of these conferences that if your mother brought the information, the defence of truth and public benefit could not be used, because she is a private woman?
> Wren, Jr: Not to the best of my recollection.[7]

Mr Campbell then suggested to Wren, Jr, that his mother had been pushed into the action for this reason, but he denied this. When asked if his mother and father had read the book, he answered that his mother had, but not his father. Mr Campbell said, 'You were not serious when you said that your father had not read this book were you?'. Wren, Jr, replied, 'I was completely serious'. He said that his mother had told him she had read the book about three or four weeks prior to the information being issued. In reply to further questions, he admitted that he had acquainted his father of the tremendously serious allegations made against him. He agreed that the book accused John West of being concerned with the bribery of police, bribery of justice and bribery of officials. Mr Galbally interjected at that point, 'I think this is scandalous'. Mr Jackson reprimanded him and said he would not have that term used in the court. Mr Galbally told Mr Jackson that John Wren, Sr, 'may have set his face against reading the book'.[8]

Mr Campbell resumed his cross-examination of Wren, Jr; he said that John West 'was concerned with two murders, and involved in a nefarious manner with the Milk Commission'. Wren, Jr, agreed that the book had said that. Mr Campbell asked a series of questions—that he [West] was concerned with the ringing-in of a racehorse—that the book had alleged that before he had started his tote, 'your father had rigged a pigeon race'—it was alleged that he rigged and won £60 000 over the Austral Wheel Race, and also that he rigged the Caulfield Cup the year a horse called Whisper won. To all these questions Wren, Jr, answered, 'The book says that'.[9]

It is of interest that Mr Campbell at first questioned Wren, Jr, about John West's activities, but soon after used the term 'your father'. Was this a lapse, or a deliberate ploy, by the defence counsel to unsettle the witness? Mr Campbell suggested that Wren, Jr, had told his father about some of the allegations. Wren, Jr, agreed that he had mentioned the one about Whisper. He told Mr Campbell that his father was not aware, at that time, that his wife had read *Power Without Glory*. She had kept it hidden from her husband; later she had burned the book. He said it was possible that he may have suggested to his father that he should read the book himself.[10]

People in the court and the members of the press were aware that the events they were witnessing were quite extraordinary.

Melburnians were intrigued by the reports of the first day's hearing. Headlines proclaimed that 'Mrs Wren "Read, Hid and Burned" Hardy's book'.[11] Not only in Melbourne, but nationally, evening and morning newspapers were read avidly, and people gathered to listen to the radio broadcasts. John Wren had been the mysterious, millionaire entrepreneur for half a century. Now, Frank Hardy had lifted the veil on Wren's activities and his family, and Hardy was likely to go to gaol for his trouble. As disclosure followed disclosure in the City Court, the informed and uninformed nodded their heads. Some raged against Hardy's treatment of Mrs Ellen Wren; they felt she should not have been mentioned. Others did not mind Hardy exposing Wren's shady involvements, as it was time he got his 'come-uppance'. Wren also had some who defended him; they recounted stories of his generosity to those down on their luck in Collingwood and Richmond. While others were Hardy's fervent supporters; they believed the book was long overdue. John Wren and Frank Hardy had a similar standing in the community; they were either admired, feared or hated.

At the end of each day, there would have been little rest for Ross and Frank. Their maisonette was filled to overflowing; for months the seamen who were guarding them had moved in and moved out when it was time to return to their ships. Their daughter, Frances, had clear recollections of these men. She was also aware that there were guns in the house. Frances said that she had liked some of the seamen who taught her things, but it was a confused and troubled time for an eight year-old child. Alan Hardy was then almost five years old, and his memories of that time are not clear, and consequently less troubled than those of his sister.[12] The tension engendered had placed incredible strains on both Frank and Ross.

On the second day of the hearing Wren, Jr, was again in the witness box. He made allegations that his father had received a £100 000 blackmail demand, together with extracts from the book, before its publication. He said that his father had been told that if he paid the money the book would not be published. Mr Campbell read an extract from *Power Without Glory* that described a meeting at which Archbishop Malone, John West and others discussed the communists and militants in the unions and the role of the ALP Industrial Groups. When Mr Campbell finished reading the extract he asked Wren, Jr, if he remembered reading it. He burst out angrily, 'That was the extract for which they tried to blackmail my father for £100 000'. Mr Campbell replied, 'You will be getting into trouble if you say things like that. That is not an answer to my question'. Mr Galbally replied that Wren, Jr, believed the reference was put in [*Power Without Glory*] to blackmail his father. Mr Campbell requested that the reference to blackmail be struck out. Mr Jackson agreed. Later several further references to blackmail were also deleted from the proceedings.[13]

If the claim made by John Wren, Jr, was true, then who was the blackmailer, or blackmailers, who could have stopped the publication of *Power Without Glory*? The person or persons could only have been someone close to either Frank Hardy, the Victorian CPA leadership, or the National CPA leadership. Who else would have had access to a section of the manuscript, and who could have stopped publication? A hundred thousand pounds was a huge sum of money in 1949–50.

Hardy's literary biographer Paul Adams has stated that Hardy was convinced that Ted Hill and CPA organiser Frank Johnson were responsible for the blackmail threat made to John Wren. Johnson had retained part of the manuscript loaned by Hardy months before. Hardy believed that Johnson and Hill realised that Frank would be held responsible. Hardy had long entertained doubts about Ted Hill; but party loyalty obviously prevailed at that time.[14]

During Mr Campbell's cross-examination of Wren, Jr, the question again arose as to why Mrs Wren rather than her husband had taken proceedings. Wren, Jr, denied that his mother was under his father's domination. He said they were a devoted couple, but agreed that they had occupied separate bedrooms since about 1918, when an open-air bedroom was constructed. He denied vehemently that his parents, for a time, did not eat at the same table, and that Wren, Sr, only spoke to his wife in the presence of visitors, or when he could not avoid it. Mr Campbell said that his advice was that John and Ellen Wren had been seriously estranged since the birth of the child Xavier. Wren, Jr, shouted angrily from the witness box, 'That's a filthy lie'. Mr Jackson asked him to please remain quiet, whereupon he apologised, and he was reminded that it was not his place to interfere.[15]

Mr Campbell continued to question Wren, Jr, about the characters in the book, and whom he believed them to be in real life. He identified Snoopy Tanner as the well-known criminal Squizzy Taylor, asserting that his father knew him only to the extent that he had once ordered him off one of the Wren racecourses. Mr Campbell proceeded to read an extract from *Power Without Glory* which began:

> John Wren [incorrectly named in the *Argus*, should read 'West'] was under sentence of death: Snoopy Tanner had threatened to murder him! . . . Tanner had been drinking and was in a violent mood. John West threatened to call the police. 'So the great J.W. will call the coppers! Well, the coppers won't save you! Either yer lift the ban or yer die!' . . . Next day, up the grapevine from the underworld, came to Frank Lammence the news that Tanner was on a drinking bender and bragging that he would murder John West.[16]

Wren, Jr, identified Lammence as the late Frank Lawrence, his father's secretary. Mr Campbell continued to read: '. . . For two days and nights Arty West and another gunman hovered close to John West'. Again Mr Campbell questioned Wren, Jr, 'Whom do you understand to be Artie West?' He replied, 'My late Uncle Arthur'. Mr Campbell read on '. . . Rumours from the underworld became more ominous . . . John West sat thoughtfully for a while caressing his revolver . . . he put the revolver under his pillow'. Wren, Jr, stated that he did not know if his father slept with a revolver under his pillow, but he was aware that his father owned a revolver.[17]

Mr Campbell read more passages from the book and asked Wren, Jr, to identify the characters. John West had decided that he, one of the most powerful men in Australia, should not live in fear . . . Clive Parker stood under a shop verandah in a shabby suburban street . . . Clive Parker was married to Ronald Lassiter's . . . granddaughter . . . 'old Ron' was proud of his reporter grandson-in-law . . . This was the biggest story yet—if it came off . . . First on the scene of the death of Snoopy Tanner. Mr Campbell continued to read from the book. Wren, Jr, said that he believed Parker to be Clyde Palmer, a Melbourne journalist, and Ron Lassiter to be Con Loughnan. Then Mr Campbell identified Loughnan as being associated with the Richmond Council. The reports of that day's events show that, despite Mr Galbally's protests, Mr Campbell was not deterred, and he continued to read from *Power Without Glory*, and direct questions to Wren, Jr:[18]

> John West's plan to dispose of Snoopy Tanner had succeeded . . . Tanner was dead when he reached hospital . . . At Frank Lammence's request, friendly detectives had spread the word through their pimps in the underworld . . . Tanner could be murdered and no questions asked . . . a Sydney gunman, who had been 'shelved' by Tanner five years before had done the rest for £500.[19]

Again Mr Galbally interjected, 'If we are going to have this going on the matter will be interminable!'. Wren, Jr, 'I think so'.[20]

Mr Campbell was not daunted; he proceeded to read from the book and to cross-examine Wren, Jr. In reply to a question, Wren, Jr, agreed that his father had a great interest in politics. Mr Campbell then asked: 'And that your father ran politicians for Parliament?'. Wren, Jr, replied: 'That is stated'. When Mr Campbell asked if Wren, Sr, had used the gang of which Snoopy Tanner [Squizzy Taylor] was the head to terrorise his political opponents, Wren, Jr, replied: 'The book alleges that'. He agreed that this was an allegation against his father of having instigated a foul, brutal and horrible murder. Mr Campbell asked Wren, Jr, if the book had portrayed Nellie West as a woman more sinned against than sinning, and as a good woman interested in her home and children, he replied, 'The book says that'. When asked if he remembered the incident in the book which had stated that West instituted the bombing of Detective O'Flaherty's house, he agreed that he did. Mr Campbell then asked if he remembered that 'your mother was driven nearly crazy with fear over what had been done?'. Wren, Jr, replied, 'The book says that'. Mr Campbell continued, 'Do you regard murder as more serious than adultery?'. Wren, Jr, replied, 'In some circumstances, no'. He also agreed that the allegation of the murder of Squizzy Taylor, who had once been his father's trusted employee, was particularly foul[21]—thereby contradicting his evidence given earlier that day that his father had once ordered Taylor off one of the Wren racecourses.

Mr Campbell's cross-examination continued. At one stage of the hearing he submitted to Mr Jackson, SM, that Wren, Sr, had 'dragooned' his wife into issuing the information. He said he would attempt to show that Wren, Sr, had not issued the information himself because of his 'underground activities, and control of a certain section of the Labor Party'. Mr Galbally replied that that was only a matter of scandal. However Mr Campbell seemed determined to extract an admission from Wren, Jr, that his father had his own reasons for not taking out the information. He badgered Wren, Jr, on several occasions during the cross-examination. Was this deliberate repetition of the same, or similar questions, intended to elicit the desired response? Wren, Jr, in response to Mr Campbell's remark that his mother had only agreed to issue the information if she did not have to come to court, said that she would be quite willing to give evidence.[22]

The atmosphere in the court remained tense throughout the day. Wren, Jr, said that the character Barney Robinson was Barney Reynolds, a member of his father's staff. He believed that the boxer Lou Darby referred to in *Power Without Glory*, who had quarrelled with John West, had subsequently stowed away on a ship to America. He believed that the character Darby was Les Darcy, former middleweight champion of Australia, who had died in America. Just prior to the conclusion of Mr Campbell's cross-examination of Wren, Jr, he was asked if his father had ever made payments of money to racing clubs. Wren, Jr, replied that his father had been told that, if he paid over £100 000, the book would not be published. Mr Galbally interjected: 'There was no question of proceedings by your father or yourself at that time?'. Wren, Jr, replied:

'No. My father had no intention at that time of taking other proceedings, but he has now instructed you to take proceedings for blackmail'. Mr Jackson, SM, asked, 'How do you know that, Mr Wren? Were you present when those instructions were given?' 'As a matter of fact, I was,' replied Wren, Jr. Mr Campbell protested at the reference to blackmail. Mr Jackson ordered that it be struck off. John Wren, Jr, then left the witness box.[23]

The second witness to be called on the afternoon of the second day of the committal hearing was Bernard Nolan, barrister and solicitor. He was not only John and Ellen Wren's solicitor, but also a long-time friend and neighbour, who visited their home once a week. The following morning, the front page of the *Argus* carried a headline: ' "Power Without Glory"—"I'd kick him to pieces" —court flurry':

> The 'Power Without Glory' criminal libel hearing in the City Court yesterday assumed a violent note—a witness said that if he had been locked up with the author, Frank Hardy, he would probably have 'kicked him to pieces'.
>
> The witness, Bernard Nolan, a friend of the Wren family, said that this was his reaction after reading the book.
>
> Nolan, who was repeatedly told by Mr Jackson, S.M., to keep cool, stated that, in saying this, he meant that he would have liked to kill Hardy.[24]

The front page showed a photograph of Nolan leaving the court. Page four carried a full-page report of the proceedings, and a photograph of Hardy leaving the court; a third photograph showed an armchair bearing the Wren crest and the framed print of Beethoven that were exhibits in the case. The translation of the inscription of the crest read 'Wren to Victory'. In *Power Without Glory* the chair described had an inscription 'West to Victory'. A photograph of the chair and the crest was also reproduced on the front page. Page five carried the headline '. . . Sensational evidence during second day', together with photographs of Sir Gilbert Dyett, Mr S. Keon, Mr E. G. Theodore, Mr R. Lean, Sir Albert Dunstan, Mr T. Tunnecliffe, and Mr C. Loughnan.[25]

When Nolan entered the witness box to answer Mr Galbally's questions, he was carrying a copy of *Power Without Glory*. In response to questions, he frequently read at length from the marked passages in the book. He replied that, to his knowledge, John and Ellen Wren had never been estranged, nor did Wren dominate his wife. He identified Mrs Ellen Wren with Mrs Nellie West. He stated that he identified the character of John West with that of John Wren, Sr, and that the description of the West home fitted that of Wren's home. He identified other characters who appeared in the novel as being real people:

Sol Solomon—the late Mr. Sol Green.
Barney Robinson—Mr. Barney Reynolds.
Richard Lamb—Richard Lean, present manager of Stadiums Ltd.
Thomas Trumbleward—the late Mr. Tunnecliffe, M.L.A. member for Collingwood.

Godfrey Dwyer—Sir Gilbert Dyett.
Murkett—partner with Wren in ownership of the Brisbane *Mail* newspaper—Sir Keith Murdoch.
Patrick Corry—Mr. Patrick Cody.
Frank Lammence—the late Mr. Frank Lawrence, former secretary to Mr Wren.
'Red Ted' Thurgood—the late Mr. E. G. Theodore, M.H.R.
Tinn—Ted Thye, wrestler.
Vera Maguire—the witness, Nolan's, wife.[26]

When pressed by Mr Campbell for an explanation of his wish to be locked up with Hardy after reading his book, Nolan said: 'I mean I would probably kick him to pieces'. He said that the book had disturbed him very much, as the Wrens were great personal friends. When Mr Campbell suggested that he was much more upset than the average reader, Nolan debated this fiercely. Mr Jackson again intervened; he asked Nolan to keep cool and answer the question. When Nolan repeated that he would have kicked Hardy to pieces had he been locked up with him, and he would like to kill him, Mr Campbell replied, 'That is a gross exaggeration'. Nolan said that it was not. Mr Campbell said, 'As a result of what is stated in the book about Mr West and Vera Maguire, has it made you more angry?'.[27]

Nolan claimed that the relationship between Vera Maguire and John West, as depicted in the book, was a pack of lies. Mr Campbell further suggested that his anger about the book would have not been so great had it not mentioned Vera Maguire, whom Nolan believed to be his wife. Nolan agreed that he would not have been so concerned had only Wren, Sr, been mentioned. He said, 'My state of mind would have been pretty bad if any decent woman I knew had had that accusation written against her'.[28]

Mr Campbell asked Nolan if Wren, Sr, had spoken to him about the book. Nolan replied that he had not done so until after the proceedings had commenced, when they were on their way to the Stadium. Mr Campbell queried whether Nolan had discussed with Joseph Wren (one of his employees and a son of Wren, Sr) whether his father or his mother should bring the action. Nolan denied this. When Mr Campbell asked whether Joseph Wren had told him why his father was not bringing the action, Nolan replied: 'No. If he would take my advice he would bring a lot more proceedings against a lot more people'. Mr Campbell replied that he had not asked for his advice, but he did ask whether he had attended any of the legal conferences before the information was laid by Mrs Wren. Nolan said he had not. But he agreed that he knew, prior to the information being issued, that Mrs Wren was going to bring the action, but he did not have a diary entry about it because he was not in the case. The hearing was adjourned until Thursday, 18 January, to enable depositions to be read back the following day.[29]

Newspaper reports of the first days of the committal hearing give some indication of the sensational revelations that continued to unfold in the court. The *Power Without Glory* case confirmed the *Argus* journalist's prescience; it was rapidly attaining the status of a literary *cause célèbre*. Each day's newspaper reports confirmed, in the minds of many readers, that the innuendoes and gossip which had linked certain public figures to corruption and crime were, in fact, well founded.

Thursday's hearing was reported in the *Argus* the following morning with a photograph on the front-page of Patrick Francis Cody leaving the Third City Court—the caption read 'Wren Case—I'D HAVE TAKEN LAW IN HANDS'. Page four bore a heading 'Leading public figures mentioned in . . . S.M. SHOUTS "SIT DOWN!" IN FIERY COURT SCENE. It also showed a photograph of Joseph Wren leaving the court, together with some photographs of prominent Australians, and a list of those who had been identified by witnesses as characters in *Power Without Glory*:

> **William Brady**—*Mr. Barry, M.L.A. for Carlton, former Minister for Housing in the Cain Government.
> **Dr. Devlin**—Sir Hugh Devine, a leading Melbourne surgeon.
> **Blair**—*Field Marshal Sir Thomas Blamey.
> **Paddy Kelleher**—*R. P. Kennelly, M.L.C., former secretary of the Labor Party in Victoria, now general secretary of the A.L.P. Former State Minister.
> **Archbishop Conn**—*The late Archbishop Carr, a former Archbishop of Melbourne.
> **Jim Summers**—Mr. James Scullin, former Labor Prime Minister, and M.H.R. for Yarra.
> **T. J. Real**—The late Mr. T. J. Ryan, former Labor Premier of Queensland.
> **Sir Samuel Gibbon**—Sir Samuel Gillott.
> **Father Jesper**—Father Jerger.
> **Sandow**: Ad Santel, a wrestler.
> **Frank Ashton**—*The late Mr. Frank Anstey, M.H.R., famous Labor orator.[30] [* denotes those whose photographs appeared in the *Argus*].

Page five of the same edition carried a banner headline: 'Witnesses allege book written as "Communist propaganda"', and photographs of Frank Hardy and his counsel Mr Campbell, KC, and Bernard Nolan. A. M. Harold and K. C. Wilkes, co-editors of the Melbourne University student paper *Farrago*, who were to be called as witnesses the following day, were also shown.[31]

Before the hearing resumed that morning, John Andrew Dodds, a clerk in the Government Statist's Office, was called by Mr Galbally to produce a registered certificate of marriage, dated 31 December 1901, between John Wren and Ellen Mahon. When Bernard Nolan, barrister and solicitor, was asked to identify the handwriting, he said it was that of Mr and Mrs John Wren. Patrick Cody, a wine and spirit merchant, was called as a witness. He said that he had attended the church with his father when Mr and Mrs Wren were married, and he identified the writing on the certificate.[32]

Nolan was then recalled to the witness box to resume his evidence. During the course of the cross-examination Nolan was asked by Mr Campbell if he considered some of the incidents in the book as fiction:

Nolan vehemently: I did not regard it as fiction. I regarded it as deliberate Communist propaganda, and the technique of that book is common throughout the world.

Mr Campbell: Do you think that was an answer to my question? Was it not an endeavour to get in an accusation of Communism against this defendant?

Nolan: No, it was not!

Mr Jackson: The second part of the answer was improper.[33]

Mr Galbally jumped to his feet and protested that Mr Campbell was about to read 'grossly defamatory passages' from the book. He would then link them up with prominent people. Once these passages were quoted in newspapers, the people mentioned would have no remedy. As the cross-examination continued, there were frequent heated exchanges between Mr Campbell and Mr Galbally. Mr Jackson warned that it had not been a very pleasant hearing, and he would not hesitate to use stringent powers to, if necessary, adjourn the inquiry. As Mr Campbell's cross examination proceeded, he elicited from Nolan the fact that he was aware that Wren, Sr, had an interest in politics, but that he was not aware that Wren, Sr, was exercising a large underground influence. He did know that Wren, Sr, had provided some expenses for candidates. He reiterated that he considered the book to be a work of communist propaganda. Nolan agreed that the section of the book regarding the death of Snoopy Tanner was purporting to give a description of the death of real-life criminal, Squizzy Taylor. In reply to a question by Mr Galbally, Nolan stated that he believed that the author was trying to portray certain events and certain people in a defamatory way. He was then allowed to leave the witness box.[34]

Patrick Francis Cody, who had earlier given evidence about the Wren marriage certificate, was recalled to the witness box. He said that all the Wren family were well known to him. He used to drive his father, who was a business associate of John Wren, Sr, to the city. He frequently picked up Wren, Sr, on the way. In response to Mr Galbally's question, he agreed that, after his father had died in 1933, he had become more closely associated with Wren, Sr, in the Australian distilling industry and other types of business, including the manufacture of yeast and the Fiji gold industry.[35]

He said that he had read *Power Without Glory*. In response to a question by Mr Galbally, he said he had received it by registered post. He did not know the name of the sender. He had identified John West as John Wren, Sr, and Nellie West as Ellen Wren. He thought the Wrens were a happily married couple, and it was not true that they rarely spoke to each other. He had heard Wren, Sr, talking and joking with his wife, and it was untrue that the Wrens did not take their meals together. He identified the description in the book of the embroidered chair with the motto 'West for Victory' as referring to the chair in the Wren home bearing the motto 'Wren for Victory'. In response to further questioning from Mr Galbally, Cody said that he believed that passages in the book related to actual events and people. His belief that John West referred to John Wren, Sr, had been confirmed when he had recognised the black and white colours mentioned, as the Collingwood Football Club; also the description of Wren, Sr's bedroom, his enlistment during World War I, his business interests and the names of five members of his family. In his opinion Mrs Moran was Ellen Wren's mother, Mrs Mahon. In reply to further questions by Mr Galbally, Cody said that he had identified Pat Corry as himself.[36]

A list of twenty names, which was not exhaustive, was submitted to the court. Cody said he could identify the real people (and places and companies) from characters in the book:

Frank Ashton—the late Frank Anstey, M.H.R.
Pat Corry—Patrick Francis Cody.
Archbishop Conn—Archbishop Carr.
Chirraboo Mines—Chillagoe Smelters.
Carringbush—Collingwood.
Dr Devlin—Sir Hugh Devine.
Sir Samuel Gibbon—Sir Samuel Gillott.
Ned Horan—Edward Hogan.
Father Jesper—Father Jerger.
Frank Lammence—the late Frank Lawrence.
Richard Lamb—Richard Lean.
Keith Murcutt—Sir Keith Murdoch.
Mulgara Mines—Mungara Mines
T. J. Real—the late T. J. Ryan, former Queensland Premier.
Pat Ryan—Paddy Kelly.
Jim Summers—James Scullin.
Sandow—Ad Santel, a wrestler.
'Red Ted' Thurgood—the late Mr. E. G. Theodore, M.H.R.
'Sugar' Renfrey—'Sugar' Roberts.
Blair—Field Marshal Sir Thomas Blamey.[37]

Some of these names had been identified earlier by John Wren, Jr, and Bernard Nolan. Mr Galbally then asked Cody if he regarded the book as a work of fiction. Cody replied: 'No, I regarded it as communist propaganda'. At this point, Mr Campbell objected, because 'every single, solitary witness has given the same answer'. Mr Jackson ruled out the question.[38]

When Mr Campbell asked if Cody had owned racehorses, he agreed. Mr Campbell mentioned an incident in the book about Whisper, a racehorse owned by John West, which had won the 1904 Caulfield Cup. The race had been rigged, and two jockeys had been bribed by West to let his horse win. This incident was alleged to refer to a horse owned by Wren, Sr, Murmur, which had won the 1904 Caulfield Cup. Cody, in reply, said he did not think that was in the book. Mr Campbell then read passages from pages 169, 281 and 165 of *Power Without Glory* which outlined how the race was rigged for West's advantage. When Cody was asked if he understood that the book was making 'an allegation that John Wren had rigged the Caulfield Cup of 1904 by bribing the jockeys of the leading favourites', he said: 'You could put that interpretation on it'.[39]

Mr Campbell then closely questioned Cody on the allegations of adultery made in the book. Mr Campbell claimed that the book portrayed Nellie West as a woman, attentive to her religious duties and a good mother fond of her children, apart from the section on her adultery. Cody agreed that that was correct. He also agreed that as she was portrayed, she was to be pitied. Mr Campbell then asked Cody: 'When you read the entire book did you think Mrs Wren was represented as a woman driven into adultery by the conduct of her husband?'. He replied: 'I agree that she did not seem to have a happy life'. Mr Galbally claimed that, in his opinion, no one is ever driven into adultery. Mr Jackson disagreed; a person could be driven into such an act in certain circumstances.[40]

When Mr Campbell questioned Cody as to the shocking allegations made that John West had instigated the murder of Squizzy Taylor, he chuckled as he replied, 'Yes'. Mr Campbell reprimanded Cody for laughing about a serious matter. He asked if Cody considered that allegations of murder and attempted murder against John West were more serious than accusations of adultery against Nellie West, he replied: 'I regard them all as extraordinarily serious, but I suppose, in the eyes of the law, murder would be regarded as more serious'. In response to further questions about the murder allegations, Cody said he considered the book as so much trash and untruths. When Mr Campbell asked him if he considered the allegations of adultery against Mrs West as so much trash, Cody said he did not. He regarded them as a serious reflection on a decent woman. He said he had not given any thought to which was more serious, murder or adultery. But he felt that a man could take a murder allegation much better than a woman accused of adultery.[41]

Cody conceded that he had discussed the book with Wren, Sr, and members of his family on about half a dozen different occasions. He admitted to Mr Campbell that he had discussed it with Wren, Sr, the previous evening, and he had read the account of the evidence given by John Wren, Jr. Mr Campbell asked Cody why he had been ordered out of court. Cody replied that he had assumed that it was to prevent him from hearing other witnesses' evidence. In that event, Mr Campbell asked, '. . . why did you read the newspapers, and read the account of everything that had been said by John Wren [Jr] in his cross-examination?'. At this point Mr Galbally interjected: 'I don't know of any power to stop witnesses reading newspapers'. Cody agreed that he had seen John Wren, Jr, after he had given his evidence, and he did not believe there was any harm in reading the newspapers.[42]

Cody denied that he had ever discussed the book with Ellen Wren, and he said Wren, Sr, appeared to know very little about what was in the book. Once he had read the 'shocking' allegations of adultery against Mrs Wren he had decided not to mention the matter to Wren, Sr again. 'The allegations were raised after a meeting when Mr Wren [Sr] and myself were going home,' Cody said. This was after his brother had come up to the car and asked if he had heard about the book. It was then that he had his first discussion with Wren, Sr. The Wren family, or their solicitors, had not mentioned that Wren, Sr, might bring an information for libel. Nor had Wren, Sr, told him that Mrs

Wren intended taking action for libel; nor had he mentioned that he was not going to bring the information, because the defence of truth and public benefit could be raised. In answer to further questions Cody repeated that Wren, Sr, had not told him that Mrs Wren was going to take out the libel. He agreed with Mr Campbell that he drove Wren, Sr, home practically every night, but the first he knew about the information was when it was issued. Cody told Mr Galbally that he regarded certain passages in the book referring to Mrs Wren as 'definitely defamatory'. When Mr Galbally asked him his reaction to the references of adultery, Cody replied: 'It was one of extreme anger, and I was tempted to take the law into my own hands against the person responsible'. Mr Starke questioned Cody about Bernard Nolan, the Wren family solicitor, who had made similar remarks. Cody agreed that Nolan was a red-blooded individual, quick to anger. Mr Starke then asked if Cody himself was a cool type? 'I am pretty fiery at times.'[43] The court then adjourned.

When the court resumed on Friday, 19 January, Mr Galbally urged that the hearing be settled as quickly as possible, as other actions were pending. John Wren, Jr, was recalled to the witness box to identify a framed picture of a former Collingwood footballer, Gordon Coventry. Wren, Jr, said he had brought the photograph from his father's office, where it had hung on the wall. Mr Galbally then read from page 346 of *Power Without Glory*: 'Three months had passed since Barney Robinson had been murdered, and his photo had joined the footballers and racehorses on the wall of John West's office'.[44]

The next witness called by Mr Galbally was Anthony Manum Harold, a law student, who said he was the editor of the Melbourne University weekly newspaper *Farrago*. He gave evidence that when Hardy had spoken at the University at a meeting organised by the University Labor Council, he had said that 'he did not accept the laws of libel because they existed only to preserve the status quo'; he had also stated that 'bourgeois fossilised professors might take his book to be propaganda and had added that *Power Without Glory* was the first of a trilogy'. Harold said that Hardy had stated that he was meeting with obstruction in publishing his book. Hardy, when commenting on Mr Winston Churchill's memoirs, had said, 'It took the Tories to get us into trouble and the Reds to get us out'.[45]

Harold did not think that Hardy had mentioned the printing of a second edition. Mr Galbally pursued the matter, asking, 'But did he say how many books in the first edition had been sold?'. Mr Campbell objected; the only question to be decided was whether Hardy was the author. He said that Hardy would definitely be pleading not guilty. It was immaterial how many copies of the book were sold. Then Mr Galbally submitted to Mr Jackson that the more widespread the publication, the more likely that would lead to a breach of the peace. Under further examination, Harold said that he and his co-editor had written an article in *Farrago* under the heading, 'Author Gives the Bird to Wren'. Mr Galbally questioned Harold as to whether he believed that the character in the book, John West, was a reference to John Wren, Sr. He agreed.[46]

The next witness called by the prosecution was Cyril Augustine Burley, a journalist who had formerly been employed by the *Age* newspaper. He gave evidence that he had attended a meeting at the Athenaeum Gallery on 29 September 1950, which Hardy had addressed. During the course of his speech Hardy had said he had never invented a character in his life; they were real people. There was laughter in the audience. Burley said he had been asked by the chief of staff to attend the meeting. He had not taken full shorthand notes, but after writing the story, he had destroyed them. He said he had been asked to give evidence about two months ago. He had never met any members of the Wren family, nor had he had any business with them.[47]

Alfred Gordon Andrew-Street was then called for the prosecution. He said he had been a friend of John Wren, Jr, since meeting him in New Guinea during the war. Wren, Jr, had asked him to attend the New Theatre in Melbourne on 14 November 1950. Copies of *Power Without Glory* were in two piles; he estimated that about one hundred copies had been sold that night. He purchased a copy for twenty-five shillings, and Hardy autographed it in his presence. At that meeting Hardy had told the audience that he had hidden his handwritten manuscript in a very safe place, and that he had taken years to research the book.[48]

Detective Henry Murfett gave evidence of his attendance at a Communist Party meeting of between 300 and 400 people at the Yarra Bank on 12 November 1950. Mr Starke (junior counsel for Hardy) objected to Murfett reading from notes made at the meeting. Mr Jackson ruled against the objection. Reading from his notes, Murfett said that Hardy had claimed that the Crown had promised him full assistance in the case, but they were now ignoring him. 'There's one thing in my favour. Writers from all over Australia have banded together to help me'. Hardy also said that only a couple of dozen members of Parliament were worried about the book. He then stated that 'I am proud to admit that I am a communist. I wrote the book under the laws of Marxism'. Mr Starke asked Murfett if he had endeavoured to conceal his note-taking; Murfett denied this. He agreed that he had attended other meetings where Hardy was speaking, including one at Unity Hall. Mr Starke suggested that Murfett was hiding outside the window; Murfett said he was inside the hall. Mr Starke asked Murfett if he recollected that several members of Parliament, under Parliamentary privilege, had made outbursts against Hardy. When Mr Galbally objected, Mr Starke said that it was a fact. Mr Galbally denied this, and said that Mr Starke should not refer to 'outbursts' by members of Parliament. When Mr Jackson stated that members of Parliament were not 'a breed of divine persons', Mr Campbell interrupted: 'Neither are MLC's!' At this time Mr Galbally was a member of the Legislative Council. Murfett said he had recorded that Hardy had said: 'I will challenge Wren to prove he is "West, in the book", it might have been . . . that she is "West in the book"'.[49]

Senior Detective John O'Connor of Russell Street stated that he met Hardy by appointment at 4 p.m. on 25 October 1950 at the office of his solicitor in Queen Street. Hardy admitted that he was the author of *Power Without Glory*. O'Connor said that after he arrested Hardy and took him to the Watchhouse, he found certain papers in Hardy's possession. Hardy said they were mostly about the book. When O'Connor produced five large sheets in triplicate,

Mr Starke objected that they might be irrelevant and improperly admitted. Mr Jackson read the documents and said that some were admissible. Mr Galbally then produced another document; Hardy had told O'Connor that this contained details of the printing of the second edition. Hardy had also said that he was upset that he had left these documents in his pockets. Mr Starke questioned O'Connor as to his length of service in the police force. O'Connor replied: 'Fourteen years'. Mr Starke suggested that it was almost unheard of for a police officer to question an accused person after he had not only been, in fact, charged, but after, in fact, he had been arrested. O'Connor replied: 'No. There are instances of it'. Mr Starke: 'Very, very few, aren't there?'. O'Connor: 'Yes'. Mr Starke continued to challenge O'Connor on the procedures adopted when Hardy was arrested. It seemed clear from the examination and the answers given, that usual fair procedures had not been followed. O'Connor told Mr Starke that he had not been in contact with any legal adviser of the Wren family before the arrest, but he did acknowledge that the following morning he had run into Mr Galbally in the City Court. He then related how he had told Mr Galbally all the details of the events that had taken place the day before. He said that after that he had left the conduct of the case with Mr Galbally.[50]

Mr Starke further questioned O'Connor on the documents which had been taken from Hardy. When Mr Dall, Hardy's solicitor, had talked to O'Connor about these documents, he had said it was nothing to do with him; Mr Dall would have to ask Mr Galbally. O'Connor said he had not used those words. Mr Starke again asserted that O'Connor had told Mr Dall that he would have to see Mr Galbally to get the documents back. After a lengthy interrogation, O'Connor revealed that after he had arrested Hardy, he had typed out his statement. Mr Galbally had one copy, and the witness had another. This startling disclosure drew a question from Mr Starke: 'You handed the solicitor for a private informant the police brief?'. O'Connor replied: 'We gave him the statement approximately a month later'. Mr Starke later asked the question: 'Did you know whether other statements taken by the police were handed to Mr Galbally?'. 'No, sir'.[51]

When O'Connor had finished his evidence, Mr Galbally announced that he had completed his evidence for the prosecution. The hearing was then adjourned until Thursday, 25 January 1951.[52]

The report of that day's proceedings were headlined in the newspapers. 'Other actions are coming' . . . WITNESSES DESCRIBE MEETINGS IN CITY . . . DETECTIVE CHALLENGED ON HARDY'S ARREST.[53]

Before the seventh day of the hearing in the City Court began, the public gallery was packed, and many people were unable to gain admittance. As on other days, some waited outside the court. The interest that the case had generated grew as each day's evidence unfolded.

Mr William Barry, MLA, deputy leader of the Parliamentary Labor Party, who had already been identified as 'William Brady', was in the court, and conferred briefly with Mr Galbally before proceedings began. Mr Galbally then said to Mr Jackson that it seemed open for the defence to submit that the evidence, as disclosed by the prosecution, was deficient. It was open for Mr Campbell to submit that there was neither evidence of defamation or publication.[54] Mr Campbell addressed the court:

He said he proposed to make certain legal submissions to prove that on the evidence, at present before Mr Jackson, the Court could not find that there was a strong presumption of guilt.

The question whether there was any evidence upon which Mr Jackson could commit Hardy for trial was always one of law.

Mr Campbell then quoted legal references to support his submissions on the duties of a magistrate.

He said that, paradoxically, the Wrongs Act of 1928 gave a person charged with criminal libel the right to raise a defence of truth and public benefit, but the authorities seemed to preclude that defence being raised before committal.[55]

Mr Galbally interjected: 'Mr Campbell has to prove that the evidence is deficient—not raise the issue of truth and benefit'. Mr Jackson asked: 'How can that come into the present situation when there is no case to answer? This submission of Mr Campbell's might be relevant later'. Mr Campbell replied that he did not want to suggest that this had not been raised at that time. He said he did not intend to argue the question of publication, but he did not believe that a statutory charge of criminal libel had been proved. The prosecution case rested on the evidence of three witnesses, John Wren, Jr, Bernard Nolan and Patrick Cody.[56] Mr Campbell further submitted that

The evidence of these three main witnesses appeared to be fully hallmarked with the grossest exaggeration, and was full of the grossest inconsistencies . . . The evidence of each one of the witnesses and of all three taken together reeks of improbabilities . . . Transcripts of testimony show a studied and carefully prepared design to raise a false issue. It is an illicit attempt to gaol Hardy because of his Communist beliefs . . . Mr Campbell reminded Mr Jackson, that earlier in the hearing, he had protested that Hardy's political beliefs were irrelevant and immaterial, and that Mr Jackson had ruled accordingly.

Every one of the three main witnesses went out of their way to make a charge of 'Communist propaganda,' . . . then quoted from transcripts in which John Wren junior said that his mother had told him that she had laid the information against Hardy because she regarded the book as 'a Communist plot'.

Bernard Nolan said: '. . . I regarded the book as Communist propaganda'.

In other transcripts Patrick Cody said that he did not regard the book as a work of fiction, but as 'Communist propaganda'.

Mr Campbell said: 'It is beyond the bounds of credibility that three witnesses such as these, one a son of the informant, and the other two great personal friends of the informant and her husband, should each give precisely the same reaction to the book'.[57]

Mr Campbell further submitted that the information laid by Mrs Wren was, in truth and in substance, a proceeding taken by John Wren, Sr. Mr Campbell said that Wren, Jr, had never given specific evidence that the allegations about his mother had caused him 'to want to smash up Hardy'. Therefore it must be presumed that it was the serious nature of the allegations against his father that had caused this reaction.[58]

Similarly the witness, Bernard Nolan, had given evidence of 'wanting to kick Hardy to pieces' or to kill him. Mr Campbell submitted that that was not because of the allegations regarding Mrs Wren, but because Nolan believed that a character in the book, Vera Maguire, referred to his wife. 'It is quite reasonable to assume that in the portrayal of that character, he has wrongly seen something sinister in her association with John Wren senior [sic], whereas all the book does is portray a purely good and moral relationship between John Wren senior [sic], and Vera Maguire.'[59]

Mr Campbell had again referred to the character John West as John Wren, Sr. It must be presumed that he maintained this device of substituting the character John West with John Wren, Sr, for his own legal purposes. Mr Campbell said he would try to show that the information was not genuine; Mrs Wren had only been the figurehead. The purpose was to gaol Hardy because of other passages in the book attacking John West, whom the prosecution had identified with John Wren, Sr.

Mr Campbell referred to the evidence given by Cody; he said it was nearly a year since the book had been published, and there was no evidence of a breach of the peace as a result.[60]

Mr Jackson would not permit either counsel to address him on the question that Mrs Wren was under duress, saying that he did not require their advice. Mr Campbell said he believed that this was a complete denial of justice, because he could not then make his strongest arguments. The non-appearance of Mrs Wren in court had indicated to Mr Campbell that she was under duress. Mr Campbell pointed out the discrepancies in the evidence of John Wren, Jr, regarding discussions with his mother and father about who should bring the information. Later he had denied that they had ever discussed the matter. Mr Campbell said there were twenty or thirty other facts which he could illustrate, but the fact that the informant had not come to court, and her signature had to be proved by a witness, could only lead to the conclusion that John Wren, Sr, was the real prosecutor.[61]

Mr Jackson said he would not allow Mr Campbell to address him on the probability or improbability of evidence. Even if the witnesses's evidence had been inherently improbable, inconclusive and shuffling, it would not necessarily be evidence of duress. 'I have heard the witnesses. Their evidence is not such that I would reject it on the grounds that it is inherently improbable, shuffling, and self-contradictory'. He added that he would not debar Mr Campbell from addressing him, but not on the question of attempting to allege duress.[62]

The second submission on behalf of the defence was that there had never been any reported case, that an allegation of adultery against a married woman was the proper subject for criminal libel proceedings. Mr Campbell quoted from a number of legal authorities to support his admission that a civil remedy could have been sought by the informant. He said there were hundreds of divorce cases each year in Victoria, 'so few mere allegations of adultery against women were made the subject of criminal libel allegations. There would be thousands of criminal libel actions if everybody who was called an adulterer or adultress took proceedings'. The subject of criminal libel was only brought on rare occasions and in uncommon cases.[63]

Mr Campbell then submitted that Hardy should not be committed for trial, unless there was a strong presumption that the statements referring to Mrs Wren were intended to cause a breach of the peace. He said there had not been a 'tittle of evidence that it would cause of breach of the peace, the evidence is all the other way'. He further submitted that only the witnesses John Wren, Jr, Bernard Nolan, and Patrick Cody had spoken in regard to a breach of the peace. Nolan had made a specific reference to his feelings about committing a breach of the peace. Mr Campbell claimed that Nolan's evidence must be disregarded, as it was contradictory and unreliable as befits 'a very angry man who spoke before he thought. His general conduct in the box showed that he really was beside himself with rage'.[64]

John Wren, Jr, had denied that the question of raising the defence of truth and public benefit had ever been discussed before the information was made. Mr Campbell said, 'All I have to say about this is that Your Worship did not come down in the last shower'. Mr Galbally then attacked Mr Campbell on the grounds of his aspersions about the reliability of the witnesses's evidence. He said, 'It seems to me that Mr Campbell has now embarked on general character assassination'. Mr Jackson did not agree.[65]

Mr Campbell submitted that Wren, Jr, had given evidence that he had read the book, in which accusations 'of bribery, corruption, race-rigging, instigating murder—all shocking allegations', had been made against his father. But he had denied that his father had read the book, even though John Wren, Sr, had been threatened that, unless he paid £100 000 blackmail, the book would be published. There was, he said, no suggestion that Hardy was implicated in the blackmail threat. Mr Campbell suggested that the allegations of blackmail 'were a sheer invention or exist only in the minds of the witnesses. We say it is sheer invention, and that it is utter nonsense'.[66]

Mr Campbell referred to only some of the evidence of Wren, Jr, as he suggested it was thoroughly unreliable. He discussed Patrick Cody's evidence, who was 'obviously partial to the Wrens'. Cody and Wren, Sr, had a number of discussions before the information was issued. Mr Campbell said that Cody had read the book, but he had no recollection of mentioning the murder incident to Wren. Mr Campbell then read part of Cody's evidence to the court. He suggested that he was not a frank witness, or a reliable witness.[67] Mr Campbell continued:

> The real charge here is not an allegation that the libel on Mrs Wren would be likely to lead to a breach of the peace in reality. It is an information on behalf of John Wren, [Sr], who is trying to put Hardy in gaol for what Hardy said about him.
>
> Mr Jackson: There is no evidence of that.
>
> Mr Galbally: John Wren [Sr] is not a party to these proceedings, and it is infamous for Mr Campbell to stand up and say that a citizen of this community is trying to put Hardy in gaol. I think he should withdraw.
>
> Mr Campbell: I don't withdraw it. I emphasise it.
>
> Mr Galbally said that it was a shocking thing for counsel to make reflections on a citizen. Those reflections were intended for the Press, and would receive wide publicity.
>
> Mr Campbell: I reaffirm it very strongly, because it is all based on my submission that this libel action, which has been brought as relating to statements in the book about Mrs Wren, is not the real reason for this evidence, or for these witnesses' states of mind.
>
> Mr Jackson: I do not know that I have the power to make you withdraw that statement, but I do desire to intimate that there is not a word of evidence before me that John Wren [Sr] is seeking to put this man in gaol.
>
> Mr Campbell: I do not withdraw. We have only to refer to the repeated opposition to bail, when John Wren [Sr] was sitting behind my learned friend [Galbally].
>
> Mr Jackson pointed out that John Wren senior [sic] was the husband of the informant and would naturally have an interest in the case.[68]

Mr Campbell further submitted that the witness Cody had claimed that he could not recollect the parts of the book which had shown the character of Mrs West in a favourable light. Mr Campbell said had he done so, there would have been no cause for an action. He did not believe witnesses who had claimed that the fifty-year relationship between John and Ellen Wren had been 'idyllic, and there has never been a cross word between them'. Mr Campbell said that the book had represented Mrs West as a 'moral woman attentive to her home, her children and her religious duties'. He said that reading the book as a whole showed that there was nothing to suggest that a case for an alleged breach of the peace could be submitted to any jury. Nor were there grounds to regard a libel as a fit subject for criminal proceedings. Mr Campbell added: 'Your Worship realises that if civil proceedings are brought then, of course, the libel could be justified'. Mr Galbally objected to the reference to a civil suit being brought. He said the reasons she [Mrs Wren] took these proceedings is because the defendant was a worthless fellow. Mr Campbell objected to this remark; in reply Mr Galbally said that he meant that the defendant was a man of straw. In response Mr Jackson said 'You said "a worthless fellow", which is a totally different thing'. Mr Galbally replied:

He is a man of straw. Where the civil remedy is likely to be abortive, the only remedy is to take criminal proceedings.

Mr Campbell: It is quite improper to make a statement that a man is worthless financially when there is not the slightest evidence of it. If Mr Galbally got into the witness-box on this I would be happy to cross-examine him.[69]

Mr Campbell then made his final submissions on two grounds:

The first, he said, was the legal ground that an allegation of adultery against a woman had never succeeded as the basis for criminal libel proceedings, and the second was the factual ground that Nellie West, in the book, had been portrayed in a favourable light.

For these reasons, I submit that Your Worship should clearly, in this case, exercise your discretion by refusing to permit this case to come to trial.[70]

Mr Galbally, in reply to Mr Campbell's submissions, detailed at great length that, in *Power Without Glory*, Mrs West was painted as a woman given to seduction, a woman who had singled out a bricklayer working at her home, who bought him gifts, and was prepared to leave her 'flock of little children'. He did not consider Mrs West was shown in a favourable light. In reply to Mr Campbell's criticism of John Wren, Jr's evidence, he said, 'I hope there will always be John Wrens in the community, prepared to take that attitude when their mother's honour is questioned'.[71] Mr Galbally said that there had been no apology offered, and Hardy had published a second edition of the book and addressed numerous public meetings at which he had said, 'It is all true'. Mr Galbally then quoted from another leading case in which the defendant 'had been putting money in his pocket all the time, by the libel'. Hardy was able to make money and sell his book. A civil remedy in this case 'would be worthless'. Mr Galbally said:

Hardy is a man of no substance, and judgments could be plastered on the wall against him to no avail . . . The only thing to do is prosecute him and put him in gaol . . . He said he hoped to produce evidence that even Hardy's word as his bond was worthless, because he had been selling copies of the book.[72]

Mr Starke objected that 'these observations were not directed to any issue which Mr Galbally was arguing'. Mr Jackson, in reply, stated that they might possibly apply later. Mr Galbally said that Hardy had continued to repeat the libel, and when he spoke to students at the University of Melbourne he had 'mocked the laws of libel'.[73]

Mr Galbally told the court that he had been responsible for not calling the prosecutrix, Mrs Ellen Wren. He said it was a risk that a public appearance might cause suffering, and it was not an exaggeration to say that 'it might have resulted in her death'. Mr Galbally then submitted that Bernard Nolan's belief that the character Vera Maguire in the book, was his late wife was justified. He quoted from page 559 of *Power Without Glory*:

> '. . . They talked mainly about sport. He (John West) found her company stimulating. He looked forward to seeing her (Vera Maguire). Though he was sexually impotent, she aroused passion in him. He tried to kiss her in the car in front of his home one night. She rebuffed him gently: "Naughty boy; we're getting too old for that sort of thing".'

Mr Jackson, at this stage of the proceedings, said that he found nothing in the book which suggested that Mrs Nolan, assuming she was 'Mrs Maguire', had been impugned.

Mr Galbally: If the citizen were not given some remedy to take action there would be 'lynch law' in the community.[74]

Mr Galbally submitted that the question of duress would no longer apply if Hardy were committed for trial. Therefore, it would be fair to the Wren family if the defence was asked either to withdraw the allegation or else to prove that it was bona fide. In reply to the prosecution witnesses who had referred to *Power Without Glory* as 'Communist propaganda', Mr Galbally said:

> What they are saying, in effect, is that 'we believe this book to be about living people, and that it is part of a Communist plot to turn people against our public institutions and the Government . . . that allegations which had been made against a number of people's characters had been published in the Press . . . We even went back to the alleged rigging of the Caulfield Cup in 1904'.

Mr Jackson assured him that the allegations were 'just something referred to in this court. I neither accept nor reject them'.[75]

In his conclusion, Mr Galbally stated that 'a clearer case of criminal libel could not be made out against Hardy. There are certain fundamentals in our society, and I suggest that marriage is one of them'.[76] Mr Jackson stated that he 'reserved his decision', which he would announce when the court resumed the following morning.[77]

On Friday, 26 January 1951, Frank and Ross Hardy travelled to the City Court. Who could know how they felt as they sat quietly in the court waiting for the magistrate's decision? They had heard the prosecution and defence counsel locked in combat. Just as the condemned person hopes for an eleventh hour reprieve, perhaps the Hardys, too, hoped that Mr Jackson might rule that there was no charge to answer. For four years Ross had worked with her husband transferring information on to thousands of cards, typing drafts and revised drafts, and more than a thousand pages of a manuscript which was later discarded. She had typed, on a manual typewriter, the 672-page manuscript of *Power Without Glory* not once, but twice. The physical printing of the novel was another time of anxiety for the couple. Ross had been part of the whole project; she had eased Frank through periods of despair. Her role had been unsung; she had suffered many of the tribulations, but few of the pleasurable social aspects of the production of *Power Without Glory*.

Ross had been under a great strain, but so, too, had Frank Hardy. During the period of research and writing, he had infiltrated a world of intrigue and corruption, and he may have put his life at risk. He had written and rewritten, learning 'the hard way', until *Power Without Glory* was completed. Then he had struggled to transfer the manuscript to the printed pages. It is not a histrionic claim that, once suspicions were aroused in some quarters, and certainly after the novel had been published, there were those who wanted him silenced by whatever means. Despite his concern for what might await him, Hardy believed that he had, with the help of the CPA, produced a novel that had revealed the sordid underbelly of a capitalist society.

Ross and Frank Hardy listened intently as Mr Jackson delivered his decision. He said:

At this stage I am called upon to decide a submission made by Mr Campbell, for the accused Hardy, that there is no case to answer.

On that submission I find that there is a case to answer.

I do not intend to traverse all the arguments put to me, but I feel I should rule briefly on two of Mr Campbell's submissions.

The first ruling is that I am clearly of the opinion that the allegations against Mrs West, or Wren, that she seduced Bill Evans, and committed adultery with Bill Evans, is of such extreme gravity that it has been properly the subject of the present proceedings.

The second ruling is that, if there is need for me to find that it is a defamation calculated to cause a breach of the peace, then I so find.[78]

Mr Jackson then formally committed Hardy for trial in the Supreme Court. Hardy stood impassively in the City Court, with his hands clasped in front of him. When asked how he pleaded, he replied, in a clear voice, 'Not guilty'. He was then taken from the court in the custody of Senior Detective John O'Connor, who had been a witness in the trial. Mr Starke then applied for unconditional bail for Hardy. When he stated 'that the maximum penalty for criminal libel was one year', Mr Galbally interjected: 'It is incorrect. In common law the penalty is unlimited'. Mr Jackson said the discussion was academic.[79]

When Mr Starke applied for bail for Hardy to Mr Justice Hudson in the Supreme Court that afternoon, the Attorney-General was represented by Mr J. V. Dunn:

Mr Starke objected to the appearance of Mr A. J. Gillard, KC, and Mr B. Shillito [sic] for the informant, Mrs Wren.

It was for the Attorney-General and the Crown Prosecutor to decide whether the trial should proceed, he said. Legally, the question now had nothing to do with the Wren family.

Mr Starke, applying for unconditional bail, produced a copy of 'The Age' newspaper.

In it, he said, the complete information was set out, word for word. Every sensational feature had been published in the Press.

Because of this, it would be futile to attach conditions to the bail.

Mr Starke said every syllable of the book would be read by the Crown to the jury at the trial.

Any newspaper trying to lift its circulation could put in a special 'lift out' section, and publish the whole of the book.

Mr Justice Hudson announced that he proposed to grant Hardy bail until the trial or until further order. A bond of £250 with a surety of £250 would be sufficient.[80]

The following morning the *Argus* newspaper carried two photographs bearing the captions 'HARDY GOES "IN"—AND COMES "OUT"'. The first image showed Hardy being hustled out of the City Court by Senior Detective O'Connor, and the second showed a smiling Hardy leaving the Watchhouse with his solicitor, Mr T. Dall. Hardy had spent seven and a half hours in custody in the City Watchhouse.[81]

The prosecution barrister and the witnesses for Ellen Wren had been so carried away by their mission to have Hardy committed for trial, and ultimately gaoled, that caution frequently became a casualty. The public were titillated, intrigued and shocked by the evidence which linked John Wren, Sr, not only to nefarious deeds and deals, but also to premiers, politicians, financiers, businessmen, doctors, Catholic clergy, municipal councillors, police, judiciary, military leaders, and members of the harness racing, horse racing, bookmaking, wrestling, boxing and cycling industries. Hardy's counsel—Mr Campbell, in particular, but also Mr Starke, his junior counsel—had, by their adroit examination of the prosecution witnesses, managed to reveal much that had previously been hidden from public gaze. This ploy would not have been acceptable in the Criminal Court, where Hardy would be tried.

It was to be five months before Frank Hardy came to trial. The delay was another bonus for the Frank Hardy Defence Committee; it was able to gather more supporters, more money and a significant public image, as it linked the charge against Hardy the writer with the perceived general assault on democratic rights. Ross and Frank Hardy were exhausted; now they had to rally their reserves to further participate in the campaign.

Meanwhile, *Power Without Glory* became highly sought after; its success as a best-seller in Australia, and in some overseas countries, was assured.

Chapter Ten

THE TRIAL

DURING THE COMMITTAL PROCEEDINGS, Hardy had become a focus for the nation's press. The months that followed were to be exhausting; he travelled all over the country, making speeches in halls, streets, factories and private homes, often sleeping in strange beds in strange towns. Meanwhile, the Frank Hardy Defence Committee had stepped up its fund-raising campaign, and more people became aware of the heavy legal expenses involved. The New Theatre contributed the proceeds of one night's performance. The Sydney branch of the Defence Committee set up rooms in 188 George Street, and writer Zoë O'Leary became the organiser. The Seamen's Union contributed £50, and a further £13 was donated during a stopwork meeting. The NSW Building Workers' Industrial Union (BWIU) donated £25.[1]

On 4 February 1951, 4000 people gathered in the Sydney Domain; they unanimously carried a resolution that the Victorian Attorney-General should withdraw the charge of criminal libel. Ross and Frank had been in New South Wales for a five-day lecture tour organised by the Sydney Defence Committee. The couple had received enthusiastic receptions at the fifteen meetings held. One hundred and fifty members of the BWIU at Villawood passed a resolution demanding withdrawal of the charge; they requested subscription lists to aid Hardy's defence. At a pit-top meeting at Coalcliff, 300 miners voted for a compulsory levy of two shillings per man to raise funds. Hardy addressed the United Association of Women, and they asked for lists to collect money. There were cottage lectures held at Roseville and Vaucluse, at which contributions of £76 were made. A public meeting was held in the Ironworkers' Hall, and the sum of £71 was collected. This meeting carried unanimously the following resolution:

> In view of the fact that so many people prominent in the political, sporting and business life of Australia claim to have recognised themselves in Frank Hardy's novel *Power Without Glory*, and in view of the corruption in public places thereby implied, and because prominent public persons in no less than three States are involved, this meeting demands that the Federal Government appoint a Royal Commission to inquire into all aspects of this case.[2]

Two members of the Sydney Defence Committee, Tom Lewis and Zoë O'Leary, addressed thirty seamen and firemen from SS *Rona*, and a motion was passed to send a telegram to the Victorian Attorney-General demanding the withdrawal of the charge against Hardy.[3]

The Defence Committee in Victoria had not been idle while Frank and Ross were interstate. Meetings were held at factory gates, homes and in back streets. A meeting in Hawksburn attracted 150 local residents, and at another in South Yarra the citizens listened and questioned the author. Substantial contributions were made to the defence fund. The Defence Committee announced that the appointment of a Royal Commission was the least the government could do to satisfy the people of Australia. Such an action would indicate that their concerns were being heeded.[4]

'Hardy Stories Published—"The Man From Clinkapella"'—this headline announced the publication of a collection of Hardy's four prize-winning short stories. The foreword had been written by 'the eminent Australian writer, Alan Marshall, himself outstanding in the art of the short story':

> In this collection . . . Hardy reveals those qualities that finally reached their highest expression in the novel 'Power Without Glory'. In this work Hardy emerged as a writer of great significance in the Australian literary world.
>
> Referring to the story 'The Load of Wood' particularly . . . Hardy's ability to create a three-dimensional character, his great skill with dialogue and his handling of atmosphere are shown at their best in this fine story. The tale captures something of the charm of a folk tale and could well become part of our folk lore.[5]

'Illustrations by artist, Ambrose Dyson, faithfully evoke the atmosphere of Hardy's stories.' The Defence Committee had been responsible for its publication and for sales. It was also available on sale at the International Bookshop. The price was 2s 6d. The publication could, more properly, be described as an attractive folder with card cover and insert sheets. It carried only the name of the printing company.

The Man From Clinkapella was an immediate success, and 4000 copies were sold in the first week. The Wonthaggi coal miners had sold fifty copies at a meeting. Similar sales were reported from other job sites.[6]

There was little respite as the campaign gained momentum; Frank, Ross and other speakers were constantly on the move. The Preston Branch of the BWIU carried a resolution demanding the immediate repeal of the archaic law of criminal libel and the withdrawal of the charge. Meetings were held at Smorgon's Canned Meats and Hutton's Bacon Works, where resolutions were carried that the charges be dropped. At a private home in Murrumbeena, sixty citizens attended a meeting; a resolution was passed to write to the State Attorney-General urging that the charge should be abandoned because 'this archaic law is foreign to democratic traditions'.[7]

From the time Hardy was first arrested on 25 October 1950, the immediate question of how to fund the legal proceedings loomed large on the agenda, as well it might have done, given the conditions under which his counsel, Mr Don Campbell, KC, and Mr John Starke as junior, acted on his behalf. Many years later, Sir John Starke was asked whether he was concerned that he was defending Hardy who had attacked the Establishment of which his family was a part. Sir John replied:

> It didn't concern me. I was getting paid to appear for a client. I'll tell you a funny thing about it. Our fees were being paid by the Communist Party. We knew that, and Don had no particular affection or admiration for the Communist Party. And at the conference one day he said to Hardy, 'Hardy,' he said, 'my fees and Jack Starke's fees are to be paid to our clerk', we happened to have the same clerk, 'at ten o'clock each morning of the trial'. And Hardy looked a bit taken aback. He said, 'And what will happen if they're not, Mr. Campbell?'. 'Oh,' he said, 'don't you worry, Hardy, don't worry at all.' He said, 'On that day Starkey and I won't be appearing for you'. The fees were paid at ten o'clock every morning, I can tell you that.[8]

Hardy has attributed credit to George Seelaf for the collection and payment of money for the legal fees; it was he who found the money every day to pay the lawyers before they went into court each morning.[9]

The CPA may well have assigned Seelaf to pay the legal fees each morning, and it is certain that Seelaf did collect money. The Defence Committee spearheaded the campaign to free Hardy and raise funds for his defence, but the CPA Executive could not have risked depending entirely on the day-to-day donations of pounds, shillings and pence. The method adopted to maintain a pool of readily available and ongoing funds was not new to the CPA. The well respected and admired Ralph Gibson, for one, had a most effective and persuasive means of extracting large contributions from wealthy middle-class communists, sympathisers and fellow travellers. A tireless walker, Gibson would appear, unannounced, at people's front doors, wearing his trademark crumpled, shabby suit and pullover.[10] Within left-wing circles, Gibson was renowned as the philosopher who had renounced the comfortable academic life to dedicate himself to the emancipation of the working class and the attainment of world peace and socialism. 'Talented, dedicated, utterly incorruptible, energetic, gentlemanly, he had a charisma which inspired awe. His rapid-fire, no-notes oratory excited thousands. Militant workers revered him, colleagues protected him. While he got much applause, sometimes there was abuse and missiles and arrest—and infrequently indifference.'[11] People found it difficult to resist Gibson's appeals; he unknowingly projected the image of the ascetic, a man who never sought anything for himself. He was equally successful in his approaches to less affluent CPA members and sympathisers, when he recruited them to provide manpower and resources. From the beginning Hardy had been under the tutelage of Gibson. It was a natural progression that Gibson would consider his task also included the provision of funds to ensure that Hardy had access to good legal counsel. There were many trade unionists, communists and sympathisers, too, who had lent or given money to Hardy during that critical period. Cedric Ralph, CPA solicitor, wrote:

> An entirely different aspect arises from the question of finance. Of course Frank was in trouble, of course he badly needed funds. And so, many comrades gave him generous support. I think I advanced him £300 or £400. Many others gave substantial sums.
>
> After his trial was over, and the period arrived when Frank was in receipt of royalties in plenty, one day he came into my office and repaid me whatever it was I had contributed. Naturally I thought he was repaying everybody. It was some years, I think, before I found out that many people knowing Frank was in the money had asked him for repayment, but not one got anything out of him. I have made it a rule of life never to be embarrassed, but if ever there was an occasion when I was tempted to forego that rule was over that detail that I was the only one of the multitude to get repayment. I had never asked for repayment and in fact never expected it. The question remains: why did he favour me? Echo answers 'Why?'. Of those not repaid, some in desperate need: in them, Frank took not the slightest interest.[12]

Did Hardy repay him because he was a solicitor who had ready recourse to the law, or because Cedric Ralph was a close friend and associate of CPA Executive member Ted Hill? Did Hardy believe that he might again need their support in the future?

As the Defence Committee's campaign developed momentum, Hardy gained support from wide sections of the community. It was not long before literary communities abroad became aware of Hardy's plight. Hardy received a letter from the London-based Australian author Jack Lindsay. He wrote:

> I have just read your book 'Power Without Glory', and feel that I must send you a message of congratulation on its fine literary quality . . . I feel that it founds the fully-matured novel that we have all wanted to see for so long . . . With fine courage, you have tackled in [an] epical theme, and you have risen to the demands that it makes. I gather that some emasculated critics have thought its style rough in parts. Take no notice of them . . . your basic structure, your power to define character and to link event with event in a single significant definition, show literary mastery of a very high order . . . I should be proud to be associated in any way with the defence of this work.[13]

The Defence Committee also received a letter from the American novelist Howard Fast. He wrote:

> I have your letter concerning the case of Frank Hardy. How familiar the story sounds in terms of our own scene! However, the fact that this process is so accepted here in the US does not lessen its terible [sic] dangers to your own people.

Can you tell Mr. Hardy that all of my sympathies and support are with him? The action taken against him is precisely the type of action which has become so typical of imperialism in these last miserable moments left to it. How they fear books in these times! How eager they are to destroy the few voices that still speak up with courage and with integrity![14]

Among other letters and cables received from abroad was a cable from Poland addressed to the Defence Committee:

Union of Polish writers expresses its indignation at vile attack of Australian reactionaries against Frank Hardy. Please convey to author of 'Power Without Glory' our cordial fraternal greetings. We hope the knowledge that Hardy's struggle is [the] struggle of progressives the world over will add to your strength and fortitude in the defence of this fighter for Australia's freedom.[15]

The Fellowship of Australian Writers held a public meeting, addressed by the president, Bartlett Adamson, and Rupert Lockwood; the audience contributed £72 to Hardy's defence fund.[16] A group of Australia's best-known writers, artists, scientists and members of the liberal professions decided to petition the Attorney-General of Victoria, Mr Thomas Mitchell, to withdraw the prosecution against Hardy. The preamble of the petition stated:

- that civil proceedings for individuals are adequate to vindicate their honor [sic].
- that no action for criminal libel has been laid in Victoria for more than thirty years.
- that the revival of this antiquated legal process threatens freedom of expression and literary creation.
- that the petition is a defence of Australian traditions.[17]

Over one hundred people had signed the petition, an indication of how seriously they had viewed what was perceived to be a grave threat to democratic freedoms. The names of some signatories are of historical interest:

Professor Walter Murdoch, Nettie Palmer, Vance Palmer, Eleanor Dark, Douglas Stewart, (Editor The Red Page, Sydney Bulletin), Kylie Tennant, Flexmore Hudson, Bartlett Adamson, Alan Marshall, Will Lawson, Frank Dalby Davison, John Morrison, Judah Waten, W. Barratt, C. B. Christesen, Bertha Lawson (widow of late Henry Lawson), Lady Beeby, Brian Fitz-patrick, David Stead, Professor Manning Clark, D. E. P. Dark, Miss Ada Bronham, Max Meldrum, Professor O. Oeser, Professor Mohr, Rev. Victor James, Rev. S. Yarnold, Rev. Paul Baker, Rev. D. Munro, Dr. D. F. Lawson, Archer Russell, Muir Holborn, Alan Nichols [Nicholls], Roland E. Robinson, Ian Mair, William Lynch, Bernard Smith, Dr. Clarke (zoologist), Dr. Peter Russo, Dr. R. C. Traill, Dr. Guy Reynolds . . . The following signatures have been forwarded from London: Jack Lindsay, John Summerfield, Randall Swingler, Montagu Slater and David Martin.[18]

Not all of the signatories wholeheartedly endorsed the terms of the petition, while others did not agree with its precise wording. 'There is unanimity, however, that the charge would best be withdrawn.'[19] Short extracts from some of the viewpoints, as quoted in the *Guardian*, are revealing:

> **Mr. H. M. Green**, noted authority on Australian literature said: 'I am glad to support your appeal against the criminal prosecution of Mr. Hardy. But (and I must ask you to mention this qualification if you include my signature) I wish to make it quite clear that my support is confined to this matter of principle and is not based on political or literary grounds.'
>
> **Mr. Rex Ingamells**, poet, who criticises some aspects of 'Power Without Glory' concludes: 'Although I cannot associate myself with the precise viewpoint of the Frank Hardy Defence Committee's Petition, I state that I consider that the criminal charge would be best withdrawn.'
>
> **Kylie Tennant**, novelist, after criticising Hardy's book in some respects said: 'None of these criticisms effect [sic] the issues involved. One should oppose a law because it is an unjust law in all cases irrespective of the particular cases. Laws which jail men for expression of their opinion, whether they operate in America, Russia, or Australia, are an insult to be resented and a menace to be fought'.[20]

Jack Lindsay had informed the Defence Committee that he had written to the *New Statesman*, and author Dymphna Cusack was a co-signatory; they had requested help for Hardy. Lindsay had also written to International Poets Editors Novelists (P.E.N.). The Committee had a message from leading Soviet writer Alexander Fadeyev, that strongly condemned the criminal libel process. Louis Lavater, the veteran composer, wrote, 'If things are as I surmise there will be plenty of pay for lawyers on the one side and a consequent dearth on the other—if the case is prolonged. This is certainly a great disadvantage. My vote is for the Defence of Frank Hardy'.[21]

Despite all the support given, Hardy remained under extreme pressure. In *The Hard Way* he referred to his irritating attacks of hives and a nerve rash that affected his legs and feet, probably a manifestation of his anxiety. CPA organiser John Arrowsmith had travelled with him around the country addressing meetings to enlist support. Arrowsmith had clear recollections of watching the exhausted, nervous Hardy sitting on a narrow hotel bed as he rubbed gentian violet on to his legs and feet, in the hope that the purple antiseptic would ease the itching.[22]

Shirley Pinnell remembers how it was general knowledge within her family that her uncle, Royce Hovey, who worked for the Victorian Railways in Maryborough, acted as a bodyguard for Frank Hardy at that time. He would accompany Frank as he journeyed from place to place, addressing meetings, collecting money for his legal fees and seeking support for the Frank Hardy Defence Committee. Hovey later admitted that, because the situation was so tense, it was believed that an attempt could be made on Hardy. For this reason he carried a gun when he was with Frank.[23]

Ross, too, had her share of tribulations as she addressed meetings in the country. Bill Smith, another CPA organiser, accompanied Ross to Gippsland, where she conducted a series of successful assemblies. However, at one meeting in Morwell, Ross was howled down by a group of hostile locals. Ross and the chairman finally left the stage. Smith said he had no alternative but to follow Ross's instructions and close the meeting. He said it was a distressing experience for her, as she was such a retiring person. Only her loyalty to Frank drove her on to public platforms to plead her husband's cause.[24]

Joseph Waters, Hardy's book distributor, also had problems. During the legal proceedings he had received a visit from two detectives who had asked him why *Power Without Glory* was being sold outside Flinders Street Station for £5 a copy, when sales were banned by the court injunction. Waters had vehemently denied any knowledge. The printed sheets were awaiting collating and binding in a small printery in Port Melbourne, pending the outcome of the trial. The detectives had said, 'We thought that, we understood that'.[25]

The Defence Committee and Hardy, in particular, had been linking the criminal libel charge with the Communist Party Dissolution Act—the so-called 'Red Bill'. On 19 October 1950 the Senate had finally passed the Bill; but, soon after the CPA had challenged its legality in the High Court. In March 1951 the High Court, with a majority of six to one, ruled that the Act was unconstitutional and therefore invalid. The Menzies government was not deterred; it called an early election in April 1951. Anticommunist propaganda was the big election issue, and voters were asked to 'free Australia from the communist menace'. The Menzies government's success at the polls allowed it to introduce a Bill for a referendum to amend the Constitution to ban the CPA and further legislate against communism. It was little wonder that the CPA and Frank Hardy both felt extremely threatened when a 'public opinion poll in May showed that 80 per cent of the people favoured the banning of the party . . . The referendum was to be held on 22 September 1951'.[26]

This gave added impetus to the Defence Committee, as there was growing disquiet in some sections of the community that the broad nature of the powers inherent in the Bill posed a grave threat to civil liberties. As the 'Vote No' campaign snowballed, so, too, did the Defence Committee hasten and broaden its activities. Frank and Ross continued to address meetings and collect money for legal fees, as did their supporters. There must have been moments of quiet despair, despite the outward optimism, that Hardy's freedom was in great jeopardy.

The tension, exhaustion and uncertainty were to continue as the trial was delayed for various unexplained reasons. It was not until 12 June 1951 that Hardy was brought to trial in the Criminal Court in Melbourne. The prosecution was launched by the McDonald (Cain [Labor] supported) Government. Mr H. A. Winneke, KC, with Mr F. R. Nelson and Mr J. M. Young were the prosecutors. Mr D. M. Campbell, KC, and Mr J. E. Starke acted for the defence. They appeared before Mr Justice Martin.[27]

It was not the first time that Mr Justice Martin had been involved with charges against an author. In 1946 Robert Close was charged with obscene libel following the publication of his novel *Love Me Sailor*.[28] His first trial had been aborted when the judge, Sir Edmund Herring, Chief Justice, following advice from the prosecutor, had decreed that the trial should be abandoned, because the foreman of the jury had been seen in the company of:

> . . . a literary critic known to both the author and the publisher. The man was Ian Mair . . . [who] had filled the wanton hours listening to the trial of his old mate Bob Close. On the first day of the trial, according to Mair, he had recognised the foreman of the jury as someone he had known . . . He had a beer with him on the strength of it. The Crown had known of this encounter for four days, but had allowed the defence to present its entire case before bringing the juryman's encounter to the attention of the court. When the prosecution did raise the matter, Sir Edmund Herring decided that he had no option but to discharge the jury and order a new trial. At this second trial the Crown was able to avoid the pits into which it had fallen during the first. Close was convicted and sentenced to a fine and imprisonment for three months. He was led away in handcuffs.[29]

Mr Justice Martin presided over Close's second trial.[30]

Whether the delays in finally bringing Hardy to trial were due to machinations by the Crown to ensure that a preferred judge was appointed cannot be determined; nor can the possibility be dismissed.

With hindsight, Sir John Starke's view was that 'he was a bad tempered old fellow, not much of a lawyer. He and Campbell did not get on well, and he conducted the trial, in my opinion, very unfairly. He and Campbell were having rows all the time . . .'.[31]

The court was already crowded when Frank and Ross arrived. When Hardy wrote about the trial he noted that it was like the re-run of a film, with some actors saying much the same things as at the January committal hearing, although there were exceptions.[32] Newspaper reports confirmed Hardy's comments.

Mr Justice Martin entered the court, and the Judge's Associate began the call for the selection of jurors. Mr Carroll, on behalf of the Crown Law Department, was challenging on behalf of the prosecution, and Hardy on behalf of the defence. Eight challenges for the defence were allowed and twelve for the prosecution. Hardy exhausted his challenges first, and the jury was finally empanelled.[33]

Mr Winneke, in his opening address, outlined how the charge of criminal libel was an old charge from English common law. It was quite a simple concept: the publication of written defamatory words about another person, which had a tendency to disparage the character or reputation of the person about whom they were written. Mr Winneke said:

They are words which take away the good name and reputation of another person.

Criminal libel was the publication of words which tended to hold up a person to public hate, ridicule, and contempt.

Might I say this quite openly to you . . . It is of the utmost importance in this case, to the accused man first of all, and to the community, from which you are drawn, 'that you should come to your responsible task with minds which are completely unprejudiced'.[34]

Mr Winneke then detailed the problems associated with this case which had been given very wide press publicity; these were likely to create factions, either political, sectarian or social. He mentioned that writers, journalists and people who were engaged in newspaper work, might feel that the charge against Hardy was an attack upon liberty, speech and freedom of expression. He claimed that the charge of criminal libel, far from being an attack, was present to preserve and protect 'the most cherished liberty we have—the liberty of the individual'. Mr Winneke said that the case was no longer one of private litigation, between 'Mrs. Ellen Wren on the one hand and Mr Frank Joseph Hardy on the other. It was now between His Majesty and Frank Joseph Hardy'. He read passages from *Power Without Glory* which referred to Nellie West, her advances to Bill Evans, the bricklayer employed by her husband, his ultimate seduction, and the subsequent birth of the child Xavier, the product of this liaison.[35]

After concluding his reading of the long extracts, Mr Winneke submitted that the true meaning of the words was that this woman was an adulteress, and that she had made advances to a workman employed by her husband. The second issue the jury would have to consider was whether the words referred to Mrs Ellen Wren. 'The law did not allow anybody to attack the character of a person then avoid the consequences of that attack by adopting a "thinly veiled artifice"'. Mr Winneke said that the test which needed to be applied was whether 'reasonable and sensible people, knowing Mrs. Wren, and reading the book, took the words as referring to Mrs. Wren'. He said witnesses would be called, and they would swear that they had little difficulty recognising that Nellie West referred to the living Mrs Ellen Wren. The third issue the jury had to consider was whether Frank Hardy was responsible for publishing, for the purpose of the charge, and making known the libellous words to some third person. It meant 'communication'.[36]

Mr Campbell then rose to his feet, because he believed he should make a submission to the 'three issues'. He said:

As the case unravelled itself . . . it would be seen that it was essential for the Crown to show that the defamatory words were clearly calculated to cause a breach of the peace.

Much of the cross-examination which will be directed at witnesses called by the Crown will be directed at that issue.

We say there are four elements in the case and it is essential for the Crown to prove the words were completely 'and clearly a breach of the peace'.

Mr Winneke said the Crown did not consider that fourth element was a content of criminal libel.[37]

The entire proceedings for the afternoon were taken up by legal argument between Mr Winneke and Mr Campbell. Mr Campbell submitted that it was necessary for the defence case that all but 150 pages of the book be read aloud to the jury. It would be found that the defamatory words complained of, 'far from being calculated to cause a breach of the peace, would cause a feeling of pity for the character'. If the book were read, he said:

> It would show that Nellie West was not an immoral and bad woman, but a good, kind-hearted, and religious woman, who had been driven into the arms of another man to seek the love and comfort that her own husband had failed to provide.
>
> Reading of the book would also leave open for the jury to decide that the words complained of were not likely to cause a breach of the peace.[38]

Mr Justice Martin ruled on the defence claim; he said that the defence was not entitled to read the book as a whole. He further ruled that if the basis of the complaint had been on a libel of John Wren, then it could have been read. But, as the court was dealing with the character of Mrs Wren, he said the defence was not entitled to read the whole of the book. Only those passages that 'really touched' on the allegations in the presentment could be read.[39]

Mr Justice Martin reserved his decision until the following morning as to whether Hardy could call evidence to show that the libel was of a trivial nature. He also ruled that the prosecution did not have the onus to prove that a libel was likely to cause a breach of the peace.[40] The court then adjourned until the following morning.

John Wren, Jr, spent almost that entire day in the witness box insisting that John West in the book was, in fact, John Wren, Sr. His evidence was similar to that given at the committal hearing. The armchair bearing the Wren crest and the Beethoven print were carried into the court, and he identified them as belonging to his father's home. Mr Nelson (for the Crown) read selected passages from the book, and Wren, Jr, continued to identify characters as being real people, either members of his family, or friends and business associates of his father.[41]

When Wren, Jr, had finished his evidence-in-chief, Mr Campbell asked Mr Justice Martin's permission to read extracts from the book. Mr Campbell said:

> Wren [Jr] was purporting to ally the identity of Nellie West in the book with the living character of Ellen Wren, his mother, by linking John West in the book with the living character of his father.
>
> It is impossible for me to cross-examine Wren [Jr] without reading in full the passages already referred to in evidence.[42]

Mr Justice Martin did not see the need to read hundreds of pages. He said Mr Campbell could challenge the identity of John West as John Wren [Sr], or Nellie West as Ellen Wren; 'you can refer to those passages which you say are inconsistent with their being so . . . I am not going to have all these conversations between 'Cauliflower' and 'Piggy', and all those people *ad nauseam*'.[43]

Conversations alleged to have taken place between the man whom Wren, Jr, considered portrayed his father, and other fictitious characters were 'lies'. But, 'John West is not fictitious,' he added. Wren, Jr, identified and named characters in the novel as real people and real incidents. There were some characters and events he said he did not recognise. For most of the day Mr Campbell was frequently interrupted by Mr Justice Martin when he attempted to read passages from the book. There was an angry clash between counsel and the witness. Mr Campbell shouted, 'Lies, lies, lies! Do you know any other word, Mr Wren?'. 'In this case, no,' replied John Wren, Jr.'[44]

On the third day Patrick Francis Cody appeared for the prosecution. His evidence was similar to that given in the committal hearing, except that he did not repeat that he had felt tempted to take the law into his own hands. He said the book had set out to hurt John Wren's reputation, and he 'never knew John Wren senior to do anything wrong'. Bernard Nolan was called as a witness for the prosecution; his answers to questions closely followed those given in his earlier evidence. Mr Campbell reminded him that he had said, at that time, that his reaction was to kill Hardy. He denied that that statement was a gross exaggeration; that was how he felt at the time. He admitted that John Wren, Sr, had presented his wife [Mrs Nolan] with a Buick car. In the earlier hearings Nolan had identified the character Vera Maguire as being his wife. Nolan admitted that the character of Nellie West did not depict her 'as either a good woman or a bad woman, apart from the Evans incident'.[45]

Wren, Jr, was recalled to answer further questions from Mr Campbell, who first outlined a summary of the libels or allegations against John West in the book, including:

> Running an illegal tote and cheating customers; bribing police; attempted bribery of judges; suborning; rigging a pigeon race, a bicycle race, and the Caulfield Cup race; being responsible for the attempted murder of a detective, and being concerned in two other murders.
>
> Wren, junior, said he identified a character in the book, named 'Snoopy' Tanner, as 'Squizzy' Taylor.[46]

Mr Campbell then asked Wren, Jr, if he believed that his father was behind the political scenes. He denied this. Mr Campbell asked whether his father had ever had anything to do with shipping 'poor quality' liquor to America during the prohibition era. Wren, Jr, replied, 'No'. Campbell challenged him over his statement that the libel against Nellie West was 'the greatest libel in the book', Wren, Jr, interjected hotly, 'How would you like it if your mother . . .'.[47]

Witnesses for the Crown who had appeared at the committal hearing were called. Alfred Andrew-Street, an employee of John Wren, Jr, gave evidence that he had attended the New Theatre, at the request of Wren, Jr, but he had not been paid. He had purchased the book, and Hardy had autographed it. Cyril Burley, a journalist, repeated his evidence that he had attended a meeting addressed by Hardy, and a report had been published in the *Age* newspaper the following day. He claimed that Hardy had said that the characters were based on real people and that the main character appealed to him 'as a very colorful personality'. Burley said that Hardy had told the meeting that he had not intended to do that character any injury. The third witness for the Crown, A. M. Harold, former co-editor of *Farrago*, the University of Melbourne student newspaper, stated that he believed that the book was 'partly fact, partly fiction'.[48]

On the fourth day the public gallery was again packed, and special police had been posted to keep control. Barristers pressed into the court ante-room to listen. 'The Crown case was closed and no evidence was called for the defence, nor did Hardy make a statement from the dock.'[49]

Mr Campbell asked the court why John Wren, Sr, had not been called, nor the one woman alleged to be defamed. Mr Campbell added that the woman alleged to be defamed, and John Wren, Sr, were both quite fit to come to court. The reason why Hardy did not give or call evidence was because 'There was nothing I could put Hardy into the box about . . . The evidence about the publication he was not going to deny, and there was not another issue on which he would be allowed to give evidence'. Mr Campbell attacked the credibility of the main Crown witnesses; John Wren, Jr, had shown himself, under cross-examination, to be a person whose evidence reeked of wild improbabilities. He had considered the alleged adultery of his mother to be a gross libel, even when compared to the allegations of murder, race rigging, robbery and so on made against John West. Mr Campbell said that the witness Bernard Nolan had behaved like a 'hot-headed Irishman' and had given answers that resembled the currently popular song: 'The Answer She is 'Yes'—'No'?'. Mr Campbell finally asked the jury for a verdict 'that common sense, the evidence, and justice demand—a verdict of not guilty'.[50]

Mr Winneke made his address to the jury; he reminded them of his prediction that they would be faced with only three issues—'Was the woman in the book (Nellie West) libelled? Did the words refer to Mrs. Ellen Wren? Did Frank J. Hardy publish them?'. Mr Winneke then referred to passages from the book and to the evidence of identification that Ellen Wren was Nellie West, and John Wren was John West. Mr Winneke continued:

> There is not one tittle of evidence in this case that one of the incidents in the book is true about this woman.
>
> It is not in issue, and it does not concern us.
>
> But in any event there is not one shred of evidence or piece of evidence that would justify you for one moment in thinking there is one atom of truth in these words complained of.[51]

After a lengthy address which touched on evidence given by witnesses, Mr Winneke voiced his admiration for John Wren, Jr, who had defended his mother and spent gruelling hours in the witness box. In his conclusion Mr Winneke told the jury that the criminal libel was 'gross, scurrilous, and scandalous'.[52]

When Mr Campbell began his address to the jury he began by saying that 'The charge of criminal libel is a legal anachronism. It is completely out-moded'. He suggested that the jury might well think that the 'fire and fervor' shown by Mr Winneke in his closing address had not 'rung true'. Mr Campbell said that a fair-minded man could not agree with the bulk of what the Crown Prosecutor had said:

> We submit that if you decide this case on the evidence before you, and the strong and intrinsic evidence from the book—from the cross-examination of witnesses—you will have little doubt that this man should not be deprived of his liberty . . . The jury, he went on, should discard any politi-cal or other such considerations in reaching their Verdict, no matter how strongly they might dislike the considerations involved . . . You may have a strong hatred for Communism . . . A verdict of common sense and justice, he said, would be one of 'not guilty'.[53]

Mr Campbell referred to the many anachronisms in our laws, and he pro-ceeded to cite some. This led to heated exchanges between Mr Justice Martin and Mr Campbell. Mr Campbell had claimed that there was a law, another anachronism, which enabled a judge to put a convicted man in irons. Mr Justice Martin informed Mr Campbell that there was such a section, but it was repealed some years ago. He said:

> 'So you can see that, even in the ranks of KC's a little learning can be a dangerous thing, and it is no longer upon the judge, if he felt so inclined, to say that a man can be put in irons for certain offences' . . . The judge then dealt with the portion of Mr Campbell's address that truth was, in this particular case, no defence . . . 'You were told that the greater the truth the greater the libel . . . That had been so . . . but it had been altered when Queen Victoria came to the throne about 110 years ago. An act was passed then which allowed a person charged with criminal libel to prove that he was writing the truth and published it for the public benefit . . . When Victoria became a State that legislation was kept, and it left open the defence of having the truth for the public benefit . . . And if he can prove those things, he is entitled to be acquitted.'[54]

Mr Justice Martin then noted that the three issues as submitted by Mr Winneke had to be proved before Hardy could be convicted. He continued to clarify points of law. He had begun his charge to the jury at ten minutes after noon, and just before five minutes to one o'clock he said that if the words were found to be libellous, and Hardy did publish them, and they were found to refer to Mrs Wren, then the jury would find the accused guilty. If the jurors were not satisfied on any of these matters, then they should find him not guilty. He sent the jury out to consider its verdict.[55]

As Hardy was being taken to the cell under the courtroom, Ross left her seat hurriedly and handed him a lunch bag.[56] For months there had been tasks to perform, meetings to attend, leaflets to be written and distributed, money to be collected and legal conferences. Now there was nothing to do but wait. Hardy's fate was in the hands of those 'twelve good men and true'.

Had Hardy's counsel prepared him for the possibility of a guilty verdict? Sir John Starke said:

> Oh, I don't know whether we told him [Hardy]. Campbell thought he would get five years. But the only thing I said, and Campbell rebuked me for it, was on the last day before he went home. The verdict would have come on the next day; I said to him, bring your razor and tooth-brush in, Frank. He turned a bit pale and went off. Campbell said, you should not have said that. I said, well, God damn it, Don, one of the things that may happen is that he may be convicted. Campbell said, of course he might get convicted but there's no need to tell him so.[57]

Hardy's recollections were that he had brought his toothbrush and razor, together with several packets of his favourite *Turf* cigarettes secreted in the lining of his jacket and in his pockets.[58] At two o'clock Hardy was taken back to the court. Mr Justice Martin resumed his seat; soon a knock was heard from the jury-room door. The twelve men filed in and stood in two rows in front of the jury box. The Judge's Associate asked, 'Gentlemen of the jury; have you considered your verdict?'. 'We have.' 'And how say you? Is the prisoner guilty or not guilty?' The jury foreman answered quietly, 'Not guilty'.[59]

The verdict may not have been a surprise to some people. Les Barnes had a relative, a fireman, who was selected to sit on the jury for the Hardy trial. He later related to Barnes that he had received a message from his workmates to the effect that if 'Hardy is found guilty, don't bother to come back to work'.[60] When John Starke met the foreman of the jury some years later, he asked, 'Why did you acquit him?'. 'Well', he said, 'Old Wren had been a bloody scandal all his life and the first time he's hurt by anything, he rushes to the law for protection, and we thought "to hell with him"'. Starke felt that both Frank Hardy and he had had a good result. 'We both did well out of it, Frank got publicity for his book and it helped my career.'[61]

The events that followed can best be gauged by a report published on the front page of the *Argus* the following morning:

JUDGE SILENCES CLAPPING, AS JURY FINDS AUTHOR NOT GUILTY OF CRIMINAL LIBEL.
HARDY SEEKS 'QUIET' TO WRITE NEW BOOK
FIVE-DAY TRIAL ENDS.

* Wave after wave of wild clapping filled the Criminal court yesterday as the jury found Hardy, author of 'Power Without Glory,' not guilty of criminal libel.

The Court proceedings were drowned in the extraordinary outburst from the public gallery, and Mr Justice Martin joined with his associate, the Court crier and policemen in calling for 'Silence!'.

Hardy did not smile until he left the dock and caught hold of his wife's hand.

* At his home in quiet tree-lined Hillard st., East Malvern, last night, Hardy said: 'Most of all now I want peace and quiet to continue work on my new book.

My only reaction to the case is to forget it, but I will never forget the countless thousands of ordinary Australian people who have stood behind me.'

Today, for the first time in months, the Hardy household will be back to normal as their two children return home.[62]

Hardy had also stated that '7000 copies of *Power Without Glory*, the available balance of the second edition, would be on sale today, and the price would probably be less than 25/6'. These copies had not been able to be sold under the terms of his bail. He also said he could not afford to bring out another edition, but before the trial eleven countries, including France, Holland, Czechoslovakia and Germany, had accepted the book for publication. Ross Hardy's comments to the press on the verdict were of a personal nature. She said, 'It was the most wonderful feeling when Frank was acquitted. I didn't know whether to laugh or cry. I feel better now, but I can't wait till we get the children home tomorrow'.[63]

So ended one of the most extraordinary and sensational chapters in Australian literary and political history. The prelude to the trial had elicited a great range of emotions and responses from broad sections of the public. The committal hearing that had extended, with adjournments, from November 1950 until late January 1951 and the five-day trial in June 1951, were estimated to have incurred legal costs of £3000. What cannot be estimated in financial terms, time, energy and stress, was not only the incalculable contribution of the CPA leadership and its members, but that of those others who supported Hardy, even though some did not share his political beliefs. The Frank Hardy Defence Committee was the spearhead, but various organisations and people gave their time and resources to ensure that, in those critical times when democratic rights were being assailed, writers would never again be brought before the courts on charges of criminal libel.

A few days later, a celebration of Hardy's acquittal was held at the Masonic Institute at the top of Collins Street. Realist writer Hugh Anderson was among the group that moved to the home of writer Bill Wannan near the corner of Glenferrie and Dandenong Roads, Caulfield. Anderson said that the party was quite spontaneous, there was little to drink (the pubs had long closed), and Frank, in particular, was soon roaring for anything with alcohol. The yarning began simply as just that, but it was not long before each story became a sort of 'top this' competition. One by one the participants, among them Alan

Marshall and Judah Waten, dropped out until Hardy was the sole performer. He continued on, really acting out the characters in the tales, by turn pathetic and hilarious. They were mostly centred on Bacchus Marsh and the Depression years. Hugh remembered thinking at the time, 'If only he wrote as well as he tells the stories'. There was an air of great elation; the tension that had gripped Hardy and his supporters for so long was at an end. In 1997 another participant, Dawn Anderson, remembered 'that it was a wonderful night'.[64]

Chapter Eleven

AFTERMATH

NOW THAT Frank Hardy had been found not guilty, it might have been assumed that his concerns with the law were over. But on the day following his acquittal, Lawrence Kay, printer and publisher of the *Sun* newspaper, was fined £50 for contempt of court by Mr Justice Martin in the Supreme Court. Hardy had alleged that an article published in the *Sun* had tended to prejudice his pending court appearance on a charge of criminal libel. Kay gave evidence that he was not on duty on the day on which the article was written, nor did he have jurisdiction over the editorial staff. The acting editor, Mr F. Daly, stated in an affidavit 'that he did not regard the article as prejudicial to Hardy's fair trial'.[1] There was a feeling among Hardy's supporters that this hearing had been held over until after the trial.

On the same day two detectives went to the office of the Frank Hardy Defence Committee; they left a message saying that they would question Hardy at his home the next day. Later Superintendent F. W. Lyon, chief of the CIB, denied that his detectives were involved. On the following day Senior-Detective W. Garvey and Detective D. J. Swanson interviewed Frank and Rosslyn Hardy at the offices of Hardy's solicitors, Dall and Alway; they declined to answer questions. Later that day the detectives questioned the author Alan Marshall and Clem Christesen, editor of the literary journal *Meanjin*. Christesen said, 'I was visited by two detectives, who showed me a pamphlet I had never seen before'. The pamphlet had been published in defence of Frank Hardy who had, at that time, been on bail awaiting trial.[2]

John Selig, who worked in his family's printery in Russell Street, was also questioned by detectives about the pamphlet. He told them that he had been approached by a Mrs Booth [an organiser for the Frank Hardy Defence Committee] to print 15 000 leaflets. When he saw the copy he was not happy, because it mentioned Hardy's impending trial. On 25 May 1951 he rang Francis Patrick Mortimer, officer-in-charge of criminal prosecutions in the Crown Solicitor's office, who told him that he would not touch the job 'with a 40 foot pole'. When Selig discussed this with Booth, she assured him that there was nothing he could get into trouble about. Later she returned with the copy because she had failed to find a printer. She asked him to do it as 'an outside job' for the Capricorn Printing Company. The pamphlet would bear their imprint, and she would take full responsibility for it; but he remained reluctant. Booth took the pamphlet away to get it printed elsewhere. She called again, and Selig told her, as an excuse, that he had not been able to get the linotyping done. She said, 'Apparently Mr Wren has even got the linotypers bluffed'. Selig said, 'I told her no one had me bluffed and, after that, Mrs Booth took the copy away and came back with the type set-up'. Selig printed 28 418 pamphlets in all.[3]

When he was later questioned by detectives, he explained that he could tell them nothing about Booth except as described in her visits to his premises, and that she had worn a green raincoat. When word leaked out that the police were looking for 'a woman in a green raincoat', Booth was called urgently to the CPA headquarters in 49 Elizabeth Street, when Ted Hill advised her to keep out of sight and dispose of the incriminating raincoat. She had suggested to Hill that she should accept responsibility for her actions.[4]

On 4 July 1951, Selig was called upon in the Practice Court 'to show cause why he should not be committed for contempt of court'. Selig was committed for imprisonment for 'no longer than three weeks'. He was also ordered to pay costs. Although Justice Dean considered that Selig had been an 'innocent tool' who had no communist affiliations, he must be punished. Selig's affidavit, which was read to the court, tendered his sincere apologies.[5] He served one week in prison.

Booth continued to feel embarrassed about the part she had played. She understood that Selig had eventually received some financial compensation from the CPA.[6] But that must remain a matter of conjecture. What is demonstrated by these events is the powerful influence that Hill had wielded over party members.

When *The Hard Way* was published in 1961, the *Bulletin* reviewer attacked the work in vitriolic terms; in particular, he made scathing comments on the Selig affair: 'But the most detailed treatment is given to the promotion of contempt for law. This is not only seen in systematic "contempt of court" in the legal sense—the issuing of pamphlets while the trial was still on to show Hardy was not guilty.'[7]

A reviewer in the British *Times Literary Supplement* had accepted most of what Hardy had written, but was interested in how Hardy had viewed his role in relation to the Defence Committee and its legal implications: 'He [Hardy] seems to have been largely responsible for the success of the "Defend Hardy Campaign". This conducted a vigorous campaign outside the court, which surely would have been considered as brazen contempt in this country'.[8] Perhaps the words of Ted Thompson, who then worked at the CPA press close by Selig's premises, best sum up the pamphlet episode. He said, 'It was a bloody shameful thing for the party to do'.[9]

Immediately after Hardy's trial Joseph Waters, the distributor of *Power Without Glory*, had been inundated with orders for copies of the book from Victorian and interstate booksellers. The balance of the second edition had already been promised to buyers before the case ended. On the day after the trial copies were on sale in the International Bookshop and Franklin's Library Supply. Two days later Myer's, N. H. Seward's and Hall's Bookshops in Bourke Street were also selling the book. Waters had received orders for 2000 copies from England and another order for 6000 copies from the United States.[10]

Waters had despatched 500 copies to a left-wing distributor in the USA, but the consignment was impounded by the authorities and thrown into the sea, and not one copy reached the US market. Waters arranged that the printer in Port Melbourne who had been holding the unbound printed edition should proceed. When the delivery was made, Waters found that there were 250 copies missing. He then knew that the printer must have collated and bound these copies and sold them 'on the side'. This explained the earlier visit from the police about copies being sold illegally outside Flinders Street railway station for £5. He sent an invoice to the printer, but by the time the nominated payment date arrived, he had disappeared, never to be seen again! Waters said that £1250 was a lot of money in 1951. Between the Port Melbourne printer and the US authorities, Waters had lost 750 copies of the highly sought-after novel. 'As soon as the case was ended there was a tremendous demand for it . . . You had a book which was in great demand, and you lost money on it because peculiar things happened.'[11]

The novel had been openly displayed for sale in the window of the CPA's Current Book Distributors in Sydney, and was being sold in Victoria; this was at a time when an injunction had been imposed by the Court in Victoria.[12] That the injunction failed to stop the sales of *Power Without Glory* demonstrates that

> . . . censorship is a self-defeating thing. Nearly all forbidden things are attractive by definition, so it is the most nonsensical law because it has its own in-built self-destruction in it. If you ban a thing, you actually draw more attention to it, so you wind up by doing the opposite. A book should be judged on whether it's entertaining or whether it's useful or whether it's well written.[13]

Many people expressed the opinion that the Wren family and their associates had displayed poor judgment in initiating proceedings against Hardy. Others believed that the Crown was unwise to take over the prosecution, as the case might have lapsed. Had there been no prosecution, *Power Without Glory* might have slipped into obscurity. By the time the trial was over, supporters, quite apart from CPA members and trade unionists, had accorded Hardy the status of a folk hero. Such was the feeling that Hardy was in the position of being like the bridal couple at a traditional Greek wedding, where well-wishers pin money to their clothing. People offered and, indeed, pressed money into Hardy's hand or pocket, often the small savings of working people who were willing to wait until the book royalties came in. Others neither expected nor wanted repayment.

For the CPA Executive Hardy had become their 'show pony'; his novel and the events preceding and following his trial were seen as a great success for the working class, guided by the sure hand of the CPA. People were still donating money to the Frank Hardy Defence Committee months after the trial.[14]

When Willie Gallacher, former Communist member of the British House of Commons, and his wife Jean, who had been sent on a cruise following his electoral defeat, arrived at Port Melbourne on 5 March 1952, they were met by party members. Among them was Waters, a former resident of Tyneside, England, who was in charge of their itinerary. On the following day CPA solicitor, Cedric Ralph, took the couple for a tour which naturally included the locations mentioned in Hardy's novel, first to Collingwood (Carringbush), when they were shown the shop where John Wren had started his illegal tote. They were then driven to view Wren's mansion and Archbishop Mannix's residence, Raheen, in Kew. In a letter written en route to Sydney, Gallacher made pithy comments about Wren, 'the gangster', and Archbishop Mannix, 'a close pal of Wren's. He is not waiting for "a mansion in the sky"—He's got it right there in Melbourne . . . [and] he is reluctant to transfer'.[15]

Joseph Waters was aware that Hardy was worn out after the trial which had 'dragged on and on'. He said, 'It had an effect . . . and arrangements had to be made, as a matter of fact, to get Frank Hardy out of things, and he went to England'.[16]

In 1987 Hardy was to claim that he and Rosslyn left Australia for the good of their health.[17] In 1969 Hardy mentioned that his reason for leaving the country was that he would become a victim if the referendum to ban the Communist Party had been successful. He returned to Australia only after the people voted No in the referendum.[18]

It is difficult to give credence to these claims, as his children, nine-year-old Frances and five-year-old Alan, were left behind with 'good friends, Betty and Les Boyanton' in the Neerim South district in Gippsland. Would parents leave two small children in a country in which their father's life was in danger? In the event of the referendum being passed and with a resulting deteriorating political climate, the Hardys could have been separated from their children for an indefinite period.

However, some weight must be given to Hardy's assertion, given the contents of this extract from a roughly prepared document signed by W. G. Smith, who had, at Hardy's request, accompanied him to a meeting in December 1979:

> [With] James A Loughnan at 5 Waltham St Richmond . . . I already knew something of the Loughnan family's participation in local and State politics, and had on occasions met Jim's brother Con. Jim himself had served for years as a Richmond councillor, had been a Mayor, and at the time of our visit was a Justice of the Peace.
>
> The conversation turned to the 'Power Without Glory' case. Loughnan revealed that it was he that speeded up the taxation clearance to enable Hardy to leave the country in haste after the trial in 1951. 'You would not have lived if you had stayed around, he said, none of us expected you to win that case, and Bill Barry had it all arranged that when you went to

Pentridge you were never to come out alive'. 'You mean Bill Barry, the member of the State cabinet at that time, later a member of the D.L.P.?' When Frank asked the question he appeared more inquisitive than upset.

'That's the man,' Loughnan said grimly, 'and when Barry made arrangements they were usually carried out, so now you know how lucky you were.'

As we left the house Frank muttered quietly, 'What do you reckon about that, the Attorney-General arranging a murder, people will never believe it, and to think that I thought in prison I would be able to make it pay by applying myself to my writing, how lucky was I?'

We walked the rest of the distance to the car in silence.[19]

Hardy's memory was faulty, as Barry had never held the office of Attorney-General; during and during Hardy's trial the Attorney-General in Victoria was Thomas Mitchell.[20]

Criticisms had been levelled at Hardy, but he was in an unassailable position; he continued to be 'a valued and favoured son' of the CPA Executive. Any rents which appeared in the fabric of unity were soon cobbled together.

In early July 1951 Frank and Rosslyn Hardy left Australia to attend the World Youth Festival in Berlin. At a meeting in Unity Hall eight hundred people gathered to farewell the couple; Hardy told them that when he had started to write he had set out to serve the working people, and his trip to the World Youth Festival would enable him to serve once more. The speakers included Clem Christesen, Alan Marshall, Vance Palmer, George Seelaf, Lester Allan and Ted Hill.[21]

At the time of the couple's departure the *Herald* 'sneeringly referred to their first-class passage, and rumours were put around that money raised for Hardy's defence was used to pay his passage to Europe'. These comments brought an angry response:

A spokesman for the Frank Hardy Defence Committee told *The Guardian* this week: 'The facts are that when Mr. Hardy, exhausted after the strain of recent months, and wanting only to rest and write, allowed himself to be persuaded to go to the World Youth Festival to play a part in preserving peace, he went to the shipping office to book second class passages for himself and his wife. There were none available. He had the alternative of going by air or of taking first class passages. He took the far cheaper course.

The money for his fare was lent by his close friends. Most of it will have to be repaid from the income of his future books'.[22]

Given that Hardy did have the best intentions about repayment of loans from future royalties at that time, it was some years before he wrote another book, apart from the ill-fated *Journey Into The Future*.

Frank and Ross travelled first to England where accommodation had been arranged with Barney Letski, a family connection of Joe Waters. He was Jewish, a successful businessman and a member of the Communist Party of Great

Britain (CPGB). He lived near Harry Pollitt, the secretary of the CPGB, who arranged that Frank and Ross would travel to the Soviet Union after the Youth Festival in Berlin. Hardy was not an easy guest. Letski liked to get up early and had 'a tendency, when getting breakfast, to sing arias from operas'. Whereas Hardy liked to stay up late and get up late; he was irritated by Letski's habits, and complained bitterly, not only about the singing, but of its quality.[23]

A few days after their arrival, Frank and Ross departed for the Youth Festival in East Berlin. The *Guardian* published a cable sent by Hardy, which warned that there was a real danger of war, and Berlin was likely to explode, despite the fact that it was the location for the great Festival for Peace. He glorified the efforts of the people of the German Democratic Republic and claimed that fascism no longer existed there, that food was plentiful and that West German workers' wives travelled to the Eastern sector to purchase cheap food, but were frequently accosted on their way home by the Americans, who confiscated their parcels.[24]

Frank and Ross went on to travel extensively in the Soviet Union, where they visited schools, theatres, hospitals, universities, kindergartens, pioneer children's camps, creches, theatres, football matches, basketball stadiums, harness-racing and all the usual sights. Hardy was impressed by the living standards there, which he considered were better than anywhere else in the world. He was amazed at the speed at which construction work was going ahead, far faster than in Australia or any other country he had seen.[25]

On 20 October 1951 the couple were guests of honour at a farewell dinner organised by the Soviet Writers' Union. The following morning friends drove Frank and Ross to the airport, where they met a group of Australians who were going to London, but they were en route to Warsaw and then to Czechoslovakia.[26]

While in Europe Hardy met a Melbourne woman who was a student at the Budapest University. She was delighted to meet Frank; she told him how a copy of *Power Without Glory* had been sent to her from Australia. She explained that she was the person who had taken his book to Szepirodalmi Könyvkiadó, who were publishers of literature in Budapest. When she had informed them of the events surrounding the novel and Hardy's trial, they had agreed to publish the work in Hungarian, and it was arranged that one of the best translators in Hungary would undertake the task. She was requested to write the foreword on the events of Hardy's trial, for which she received a fee. The foreword ultimately became an afterword, when the novel was published under the title of *John West Hatalma* [*The Power of John West*]. It sold very well, and she said this was the first European translation of Hardy's novel. When she informed Hardy of the events, he was pompous and dismissed her by saying, 'My book is being published everywhere!'. She said that Hardy appeared to be very prosperous at that time. In 1964, *Nehez Út* (*The Hard Way*) was published in Budapest by Kossuth Kiado.[27]

After three months the Hardys returned to London. Once again they were welcomed and feted. In early December 1951 Noel Counihan, Australian artist and CPA member, held his first exhibition in London at the Irving Galleries in Leicester Square. The show was opened by Jack Lindsay, and Frank Hardy spoke on the second night, with 'a giant copy of . . . *Power Without Glory* terrifying an assorted group of churchmen, businessmen and politicians'.[28]

Early in 1952 Frank and Ross Hardy boarded the SS *Orcades* for their return trip to Australia. When *Journey Into The Future*, Hardy's laudatory account of life in the Soviet Union, was published a few months later, he mentioned his excitement and elation as he was driven home through the streets of Port Melbourne.[29] Did Ross Hardy guess that her husband's travels had only just begun? It is unlikely that she any longer nurtured thoughts of a more settled family life.

The CPA Executive and party members had rejoiced when Hardy was acquitted; their mood was high again following the defeat of the Communist Party Dissolution Act Referendum on 22 September 1951. Hardy was welcomed back; he was a valuable asset to the party, and his appearance at any function or rally, large or small, guaranteed a big attendance.

Plans were under way for the formation of the Australasian Book Society (ABS), in which Hardy was to play a prominent role. There is some confusion as to the precise date that the Society was founded, but a meeting had been held on the initiative of Joseph Waters on Anzac Day, 25 April 1950, in his office in Collins House, 360 Collins Street, Melbourne, and there was another meeting on 1 February 1952. According to Waters, 'At this stage, the Communist Party was not formally involved, although it is likely that everything was planned by the Party and its fraction'.[30]

Hardy had not long returned to Melbourne before he went to Sydney to help with the Eureka Youth League's Youth Carnival for Peace and Friendship. Eric Lambert was a member of the committee, which was facing heavy attacks from the press and obstruction by the authorities. Permission to use or hire certain venues had been revoked. Howard Fast and Paul Robeson had been invited to attend and speak at the Carnival, but the US government had refused to give them passports. Despite all the difficulties encountered by the organisers, the Carnival commenced on 15 March 1952.[31]

After the Carnival, a writers' conference was opened by Dame Mary Gilmore; 'under discussion was the formation of the Australasian Book Society (ABS), a co-operative publishing venture initiated by a number of Australian writers, as a means of widening the field of possible publication for new Australian books'.[32]

Frank Hardy and Eric Lambert both addressed the conference on the subject of self-publishing. Hardy gave a detailed account of his own and others' struggles to get their books to the public. Some members of the audience were critical that writers from States other than Victoria had not been given an opportunity for input, but they concluded that it was a 'step in the right direction. A co-operative publishing house of this nature would be a useful avenue for new writers with something to say'.[33]

Joseph Waters had been impressed by *Power Without Glory* and Lambert's *Twenty Thousand Thieves*; he believed that there was an immense amount of important writing which had not been published. In discussions with Andrew

Fabinyi of Cheshire's and Vance Palmer about the formation of the ABS, they both asked him the question, 'Where are you going to get the manuscripts?'. He told them there were cupboards full of them. Palmer replied, 'Look, Joe, they aren't there you know . . . Frank Hardy and Eric Lambert are exceptions'. Fabinyi said the same thing. One of the reasons that the idea of an ABS appealed to Waters was that he was the Australian agent for the British Book Society, a very large and most successful organisation. It had a lot of support in Britain, and he felt this might be the way to go in Australia.[34]

When Hardy was writing *Journey Into The Future*, Arthur Phillips, Leonard Mann and Alan Marshall, the ABS selection panel, had already chosen Ralph de Boissière's *Crown Jewel* as the Society's first publication. At a CPA literary fraction meeting of the Realist Writers' Group, Waters had opposed the CPA's decision that the ABS should give priority to Hardy's work. He had moved a motion rejecting the proposal, but he did not get a seconder. 'They all agreed that it should be published by the ABS, and the CPA laid it down that it should be published by the ABS.' Waters had suggested that an alternative publisher could be used. 'Well, automatically Arthur Phillips came to see me and said he was finished, so did that fellow Mann. Alan Marshall was more willing to go along with us, but had to resign as well.'[35] The ABS was left without a selection panel. The will of the CPA had prevailed, and *Journey Into The Future* and *Crown Jewel* were launched almost simultaneously.

As time passed, Hardy was to distance himself from *Journey Into The Future*, referring to it as a 'travel book', and eventually it disappeared from the list of his published works.

Ralph de Boissière arrived in Melbourne from Trinidad in January 1948, and first met Hardy in a lift in an old building in Collins Street, where the Fellowship of Australian Writers held its meetings. It was Frank who recruited de Boissière to the Realist Writers' Group, and he attended the next meeting. In recounting this first meeting, Ralph wrote:

> Very early Frank struck me as epitomising the working-class Australian I was getting to know—anti-authoritarian, militant and committed to a betterment of living conditions. I had come to a completely different world . . . Frank to a large extent educated me in its ways. At that time he had the truth—as we all had—and was abrasive, quite unreliable and seemed to live by and for gambling. If you arranged to meet him at twelve, he might turn up at one, or not at all. At that time he was busy meeting various characters in secret places who were able to give him first-hand information on the past life of the central figure in his book. He and Amby Dyson were always discussing the latter's cartoons for it.
>
> In a pub with him and others I saw him at his best as a raconteur. He could hold his audience, and they listened eagerly. Getting away with something not necessarily illegal, but just for the hell of it, like down the boss—that kind of yarn always went over well. Frank knew his audience.
>
> He was a great admirer of Balzac's novels. At this time, late forties, early fifties, he had ideas for a Human Comedy of his own, but the

enormous strain of the case over his book probably dashed those early plans.

He, too, believed that 'in another ten or fifteen years we'll have socialism in this country'. Three years later Stalin died. When some days afterwards we happened to be together in Collins Street, he said to me: 'He ruled that country for thirty years and never made a mistake'. I don't think he could really have believed that. It was a way of expressing his enthusiasm, at that time, for the Soviet Union. That country of which we really knew very little.[36]

Frank took the ABS books to the workers. He spoke at open-air meetings with seamen on the docks, and at various factories and workshops. Waters remembered 'how writer David Martin was so impressed by this that he wanted to be in it. So he went around, and there was this feeling that ordinary workers read books'. In 1952–53 Hardy undertook tours throughout the country to address groups and increase the membership in the ABS. Hardy's enthusiasm for the ABS may have involved some self-interest, but there is no doubt that he contributed a great deal towards the success of the membership drives in those early years. In 1987 his recollection was that he had visited the eastern States and Adelaide and 'joined up 4000 members'.[37] This claim was extravagant as the ABS membership, at its peak, barely exceeded 3000.[38]

At this time the CPA press was engaged on printing further editions of *Power Without Glory*. An arrangement had been made for Ross Hardy to work at the Federal Press on a part-time basis. Why did the CPA not seek a position for Ross, a competent stenographer, in one of the communist-led trade union offices, where she would have received equal pay? This was at a time when secretaries and stenographers were highly sought after. In 1952 Eileen Capocchi worked for some months with Ross, whom she remembered as being very quiet and diligent. She recalled that the nature of their work did not allow for much conversation, and at day's end they both had to hurry home to young children.[39]

Alvie Booth had warm memories of how helpful Frank Hardy was to other writers at that time; she particularly mentioned how he had arranged for Ross to type the manuscript of *Voices in the Storm* by former 'Dunera Boy' and Realist Writer Walter Kaufmann.[40] It would seem that little had changed for Ross. It was fortunate for her that she had accompanied Frank to Britain and Europe, and that she had the opportunity to relax and enjoy the forward and return voyages. Although there is no record of how Hardy had behaved on board, it is likely that he had revelled in revealing to the first-class passengers that he was *the* Frank Hardy, the communist writer who had just been found not guilty of a criminal libel charge. If he did maintain a low profile, then it was completely out of character with the public Hardy.

Hardy resumed his participation in the Realist Writers' Group after his return from Britain. The first edition of the duplicated journal *Realist Writer* was published in 1952. Hardy, with other members, continued to embrace his early views that their stories were written about the working class, by the working class, for the working class. In a study of the Realist Writers' move-ment, Ian Syson wrote, 'From the outset the Realist Writers' movement incor-porated twin aims: the encouragement and development of worker-writers and the continuation of a perceived national, democratic and realist tradition'.[41]

In 1953, notwithstanding Hardy's deep involvement with the Realist Writers and the ABS, he decided to become a seaman. His entry and union membership was almost certainly arranged by the communist-led Seamen's Union. On 9 July 1953 he embarked on the SS *Carcoola* as a crew attendant. He was discharged in Sydney on 22 September 1953. Two months later he started work as a coal trimmer on the SS *Iron King*, but less than a month later he was discharged in Port Kembla. On 31 January 1954 he shipped on the SS *Bungaree*, again as a coal trimmer, but discharged himself in Sydney eight days later.[42] These days aboard were to provide the material for his play *The Ringbolter*.

Hardy became unpopular with the crew members, as he was considered, as a crew attendant, to be 'a hygiene hazard—he believed he had the right to stay in his cabin all day and tinker with his typewriter'. What finally alienated him from the crew was 'his immense capacity to be a "super-snip". He enjoyed living out of other people's pockets; he'd put the "bite" on anyone and every-one'. For a while seamen honoured some of his dud cheques that covered the land. When he worked as a coal trimmer, his job was to wheel the coal from the bunkers to the stokehold. He swiftly 'earnt the nick-name [sic] of Norman Von Nida [a world champion golfer] because he was "never caught in the bunkers".'[43] Perhaps Frank saw himself as the 'writer on board', rather than a seaman. It is unlikely that the seamen lodged any formal complaint to the Sea-men's Union regarding Hardy's poor performance.

On his return to Melbourne in February 1954, Hardy resumed his activities with the Realist Writers' Group. By then serious rifts had developed within the membership on the question of socialist realism, and John Morrison felt com-pelled to express his doubts:

> Statements concerning the place of the writer in society, on socialist-realist etc. with which I do not find myself in complete agreement have appeared in the REALIST WRITER [sic] from time to time, but I have resisted an inclination to join issue because I believed that my limited studies in what has become the exact science of writing (art no longer) did not qualify me to speak with sufficient authority. Some protest, how-ever, must be made by somebody against the views put forward in the last issue by Vic Williams.
>
> Here in the baldest possible terms is set out an attitude to writing which I have seen growing up over a number of years, and which I believe more than ever before leads straight to literary damnation. An attitude which maintains that literature should be regarded as an instrument in the social struggle and as nothing else. As a matter of fact Williams goes even further, arguing as he so clearly does that writing is good only in the degree in which it serves the needs of a given moment . . . Am I commit-ting a heresy when I suggest that the function of the artist, no matter

through what medium he works, is to move his audience emotionally. If a man has a message and will not or can not convey it on these terms, then he is not an artist, and would be better employed trying to reach his audience through straight-out reportage or oratory. (And why not?—there is room for every talent in the task before us.)[44]

The divisions within the ranks of the Realist Writers' Group have been well documented in a number of other publications.[45] David Carter asserts that while most members of the Realist Writers' Group were communists . . . 'it was not a Party or front organisation'.[46] However, Les Barnes had been directed by the CPA to join the newly formed Realist Writers' in 1944 'to organise the writers', and the party's influence could not be underestimated.[47] Some members of the CPA fraction within the Group were adherents of Andrei A. Zhdanov, the head of the Union of Soviet Writers, who had interpreted the meaning of Stalin's view that writers were 'the engineers of the human soul' to mean:

. . . in the first place, that you must know life to be able to depict it truthfully in artistic creations, to depict it neither 'scholastically' nor lifelessly, nor simply as 'objective reality', but rather as reality in its revolutionary development. The truthfulness and historical exactitude of the artistic image must be linked with the task of ideological transformation, of the education of the working people in the spirit of socialism. This method in fiction and literary criticism is what we call the method of socialist realism.[48]

The theory of socialist realism 'appears to have been devised by [Maxim] Gorky in consultation with Stalin' and 'promulgated by Zhdanov, who made his debut on this occasion as Stalin's great panjandrum in cultural matters' at the First All-Union Congress of Soviet Writers in 1934.[49] He pronounced that 'The present position of bourgeois literature is such that it is already incapable of producing great works'.[50]

'The authority of the Party over literature had been reasserted by Zhdanov after the war.'[51] His discourse was published in the *Communist Review* in February 1947, and his views on socialist realism were embraced by the leadership of the CPA. '. . . Miles [J. B. Miles, CPA General Secretary] pronounced it with all the authoritarian certainty that a Communist Party hierarchy can muster when it feels it must, socialist realism of the Soviet kind.'[52] This was to have a profound effect on some of the Realist Writers.

Hardy had clearly expressed his views on the socialist realist debate in the *Communist Review* No. 32, December 1952. He believed only Marxist-Leninist writers, who wrote from the point of view of the working class, could produce worthwhile literature. He criticised some party members who preferred to be accepted by bourgeois publishers. Writers needed to be mindful of Comrade Lenin's behest that 'literature must become part and parcel of the general proletarian cause'.[53]

Hardy's contempt for bourgeois publishers did change, as *The Four-Legged Lottery* (1958) and *The Hard Way* (1961) were first published by T. Werner Laurie Ltd in London, although arrangements had been made to print special editions for the ABS members. These assured pre-publication sales were an incentive for T. Werner Laurie. Despite his forceful rejection, Hardy was to have ongoing, if turbulent, relationships with a long list of so-called 'bourgeois' publishers, outside the Soviet Union and Eastern Europe, until the end of his life. The author/publisher relationship was constantly sullied when Hardy received advances for work planned, or work in progress. Problems and disputes arose when there were inordinate delays, or the manuscripts failed to materialise. Some of Hardy's later work failed to conform to Zhdanov's socialist realist gospel.

As a result of the dissent within the Realist Writers' Group, the *Realist Writer* was subsumed by *Overland*; the first edition was the Spring issue of 1954 with Stephen Murray-Smith as its editor. Subsequently, 'Hardy offered to cooperate with him if he would agree to accept a joint editor and/or appoint a representative editorial board and return to its original policies.'[54] No accommodation was reached.

In 1987 Hardy mentioned that in 1952 Rosslyn and he had made the decision, partly for the sake of the two children, Alan and Frances, to move to Sydney.[55] Frances remembered when her father was arrested, 'One of my mother's friends told me that . . . I used to cry every day when I came home from school, the other children would say, 'Your father tells lies and we hate you, and all that sort of stuff'.'[56] When the Hardys announced their intention to Ted Bull, an ex-serviceman and an official of the Waterside Workers' Union, he prevailed on them to let him, his wife and their several children move into the Hillard Street maisonette without the owner's knowledge. The post-war housing crisis was such that the Bull family had been living in two rooms. Bull managed to retain the tenancy, and he remembered just how hostile the neighbours were to his family. The neighbours refused to talk to them; the anti-communist feeling was very much alive in middle-class East Malvern.[57]

Hardy's children might have played some part in the decision, but it seems likely that other events were the determining factors. There were murmurs from his creditors; *Power Without Glory* was selling well, and it was not unreasonable to expect that some efforts were being made to repay loans. The divisions within the Realist Writers' Group and the loss of the *Realist Writer* had been devastating defeats for Hardy. When he had shore-leave periods in Sydney, did it beckon as a place where his talents and interests could be better promoted? It was also where the national headquarters of the CPA were located. Perhaps he felt his star had set in Melbourne, but it can only be conjectured why he made this decision.

Former CPA member Amirah Inglis has clear recollections of being given a lift by Hardy when he was taking his papers to Sydney. During the journey they heard an ABC news flash that announced a defection from the Soviet Embassy staff in Canberra. The staff member was Vladimir Petrov, whose defection was announced on 14 April 1954.[58]

Soon after, Frank, Ross and Alan drove to Sydney. They moved into a house, 'Horizon', in Powderworks Road, Narrabeen North, about twenty miles north of Sydney. Twelve-year-old Frances remained in Melbourne with her maternal grandparents, to complete the school year. Alan Hardy said his father had told a story, which was probably true, of how he won the deposit on the house at the races. He was on his way to the pictures with Ross one Saturday afternoon, when a friend pulled up and asked them to go to the races instead. In a series of bets Hardy won £1000. Ross stuffed all the notes into her large black handbag. Her parents were opposed to gambling, and when Frank announced that there was a report in the newspaper of their win, she was very upset. 'He was just kidding,' said Alan. 'It was a lovely house, a really classic 1950s with polished floors, sloping ceilings, and a bush garden.'[59]

Vic Little stayed with Frank and Ross in their Narrabeen home, and he later described it as 'a beautiful house'. Hardy had told Little how he had got the house; this was a variation of the story he had told his children. This version was that he and Ross were driving along in his old car in Flemington when they saw a mate of his running for his life, so he pulled up, and his mate said, 'Frank, can you run me to Moonee Valley Racecourse?'. 'Why?' said Hardy. 'I've got a hot tip in a race that is coming up in about half an hour.' His mate told them that the tip was straight from the owner. Hardy asked Ross how much money she had left, and she said twenty pounds. Hardy put the lot on the horse, and it duly won. Then he proceeded to back more winners, until they didn't know where to put the money. On the way home they were sitting at the traffic lights, and the bookmakers were looking over from their car, 'this is what Frank said, and it might have been one of his [stories] anyhow, and there was his wife counting all the bloody money'. Little said that that was how Frank was supposed to have got the money to buy the house.[60]

Rumours circulated in CPA circles that Hardy had financed the house with money from Moscow which had accumulated from his *Power Without Glory* royalties, to which Hardy had clear entitlements. Presumably this was organised in the same manner as when CPA functionaries attended conferences and meetings in the Soviet bloc. The practice was for money to be transferred through the Soviet Embassy in Canberra. It is understood that when writers were invited as guests of the Union of Soviet Writers, money was made available for airline tickets and travelling expenses. If a private visit was made, a writer could use accrued royalties for living and travel expenses and for a return airline ticket to Australia. In some cases prior arrangements were made to give other visiting Australians access to writers' funds to pay their expenses within the Soviet Union; on their return they would reimburse the writer in Australian currency.[61] It is impossible to verify just how these matters were negotiated, and there is no way of establishing how the Narrabeen house was financed.

The Hardy family was reunited when Frances came to Sydney at the end of the school year. On 8 February 1955 Ross gave birth to a daughter, Shirley. Rumours trickled back to Melbourne comrades that Hardy had, in Churchillian manner, built himself a tree-house where he could retreat and write. Alan and

Frances said however that a small studio in the garden, facing into the bush, had been built where their father worked. The tree-house appears to have been the figment of an over-active imagination of someone who might well have been an anxious creditor.

Hardy was no newcomer to Sydney, and he quickly became involved in local and literary affairs. In 1952 the first Sydney Realist Writers' Group had been formed, but had soon lapsed. Marjorie Pizer and Muir Holburn had invited Vera Deacon, later National Secretary of the Group, to a meeting held on 27 September 1954 to form another Sydney Realist Writers' Group. The meeting was chaired by Edgar Ross, editor of the miners' journal *Common Cause*, and Hardy outlined the proposed aims and activities of a revived Group. He attended most meetings, and fired the beginning writers to 'have a go'. At one meeting he read the early draft of a story in which he posed, among other things, that 'male mateship often took precedence over the love of a man for his wife'. 'This caused a stormy debate led by two women!' Deacon recounted how Frank had offered positive encouragement to the other writers, and if one of their number had a success, he would send a congratulatory telegram.[62]

In 1954 Hardy was invited to attend the All-Union Congress of Soviet Writers, but his application for a passport was refused. He volunteered to appear before the Royal Commission into Espionage. He hoped this would absolve him from any involvement in the Petrov affair. However, a few weeks before the date of the Congress, Hardy was informed that passports could not be issued to communists who desired to travel to Communist countries.[63]

Frank renewed his friendship with Dame Mary Gilmore. In a letter to a friend she mentioned that the ABS was giving a party on 23 August 1954 in honour of her eighty-ninth birthday, which had occurred on 16 August; 'Frank Hardy will call for me and bring me home'.[64] Gilmore's long-standing friendship with Henry Lawson was of great interest to Hardy, as he had plans for a work on Lawson.

In 1955 he failed to be elected to a position on the National Committee of the CPA. He stood as a communist candidate for the seat of Mackellar in the December 1955 Federal elections; again his candidature was unsuccessful. Frances was embarrassed. 'Walking down the street every day, I saw Vote 1 Hardy Communist Party on every single telegraph pole. Can you imagine, I'm new to the school, year seven?' However, only one school friend ever asked Frances if Hardy was her father, and this girl's brother had asked her brother, Alan. At the time Frances did not know that Alan had been affected, but, in later years, he had told her he 'was more upset than she had realised'.[65]

Alan's childhood memories of Melbourne had been happy, except when he lived in the country while his parents were overseas. There were no happy times then, he was 'terribly homesick', but he said the Boyantons were marvellous people. Whereas Frances had enjoyed living and going to school in the country. Alan remembered occasional Sunday lunches at 'Nanna' Hardy's house in Martin Street, Gardenvale. His father and brothers would play cricket in the back garden, and he was allowed to join in. He would sometimes go to the upstairs 'printery', where his mother was working on binding *Power With-*

out Glory. He recalled that there always seemed to be parties and many people at Hillard Street. He was aware that there was a rifle in the house. He had been told it was his father's gun from the war. He knew there were sailors who came to stay, but he now knows they were also bodyguards. Generally he was just living the life of a small boy, and he knew that sometimes he had to be quiet as father was working in the back room.[66]

The children had seen their maternal grandparents more often, as they came to visit them every Wednesday. Alan Hardy said this warm relationship was maintained after they moved to Sydney, as they stayed with them during the Christmas holidays at their home in a Melbourne bayside suburb. Following his father's trial, relations had become strained with the Hardy family, although Winifred Hardy had attended the court on one occasion. She died on 28 May 1958.[67] The Hardy family had a keen sense of humour. Alan thought his father and his Uncle Jim were humorous, but Uncle Gerry, in his opinion, was the funniest member of the Hardy family.[68]

By 1956 the family were well settled into the ebb and flow of life in Narrabeen. Hardy was invited to travel to Moscow and Eastern Europe. When the idea was first raised, Ross insisted he could only go if he bought the family a television set. Alan said it was probably on hire-purchase; they were only the second family in Powderworks Road to have a set, and from this stemmed 'his lifelong obsession with television'.[69]

Hardy had also received an invitation to be the guest of the Institute of Cultural Relations in Budapest. He travelled first to London, and again when he returned from Europe. During his period in Europe he met Rumanian actress Elena Arama, with whom he had an affair. It is probable that she later appeared in *But/The Dead Are Many*, in the roles of Anna and Elena Buratakov. When Little had visited Narrabeen during that year:

> Hardy was doing research for a book, or at least his wife was doing most of the researching in at the Public Library on Henry Lawson . . . she [Ross] did a hell of a lot of the research for it . . . He had got Frankie Flannery [a champion boxer] to stay with him for a fortnight . . . to get stories about the fight game . . . he [Frankie] was working down on the waterfront doing a bit of work there. He had given up fighting at the time; he was a bit punchy, but he had a tremendous vocabulary of sayings of the waterfront, not just the waterfront, but the knockabout blokes . . . rhyming slang. One expression that caught my imagination I remember—someone who was 'Sharp as a Fitzroy razor'. The razor gangs were around in the twenties.
>
> Wherever he [Hardy] used to go, he would have a little book, [it] would only be a small book. If he heard something in a pub, if he heard a good little story, he would ring it in somewhere in the future . . . He was in with a group of people, and that is how he got that story about these blokes on the garbage trucks down the pub at Narrabeen. It all happened there. It was happening at the time I was there. I heard him talking about it, and he was gathering information.[70]

In 1971 Hardy's *The Outcasts of Foolgarah* was published; if Little's recollections are accurate, then the real-life adventures and struggles of the Narrabeen 'garbos' were transformed into fiction.

The house at Narrabeen, just like the Hillard Street home in Melbourne, became a meeting place not only for left-wing writers and friends, but also for the 'Powderworks Road Transport Committee' that had been formed to obtain a permanent bus service in the district. The Honorary Secretary was Frank Hardy.[71] There is nothing to suggest that money was any more plentiful in Narrabeen than it had been in East Malvern. According to Vic Little, 'Gambling remained his first priority'.[72]

Hardy was working on short stories and *The Four-Legged Lottery* at this time. Joan Hendry, Sydney Realist Writer, used to visit the Hardy house, 'where Ross would be sitting on a stool at the kitchen bench with a little typewriter' working on one of the eleven drafts of *The Four-Legged Lottery*.[73]

During the years at Narrabeen, Hardy contributed a number of articles to the *Communist Review* on art, literature, cultural and ideological matters.[74] These articles were written from the viewpoint of the socialist realist theoretician. Hardy was obviously in favour with the CPA, as publication in the *Communist Review* was highly sought by dedicated comrades. Hardy frequently received requests to write articles for Soviet and Eastern European newspapers, journals and magazines. As copies of the *Communist Review* were sent to these countries, Hardy's inclusion would have boosted his image as a culturally and ideologically correct writer/comrade.

The divisions within the ranks of the Realist Writers and the events surrounding the birth of *Overland* were to be exacerbated when Soviet tanks rolled into Hungary on 26 October 1956 to quell the uprising for a democratically elected government. The CPA was in turmoil following the Hungarian revolution. Many CPA intellectuals and others were no longer prepared to accept the official party line that the Soviet was defending socialism, and that the US Central Intelligence Agency had organised counter-revolutionary upheavals. Hardy's political stance may be gauged by Dorothy Hewett's recollections:

> A meeting of the Realist Writers at Frank Hardy's is interrupted by a phone call from Ian Turner, member of the Victorian State Committee [CPA] and secretary of the Australasian Book Society, in Melbourne. Eric Lambert, the left-wing novelist famous for his war novel *Twenty Thousand Thieves*, is imprisoned in Hungary for demonstrating with the 'counter-revolutionaries'. What are the Party writers, and Frank Hardy in particular, going to do about it?
>
> 'Nothing,' says Frank. 'It's all bullshit. Lambert was always a lying bastard.'[75]

It was ironic that Hardy should apply the epithet of liar to his once close friend. Biographer Zoe O'Leary wrote that Lambert 'must be held responsible for much of the false information, particularly the histories which were compiled by him; but there was always a vestige of truth behind these recorded activities'.[76] So, too, did Hardy share the reputation of being an unreliable recorder. The two men were never to be reconciled, although Ross Hardy and Joyce Lambert maintained their friendship.[77]

By the late 1950s, Frank and Ross had encountered grave financial problems, and the house at Narrabeen had to be sold. Alan Hardy said they moved first to Collaroy, to 'an old-style 1920s fibro-cement beach holiday house that had an enormous living room as big as a dance-floor, but with poky bedrooms. You could step down from the verandah onto the beach'. As their fortunes declined, they moved to another house in Collaroy: 'a tiny, horrible place, on the beach again, and I had to sleep on a platform behind the couch; I didn't mind this, because I could watch television'. Before long they were obliged to move to 38 Ocean View Road, Harbord, where Alan once again had to sleep in the same room as the television set.[78] During that year, 1958, *The Four-Legged Lottery* was published.

Historian Michael Cannon in *That disreputable firm . . . the inside story of Slater & Gordon* has disclosed that:

Phone taps [by ASIO] reveal that the close relations between Hill and Hardy (whom Hill called 'son') continued for some years. [16] An intercept in November 1958 showed that Hardy consulted Hill about his new book, *The Four-Legged Lottery*, probably for advice on defamation. [17]

The following year, Hardy again approached Hill, no doubt about a proposal that Hardy should write his autobiography. The listeners reported that 'HILL is not over enthusiastic about this project', and asked Hardy to consider whether he 'should continue and complete the project as an individual'—in other words, without Party backing. [18] In 1960, Les Harsant of the Communist-controlled Australasian Book Society asked Hill for a legal opinion on Hardy's completed manuscript. [19] From the fact that Hardy was finally forced to go to T. Werner Laurie in London to publish *The Hard Way* in 1961, we can deduce that Ted Hill had turned thumbs down on what was a most illuminating manuscript. Hill and Hardy fell out, partly over Hardy's casual attitude to personal loans and gambling. Later, Ted Hill refused a request by Hardy to facilitate a visit to China.[79]

By 1960 the family had moved to Flat 4, 37 South Steyne, Manly. The entrance to the block of flats was a doorway inset between two shops, one of which was a Chinese café. The front windows of the flat overlooked the landmark Norfolk Island Pine trees, the sand and the Pacific Ocean. When Hardy had lived in Melbourne he was conservative in his dress; he wore three-piece suits, or neat sports trousers and jackets. When he became a resident of the beach areas, he had quickly adopted the dress of a 'beach bum' with shorts and comfortable shirts.[80] Manly, with its semi-tropical climate, beach, hotels, cafés, clubs, SP bookmakers, tourist shops and the bustling terminal where the ferries discharged, not only the commuters, but the crowds of excited holiday makers, gave it a cosmopolitan air. This suited Hardy's temperament far better than ordinary suburban living, and he soon became an identity, Manly's own writer-in-residence. Number 37 South Steyne was to be the last place in which Frank, Ross and the children lived together as a family.

Chapter Twelve

THE TURBULENT SIXTIES

WHEN FRANK HARDY moved to Manly, *The Four-Legged Lottery* had only recently been published. The novel was mainly ignored by the critics, or given a lukewarm reception.[1] Nor did it please the CPA. The novel revealed Hardy's understanding of the forces that drive a gambler, but the intrusive political rhetoric interspersed in the text did little to enhance it. As a socialist-realist writer, Hardy was motivated either by conviction, or by his desire for the approval of the CPA, or both. But when he wrote from his own knowledge, as in chapter eight, the novel becomes compelling.[2] This chapter later appeared in *Legends From Benson's Valley* under the title 'The Gambler'. When Hardy wrote *Up the Garbos*, 'He gave it to the party to read and O.K. They were scathing in their criticism that he had "portrayed the worker in a bad light". Hardy accepted the criticism and shelved the book.'[3]

Ross accepted a temporary full-time job as a stenographer with the Amalgamated Engineering Union; she became a permanent staff member for about twenty years until her death. She continued to act as Frank's secretary; her workload grew as the volume of local and international correspondence increased, and there was a constant backlog of manuscripts.[4] Realist writer Vera Deacon recalled how Ross thought one of the best things about the job, apart from earning money to keep her family, was that it enabled her to type Frank's manuscripts during her lunch hour. Deacon often wondered how this undernourished-looking, birdlike woman coped with all the demands made upon her. Deacon had first met Ross when she visited Sydney with Frank late in 1953, and they stayed overnight at her home. Deacon greatly admired Ross Hardy's loyalty to Frank and her children. She believes that Ross's huge contribution to Frank's work and to *Power Without Glory* in particular, has never been properly acknowledged.[5]

Hardy had been appointed advertising manager for the *Maritime Worker* and the *Firefighter* union journals, on a commission basis. He was working on *Legends from Benson's Valley. The Hard Way* was in progress, and extracts had been published in the weekly publication *Nation*. He was the Vice-President of the Fellowship of Australian Writers. It is is not clear why he decided to go to sea again. Certainly he was being pursued for payment of debts that dated back to his trial. Norman Jury, a CPA member and State Electricity Commission linesman in Melbourne, had lent Frank a large sum of money in 1950–51. Ten years later, long after Jury's retirement, Hardy still owed him about £600. Jury had requested payment on several occasions, but he was always assured that the debt would be settled when Hardy's next book was published. Sometimes he received £10 or £15 on account. It is believed that he died before the debt was fully redeemed.[6] Frank had left many debts behind in Melbourne, but he had made new friends and contacts, some of whom were prepared to advance him money. Did he hope to gain writing time, or did his innate restlessness compel him to seek a change of scene?

Whatever his reasons, he signed on in Port Kembla as a crew attendant on the SS *River Fitzroy* on 11 November 1960; he was discharged in Melbourne on 8 December 1960. Six months later Hardy was engaged in Port Kembla as a crew attendant, this time on the SS *Daylesford* on 26 July 1961, and thirteen days later he was discharged in the same port. That was the last occasion that Hardy went to sea. Hardy had served 155 days, including ten days embarking and arriving in ports, between 1953 and 1961.[7]

While Hardy was completing *The Hard Way*, the Amending Crimes Bill was before the Federal Parliament. A procedural section indicated that literary and journalistic works could come within the provisions of the Bill. Writers who did not wish to follow conventional ideas might well come under the surveillance of the judiciary. Journalists and thirty leading authors signed a petition demanding withdrawal of the Bill. Frank was among the signatories.

When *The Hard Way* was published it received a mixed reception, as disclosed by some reviews.[8] In August 1961 Hardy made a three-State tour to promote his new book.[9]

Clement Semmler, who became Hardy's advocate and friend, recalled their first meeting:

We first met in the Adams Marble Bar in Pitt Street, Sydney. I think it was Cyril Pearl who introduced us, or it may have been George Finey. Hardy, lean, quizzical and carelessly dressed, radiated warmth and good-natured fellowship to which it was impossible not to respond instantly. I don't remember at this distance much of what we talked about except that he knew I was head of ABC television and asked me if I was interested in 'a bloody good idea' for our programs. 'Try me,' I replied.[10]

This led to the production of several television series based on Hardy's creation *Billy Borker*, with actor Peter Carver in the title role. Semmler sent Hardy to Western Australia to 'satisfy himself about the cast and production of the first few episodes and to give advice where necessary. From what I heard later, he practically ran the show'. There were moves afoot to have the first series banned because Hardy was a communist. Semmler believed that 'McCarthy was surely riding again . . . I'm glad to say there was no more of this nonsense'. The first of several successful series appeared in 1964. These were followed by the publication of *The Yarns of Billy Borker* introduced by Semmler,[11] and a sequel, *Billy Borker Yarns Again*.

It might have been assumed that Hardy's fortunes had improved; in addition to the *Borker* television series, *The Four-Legged Lottery* and *The Hard Way* had been published in Britain, Australia and Eastern Europe. By this time *Power Without Glory* had appeared in fourteen languages. Whatever his financial successes and rewards, Hardy's gambling gave him an insatiable thirst for more and more money which disappeared into the bookmakers' bags, or the gambling clubs' coffers. He would fly to Melbourne to attend race meetings.[12] On occasions Hardy would meet Bob Hawke at the races, and they would later adjourn to the John Curtin Hotel in Carlton. This friendship was not to endure after Hawke became Prime Minister. Hardy believed that Hawke had turned his back on labour principles.[13]

Credit must be given to Frank Hardy for his ability to create the right impression, and to adapt to the company in which he found himself. Clement Semmler said that 'Frank always maintained that gambling among working men wasn't so much a vice as a desperate attempt, with all other avenues denied them, "to make a few bob". We were both, in fact, what was then known as "five-bob punters" and tipped each other winners and losers'.[14]

Hardy had claimed to Semmler that 'he had been a "social leper" . . . after he wrote *Power Without Glory*'.[15] Could this be interpreted as a bid to gain his friend's sympathy? Semmler was a loyal friend who considered Hardy to be 'one of the most gentle, generous and understanding of men, in all the time I have known him, showed bitter anger only once and that was on a matter arising from this'.[16] Hardy's first literary grant had been vetoed. Many Australians had helped Hardy, and they held him in great esteem. During his five known visits to the Soviet Union and Eastern Europe between 1951 and 1968, he had gained a high profile, and his work had a wide readership. His stories were used for radio and television programs. His birthdays were marked by congratulatory cables from the Union of Soviet Writers, other organisations and prominent individuals. He was treated with deference as the working-class Australian writer who had been tried for criminal libel by the capitalist courts. He also spent time in Britain on each occasion that he travelled during the 1950s and 1960s. There he had found acceptance and made valuable contacts with members of the British aristocracy who became friends. He met and became part of a circle of writers, journalists, artists, publishers, businessmen and leading and influential members of the Communist Party of Great Britain. He became a member of several London gambling clubs, among them the Playboy Club. Rather than cast himself in the role of a 'social leper', might not Hardy have marvelled how he had been warmly embraced by such diverse groups of people?

There were two known occasions when Hardy might have felt excluded by his contemporaries. Fellow writers Clem Christesen and John Morrison recalled how they had, on different occasions, been billeted to share a room with Frank Hardy. His drinking and coarse behaviour was such that they requested transfers to other rooms. Christesen also recalled how he had attended the launch of *The Hard Way*; Frank had failed to give any acknowledgement to the prominent role that he had played in the Frank Hardy Defence Committee.[17]

Following the launch of *The Hard Way* in 1961, Hardy's play *Black Diamonds* was produced for Czech television. He was invited to the Soviet Union for six months as a guest of the Union of Soviet Writers. He was also appointed as a delegate for the New South Wales Peace Committee for International Co-operation and Disarmament to attend the World Peace Congress in Moscow in July 1962. During his absence Hardy was awarded equal second prize for a story, 'The New Policeman', submitted for the 1962 Dame Mary Gilmore Awards.[18] On this occasion in 1962–63, he spent eight months in the Soviet Union and Eastern Europe. It was during this period that he suffered a breakdown and spent a prolonged period in a sanatorium. Realist Writer Ali Verrills said that Hardy had later confided in her about his illness. She was very sympathetic to him, and continued to assist and give him support, even when he fell out of favour with some Realist Writers over the alleged misappropriations of funds.[19] Hardy 'organised some sort of deal' with Air India for Ross, Alan and Shirley to travel via India to join him. Frances, who was studying at that time, remained in Manly. When they arrived, Alan was seriously ill with an infection contracted en route, and he spent some days in a Moscow hospital. Although of short duration, the family's visit was successful. For the teen-age Alan it was a memorable experience.[20]

Hardy later travelled to London, where he was able to meet old friends and make new contacts, before returning to Australia in March 1963. He resumed his many activities in Sydney. He was involved with a number of literary groups, and he had recently joined the newly formed Society of Authors. He became an identity in the War Memorial, Anglers', Amateur Fishermen's and the Pipe Smokers' Clubs in Manly. During that year he appeared on three television programs including an ABV2 social comment series 'Four Corners'. *Legends from Benson's Valley* was published in Britain; not only did it find an admiring audience among Hardy devotees, but it received thoughtful reviews; Nancy Cato wrote in the *Australian Book Review*, 'These stories are in the Henry Lawson tradition. A delightful wry humour pervades them, the dialogue is laconic, blasphemous, moving by turns; and under all is a wistful sorrow for the human lot, for women betrayed, men without work, the despair of old age'.[21]

In *Overland*, David Forrest wrote that he did not believe that Hardy wrote in the Lawson tradition, but he did concede that 'Since my earlier readings of Frank Hardy, something significant has happened. It is as though a man has begun to be aware of the full resources of his intellect, and begun to put them to use'.[22]

In 1972 an unexpurgated version of the *Legends* was published under the title *It's Moments Like These*, when, according to a *National Times* reviewer, 'Frank Hardy reveals himself as the only true Australian humorist today writing in the tradition of Henry Lawson'. In 1963 the uncensored series of stories were 'considered too offensive for our delicate Antipodean sensibilities'.[23]

Meanwhile, an event occurred that was to have far-reaching effects on all Australian communists. From its inception in 1920 the CPA had suffered internal power struggles. The exodus of many intellectuals and other party members, either by resignation or expulsion, following the disclosures at the Communist Party of the Soviet Union's Twentieth Congress in 1956 and the Soviet Union's invasion of Hungary, had exacerbated the existing dissension within the CPA. By 1962, with the development of the Sino-Soviet split, the CPA was divided into two factions: those who supported the official party line behind the Soviet Union, and those who supported a pro-Chinese group led by lawyer Ted Hill, once 'described as "a man who could make a crowbar sweat"'.[24] Hill had built a powerful base in Victoria. The Hill group numbered about a quarter of the membership, but it had only sixteen delegates at the State Conference which took place in Melbourne in April 1963. Following bitter debate the inevitable happened, and the Victorian CPA split, 146 delegates for, and 16 against, the party line. It was not long before 'about two hundred members either left or were expelled from the CPA in Victoria'. Soon after, Hill and his supporters formed their own party, the Communist Party of Australia (M–L).[25]

There is little doubt that Hardy had been disturbed by the events occurring in the Soviet Union and China, and the schisms developing in the CPA, long before he went overseas in 1962. International and CPA politics aside, it is certain that he was chafing under the CPA yoke. After the split, it is unlikely that Hardy ever again submitted his manuscripts to the CPA leadership. He had chosen not to follow his former mentor, Hill, into the CPA (M–L). It cannot be determined whether his decision was based on an ideological stance, or because of his personal, publishing and financial links in Eastern Europe. But in 1964 'at a party congress Frank Hardy was criticising the tardiness of Australian CPA leaders in attacking the "China deviation"'.[26] A Peace Congress was held in Sydney in October 1964; among the delegates was a contingent from the Soviet Union. Given the CPA Sino-Soviet split, it is certain that Hardy's participation and influence in matters literary and political was carefully observed by the Soviet delegation.

Soon after, Hardy was invited by the University Extension of the University of New England in Armidale, to participate in one of the first seminars held on Australian literature in January 1965. Among others present were Max Harris, David Forrest (David Denholm), Judith Wright, Colin Roderick, John Thompson, H. W. (Pip) Piper, Derek Whitelock, Lloyd O'Neil, Andrew Fabinyi and Clement Semmler. 'Frank, not at all awed by this company, gave one of the most forthright papers of all, "Environment and Ideology in Australian Literature", in which he pointed the way in which his own writing would go.'[27] Hardy's contribution was significant; he had publicly acknowledged that the ideology he had supported for so long was not without flaws. It marked a softening of his stance since his earlier 'hardline' articles in the *Communist Review*.

In early 1965 Hardy made a brief trip to New Zealand to gather material and make contacts with publishers. In May he attended the Berlin–Weimar

Writers' Conference at the invitation of Walter Kaufmann, former Realist Writer and friend.[28] Realist Writer Bill Wannan was also a member of the Australian delegation. His association with Hardy pre-dated *Power Without Glory*; in fact he had read the manuscript and Frank had expressed his appreciation of his help and advice. Wannan had suggested a possible title, *Profits Without Honour*. He had greatly admired Hardy's talents as a raconteur. Hardy could be a congenial companion, but the ever-present need for money tended to overshadow every aspect of his life. Wannan had been aware that Hardy tended to be anti-Semitic, but this came to a head during the Conference. German writer Stefan Heym had travelled from the USA to attend. One evening he invited a number of the Australian writers to a cabaret where his wife Gertrude, the chief editor of the Seven Seas Publishing House, and his niece awaited them. Only Wannan and Clem Christesen accepted. Heym was in poor standing as some of his books had been published outside East Germany. In an aside, Hardy complained about 'this Jew bastard writer, Stefan Heym'. This was a turning point for Wannan; he felt he had to break his connections with Hardy.[29]

Hardy also visited other cities in the German Democratic Republic. He later spent time in the Soviet Union, and he visited Romania.

Soon after his return to Sydney, his friend and comrade Paul Mortier had died.

In January 1966, Frank's daughter, Frances, was married. After the Adelaide Festival of Arts, Hardy accompanied the Russian poet Yevgeny Yevtushenko, who was reading his poems in Adelaide, Melbourne and Sydney. Hardy had first met the poet in Moscow during the 1950s.[30]

Later that year Hardy embarked on a journey, a personal quest, but the purpose of his mission changed, as he became embroiled in a series of events that were, perhaps, to be the most emotionally and personally rewarding ever for him. He had told his family and friends that he intended to travel around Australia, to gain personal insight and seek topics for his future work. He went out to the highway and picked up a truck. Hardy sat up huddled in a blanket; but he had forgotten that he could not sleep without tablets. As he travelled the problems which had seemed insurmountable the day before no longer concerned him. When he arrived in Bourke in western New South Wales, he thought of Henry Lawson and recalled the years he had spent researching him. Now there was nothing but doubt.[31]

Hardy returned to Sydney within three weeks, but not for long, as he had promised to help the Gurindji people in their fight for decent wages, land and justice. He went to Wave Hill Station in the Northern Territory which was held by the British Vestey Company under a long lease. He was based at Wattie Creek, near Wave Hill, for some months, and he travelled interstate and within the Territory speaking on behalf of the Gurindji people. In February 1967 Hardy was moving around Northern Queensland en route to Darwin. At Frewena he met up with an old Melbourne friend, Fred Thompson, who was then the North Queensland and the Territory Organiser for the Amalgamated Engineering Union. Fred had warm memories of that meeting, and of Hardy's work on behalf of the Gurindji. 'Hardy was the right man in the right place!'[32] Hardy was a formidable advocate for the Gurindji people in particular, and Aborigines in general. He was firmly on the side of the Aborigines; he understood what it was like to belong to a marginalised minority. He was a public figure who knew how to engage the media, and he was not averse to challenging the law.

Hardy competed in the Australian Yarn Spinning Competition, held in Darwin in April 1967 against the reigning champion, Tall Tales Tex Tyrell, and deposed him; he was to retain the title until 1991. The publication of the *The Great Australian Lover* in 1967 was overshadowed by Hardy's involvement with the Gurindji.[33] Although it received little attention from the critics, it warranted a reprint in 1972.

Hardy's account of the Aborigines' struggles, *The Unlucky Australians*, was delayed until 1968 because of threatened legal action. This work was editor Ann Godden's first editorial job in Australia after her arrival from Britain. She has clear recollections of the Saturday morning conferences with Hardy and a lawyer. When they decided that something must be omitted, Frank would argue at length, 'But it's true'. As the time for the first race grew close, Hardy's truculence would turn to anxiety, and he would reluctantly concede. However, on some occasions, he did miss the first race. Godden said she was very proud to have been associated with *The Unlucky Australians*.[34] Reviewers were, almost without exception, prepared to ignore the rough edges and the lack of literary style; they acknowledged the immediacy of the work. No one doubted its importance. There were those who accused Hardy of using the campaign as a publicity stunt for himself, while others claimed that he did not carry out the campaign as they might have wished. He was damned if he did, and damned if he didn't. The Gurindji people valued Hardy's involvement; he was a superb publicist, and he helped focus attention on the plight of the Aborigines. The final word on this episode in Hardy's life is best summed up by one reviewer: 'Hardy's book, which will infuriate many people, and perhaps shame others, may help towards achieving a balance before it is too late'.[35]

After his return to Sydney in 1967, he attended the 21st National Congress of the CPA when the new 'soft' Italian Communist Party line was formally endorsed. This term referred to events which had taken place earlier. In 1963 Palmiro Togliatti, the General Secretary of the Italian Communist Party, was the co-author of *Testimonanze*, a work of joint Catholic–Communist scholarship. In April 1965 the Paulus Gesellschaft, a strong group of German Catholics, arranged a conference in Salzburg on the theme 'Marxists and Christians Today'. Soviet periodicals reported on the conference. Discussions continued between the Euro-Communist parties and the Catholic Church.[36]

CPA functionary Paul Mortier had long been critical of Stalinism following the events of the Twentieth Congress and his visit to the Soviet Union in 1956. In the 1960s he was further disillusioned when he was directed that he involve himself in a purge of dissident CPA intellectuals. After Mortier left the employ of the CPA in 1964, he engaged in correspondence with a Melbourne Catholic priest, Father George Maltby, about the dialogues taking place in Europe. It is significant and poignant that two years after Mortier's death the CPA formally endorsed the 'soft' Euro-Communist line.

It was interesting that Hardy was still seeking election to the Central Committee of the CPA in 1967. The following year he wrote the 'Stalin's Heirs' series denouncing the Soviet Union, and he expressed how long he had been critical of its policies. He was already engaged on the early work for *But The Dead Are Many*. But Hardy was again passed over for the Central Committee [later the National Committee], whereas fellow-writer Judah Waten was elected. Had the word been 'passed around' that Hardy was not acceptable, as it had been at the 1955 election? The reason given by a party leader then was that 'When he starts work again on the trilogy (of which *Power Without Glory* was the first), when he will do party work, then there will be a place for him on the Central Committee'.[37]

If Hardy felt any bitterness about the defeat, he did not make it public. The CPA continued to splinter; whether the combatants were aware that they were part of, and witnessing the death throes of the CPA, cannot be determined.

Hill had dedicated his energy to the destruction of Santamaria's Movement and the influence of the Catholic Church in the Victorian ALP, and to the promotion and production of *Power Without Glory*. Santamaria said, 'The Communists had a perfect understanding of the explosive potential of anti-Catholic sectarianism'. He had been and remained a bitter opponent of communism. Hill and Santamaria had been contemporaries at the University of Melbourne in the 1930s. It is not suggested that the two were 'enemies today and bedfellows tomorrow', but the capriciousness of political figures can best be illustrated by an extraordinary event that Santamaria recorded in his 1997 *Memoir*:

> Amusingly, many years later, when Hill had left the CPA, to head the breakaway pro-Chinese Communist Party, we met at lunch at the home of a mutual friend. Hill, now violently anti-Soviet, asked me to 'use my influence' to warn the Catholic Church against its policy of détente with the Soviet Union, which the latter would use only to confound it. I replied that it was he who should actually give the warning to the Catholic authorities, since he would have more influence with them than I would.[38]

Could it have been envisaged, when the CPA leadership and Frank Hardy were immersed in producing *Power Without Glory*, that such a meeting could have taken place, quite apart from Hill's request to his former adversary?

Following Hardy's defeat at the 21st Congress, despite his ties to the accepted CPA line, he was torn between old allegiances and new. In March 1968 he attended the Adelaide Festival of Arts, where he was his usual controversial and colourful self. He was increasingly in demand as a television and radio performer, and as an after-dinner speaker. He often mentioned his planned major work on the life of Henry Lawson, and he had other writing projects either under way or proposed. He maintained a hectic pace, compounded by his involvement in the Vietnam War protest movement, his political and social life, and his ongoing commitment to the Aborigines.

Following a meeting in Sydney in 1968 when Hardy had spoken about the strike of the Gurindji people, a man passed in a cheque for $300. The man

was eye-surgeon Fred Hollows. The following week a committee member telephoned Hollows to ask if he would examine two Gurindji men who had eye
trouble.[39] 'Hollows obliged, and thus began a quarter-century odyssey to save
the sight of more than 30 000 Aborigines and countless Third World people
who could not have afforded the necessary surgery.'[40] Hollows and Hardy
became friends, and for a time Hardy lived with the Hollows family.

As Hardy acquired a new public image, he became increasingly attractive
to women. Frances was aware of the humiliation and hurt suffered by her
mother. Hardy would direct Ross to the kitchen to prepare refreshments for
guests whom he considered intellectually superior to his wife. He was wont to
tell Ross how he loved young women with soft skins.[41]

How did Hardy view women? Hardy's descriptions of women, either in
derogatory or patronising sexist language, are peppered throughout his work.
He did not describe his male characters in the same vein. John Docker, in his
study of *But The Dead Are Many*, believed that 'In general in the novel, the
female characters are no more than occasional presences, figures who might
possess clues to the psychology and opinions of the men, but no personalities
in their own right'.[42]

What did attract women to Frank Hardy? Perhaps the words of a woman
who was neither wife nor lover best describe the initial impact that drew
admiring women to him, and also the reason why nearly all his relationships
with women failed:

> I sat in an armchair in the corner and listened. His capacity as a raconteur
> was unrivalled. We did not know the word then, but he had charisma. He
> revelled in his own colourful turn of phrase, his hyperbole, his humour.
> After a time the fascination began to wane, and with the years I found it
> harder to distinguish truth from the embroideries that make a good story
> hilarious.[43]

Frances and her father had a troubled relationship, and she never admitted he was her father if she could avoid it. She was fastidious and offended by
his personal habits, particularly at the table. On the few occasions she visited
him with her two sons, she was aware that he found them irritating. He
expected her to send the two small boys across the road to the beach to play
unattended, and he was piqued by her refusal. He never displayed any interest
in his grandsons, nor sent them a birthday or a Christmas gift. As she grew
older, Frances accepted him as he was, and no longer felt hatred for him. But
her sympathy for her mother, for the life she had endured, did not diminish.
She said her father never talked about her, but he was proud of having a
son, and his youngest child, Shirley, enjoyed quite a different relationship
with him.[44]

Alan remembered how he had not realised that they were poor until the
teachers called him in to provide school shoes, as he always wore sand-shoes.
Alan knew they had Morning Coffee biscuits, never chocolate biscuits, and
there was a constant shortage of money. This did not concern him, but he was

embarrassed by the teachers' intervention. He said his parents were easy-going with them, and there were very few restrictions. He had a warm attachment to his mother. 'It must have been hell for my mother, Frank was so unreliable, when he had money he gambled it. None of us kids gamble.' Alan and Frank shared a mutual interest in cricket and football. They occasionally attended matches, which were heightened by Frank's larrikin commentaries. They also spent many hours talking about politics, literature, history, the arts, television, movies and life in general. Following Alan's marriage he returned to Sydney, when he spent 'an enthralling few hours while Frank talked out the agonies he was having writing the very personal *But The Dead Are Many*. We remained that close—despite long absences from each other—until his death. For me it was a very positive experience being Frank Hardy's son'.[45] Shirley said her father had acted more like a brother than a father, and when she brought her friends home from school, he did not object if they smoked.[46]

How had Ross coped with Hardy's constant absences? After Frances's marriage and Alan's departure to Melbourne, she was alone with Shirley. Despite the years of Frank's neglect, gambling, drinking, overwork and infidelity, real or suspected, Ross stayed with the marriage. Events in Europe determined Hardy's next departure. After the freedom uprising and the tumult surrounding the Prague Spring, Soviet tanks and troops, and the armed forces of four other Eastern European countries, crossed the Czech border on 21 August 1968. Soon after Hardy went to Britain and then to Moscow, where he met Yevtushenko. He talked to his friends and acquaintances about the Czech situation. In mid-October he travelled to Prague to talk to contacts and assess the situation.

Soon after Hardy's return to London the first of his four articles were published in the London *Sunday Times* in early November over a four-week period under the banner 'Stalin's Heirs'. Adrian Deamer, editor of the *Australian* newspaper, had discussed, or arranged a similar mission with Hardy, and he was surprised that the articles appeared in London.[47] The series was reprinted in Australia in the *Bulletin*; the first article appeared in the 11 January 1969 edition.[48] Hardy explained his defection from Soviet Communism. He mentioned his first visit to Moscow in 1951, when he was seduced, as a generation of young idealists were, by the apparent vision of socialism, after which he had written *Journey Into The Future*. After he spent eight months in 1962–63 travelling in the USSR, he then decided to write a more honest account than in his earlier work. He also noted that the Soviet bureaucracy was little different to the elite in the American system.[49]

In 1962 Yevtushenko had written a poem, 'The Heirs of Stalin', which was published, at the insistence of Premier Khrushchev, in *Pravda*.[50] When Hardy chose the title 'Stalin's Heirs' for his articles, it was probably a tribute to his friend's poem. When Hardy returned to London from Eastern Europe, he became campaign director for Yevtushenko who had won the 'students' candidate' ballot in the election of the Oxford Professor of Poetry. Hardy had written an article in the London *Times* defending the poet against political attacks.[51]

On 15 November 1968 the Sydney *Daily Mirror* reported that London-based Australians, led by the left-wing author, Frank Hardy, would picket the London offices of the giant cattle company Vesteys, on behalf of Australian Aborigines' Land Rights.[52] Before his return to Australia Hardy flew to New York, where he met the dramatist Arthur Miller in his apartment in the Chelsea Hotel in Greenwich Village. They telephoned Yevtushenko and discussed political events.[53] Hardy's visa had been restricted to a short stay in New York only.[54]

Hardy's *Sunday Times* articles triggered an avalanche of newspaper and journal responses. The *Soviet News Bulletin* launched a stinging attack on its erstwhile friend, Frank Hardy:

> Thus it transpires that Hardy simply hoodwinked the *Rudo Pravo* correspondent in Prague, and his interlocutors in Moscow, when he said that he was getting the feel of the 'atmosphere' for his future novel. The writer undertook a different, a specific mission, and judging by all things, he has pleased those who had sent him.[55]

The Australian press became involved in the debate within the CPA. According to Sam Lipski in the *Australian*, 'The dispute is really about what sort of a party the CPA should be—an "independent" party, or an appendage of Moscow'. The feeling between the different factions was fuelled by Hardy's articles, and passions ran high. 'Hardy's old union, the Seamen's Union, led by E. V. Elliott, passed a resolution condemning his "false and vicious anti-Soviet articles"'.[56] Three CPA branches moved a resolution to expel Hardy at the National Committee in Sydney on 25–27 January 1969,[57] but there was little support, and he retained his membership. Newspapers had reported Hardy's possible expulsion and the result of the move.[58]

Hardy lost friends over his denunciation of Stalinism, and he forfeited royalties from the Soviet Union and the Eastern European countries. The Soviet Union announced that he would not be issued with a visa.[59] It had taken several visits over seventeen years for Hardy to acknowledge that he had ignored the warning signs, while others, who were not blinkered by party allegiance, had expressed serious concerns. Hardy had not mentioned his visit to Pankrats Prison in Czechoslovakia in October 1951, nor the appalling things he had observed, or that, over the years, he had been haunted by the experience, until his 'Stalin's Heirs' articles in November 1968. His reason was that he had been so involved with Stalinism, that it would have been anticommunist to have acted otherwise.[60] Hardy's tardiness was to be condemned, but it was not unusual. Leading members of the CPA had visited the Soviet Union before World War II; some were aware of disturbing happenings. CPA leaders Audrey and Jack Blake had studied in the Soviet Union in 1937. They lived in the Lux Hotel in Moscow, the headquarters of the Comintern and KIM—the Young Communist International. They were told not to mix with Russians. Soon after, Blake told his wife that 'Brigadirov's been taken. His room is sealed. It seems he's an agent'. 'The sealed doors became more frequent . . . our corridor became strangely deserted and the lead seal would appear outside another apartment.'

They never saw anyone taken, nor did they know that Soviet people were being put into camps, and some were foreign communists. 'We didn't read the critics of the USSR',[61] and 'yet the papers of the time were dominated by the trials of the Old Bolsheviks . . . Jack Blake's memories have a similar quality . . . he was one of the few Australians to learn Russian and undoubtedly appreciated the nightmare quality of the purges'. When Blake 'returned to Australia he cited the courtroom confessions of the Old Bolsheviks as conclusive evidence of their guilt'.[62] The Blakes did not deviate from the official CPA line for almost another two decades, and CPA functionaries trod a well-worn path to Moscow in the post-war years. If they had doubts, there were few, if any, disclosures to alert rank and file Australian comrades that all was not well in the Soviet Union and Eastern Europe.

In March 1969 the Minister for Immigration, Mr Billy Snedden, refused to confirm or deny that an advisory committee to the Commonwealth Literary Fund had recommended that a $3000 literary fellowship be awarded to Frank Hardy.[63] This raised a furore in the press and in some literary circles. Tom Uren, ALP Federal Member, asked a question in the House. 'Did the minister (Mr. Snedden) . . . veto the recommendation? . . . If so what was the reason or reasons, for refusing Mr. Hardy the grant?' Mr. Snedden said the committee's recommendations were confidential.[64] In August Hardy was awarded a $2000 literature grant from the NSW Advisory Committee on Cultural Grants.[65]

Late in 1969 Hardy was invited to attend the 1970 Adelaide Festival of Arts. The sixties had been a turbulent decade of world-wide social upheaval and unrest. The conflict in Vietnam had sparked reactions that could not have been anticipated in 1960. Frank Hardy had been part of the winds of change, and he had engaged in a number of struggles, notably with the Gurindji people. He had defected from Soviet Communism and survived the move to expel him from the CPA. Hardy had had a number of works published and won literary prizes, and he had been awarded a NSW literature grant. His stories had been televised, and he had become known to radio listeners and television viewers. Frank Hardy had a changed public profile. What did the new decade have in store for him?

Chapter Thirteen

BETRAYALS

FRANK HARDY'S major role in the struggles of Aboriginal people was over, but he remained involved in the campaign to ensure justice for them. He spoke at meetings in Sydney to rally support for their claims. In 1970 Eva Jago, a talented pianist, Jewish and the divorced young mother of three children, attended one such meeting in a private home. She had been unaware of the plight of Aboriginal people in the outback, but she knew of the appalling conditions in which they lived in Sydney. She spoke to writer–activist Faith Bandler after the meeting, offering to assist the Gurindji Committee in their work. This was her first meeting with Frank Hardy, whose work she had never read. They both lived on the North Shore, and she drove Hardy home to Manly.[1]

Jago started work with Hardy in a voluntary capacity; she did the typing and other work for the Gurindji Committee. Jago worked in Hardy's flat in Manly. She seldom met Ross, who had generally gone to work before she arrived, and Jago left early in the afternoon to be home when her children finished school. The women's paths rarely crossed. Jago became aware that Ross and Frank were experiencing difficulties. Jago knew that they lived in different rooms, but that there were times when Frank insisted on his 'conjugal rights', as he felt he had an entitlement.[2] The difficulties might have arisen as a result of Ross's hostility to Jago's presence.

Some time later, it was decided that the family would move. Hardy found a more suitable flat in Manly, and he arranged to shift the family's possessions. Frances said that Ross and Shirley did move, and her mother had believed that Frank was going to live with them. He kept stalling; he had to sort out his papers, or there was some other reason. He had a flow of excuses as to why he had not terminated the flat. 'He never came, he just never came.' After thirty years of marriage Ross was rejected in a most humiliating and cruel way. Hardy had dealt a mortal blow to what little self-esteem Ross had left. They were never divorced. Frances said her mother was very bitter about her husband's treatment.[3] Shirley stayed with her mother for a time, before leaving to live with a friend.[4]

Jago and Hardy had a stormy relationship. She maintained her home with her children in Killara, and Hardy remained in Manly. He would occasionally spend a weeknight or a weekend at her home. When she reflected on that first meeting, she could see why she was drawn to him. 'I was a pianist, so the creative personality appealed to me, whether it was a writer, a graphic artist, a sculptor or anything else. I loved first the absolute opposite to what I was not —vulgar, larrikin and bigoted.' Jago was cultured, intellectual, creative, physically attractive and twenty years Hardy's junior. She became his secretary and personal assistant. Their time together was when Hardy's career was in the ascendancy. He appeared in the very successful 'Would You Believe?' television series, and he became a frequent television and broadcasting panelist. He was flattered by the nature and the number of requests for him to speak at public and private functions. Conversely, there was a conflict, as he had played the role of the shunned writer for so long. He told Jago to advise the enquirers, as a deterrent, that his fee was a thousand dollars. However, individuals and organisations were happy to pay the fee. On one occasion, Frank was the guest speaker at a Sydney University function. It was a black tie occasion, but Hardy compromised only to the extent that Jago bought him a black ribbon for his collar. Jago felt it was fortunate that she was seated between Hardy and Chancellor Sir Hermann Black, because Hardy remained resolutely in his seat during the Loyal Toast.[5]

Jago met interesting people with Hardy: communist journalist Wilfred Burchett, Yevtushenko, writers, academics, poets, journalists, trade union leaders, artists and other prominent people. They had meals with Bob Hawke on several occasions in Sydney, and once they flew to Melbourne to dine with him. Bob was then President of the Australian Council of Trade Unions. They lunched with Hazel and Bob Hawke on one occasion at Doyle's Restaurant at Watson's Bay. Hardy could be a stimulating companion, and there was an ongoing momentum to life with him. There was always some exhilarating experience just around the corner. She discovered that the left-wing offered a rich cultural life to those who sought it.[6]

Hardy, too, gained access to another life. He was invited by Jago's family to be their guest; he was included in close family gatherings and celebrations. If he had been drinking, he was likely to make anti-Semitic jokes or remarks. If Jago voiced her disapproval, Hardy would say that he was not anti-Semitic, he was anti the State of Israel, which was not the same thing. At first, she conceded that there probably was a difference. But she grew increasingly uneasy when she was in the presence of her friends; she felt she was jeopardising her reputation. Hardy was mostly cantankerous, but when he was drinking it grew worse, and his rudeness and anti-Semitism emerged in a most unpleasant fashion. At other times, he could be wonderful company.[7]

The Outcasts of Foolgarah was published in 1971. One reviewer said that despite its weaknesses of length, unevenness in quality and tone, it was 'Thoroughly scurrilous, possibly libellous, defamatory and blasphemous . . . marvellously funny at its rude, crude best . . . [it] promises to be the publishing event of the year'.[8] Liberal Senator Magnus Cormack rebuked Labor Senator Poke for 'giving the book publicity' by asking a question as to whether the characters were clearly identifiable as members of the Government.[9] The novel attracted attention, and Hardy was interviewed on a Melbourne talkback radio program when he told the listeners that he disliked 'hardline' communists nearly as much as he disliked 'hardline' reactionaries.[10]

British actor James Mason contacted Hardy early in 1972. He spoke to Jago on the telephone. Mason's wife, Clarissa, had just read *The Four-Legged Lottery*, and they wanted to congratulate Hardy, who was extremely flattered; he probably over-estimated what the Masons had in mind. Jago was aware that Hardy was wont to do this when he met people whom he admired. He became deeply involved with plans to make a film with Mason as the star. He indicated his willingness to go to the South of France where Mason was about to make a film. In September Hardy arrived at the Nice airport where the Masons met him. They had made a booking for him in St Paul de Vence at the Colombe d'Or hotel. Actors Simone Signoret and Yves Montand had an apartment in the hotel, where they mostly lived. Hardy was exhilarated; he met the rich and famous, and extravagant plans for a film were discussed. When Hardy returned to Sydney he made premature announcements to the press; this irritated Mason. Before long, he and Hardy were communicating about their business arrangements via lawyers. There were some negotiations later, but nothing ever eventuated.[11]

In October 1972 the Commonwealth Literary Fund awarded Hardy a $4000 fellowship for six months to work on his planned book on Henry Lawson; this was extended for a further six months in 1973.[12] Hardy had received a substantial advance from the Bodley Head publishers in London; they were pressing him to submit his manuscript for *But The Dead Are Many*. Hardy decided that he would go to London with Jago, where he might find the solitude and atmosphere to complete the novel. They first stayed in a flat belonging to Murray Sayle, a journalist on the London *Sunday Times*. They hired a typewriter, but little work was done. There was a lot of talking, and a lot of fighting; Hardy took Jago's passport to prevent her from leaving. It was one of their many bad periods. After Sayle returned, they moved into another flat, but the situation did not improve. When they had tickets to the theatre or a concert, Jago would often go alone. It was at the time of the Yom Kippur War, and Hardy and Jago attended a benefit concert. Isaac Stern and two other prominent artists were on the stage. Stern was giving an impassioned speech about the situation in Israel; he voiced his concern about bombs flying and children being hurt. Hardy stood up and shouted at the top of his voice, 'Cut the Zionist propaganda and get on with the show'. Jago was desperately embarrassed, and she wished that there had been somewhere to hide. After their return to Sydney, Hardy worked on the novel. Their relationship continued to see-saw, and it foundered on a couple of occasions. But Hardy always wooed Jago back.[13]

Jago excused Hardy's behaviour on the ground that he was unsure of himself because of his working-class background, of which he professed to be very proud. He liked to be outrageous and shock people, but she had believed that this was part of his defence. He had obsessions and strange behaviour, and he indulged in game-playing. He suffered from mood swings, but Jago did not believe he was manic-depressive, although he was certainly manic most of the time. On reflection, she believed that had he ever had counselling, he would have been found to be quite unstable. This was evident in his pattern of behaviour towards people to whom he was attracted; he would go out of his way to charm them. When they were of no further use, he would discard them, and they would not know what had caused their fall from grace. He could be quite ruthless to people, young and old, whom he met casually. According to Hardy, he did not have any problems; it was always the publisher, the barman, the bookmaker or the woman with whom he was involved, who caused problems. He was never concerned about paying debts to anyone, except the bookmakers. Occasionally, Hardy would mention, without any prior discussion, that he had not gone to his mother's funeral. He was almost robotic when it came to gambling. On the one hand he was quite disciplined if he was writing, but he would glance at his watch, put down his pen and go to the betting shop. He would return, pick up the pen and continue, perhaps in the middle of a line, as though he had never left. He had a cat which was allowed to walk on his desk, and there was always a 'kitty litter' in evidence. He had an established practice of sleeping in the afternoons.[14]

Hardy's behaviour became worse. Jago knew, instinctively, that she had taken a risk when she introduced Hardy into her family's and friends' circles. She was angry that Hardy could continue to accept her father's hospitality, a man who was a leader in the Jewish community, and whom Hardy professed to admire, and yet be anti-Semitic. She found his so-called jokes unacceptable. 'A Jew can tell a joke about Jews, and a Catholic can tell a joke about Catholics, but it is not acceptable when others tell those jokes.' She felt that it was as though Hardy believed that he had 'this Jewish woman in tow, so I can afford to make jokes about the Jews'. One evening when they were dining with a Jewish friend of hers, Hardy took her partner aside, and they proceeded to make comments that 'they both had these intellectual Jewish women'.[15]

Their association remained troubled, but they were spurred on by the imminent publication of *But The Dead Are Many* in 1975. Eva Jago believed that she had made a significant contribution to the novel.

Frank Hardy and jockey Athol George Mulley co-authored a collection of stories of the racetrack, *The Needy and The Greedy,* which was published that same year; these stories had popular appeal.

Jago said Hardy had convinced her that the reason she fought with him was because she had problems with her father. Hardy was so insistent that she consulted a psychiatrist; after some months she knew she was no closer to a solution, and she didn't know why she was persevering. 'The reason became clear, I had no problems with my father, it was Hardy who had problems with my father.' Jago realised that she could not take any more; there were more lows than highs, and the relationship was very destructive. Hardy thought that he was a bush lawyer and a bush psychiatrist, and he believed that he knew enough to analyse people. Hardy's career was at its peak, the *Power Without Glory* series was about to be launched, and he was in demand.[16] He had earlier won a Logie Award for the best TV drama.[17]

It was at that high point that Jago decided to leave him. He could not understand her decision, especially as he was now so successful. 'The fact that I did not attend the launch, the fact that I was able to resist it, that was un- believable, and it bruised his ego.' He sent her letters and packages, some of which she returned. She had her calls screened, but occasionally Hardy man- aged to talk to her. On one occasion, he had told her that 'the most beautiful woman in Sydney has fallen devastatingly in love with me, and I don't know what to do'. Jago said, 'He was asking *me* what to do—that was the sort of thing he would do'.[18]

Jago had realised that Hardy knew nothing about women. He was insen- sitive and egocentric. He lived for the moment, not just sexually, but for many things. If he met people by whom he was overwhelmed, he would put on 'this wonderful, charming performance—then tomorrow, he would forget all about them, and they would still be impressed'. She met Frances two or three times, and she was aware that Hardy had a 'non-relationship with his grandsons'. With hindsight, she believed that Ross had been treated very shabbily. For her- self, she just wanted it to end.[19]

Earlier, Clement Semmler had endeavoured to have *Power Without Glory* made as a television series. After the success of *But The Dead Are Many*, he raised the matter again, and the project came to fruition in 1976. *Power Without Glory* was transformed into thirteen one-hour episodes. It was also sold to a number of overseas countries. It was very successful, and a triumph for the ABC. Hardy received large fees for the television rights and his share of overseas sales, and the series created a demand for the book itself, which was reprinted in several editions and some hundreds of thousands of copies were sold. Hardy was later the guest and the star of a lunch held by the ABC commissioners in the ABC boardroom.[20]

The success of the television series and the new editions of *Power Without Glory* prompted the re-issue of an updated comprehensive list of characters, and their alleged real-life identities, as they appeared in *Power Without Glory*, together with photographs. It was prepared by Dave Nadel and printed as a 'Special Liftout' in the Trotskyist publication, *The Battler,* in 1976.[21]

Eva Jago was not the only person who thought she had made a contri- bution to *But The Dead Are Many*. So, too, did former journalist Dulcie Mortier, the widow of Hardy's friend, former CPA journalist and theoretician Paul Mortier, upon whom the character in the novel, John Morel, was allegedly based.

In 1995 Dulcie Mortier prepared a paper for a Women's History Confer- ence to be held at the fifth Women and Labour Conference, Macquarie Univer- sity, Sydney, September–October 1995. Illness intervened, and she was unable to attend the conference. The following is a précis of her paper, entitled 'Did Anne Hathaway Write Shakespeare?':

The death of Australian author Frank Hardy in January last year led to him being lauded as Australia's best known working class writer.

I now refer to the part I played in making it possible for Hardy to write *But The Dead Are Many*. First, I must query the right of an author to use 'creative fiction' as a cover for recording apparently real-life facts about real people, who, as Rupert Lockwood said, are then defenceless victims, because if a 'fact' is wrong or invented, it can easily be explained as fiction. It is a Catch 22 for the characters.

My husband, Paul Mortier, a disillusioned leading Communist who died from an overdose of barbiturates in 1965, appears as the thinly veiled John Morel in *But The Dead Are Many*. He was Hardy's *best friend*. The story of the death was interwoven with a fictional story of Nikolai Buratakov, a leading Soviet Communist who went to his death in the 1938 purges in Russia. The book was acclaimed by some as a masterpiece.

I am concerned with the moral boundaries beyond which a writer may not go in distorting personal details of other lives—because the dead may be many, but the living are also quite a few.

I first met Frank Hardy when he was promoting *Power Without Glory*, probably in 1950. Hardy stayed with us for a weekend. When the Hardys moved to Sydney in 1954 the two families exchanged visits; the friendship between Hardy and Mortier was the mainspring. Later, when Mortier showed signs of depression, it was discovered that previous 'illnesses' had been the results of suicide attempts. My husband refused to consult a psychiatrist, nor would he talk to his comrades on the Central Committee. My approach to the Party leadership proved abortive.

Finally, I persuaded him to talk to his old friend, Frank Hardy, about his depression. I believe that one night they met in a cafe, when the matter was discussed. Later that year Paul Mortier went to the USSR, but he did not consult the doctors in Moscow as planned.

In 1962 my husband took a near fatal dose of Librium; the CPA leadership either wanted to avoid the issue, or they were not interested. This was part of the peculiar and distorted ethic of the CPA. You were allowed to have ideological 'problems'—you were allowed lots of excesses actually —but psychological problems?

That night, after the doctor and the ambulance had gone, I sat in an agony of detachment and realised that I had never felt more alone. I poured out my feelings by writing on a few scraps of paper—a long description of the events of that terrible night. These notes titled *The Intimate Stranger*, I later gave to Frank Hardy to provide insight into the events and relationships of our lives.

To ensure confidentiality, I arranged for my husband to be admitted to a private clinic under the care of a private specialist. During that time Hardy, who had not been in contact for about a year, telephoned. I felt relief, as here was someone who understood Paul's problems. We agreed to meet in an hour at the hospital. Later, for the first time, Hardy and I talked personally. It was later that evening that Hardy made sexual overtures to me and was rejected. He tried to explain his attitudes to women and sex. The author's version of this episode was later to appear in pages 196–7 in the book. When I asked him, 'Why did you write this? It never happened', he said, 'You have to put that sort of stuff in to sell the book'. I pursued it, 'But why put my character in such a bad light?'. 'It's only fictional,' was his reply.

In 1964 the strain of Paul's illness grew too great. After almost twenty years Paul gave up his work as a full-time CPA journalist. It was a nightmarish dream-time, when one of Australia's finest radical thinkers began selling first encyclopaedias, then linen door-to-door. No-one from the party ever sought a discussion with me as to our future, and they certainly did not help him. They were still banging the 'ideological differences' drum. Thankfully, this *was* a feature of the situation. For many years Paul had been unable to accommodate himself to the sycophantic time-serving of some of his colleagues. Intellectual honesty and deep disillusionment with the Socialist practice in Russia, combined with an increasing awareness of Communist double-dealing, ensured complete despair for both of us. For a psychologically disturbed personality it was too much.

When a Party 'intellectual commission' was set up, Paul was invited to attend a Saturday afternoon conference. It was arranged that afterwards several of the dissidents would meet at a Chinese restaurant—a few of us were going on later to a more exclusive discussion.

With our two young daughters I picked Paul up; we sat at a long table with a couple of other people. The unreality was back; Paul was floating out of reach. Then Frank Hardy entered, accompanied by elitist members of the radical push. Hardy glanced around, saw Paul and headed for another table. When they were seated, I looked at Paul. He was ashen. The insult was obvious. I was numb with disbelief and insisted strongly that it was because they didn't like *me*. But the damage was done.

(You cannot read a version of this incident in *But The Dead Are Many*.)

My husband died in September 1965. A few weeks later my daughters and I visited the Hardy flat in Manly. After lunch I went into Hardy's study and stared out the window at the rolling Pacific breakers. My heart felt frozen. 'Now,' I said to him in the silence, 'you must write your great novel'.

He shook his head. 'I don't think I'll ever write again,' he muttered. 'Every writer has to have an alter ego. Paul was mine. Without him, I can't write.'

I pleaded. 'But now above all, you owe it to Paul. His death must not have been in vain.' He looked at me blankly. 'What would the theme be?' he grated out. 'I have no theme.'

I recall most vividly the feeling of the warm tears on my cheeks, the sight of the blue ocean and the agony we seemed to be sharing. Without looking around, I said: 'Your theme is the loneliness of man'. I was ready to overlook his public rejection of Paul in the restaurant, for hadn't we all failed?

I had previously given Hardy files of personal letters and writings; some time later he contacted me with the news that he had made a start on the book. He was haunted by Paul's death, he said, and he had to write about it. He had ideas about linking it up with the Soviet trials in 1938 and a local hunger strike held during the war. Still traumatised, I was obsessed with the need for the real story of Paul (his pain, struggle, illness, idealism) to be written. Also, I had realised that the CPA, of which I had been a member for twenty-five years, was not like a church or some other association that had compassion for its members. Hence, despite past incidents, I saw Hardy as my only available support in setting the record straight.

A few months later he came to look through some personal files with me. He was suicidally depressed. He confessed to signing phoney cheques —now the rent, gas, power and telephone accounts were all overdue; the furniture on hire purchase was about to be seized. He claimed that his wife said she had had enough, and she was going to leave him!

Four hundred pounds would solve the immediate problems. Coincidence! I had previously mentioned to Hardy that I had just four hundred pounds in the bank. I lent him the money on the condition that it be returned by Christmas. After an unpleasant scene in November, I received a cheque for seventy pounds, which was subsequently dishonoured. The money was never returned; I might have received about one hundred and twenty pounds in total.

I continued my collaboration with Hardy on the work which finally appeared as *But The Dead Are Many* in order to give some meaning to my husband's death. It would be impossible to recount the meetings and discussions we had, for I was vitally important to the book. Where else to get the private writings of the deceased? How else to get court records of the inquest? How else to get access to private letters and my own troubled scribblings penned at crisis times? Who else could make the necessary introduction to the psychiatrist and to family members?

I was troubled about the wisdom of proceeding, but felt some compulsion to continue in order to give meaning to my husband's death. Some months later I received the manuscript; I made copious and meticulous notes as I read the work. I was appalled at the amateurish style, especially the long sections of authorial comment, based on a primitive Freudianism, explaining to the reader, for example: 'This man had an inferiority complex'. Hardy and I spent many hours with my notes going through the manuscript. We discussed at length some of the philosophical and psychological problems involved. The mystery of suicide, questions of guilt, the astounding phenomenon of Communists confessing their guilt and going to their deaths, even though they were innocent. I suggested he had no idea how to portray women. He agreed. 'I can never write women characters.'

The amended manuscript arrived; I made efforts to polish and refine so that the best possible work would result. More meetings—another manuscript. I was uneasy with the choice of names, so close to the original protagonists. I could now see no way out of the involvement. He was going to write the book; it was better if I stayed with it.

I read yet another manuscript in which the character of John Morel was trivialised. By a careful selection of the odd phrase, the odd adjective, it was clear that the author had intentions against John Morel which were quite disturbing. Under the guise of the *best friend*, the author was depicting Morel as a man driven to suicide because of the 'insurance'. He described him in physically insulting terms. The author, appearing as Jack, was of course much stronger, more together, more debonair, more gifted, more everything. The device of playing the central character, John Morel, against the author, Jack, was exactly suited to the author's purpose, which could be summed up as 'Look what a great guy Jack is alongside this poor weak bastard'. It seemed that the political backdrop was secondary to the main theme.

After months of talk we finally arrived at a mutually agreed version. He had talked to the psychiatrist and my husband's sisters—in short I had done everything possible to help Hardy clarify the facts and background.

Later, after I had remarried, I dined with my husband, Eva Jago and Hardy. We drank a toast to 'the book' that had, at last, been completed. Prior to this I had read and agreed to a final version, although I had not been totally happy with the work. I awaited Hardy's advice.

Months later I had a telephone call from a friend in Melbourne. 'Do you know Hardy's book is out?' 'No,' I said, 'I had no idea.' 'Well, it's bloody disgraceful,' said the friend, 'you'd better get a copy.' I was staggered to find that Hardy hadn't seen fit to send me the book. Another friend rang Hardy for an explanation. Hardy claimed that he didn't know the book was out, and that he didn't remember who the publisher was! My daughter, Jill, contacted Hardy and requested a copy for me. He was quite rude; he told her there were plenty in the bookshops. My elder daughter, Nikki, then spoke to Hardy and told him, 'That's not good enough, Frank'. I eventually received an unmarked copy in the mail. I couldn't look at it, because I feared the worse. But my husband started to read it, and when he was about a quarter of the way through, he said, 'This sounds like the original manuscript to me'. It was the very first discarded original manuscript with minor textual amendments and the addition of the fugue format. On pages 198–200 was a segment, reproduced in italics, *This Intimate Stranger*, which I had given to Hardy years before. Minor changes had been made, but permission had not been requested, nor was there any acknowledgement.

In view of my nine-year-long collaboration with Frank Hardy in the preparation of the book, I suppose I should not have been surprised. Truth was a casualty and Catch 22 operated to the end.[22]

Contrary to what he had told Dulcie Mortier's friend on the telephone, Frank Hardy was present when *But The Dead Are Many* was launched by poet Denis Kevans at the Intervention Bookshop, 4 Dixon Street, Sydney, on 10 October 1975. CPA member Laurie Aarons also spoke. A notice advertising the function had appeared on page seven of the *Tribune* on 1 October 1975.

Some time later a friend asked Hardy to inscribe a copy of the novel for Dulcie Mortier. The inscription, in Hardy's handwriting, reads, 'To Dulcie, Without whose advice, assistance and patience, under difficult circumstances, this book could not have been written. With deep thanks Frank J. Hardy Dec. 1975'.[23] Mortier felt outraged by what she perceived to be a betrayal. She later prepared an article for publication; she believed that Hardy had misused and distorted much of the material she had given him. Her legal advisers told her that it could be defamatory to Hardy.[24] So the matter had to rest.

Why did Hardy choose to create the character of John Morel in such an insensitive manner? Given his knowledge of the factual background and his own breakdown in the Soviet Union, he could have written a compassionate work of fiction without cheapening the lives of those portrayed.

A letter from Paul Mortier to Frank Hardy, who was in in Moscow, throws some light on the relationship that existed between the two men:

30a Asquith Street, Oatley. [NSW] February 6, 1963. Dear Frank, Your book sounds exciting. As we are not going to Moscow, I'll be here when you get back and look forward to long yarns about it. In the meantime, here are a few ideas on the first part for you to chew over till we get together. The earlier primitive communist thinkers in England that I know of emerged around the 14th century, and their ideas as expressed, particularly by John Ball, played a part in the 1381 peasant revolt. As A. L. Morton puts it: 'Quite apart from the immediate demands of the peasants, which were for the abolition of serfdom, the commutation of all services at a flat rate of fourpence per acre and the abolition of the Statute of Laborers, the rising had a background of primitive Communism, strongly Christian in character. It was spread by the poorer parish priests by the friars who, Langland wrote;

'Preachmen of Plato and prove it by Seneca
That all things under Heaven are to be common',

and to some extent by Wycliffe's Lollards, though their responsibility for the rising was probably smaller than is often supposed, and Wycliffe himself certainly gave it no countenance. 'Of all the preachers of Communism only one, John Ball, has come down to us as a living figure. Though a North Countryman he worked mainly in London and the surrounding counties, deducing the equality of men from their common descent from Adam and declaring in Froissart's often quoted words that things cannot go well in England, nor ever will until everything shall be in common.'

'The personal prestige of Ball among the rebels of 1381, one of whose first acts was to release him from Maidstone Gaol, was unquestionably great, though there is no trace of Communism in the demands they presented. These demands were probably a minimum upon which all were agreed.'

It is worth noting however that the demands of the English peasants of 1381 were not achieved in Russia till 1861. The 1381 rising was suppressed, it is true, but from then on commutation of serfdom went on steadily; so, one gets an idea of how far ahead in social development England was. (Froissart, incidentally who Ball liked to quote, was a journalist of the immediately preceding era.)

Wat Tyler, who led this revolt, also frequently used, as a sort of battle cry the very quotable couplet:

'When Adam delved and Eve span,
Who was then the gentleman?'

Then in the early days of the 16th century appeared Sir Thomas More's great classic *Utopia*. Here, indeed, was a quite developed work of utopian communism, savagely exposing the savagery of the enclosures which were then proceeding, and at the same time painting an inspired picture of what a classless society could be like. Here is just one of a dozen quotes one might make:

'For in other places they speak still of the commonwealth. But every man procureth his own private gain. Here where nothing is private, the common affairs be earnestly looked upon ... For there is nothing distributed after a niggardly short, neither there is any poor man or beggar. And though no man have any things, yet everyman is rich. For what can be more rich, than to live joyfully and merely, without grief and pensifness [sic]: not caring for his own living, nor vexed or troubled with his wife's importunate complaints, not dreading poverty to his son, nor sorrowing for his daughter's dowry?'

Then in the great bourgeois revolution of the next century, came the Diggers and Levellers. As a group the Levellers presented political demands which anticipated the Chartists by nearly 200 years. A good picture of them is given in Morton's history; but one more likely to be of your taste in Jack Lindsay's novel, *1649, A Novel Of A Year*. The Levellers were, as it were, the left wing of the bourgeois revolution, whose agitation was mainly responsible for the execution of Charles in 1649, and the adoption by Parliament and its acceptance by Cromwell of what was called the Agreement which provided for two-yearly parliaments elected by manhood suffrage for all except wage earners; complete religious toleration, democratic control of the army, abolition of tithes and all taxes, except a tax on property. Within the Levellers were the Diggers led by Winstanley who actually tried to establish a Communist utopia in England at the time.

Lindsay gives pictures of all the main leaders of this movement, Lillburne, Overton and the rest, and plenty of quotes from their writings. You'll probably be able to see Jack while you're in London, and he should be a fount of information on all this. But, if you want it when you get back, I'll dig out quotes for you.

Then we can jump to the French and British Utopians—Fourier, Saint Simon and Owen . . . there's good stuff in all of them for your purposes . . . then the Chartists . . . a wealth of material . . . by then, of course, you're up to Marx and Engels and their contemporaries. I'll be happy to give any help I can on this section. But these jottings may help for thinking purposes.

Re the IPS [International Political Situation]. I'll wait to discuss that till you get back. I just want to say at this stage, Frank, that I have learned these things are terribly complex even when only one Party is involved. But when the whole world movement is in the soup, then save me from easy generalities. I look forward to lots of yarns on it when you get back . . . In the meantime, don't worry we're not rushing any fences here.[25]

This letter clearly indicated Mortier's self-effacement and generosity of spirit towards the person he believed was his best friend, Frank Hardy. It reveals no sign of jealousy of Frank's success. Rather, Mortier continues to share his knowledge and offers assistance for Hardy's proposed work, as he had done since they first met when serving in the Army in Mataranka during the war. In the final paragraph Paul Mortier expressed his own political unease at that time.

Eva Jago was not aware of earlier events or of the extent of Dulcie Mortier's contribution to the writing of *But The Dead Are Many*. It was hailed by some as Hardy's best work. 'Whatever its faults, the virtue of Hardy's *But The Dead Are Many* is that it does face this question of revolutionary disenchantment', according to John McLaren in the *Herald*.[26] Michael McNay believed that '[it] is the first novel of any consequence by a member of a Western communist party',[27] and Max Harris that 'The introspective mood and the impressionist form bring [it] into the category of Musil, Broch, the late Thomas Mann writings, even Hesse',[28] but the commendations were not universal. John Docker wrote:

Despite what appear to be its admirable intentions, however, Hardy's book is a failure, as a literary work and as an account of contemporary communist history . . . The crucial failure is in the book's chief character . . . Morel reveals aspects of himself in some dramatic situations . . . his language rarely strays from that of abstract psycho-analytic technology . . . a repetitiveness that becomes, as the book goes on, unnervingly boring . . . What is noticeable . . . is that the present leadership of the Party is exempt from any adverse criticism . . . As it is, it is difficult not to see *But the Dead are Many* [sic] as a propaganda tract written on behalf of a victorious inner Party faction, but tendentiously disguising a local political victory as a victory of universal morality.[29]

Hardy asserted that the novel had been acclaimed in France, Italy and Great Britain as a work of great literature.[30]

Frank Hardy's two most successful novels, *Power Without Glory* and *But The Dead Are Many*, have left a legacy of continuing pain for those people who had the misfortune to have some aspects of their lives fictionalised by him. This surely raises a moral issue on the rights of an author to present protagonists who have no right of reply, because the work is 'creative fiction'; particularly from an author who, on several occasions, sought access to the laws of libel for his own financial benefit.

Chapter Fourteen

THE GHOSTS OF
POWER WITHOUT GLORY

IN THE YEARS following his separation from Eva Jago, Hardy formed a number of liaisons with prominent and not so prominent young women. One woman, a psychiatrist, later committed suicide, and this further kindled Hardy's already obsessive interest and study of suicide, which had developed during the writing of *But The Dead Are Many*.[1] Paul Adams, Hardy's literary biographer, refers to Hardy's study of suicide in some detail.[2]

Hardy met Greek singer Nana Mouskouri when she was touring Australia; he presented her with a song that he had written for her. This meeting in the 1970s blossomed into a friendship which was ongoing for a number of years. Hardy went to live in the south of France in the late 1970s; for a time he became part of the Mouskouri entourage as the show travelled from city to city. Hardy was a guest 'in her luxurious, walled villa in Monaco, and his presence titillated the *paparazzi* from the highly inventive French magazines . . . He was identified in one as a mysterious American, about to wed Mouskouri'.[3] Mouskouri's children were well known to Hardy. Jago quipped that Hardy became a 'Mouskouri groupie'.[4] Alan Hardy met Mouskouri in Europe; she was a charming woman, and he was aware that the relationship had 'gone on for a long time'.[5]

Noted media personality Phillip Adams first met Hardy in the 1950s; for a short time they shared a radio programme. Adams commented that it was easy to dismiss Hardy as a writer, but he was reminded, when he read Hardy's work, that some of it was very good. Hardy reached the peak of his career in the 1970s, and 'he was certainly one of Australia's great celebrities'. Hardy was an autodidact, something that Adams believed was worth fostering in Australia.[6]

Adams was aware that Hardy had written a song for Mouskouri, and that they had been in a long relationship. Some people found it difficult to believe, but women were attracted to Hardy, who was 'a notoriously successful seducer'. Adams acknowledged that Hardy could be amazingly good company, but the downside was that he was a great user of people. He had met him forty or fifty times, but in the end he had failed to return Hardy's calls. Adams knew Mary Hardy very well; they were both insomniacs, and Mary would frequently telephone him during the night. As far as he could determine, Hardy had not treated Mary very well, but she was certainly a handful. Nor did he know whether Mary had given her brother money, but Frank was always on 'the edge of desperation'. Adams recalled that Hardy had been paid for the film rights for one of his novels, but no screenplay was produced. 'Even worse, 'twas discovered that Frank had sold the same rights to the same book to somebody else. So, he was called in for a chat. He looked somewhat discomfited, but insisted there was a perfectly reasonable explanation. First, he had to go to the toilet, "I'll be back in a shake." Frank didn't just leave the room. 'He left the building.' Adams believed that 'Hardy would have had a more honourable reputation, and left a better legacy had he had a moral core'.[7] Eva Jago did not know whether Hardy received money from Mary, but 'he did from everyone else'.[8]

Hardy returned to Australia in 1979. While living in France he had written *Who Shot George Kirkland?* which was published in 1980. The work is an extravagant tribute to Ross Franklyn, Hardy's *alter ego*. The narrator in the novel, who is writing Franklyn's biography, pursues a quest to establish if Alan Hall, a second-hand furniture dealer, had, in the 1920s, shot a criminal, George Kirkland, with Kirkland's own gun. Hall had told Ross Franklyn (Hardy) this story in 1948. He had also informed Franklyn that his brother-in-law, Bill Egan, had been seduced by Nellie Wren when he was working on the extensions to the Wren home in Kew. Egan had told Hall that he was the father of Nellie Wren's youngest child. In the novel Franklyn had been obsessed that he had harmed a fragile old woman in an earlier work; he could not live with himself and committed suicide. In this novel Hardy referred repeatedly to the obsessions of 'Ross Franklyn', and ascribed to the character Alan Hall a psychopathic condition, *pseudologia fantastica*—meaning 'pathological and habitual lying'.[9]

During an interview with Ken Brass of the *Australian Women's Weekly* following the publication of the novel, Hardy claimed to have checked the story in 1948, but he had found no evidence that Kirkland had been murdered. Hardy said that thirty years later he had returned to the State Library of Victoria to make further investigations, and he stated that he had been able to confirm that Kirkland had been murdered by his own gun. The narrative in *Who Shot George Kirkland?* suggests that if the Kirkland story is true, then the allegation of adultery made against Nellie West (Wren) in *Power Without Glory* is also true. However, Hardy was not prepared to concede to Ken Brass that the Nellie Wren story was true, because it was possibly legally and physically dangerous for him to do so.[10]

Was the character in the novel Alan Hall the product of Frank Hardy's imagination? No! Robert Allan Hall, to give him his correct name, one of the central characters in *Who Shot George Kirkland?*, was the fourth child of Thomas George Hall and Sarah Ann Hall (née Farmer). He was born in Penshurst, Victoria, in 1887.[11] His father, Thomas, was a constable in the Victoria Police from June 1880 to October 1900. Thomas Hall's resignation pre-empted impending dismissal because of heavy drinking.[12] Robert Allan Hall's sister, Lucinda

Evelyn, born in 1883,[13] married William Frederick John Egan, in 1902.[14] Egan, a Catholic, was appointed a constable in the Victoria Police in that year. His police enlistment form shows that he was born in 1878 in Dunolly, Victoria. He was five feet ten and a quarter inches tall, eyes grey, hair dark brown, complexion dark, general appearance smart. He then lived at 99 Grattan Street, Carlton.[15] After five years' service he was dismissed following a variety of misdemeanours and offences. The official police comment was 'Conduct very bad'.[16]

By that time, Lucy Egan had three children, and the family had moved from Carlton to Richmond. Electoral rolls show that Egan became a bricklayer.[17]

The characters Bill and Myrtle Evans appear in Part Two of *Power Without Glory*. Evans, it was claimed, looked like the American film actor William S. Hart, and Evans was seduced by Nellie West in 1917 when working as a bricklayer on the extensions to the West family home in Kew. Nellie West later gave birth to a son, the product of that liaison. Chapter 4 of *Who Shot George Kirkland?* closely follows the earlier novel; indeed Frank Hardy gives acknowledgment to publishers Curtis Brown (Aust.) Pty Ltd and The Bodley Head for permission to reproduce the material from *Power Without Glory*. The work is referred to in *Who Shot George Kirkland?* as *Power Corrupts*; in this version, however, Bill and Myrtle Evans have disappeared, to be substituted with real people, Bill and Lucy Egan. Nellie West remains as Nellie West.[18]

The location of the shop occupied by Alan Hall in the novel is given as 1014 Malvern Road, Malvern.[19] However, the shop once occupied by Robert Allan Hall is at 1491 Malvern Road; now the premises of 'Creswick Antiques— Pre 1830 English Furniture', and the present owners have indicated that the shop did have a similar history of tenants and businesses as outlined in *Who Shot George Kirkland?*. These premises are not far from where Hardy lived in 1948. The physical description of both the shop and the area are identical. A close relative has confirmed that Alan Hall was the occupant of the second-hand furniture shop during the period mentioned in the novel. He said:

Most people called him Bob. Hall engaged in wild thinking—a big talker —he frequently mixed fact with fiction. He was known to Frank Hardy. He almost certainly gave Hardy the story about the alleged affair. It would have been entirely consistent with his mixtures of fact and fiction. He had odd theories about many things, and he was a great yarn spinner. Hall was a 'bit odd in his mind'. I had no knowledge of, and nor was there was ever any suggestion, that Hall was a Commonwealth policeman.[20]

There is no record of Hall serving in either the Victoria, Commonwealth or the Federal Police.[21] Another character mentioned in the novel is Detective Sergeant Ted Ethel, a policeman. An Edmond (Ted?) Ethell served as a constable from 1903 until 1933, and he died in 1955.[22] In the novel Franklyn claimed that he had seen Ethel at Hall's premises on one occasion. It is also mentioned that Alan Hall had bragged that he had shot George (Ape) Kirkland who had earlier visited his shop.[23] Hall apparently fraternised with both ex-policemen and reputed criminals.

No evidence of Kirkland's shooting could be found, but Robert Allan Hall had, indeed, shot a man named Thomas Hamill. The *Argus* of 1 January 1919 reported:

REVOLVER SHOTS AT PARTY—Young man arrested. There were exciting scenes at a party held in Abbotsford yesterday evening. As a sequel, one man was taken to the Melbourne Hospital with a bullet in his left thigh, while another was locked up.

The party was a New Year's Eve gathering at the home of Mrs. Hall, in Church street, Abbotsford. It is stated that a young man came in while the party was in progress, and began to make himself generally objectionable by quarrelling. One of the guests, Thomas Hamill, 29 years of age, living in Nicholson street, Abbotsford, who was there with his wife, remonstrated with the newcomer. The other went outside, but shortly afterwards returned and exclaimed 'Where are all your fighting men?' At the same time he produced a revolver and fired two shots at Hamill, one of which logged in the fleshy part of his left thigh, inflicting a wound which, while painful, was not very serious. The injured man was taken to the Melbourne Hospital by Constable Ripper, and was admitted there. Subsequently Robert Allan Hall, 31 years of age, was arrested and locked up at the Collingwood watchhouse on a charge of having shot at Hamill with intent to murder him. Another version of the affair is that the man with the revolver was endeavouring to defend himself against a number of assailants.[24]

A further report in the *Argus* of 20 February 1919 noted:

ABBOTSFORD SHOOTING CASE Row at New Year Party.

Robert Allan Hall, 31 years, frenchpolisher, was charged in the Collingwood Court on Wednesday with shooting with intent to do grievous bodily harm to Thomas Hamill, a brewery employee, residing in Nicholson street, Abbotsford. Sub-inspector Sellwood prosecuted, and Mr. P. J. Ridgeway defended.

Annie Hall, residing in Church street, Abbotsford, said that the accused was her son. There was a party at her house on New Year's Eve . . . a shot was fired above the witness's head by whom she did not know. She then fainted . . . Dr. D. T. Thomas, resident medical officer at the Melbourne Hospital, said that Hamill was admitted to that institution early on New Year's morning suffering from a bullet wound in the thigh. He remained a patient for six weeks, and the bullet was still in the leg . . . [Hamill said] Jean Hall advised us to be careful, as her brother Bob was coming with a revolver. He walked out with his girl, his mother remarking, 'We don't want any Dick Turpin acts here' . . . The accused said he remembered firing one shot from his revolver in the air, in order to frighten the people who were molesting him . . . Mr. R. Knight, P.M., said he believed the statement of Hall that he fired in the air, and he was satisfied the shot was not intended to injure Hamill . . . The Police Magistrate.—The case against Hall is dismissed.[25]

The question might be asked, why the charges against Robert Allan Hall were dismissed? He was certainly in possession of a revolver, presumably unlicensed, and shots were fired, a man was seriously wounded, yet he went free. Was a deal made that he become a police informer? In the novel the character Hall wears a gun in a holster.[26]

So, did George Kirkland exist? Yes! He was born in Carlton in 1878. He was convicted of housebreaking in the Victorian Criminal Sessions on 19 April 1904. The *Police Gazette* for week ending 26 July 1924 shows that on a later charge, he was discharged from prison during that week. He had been sentenced at the Melbourne General Sessions on 1 October 1923 for shooting with intent; he received twelve months hard labour. His occupation was shown as labourer. Record number 29276, George Kirkland, alias Martin Ford, alias John Bexter, alias David Farmer, revealed that he had had four previous convictions. Later reports gave his occupation as a dealer, and he lived in Brunswick.[27]

Following his release George Kirkland continued his life of crime. The *Brunswick & Leader* newspaper unfolded a sorry saga. On occasions he appeared, under various aliases, on charges of housebreaking, being in possession of an unregistered pistol and two bullets, theft from the Zanoni Hotel, North Fitzroy, and of being a suspected person and for loitering. He was charged with maliciously and unlawfully wounding his wife, Mary Kirkland, and setting fire to the family home. Mrs Kirkland was bleeding freely from a wound to her head; she was taken to the hospital by a police officer. Kirkland was later admitted to the Royal Park Hospital under a Section 45 (Involuntary Patient) on 16 June 1925, where he was treated for alcoholism. He had previously been admitted as a voluntary patient on 7 August 1923 and discharged three days later. On 6 November 1925 Judge Woinarski declared him to be an habitual criminal. He was subsequently sentenced on a number of charges; he was released from Pentridge Prison late in 1930.[28]

Who Shot George Kirkland? is centred around whether Kirkland was shot, and if so, by whom. Despite Frank Hardy's claim in 1980 that he had discovered that Kirkland had been murdered with his own gun, the narrator in the novel stated that the newspaper reports could not be located. It can only be concluded that Frank Hardy left false trails in the novel that were designed to confuse any future researcher attempting to establish whether George Kirkland was ever shot by Robert Allan Hall or any other assailant. Enquiries have not disclosed any report that such a shooting took place, and in fact, records reveal that Kirkland died in the Royal Park Psychiatric Hospital in 1944. This event proves that the story told to Frank Hardy by Alan Hall that he had shot George Kirkland with his own gun was false. Was the Bill Egan and Nellie Wren story also false?

Who Shot George Kirkland? purported to be about the nature of truth. Was this convoluted novel intended to absolve Frank Hardy for his misuse of unsubstantiated libellous information about Nellie Wren? Hardy had chosen to ignore Les Barnes's warning and protest against slandering Nellie Wren, when Barnes was engaged in composing the type for *Power Without Glory* more than thirty years earlier. When Hardy complained to the Victorian CPA leadership, they intervened with Barnes. Hardy, with their approval and that of J. B. Miles, the General Secretary of the CPA, had used information that had emanated from extremely suspect sources. In summary, who were these people? Robert Allan Hall (Alan Hall), who was 'a bit odd in his mind', someone who had carried a revolver and been involved in a shooting and mixed in dubious company. Hall had told Hardy that his brother-in-law, Bill Egan (Bill Evans), had an affair with Nellie Wren (Nellie West) while working as a bricklayer at her home. Hall's sister, Lucy Egan (Myrtle Evans), was the aggrieved wife. George Kirkland, an habitual criminal, was known to, and allegedly shot by Hall. It was not revealed in the novel that Bill Egan (Bill Evans) was a disgraced policeman.

It is possible that Egan worked on the extensions to the Wren home; he lived close by in North Richmond. Electoral rolls show that Egan did become a bricklayer after his dismissal from the Victoria Police. Lucy gave birth to her sixth child, Lucy, in Richmond in 1918. Her seventh child, Joan, was born in Collingwood during 1919. By 1920 the Egan family had moved to Eltham. Three more sons were born in 1920, 1923 and 1924.[29] If it is accepted that Bill Egan did tell a story of an affair, certain questions need to be asked. Did Egan have a personal grudge against John Wren? As a constable in the Carlton–Collingwood area in the early part of the century, Wren would have been known to him, at least by sight and reputation. What more effective way to attack a man than through his wife?

Bill Egan was living at 256 Johnston Street, Abbotsford, when he collapsed and died at the corner of Flinders and Elizabeth Streets, Melbourne, on 29 September 1944. It seems certain that the couple had separated. His wife, Lucy, was a resident of Greensborough when she died in 1953, two years after Hardy's trial for criminal libel.[30]

There is now little doubt that Frank Hardy and George Seelaf did visit Lucy Egan at her home prior to Hardy's criminal libel trial, and that she appeared briefly in the lobby of the City Court on the first day of Hardy's committal proceedings.[31] It is possible that this stratagem was designed as part of an overall plan devised by Hardy's legal team in consultation with Frank Hardy, George Seelaf, and CPA leader and lawyer, Ted Hill, to unsettle the prosecution.

So, why did Hardy revive the ghosts from *Power Without Glory* when he wrote *Who Shot George Kirkland?* thirty years later? The novel received some excellent reviews, while other critics considered that it was a rewriting of *The Hard Way*. Hardy has been criticised for plagiarism, rewriting and obsessive repetition, and his texts have become the subject of academic studies. John Frow has noted that

. . . in all the books subsequent to *Power Without Glory* there is an internal doubling of the act of writing: Paul Whittaker writes about the process of writing about his alter ego Jim Roberts in *The Four-Legged Lottery; The Hard Way* splits the author into two characters, Frank Hardy and Ross Franklyn, in an alternating narrative structure; the author F. J. Borky is seen at work in *The Outcasts of Foolgarah* on a novel which is obviously *The Outcasts of Foolgarah*; Jack self-consciously reconstructs the life of his double, John Morel, in *But The Dead Are Many*; and in *Who Shot George Kirkland?* Ross Franklyn writes about the writing of a novel called *Power Corrupts*, and after his death is doubled by a biographer who gradually comes to identify with him. Increasingly the effect of this is to produce a baroque structure of *mise en abyme*, a self-reflexive structure of obsessive repetition.[32]

Certainly, there is obsessive repetition and circularity in much of Hardy's fiction and autobiographical journalism. Hardy, of course, is not the only writer who displays one or other of these characteristics. As Chris Wallace-Crabbe has observed:

> *Watcher on the Cast-Iron Balcony* keeps returning to an ending, unable to leave it alone, somehow obliged to keep revisiting, rewriting, it. The protagonist's mother dies—or has just died—on the first page of the book, and again on page 244, and for the last time on page 253 . . . A page-and-a-half later the story comes to an end . . . In these ways, Hal Porter constructs an artful circularity which endeavours to defy ending.[33]

Whereas Porter had been unwilling to disengage from his mother's death in this instance, Hardy appeared to have found it impossible to disengage from the omnipresent *Power Without Glory*. As much of his later work reflected, he constantly returned to the well for inspiration. He had written a highly successful novel; if the formula was correct, why leave the circle and go off at a tangent? Was this his philosophy, or was it something much more fundamental? Did Frank Hardy suffer the same doubts as biographer Garry Kinnane attributed to writer George Johnston?

> It is often the working-class boy's legacy to feel that however high he climbs the ladder of success, he is never the rightful owner of the prizes, that he has gained them by default, and that at any moment his fraud will be discovered and he will be back on his arse where he belongs.[34]

There are certain similarities in the lives and work of George Johnston and Frank Hardy. They were born five years apart into working-class families, one suburban and the other rural. Both had an interest in drawing and had some ability with pen, pencil and brush. Just as Johnston had been promoted by Errol Knox, managing editor of the *Argus* newspaper, to the position of being 'the golden boy'[35], Hardy had been elevated to the status of 'favoured son' by the Victorian CPA leadership. In *My Brother Jack*, Johnston's creative imagination had transformed his brother into 'a model of heroic Australian virtues, with his belief in mateship, honesty, toughness and loyalty', and his father's 'verbal violence . . . into physical cruelty'.[36] Hardy's creative imagination had transformed his father, a farm inspector, into a hero, a leader in the 1916–17 anti-conscription struggles. In his play *Mary Lives!* Hardy had so transformed his quiet mother of eight, that a reviewer perceived her to be 'an Irish-Catholic mother with the steel of fanaticism just below the surface'.[37] Johnston never 'said or wrote a word of disrespect for her [his mother]'.[38] Hardy never wrote or expressed anything but great admiration for his father. When Johnston's father was dying, he delayed his arrival until after his death.[39] Hardy did not attend his mother's funeral.[40] The two writers were acquainted with each other, and they corresponded during Johnston's hospitalisation in Sydney in 1965.

The Australasian Book Society published Jack Beasley's *Red Letter Days* in 1979; it contained a chapter devoted to Frank Hardy. It was a deeply critical appraisal of Hardy, and led some CPA members to question why Hardy did not sue Beasley for libel. However, for whatever reason, Hardy chose to ignore this attack.

In late November 1979, just after Hardy's return from France, journalist Max Harris had criticised the existence of the Literature Board and the system of writers' grants, of which he himself had been a beneficiary in 1962. Hardy had been awarded a one-year fellowship for $10 000.[41] Harris had singled out Hardy for a vitriolic attack. He wrote:

> For most of his life old Frank Hardy devoted himself to the replacement of Australia's social democrat structure with a communist dictatorship, and here he is, milking the old social democratic cow with bucolic skill.
>
> Never mind. Frank is a tradition. Let's keep him as a reformed pet. Here's $10 000.[42]

On this occasion, Hardy understandably, if not wisely, responded by issuing a writ against Max Harris, Mirror Newspapers Ltd and Nationwide News Pty Ltd, claiming damages for defamation. It was almost two years before the case came to court, and the jury made a finding against the plaintiff. Both parties had employed Queen's Counsels, and the hearing extended over several days. Costs were awarded against Hardy.[43]

Hardy spoke to reporters outside the court when he expressed his belief that the verdict showed that, because he was a communist, he had not received the same treatment as any other citizen. Hardy sought legal advice; an appeal was lodged, but he lost the case, with costs awarded against him.[44]

It is of interest to compare Harris's article with his review of Hardy's *But The Dead Are Many* written a few years before:

> Now the dreary sod has gone and written a serious work of such originality and intense seriousness as to have ruined all my comfortable preconceptions. *But the Dead are Many* [sic] is a biographical, indeed narcissistic novel, of such refinement, such complex penetration, and such a skilful distancing of the writer from his material as to elevate Frank Hardy up the

academic charts and put him in the same honors thesis group as Patrick White, Hal Porter and Thomas Keneally . . . He is now too good a writer to waste his substance on the media exploitation . . . Or can he starve his way to the geriatric wards producing magnificent self-explorations like *But the Dead are Many* [sic]. . . Horrible choice. I'd be in favour of me old mate being kept in a state of Whitlam-sponsored luxury for the rest of his life.[45]

In December 1980 Hardy returned to Melbourne; he rented a flat in Collingwood. Three years before, the Collingwood City Council had paid tribute to Hardy, the writer who had immortalised their suburb. The Carringbush City Library was opened on 31 July 1977.[46]

It is not known what motivated Hardy to return to the city of his greatest triumph. He became involved with the communities of Carlton, Fitzroy and Collingwood. It was not long before he charmed a whole new generation of Melburnians, some the progeny of his old CPA comrades and left-wing associates. He transferred to the Fitzroy branch of the CPA, and soon after he accompanied a young man to its headquarters in Melbourne. Frank indicated to organiser Carmel Shute that he wanted to sign up this comrade. She said, 'You realise, Frank, that to sign someone up to the Party, you have to be a financial member yourself'. He whipped out his cheque book and wrote a cheque for $100. She was amazed, as Frank was notoriously parsimonious, a not uncommon characteristic of some gamblers. CPA leader Bernie Taft was very impressed for two reasons: first, that Shute had managed to extract a cheque from Frank and second, that it didn't bounce at the bank.[47]

Early in March 1981, Ross Hardy was returning from work when the ferry broke down; the passengers were transferred to another vessel. During the transfer Ross appeared to fall, but she managed to reach the terminal, when a passer-by noticed that she was ill. She had suffered a stroke. Ross lapsed into a coma and died a few days later in the Manly Hospital.[48] She was sixty-one years old. Realist Writer Vera Deacon saw Hardy at Ross's funeral; 'he was stricken'. Mary Hardy was there with 'Frank's and Ross's three lovely children'.[49]

In a television interview in 1993 Hardy talked about his marriage. He said that during his trial Ross had been magnificent, loyal, stoical and a great supporter. She was a very well organised stable character, very kind and a marvellous mother. It had been a simple marriage of a working couple who were communists. Their separation had not been acrimonious.[50] Hardy's definition of a simple marriage is an interesting interpretation given the demands made on his wife, Ross.

Frank had returned to Melbourne, but his restlessness and projects kept him on the move to and from Sydney. In those years he had a number of relationships in Melbourne and Sydney with young women, some more than thirty or forty years his junior. He found a friend in Bruce Pascoe of Pascoe Publishing, who later published a number of his books and short stories.[51]

When friend Graham Pitts had lunch with Hardy when he was writing *Warrant of Distress*, Frank was in a very disturbed state over this story which had grown into a novella. He could not get it right. Graham said, 'But you've written three hundred short stories, Frank'. But it was impossible to calm him; 'it was unbearable to be with him, and the lunch was ruined'. Pitts later used this episode to illustrate to his writing students that writing was never easy. Some people found it difficult to reconcile Hardy's different writing styles. Pitts said, 'It was hard to believe that the person who wrote *But The Dead Are Many* was the same person who had written the *Billy Borker* series'. He believed that Hardy had several personalities.[52] In 1983 *Warrant of Distress* and *The Obsession of Oscar Oswald* were published by Pascoe Publishing.

On 7 January 1985 Mary Hardy committed suicide. Her friends and fellow performers had known for some years that Mary had suffered from manic depression, but they were stunned to learn of her death. Realist Writer Vera Deacon believed that 'Mary's suicide devastated Frank, and, like most writers, I believe he tried to understand by writing the pain out of his heart and mind'.[53]

There is little doubt that Mary's death had shocked Hardy. He had read widely on psychology and suicide for *But The Dead Are Many*. He was then confronted with a suicide in his own family. It seems likely that Hardy had again suffered some form of breakdown. In that year, the writer Walter Kaufmann came to Australia from East Germany to gather material for his novel *Death in Fremantle*. After his return to East Berlin in the 1950s, he had corresponded with and met Hardy several times. On one occasion [probably 1965] Hardy had expressed to Kaufmann, in the blackest terms, his disillusionment with the Soviet Union. Hardy claimed that he had had an affair with the daughter of the late Nikolai Bukharin, who had been head of the Communist International and the editor of the *Izvestia* newspaper, who had been executed in March 1938 during the Moscow show trials.[54] [Nicolai Buratakov in *But The Dead Are Many*?] Anna Larina, Bukharin's widow, had survived twenty years in the Gulag until 1959. When Mikhail Gorbachev came to power, she was able to deliver her husband's final letter to the country; Bukharin was officially rehabilitated on 4 February 1988.[55] So, it is possible that Hardy did meet Larina on more than one occasion during his visits to the Soviet Union in 1956, 1962–63, 1965 and 1968.

In 1975, before Bukharin's rehabilitation, former CPA journalist Rupert Lockwood had deplored many aspects of *But The Dead Are Many*, particularly Hardy's excruciating metaphors, but he believed that Hardy had 'helped the tongues of the dead to speak and raise again the heartless refusal of the Soviet authorities to rehabilitate Bukharin, who was acknowledged by Mikoyan and others in the Khrushchev era to not have been a "spy" or "traitor" as alleged at his trial'.[56]

Kaufmann had had reservations about Hardy's black disillusionment with the Soviet Union, but about the time of reading Hardy's novel, he also began to have doubts about Stalinism. He believed it was a courageous book.[57]

When Kaufmann was starting out as a young writer, Frank had always encouraged him. 'In his worst times he wrote me the warmest letters, probably in his mind I was the younger writer, Wally, his mate, and he kept that attitude throughout.' Hardy suffered from low moods of a bitter and savage kind, particularly when he was in a state of hatred about somebody or something. But he was not like that to Kaufmann, who said that their friendship could be put under the heading that 'a mate can do no wrong'. Kaufmann was lenient about all Hardy's failings and tolerant of his vices, and there were many. Hardy had sent him an invitation to visit him in the South of France, and he had mentioned his relationship with Mouskouri. Kaufmann had been unable to accept the invitation. He had always considered that Frank was unbalanced to the point of hysteria, and not in control of his emotions, but still very much in control of his artistic ability when he needed it. He would go in curves, deep down and way up. During his 1985 visit to Melbourne, Kaufmann had called to see Hardy; he was shocked by what he had observed:

Hardy appeared as though he was being pursued by some forces which seemed to threaten him all day and all night. I met him when he was practically insane with fear and frenzy. He thought they [the forces] were debt collectors. He had no furniture, just a bed and the bookshelves were left, and the books were strewn all over the floor. It was a house in St Kilda on the beach. He came to the door, and he looked like a ghost. He was frenzied; he'd been up all night, and he said he was watching enemies, and he had a gun in his hand. He warned me not to stay long because it was dangerous to stay in this place, all these things were almost insane, and then I told him I was going around the corner to the pub. I told him I would wait for him there if he liked to come and have a drink. He arrived about half an hour later, looking as spruce as if nothing had happened. After the frenzy, he now became the charming Hardy, 'Where have you been all my life, let's have a drink'. We had an enormous bill which, of course, he left for me to pay.[58]

The scene, as described by Kaufmann, could have been taken from the pages of Hardy's novel *The Obsession of Oscar Oswald*, published two years earlier.[59]

During his visit Kaufmann said that Hardy had spoken in glowing terms about Mary's talents, but he did not mention how she had died. Hardy told Kaufmann that he was involved with a woman, but he did not meet her.[60]

Kaufmann's description of the furnishings in Hardy's room relate to the recollections of artist Vane Lindesay. After Hardy returned to Melbourne, Lindesay had a meal with him at a Chinese café in Collingwood. Hardy told him about his alleged affair with Mouskouri. Lindesay found it unbelievable, although he knew Hardy had never been short of female company. Then Hardy drove him to the old Wren tote in Johnston Street. He had shown him the room in Bridge Road, Richmond, where he had worked on *Power Without Glory*. By then, it was dark; Frank weaved and turned his old car through the maze of back streets and lanes, until Lindesay was uncertain of his whereabouts. Hardy took him into a flat; it was extremely squalid, very hot and stuffy, a bare light bulb, a bed, a few possessions and no beer. Lindesay was shocked, he could not see how anyone could be creative in such a barren space. Hardy kept talking. Lindesay was aware that Hardy was the supreme egotist, hence his complete lack of interest in others. He never talked about his children, nor did he ever enquire about Lindesay's children.[61]

For some months in 1986, Hardy lived in Terrigal on the NSW Central Coast; he went to Sydney to read his play *Faces in the Street* in the Harold Park Hotel. On 29 July he was arrested by twenty policemen, including members of the Tactical Response Group, for the non-payment of $8410 traffic fines arising from 111 charges. It was a fiery arrest, and his supporters followed the van. He spent three days in gaol, his second and longest incarceration. Later, his licence was cancelled after he had accrued several hundred dollars more in fines; as he faced six months in gaol, he decided to pay. He claimed 'political asylum' in Melbourne.[62] That year he appeared in a 16 mm film about Ross Franklyn, 'Hollywood Ten—Melbourne One'.[63]

Whatever Hardy's state of mind at various times, he continued to write. During the next few years, *The Loser now will be later to win*, *Hardy's People*, *Great Australian Legends* and *Retreat Australia Fair* were published. He became a columnist with the popular magazine *People*. 'The Most Australian Australian —Frank Hardy' appeared from January 1985 until 13 April 1987; and then under the heading 'Hardyarns' from 20 April 1987 until 11 October 1988,[64] when another popular magazine, *Australasian Post*, continued 'The Most Australian Australian' column. This series concluded with the issue of 30 January 1993.[65] Hardy had written a weekly column continuously for eight years and one month. He often invited readers to send in yarns and anecdotes, offering one of his own books as a prize.

On 24 October 1990 Hardy had decided to apply for his Australian Security Intelligence Organisation (ASIO) files. Soon after, Fiona Capp, who was writing a book about writers and ASIO, interviewed Hardy. She had already read Hardy's files; she told him that he had been under surveillance since 7 June 1943 when he spoke at the Prahran Town Hall in support of communist candidate Malcolm Good. When Capp asked Hardy when he became aware he was under ASIO surveillance, he replied, 'I'm never paranoid about such things; treat them in a cavalier, humorous manner'.[66]

This interview spurred Hardy to write a feature article in 1992. This was published in the *Australian* and the *Age* with a by-line, 'For decades he has been one of Australia's top authors but he's only just found out that he has also been one of Asio's [sic] favorite targets'.[67] Capp's analysis was, however, rather different. The surveillance and literary witch-hunt on communist writers had heightened during 1952 and early 1953. 'The effect on Hardy of this growing mood of paranoia and increased surveillance became apparent in March 1953 when he addressed a gathering at Queen's Domain in Hobart.'[68] Hardy's speech had been reported by an ASIO officer. Hardy had mentioned that his luggage had gone astray, and the security police were trying to find information.[69] Capp considers that 'Rather than depicting himself as a victim of surveillance, Hardy played Security at its own game, empowering himself by claiming he possessed secrets it desired'.[70]

Capp's assessment is almost certainly accurate. Hardy's 1992 statement, that he was barely aware that he had been under scrutiny, bears little relation to the speech he had made in Hobart, or the atmosphere in the CPA during those years. All CPA members were very conscious of the need to be guarded in their dealings about matters of political importance. Communist newspapers waged a campaign against the security services. CPA members practised a form of restraint on each other. If an unguarded remark was made, other members would chide, 'Security, comrade, security'.[71] Hardy's retrospective view of the climate at that time appears to be only partly in accordance with the facts.[72]

Several years before his death, Hardy had met Jennie Barrington, who was many years his junior, and they formed an enduring relationship. Barrington became his companion, manager, research assistant and driver.

In 1992 *Mary Lives!*, Hardy's fictionalised play in celebration of Mary Hardy's life, was given excellent prior publicity. One reviewer conceded that 'Hardy's "Mary" is quite exemplary'. But the play disappointed another who believed that 'The pity is that the play does not get behind the public mask and establish her uniqueness in the heartache entertainment world'. Yet another thought that it failed 'to emotionally involve the audience in a brother's tribute to his sister'.[73] Mary had had a large television and radio following in Melbourne, and the play received a good reception by audiences, who had come to pay their last tribute to a tragic, well-loved performer. It is not known how Hardy's sisters and brothers felt about the public airing of the family's personal tragedies and the harsh characterisation of the mother. In February 1994, soon after Hardy's death, his nephew Marcus Taylor wrote a bitter poem reviewing his relationship with his uncle. The poem also condemned Frank's treatment of his mother Winifred and his sister Mary Hardy. The poem was published in *Quadrant* magazine in March 1995.

Just prior to Hardy's seventy-sixth birthday in 1993, he nominated as an Independent candidate for a Victorian Senate seat. He was denied permission to launch his campaign on the 'sacrosanct steps of Parliament House' in Melbourne. He joined another protest demonstration there, but he was disappointed when he was not arrested and taken to his 'old stamping ground, the City Watchhouse'.[74] A television newscast showed Hardy delivering election pamphlets, and later, Hardy and Barrington sitting on a platform, with two or three media personnel present, in an otherwise empty hall. There was a certain bathos about the scene; here was a man waiting for an audience, who could once attract two thousand people to a rally.[75] Hardy, the old political campaigner, failed in his third attempt to enter Parliament.

Frank Hardy's time was running out. In September 1993, it was noted in the *Bulletin* that 'Writer Frank Hardy lies hospitalised in Melbourne with a stroke'.[76] Hardy was reticent about his illness, and few people were aware that he was ailing. Barrington cared for him when he was discharged from hospital. It was ironic that, soon after, he was awarded one of the major Australia

Council Literary Fellowships—$80 000 extending over four years.[77] Early in January 1994, Hardy received the first Fellowship payment of $20 000.[78] At last, he had received significant recognition of his work by the literary establishment.

On 28 January 1994, Barrington arrived in the late afternoon at Hardy's Carlton home to find him slumped in a chair at his desk, holding a racing form guide; he had apparently suffered a heart attack.[79] Frank Hardy had died quietly, just two months short of his seventy-seventh birthday.

The next morning, the front pages of most metropolitan daily newspapers across the country carried photographs of Hardy and the announcement of his death. Radio stations broadcast the news, and television channels paid tribute and profiled Hardy's life. Journals, magazines and periodicals published features about the legendary writer, communist and entertainer. *Land Rights News*, the journal of the Central and Northern Land Councils, devoted almost a full page, with a photograph, to 'Farewell Frank "old friend"'. This was the tribute that might have most pleased Hardy. One obituary offered that 'the truth was that Hardy was fast becoming Australia's most treasured red', while another featured the heading, 'A rebel author, treasured communist'. The London *Daily Telegraph* noted Frank's passing.[80]

His daughter Shirley said of her father, 'I guess he was a rascal; yes, he was a bit of a vagabond, but he was wonderful. We are all going to miss him very much'.[81]

Some obituaries were less than flattering about aspects of Hardy's life, while acknowledging his talents and strengths. Phillip Adams queried whether there had been 'Too many laurels for our Hardy'.[82]

Hardy had died quietly, but the celebration of his life at the Collingwood Town Hall was a memorable occasion. There was standing room only, people from all walks of life, friends and detractors, had come to bid farewell: the young, the middle-aged, the sprightly elderly, the old on walking sticks and one or two in wheelchairs.

Next morning, the *Age* newspaper printed a front-page colour photograph of compere Jon Faine on the stage, and Gough Whitlam, former Prime Minister, at the lectern.[83] Frank's coffin, draped in the Eureka and the Aboriginal Australia flags, a sheaf of red flowers underneath, stood before them. Actor and singer Bartholomew John sang 'Waltzing Matilda', and 'Thinking of You' from Hardy's play, *Mary Lives!*. There were a number of speakers: Jennie Barrington, members of the Gurindji people, family, politicians and friends.[84] As Whitlam delivered his address, he became overcome with emotion and left the platform close to tears. One newspaper reported that 'People had come to farewell the embodiment of the myth of the Australian rebel'. At the conclusion of the two-hour celebration, Hardy was borne away with the words of the 'Internationale', the socialist anthem, ringing from the Trades Hall Choir. Later, a large group adjourned to the Great Northern Hotel in Carlton, of which Hardy had been a regular patron, to reminisce and drink a final toast.[85]

A celebration of Hardy's life was held in Sydney on 13 March 1994, when a big gathering assembled to say farewell.[86]

Frank Hardy's remains were cremated. On 8 February 1994 his ashes were interred in his parents' grave in the Roman Catholic section of the Fawkner Memorial Park Cemetery in suburban Melbourne.[87]

In July 1999, the *Age* and the *Sydney Morning Herald* published the results of a 'Poll of the Century' questionnaire which had been directed to their readers. The question: 'What was the most influential work of fiction published in Australia during the twentieth century?'. Miles Franklin's *My Brilliant Career* was awarded first place, and Frank Hardy's *Power Without Glory* second place. The same poll was sent to 150 opinion leaders who voted *Power Without Glory* to be 'the most influential work of fiction published in Australia during the twentieth century'. *My Brilliant Career* was awarded second place. How proud Frank Hardy would have been had he lived to learn that his work had received such an accolade.[88]

EPILOGUE

WHEN FRANK LEFT Bacchus Marsh he quickly adapted to city life; his transition from practising Catholic to ardent Communist was not unusual at that time. Communism was an alternative to the ALP that was seen, by many workers, to have lost its socialist plank and interest in basic working-class needs. The CPA offered to Hardy and other recruits, a window on a world that was previously unknown to them. It was new and exciting, and Hardy embraced it with fervour.

The events leading up to and following the publication of *Power Without Glory*, his arrest on a charge of criminal libel, the protracted committal proceedings, trial and acquittal were to change the young revolutionary. John Wren's name had long been associated with rumour and innuendo. The disclosures during the committal hearings had strengthened Hardy's case. He became a public figure, a folk hero, a man who had exposed corruption and the struggle for power. There were sections of the community who despised communism, but who were delighted that Hardy had revealed Wren's shady practices. Many Freemasons, Protestants, anti-Catholics and political conservatives privately applauded what Hardy had done. He had also received support from members of the literary community and other groups active in the preservation of democratic rights.

After his acquittal he became an honoured writer and guest in the Soviet Union and other Eastern European countries until his defection from Soviet Communism in 1968. Hardy had a serious and genuine interest in bringing about the abolition of capitalism in Australia, as a means of a better life for the working class. When he embraced the cause of the Gurindji people, he was a prominent and powerful advocate. As time passed, friends and supporters were wounded by his arrogance, rudeness and lack of concern for those who had assisted him, or those who had given or lent him money. His sins of commission and omission were frequently condoned by the umbrella of 'party loyalty'.

Hardy was a highly intelligent chameleon; he had an ability to charm those he wished to impress, equally he could be abrasive towards others who had shown him generosity and friendship.

Hardy freely admitted that he had many obsessions. But his addiction to gambling was overwhelming and, in his last television interview, he described, with flamboyant gestures, that there was nothing better than going to the races with a pocket full of notes.[1] The constant need for money to feed his addiction had coloured his relationship with his wife, publishers, friends and those with whom he had financial dealings. He had an interest in seeking a better world for humanity in general, but his addiction made it impossible to apply it to people in particular. Given his political beliefs, his anti-Semitism was difficult to comprehend.

Despite his gambling addiction and his obsessions, Hardy did not resile from giving support to unpopular causes, and he was vehement in his opposition to the war in Vietnam. So, too, when he became an advocate for the rights of the Aboriginal people, and he made a significant contribution. It is not suggested that he initiated the Gurindji people's protest, but his active and ongoing participation ensured a high media exposure. He maintained his allegiance to the Aborigines until his death.

How will Frank Hardy be remembered? When his old adversary B. A. Santamaria was asked about *Power Without Glory*, he said he believed that it would be remembered as a social history of the Wren period. 'It was interesting I can tell you. It was like a Grand Final football match.' He did not think it would stay in the popular memory, but it would become a social document for history researchers.[2]

When Jim Cairns, former ALP Federal Treasurer and MHR for the seat of Yarra [once a Wren stronghold], spoke to Dr H. V. Evatt, erstwhile ALP Federal Attorney-General, he expressed the view that the Victorian ALP was 'crook' during those years. Cairns was adamant that John Wren was not involved with Santamaria's Movement. He believes that John Wren represented the worker influence in the ALP, while the ALP Industrial Groups represented the middle class.[3] This statement accords with Santamaria's remarks that Wren despised him and the Movement.

The Victorian and National leadership of the CPA had high expectations that the novel would be of significant value in reversing the powerful influence of the ALP Industrial Groups in the trade unions. Yet, perhaps without realising it, Frank Hardy had read the political scene correctly when he wrote the last chapter of *Power Without Glory*. In the novel John West (Wren) was bitterly resentful that he was expected to supply money to Catholic Action and the Movement.[4] This would have no political gain for him, in fact it was to his detriment. This confirms the statements made about John Wren by B. A. Santamaria and Jim Cairns.

The CPA leadership knew that anti-Catholic sectarianism could be a useful political tool. They were well aware of the likely results when they conceived the writing and the production of the novel. In the first flush of success it appeared that their judgment was correct, but subsequent events produced a totally different outcome, as the ALP Industrial Groups continued to flourish. It may have been that apathetic Catholics were galvanised into supporting the Groups because of their disgust at the attack on Mrs Wren's character. Jim

Cairns believes that *Power Without Glory* did not have any effect on the split in the Australian Labor Party in 1954.[5]

Whatever the political effects of the novel, there remains a blemish on the records of the Victorian and National leadership of the CPA and Frank Hardy. Les Barnes challenged Hardy about the alleged adultery committed by Nellie West (Wren), but he was over-ruled when Hardy appealed to the Victorian CPA leadership. This was reinforced when J. B. Miles, the General Secretary of the CPA, insisted that the story be included. Did the leadership ever ask Hardy to establish the veracity of his sources, and, even were the allegation true, was it not a cruel and malicious act to include it in the novel? It can only be concluded that neither Hardy nor the CPA leadership considered that a code of ethics should apply. Research has shown that the true-life characters depicted in Hardy's *Who Shot George Kirkland?* were disreputable and unreliable sources. Many of the people who put considerable effort and resources into the making of *Power Without Glory*, and the fund-raising for the subsequent court hearings and trial, were jubilant. The embarrassment and humiliation caused to Mrs Ellen Wren and her family did not concern them. During the court hearings members of the Wren family and their supporters claimed that the publication of the novel was a communist plot. Were they right?

After fifty years it could be concluded that the major effect of the publication of *Power Without Glory* was the making of Frank Hardy.

Rumours had circulated since *Power Without Glory* was first published that Hardy had not written the novel. Following his death, these rumours again surfaced in the media and in an article in *News-Weekly*, together with a full-page photograph of Hardy on the front cover.[6] Many people gave Hardy information and access to documents, while others read his manuscript. He was given financial and physical help by the leadership and members of the CPA. But extensive research has not uncovered any evidence to support the claim that Hardy was not the author. Former CPA member and Brunswick historian Les Barnes, who had assisted Hardy in his early research, confirmed Hardy's authorship when he made this statement, reported in the *Brunswick Sentinel*:

'. . . Frank Hardy really stamped his style on the material, even though a lot of people may have supplied it to him.'

Mr. Barnes said Mr. Hardy was never modest.

'He always said he was the greatest novelist Australia had ever produced . . . But *Power Without Glory* wouldn't have been published without Frank.'

'I've always said I've never met anyone else in the world who could have published that book.'

'He had the guts, the resourcefulness and the ruthlessness. He was a real scoundrel.'[7]

Hardy's understanding of Catholicism, hardship, sport and gambling had come from his early years, but his knowledge and study of how society worked was developed to a higher level by his active participation in the CPA. It was these two influences which enabled him to write *Power Without Glory*. There is evidence to support the criticism that Hardy rewrote some of his work. There was also a circularity evident, that is, he kept returning to *Power Without Glory* and the events surrounding it, as with *Who Shot George Kirkland?* It may concluded that this was Hardy's *mea culpa* to Ellen Wren. It could also be concluded that it was yet another rewriting of the original humiliation. There were accusations that Hardy had plagiarised lines, phrases and structures throughout his work; to establish or disprove this would be beyond the scope of this book. What has been established is that Hardy was guilty of plagiarism on at least one occasion when he used, without acknowledgement, Dulcie Mortier's written words in his novel *But The Dead Are Many*.

Hardy did not fulfil his life's ambition to write a comprehensive work on the life of Henry Lawson. He had, with help from his wife, done extensive research and gathered supporting material for half a lifetime. Why Hardy did not achieve his aim can be found in *The Unlucky Australians*.[8]

During a discussion on the needs of writers, Realist Writer John Morrison mentioned Frank Hardy's good fortune in having had Ross, because she was 'such a splendid writer's wife'.[9] This attribute did not save Ross from being discarded. After the break-up of their marriage, Ross formed another relationship, but it was, except for brief periods, an unhappy association. It has not been possible to establish if Hardy ever found personal happiness. The constant factor in his life, until their separation, had been Ross. He paid a belated tribute to her during his last interview. There is evidence to suggest that he suffered from periods of depression and paranoia. Did he conceal himself behind the multiple personae that he had created during his life? He had an obsessive interest in, and had read widely on, the subject of suicide. His best friend, his sister and a woman with whom he had had an affair all committed suicide.

Hardy was egocentric to the point that he was unable to make a long-term commitment to another person. His addiction to gambling was such that it over-rode every other aspect of his life. When Hardy's papers are eventually open to researchers, without restrictions, they will throw further light on this complex, maverick Australian writer.

As religious and political passions cooled so, too, did Hardy and his Catholic opponents mellow. In early May 1990, Hardy was invited to return to Bacchus Marsh as guest speaker for the St Bernard's Catholic School Hundredth Anniversary Celebrations. He was at first reluctant to attend the gathering, but eventually he arrived, somewhat later than expected. Frank was welcomed like the Prodigal Son; he was photographed and warmly greeted by old friends and new acquaintances. There were few guests who failed to be charmed by him.[10] Bacchus Marsh had reclaimed its famous Australian writer.

Hardy came to prominence early in his life. He received acclaim in Australia and abroad. Shortly before his death, he acknowledged that he had made a lot of enemies, but he had also maintained a large and devoted following throughout his life. When the CPA disbanded, Hardy still declared himself a communist.

Frank Hardy became Australia's best-known writer of the radical left. He created his own myths and legends. Hardy's words 'power without glory' have become part of our language, and his suburb, 'Carringbush', has acquired its own identity and enriched our folklore. The circumstances that enabled him to achieve such an extraordinary place in Australian society will not occur again. It is unlikely that another Frank Hardy will emerge.

NOTES

Preface

1. Marie-Louise Ayres, Supervisor, Australian Special Research Collection, Australian Defence Force Academy, Canberra, letter to PA, 25 January 1995.

2. M. H. Ellis, 'The Writing of Australian Biographies', *Australian Historical Studies*, Vol. 6, No. 24, May 1995, pp. 432–46.

1 Childhood and Youth

1. Birth certificate of Francis Joseph Hardy, Registration Number 16898/19117, Registry of Births, Deaths and Marriages, Melbourne.

2. Copy of Margaret Fogarty's birth certificate obtained from St Joseph's Catholic Church, Warrnambool, archivist Helen Price, courtesy of her sister, Mrs Marie Boyce, 15 Fairy Street, Warrnambool, Victoria 3280. Where applicable, sources of additional documents will be attributed to Mrs Boyce.

3. Copy of marriage certificate of John Bourke and Bridget O'Keefe. This document discloses variation in spelling of Bourke (Burke) and O'Keefe (Keefe), Boyce Collection. Copy of baptismal entries of Elizabeth (Eliza) Collins and Patrick Fogarty, Thurles Parish Records. Ursuline Convent, Thurles, County Tipperary, Boyce Collection.

4. Copy of marriage certificate of Margaret Fogarty and Michael Bourke, Boyce Collection.

5. Copies of death certificates of Michael and Margaret Bourke, Boyce Collection. Margaret's father registered her death and made his mark. Her mother, Elizabeth Fogarty, was also illiterate. Copies of death certificates of Patrick and Elizabeth Fogarty, Boyce Collection.

6. Mick Bourke, interview with PA, Koroit, 29 August 1994.

7. Sarah Surkitt's birth certificate, Registration Number 8396, Registry of Births, Deaths and Marriages, Melbourne. This document discloses variation in spelling of Surkit (Surkitt).

8. Copy of marriage certificate of Sarah Surkitt and James Hardy, supplied by Helen Price, archivist, St Joseph's Catholic Church, Warrnambool. Registry of Births, Deaths and Marriages, Melbourne, was unable to locate any records of James Hardy's birth. From information supplied by Sandra Salmon, Assistant Deacon, Anglican Parish of Kilmore, Victoria, 17 February 1995. From information supplied by Beverley Brennan, archivist, St Brendan's Catholic Church in Kilmore.

9. Jim Hardy, interview with PA, 1996. If James Hardy was born in Ireland, he was presumably a Catholic. Although James married in the United Church of England, his sons were baptised in the Catholic Church, and his daughters were brought up in the Church of England. This was not an uncommon practice in the case of mixed marriages.

10. Caroline Milburn, *Age*, Melbourne, 29 January 1994, p. 1.

11 Tourist brochure, Koroit Hotel, Koroit, proprietor Mick Bourke, author's collection.

12 Mick Bourke, interview with PA, 1994.

13 Marriage certificate of Winifred Bourke and Thomas Hardy, Registration Number 4056, obtained from Registry of Births, Deaths and Marriages, Melbourne. Copies of Winifred Bourke and Thomas Hardy's baptisms from register of St Joseph's Catholic Church, Warrnambool, Boyce Collection.

14 Jim Hardy, interview with PA, Dandenong, 25 January 1996.

15 Jim Hardy, interview with PA, 1996.

16 Mick Bourke, interview with PA, 1994.

17 Birth certificate of Mary Veronica Hardy, Registration Number 30342/1931, Registry of Births, Deaths and Marriages, Melbourne.

18 Baptismal entry of Francis Joseph Hardy, courtesy of Father Michael Linehan, Church of the Infant Jesus, Koroit.

19 Geoffrey Camm, *Bacchus Marsh by Bacchus Marsh. An Anecdotal History*, p. 281.

20 Jim Hardy, interview with PA, 1996.

21 Frank Hardy, *Mary Lives*, p. 12.

22 Mick Bourke, interview with PA, 1994.

23 Jim Hardy, interview with PA, 1996.

24 Camm, *Bacchus Marsh*, p. 281.

25 Camm, interview with Frank Hardy, n.d.

26 Frank Hardy, *But the Dead Are Many*, p. 264.

27 *Ibid.*

28 Interview, Hardy and Camm.

29 Jim Hardy, interview with PA, 1996.

30 Alf Walton, interview with PA, Bacchus Marsh, 11 August 1994.

31 Jim Hardy, interview with PA, 1996.

32 From records of Christian Brothers College, Warrnambool, courtesy of Brother Gerard, Treacy Centre, Parkville, March 1996. From records of Allansford & District Primary School, courtesy of Marie Ziebell, History Sub-Committee of the Allansford & District Primary School, March 1996.

33 Jim Hardy, interview with PA, 1996.

34 *Ibid.*

35 Camm, *Bacchus Marsh*, p. 281. Allansford & District Primary School records.

36 Jim Hardy, interview with PA, 1996.

37 Camm, *Bacchus Marsh*, p. 233.

38 Frank Hardy, *Legends from Benson's Valley*, p. 137.

39 Camm, *Bacchus Marsh*, p. 306.

40 Alf Walton, telephone interview with PA, March 1996.

41 Kath McFarland, interview with PA, Bacchus Marsh, March 1994.

42 Vance (Pat) Dickie, interview with PA, Bacchus Marsh, 12 August 1994.

43 Jim Hardy, interview with PA, 1996.

44 Kath McFarland, interview with PA, 1994.

45 Interview, Hardy with Camm.

46 Jim Hardy, interview with PA, 1996.

47 School records, St Bernard's Catholic Primary School, Bacchus Marsh, supplied by Mr Laurie Wheelahan, curator, the Mary McKillop Convent Museum, Bacchus Marsh.

48 Jim Hardy, interview with PA, 1996.

49 Frank Hardy, *The Hard Way*, p. 28.

50 Alf Walton, interview with PA, 1994.

51 Camm, *Bacchus Marsh*, p. 307.

52 *Ibid.*, p. 307.

53 *Ibid.*, p. 340.

54 Alf Walton, interview with PA, 1994.

55 Jim Hardy, interview with PA, 1996.

56 Hardy, *The Hard Way*, p. 30.

57 Jim Hardy, interview with PA, 1996.

58 Camm, *Bacchus Marsh*, p. 282.

59 Jim Hardy, interview with PA, 1996.

60 Frank Hardy, *The Four-Legged Lottery*, pp. 63–5.

61 Jim Hardy, interview with PA, 1996. Frank Hardy drawing of Bacchus Marsh RSL members loaned to PA for reproduction.

62 Hardy, *The Hard Way*, p. 31.

63 Jim Hardy, interview with PA, 1996.

64 Frank Hardy, *Herald* (Melbourne), 7 October 1985, p. 11.

65 Jim Hardy, *Herald* (Melbourne), 6 November 1985, p. 6.

66 James Griffin, discussion with PA, December 1998.

67 Eva Jago, interview with PA, McMahon's Point, NSW, 11 October 1995.

68 Michael Cannon, *The Human Face of the Great Depression*, p. 127.

69 *Ibid.*, p. 132.

2 Rites of Passage

1 *Radio Times*, 25 September 1937, p. 3.

2 Frank Hardy, *The Hard Way*, p. 32.

3 Frank Hardy, *Legends from Benson's Valley*, pp. 247–8.

4 Hardy, *The Hard Way* pp. 32–3.
5 Jim Hardy, telephone interview with PA, 22 November 1995.
6 Radio Times Collection, State Library, Melbourne.
7 Ralph Gibson, *My Years In The Communist Party*, p. 108.
8 Radio Times Collection.
9 *Encyclopaedia Britannica*, Vol. 11, pp. 445–6.
10 Copy of marriage certificate, Francis Joseph Hardy and Rosslyn Phyllis Couper, courtesy of Shirley Hardy-Rix.
11 Jim Hardy, telephone interview with PA, 22 November 1995. Photograph of Frank and Rosslyn Hardy, 27 May 1940, courtesy of Shirley Hardy-Rix.
12 Val Noone, *Disturbing the War—Melbourne Catholics and Vietnam*, p. 42.
13 Copy of birth certificate of Rosslyn Phyllis Couper, courtesy of Shirley Hardy-Rix.
14 Shirley Hardy-Rix, interview with PA, Doncaster East, 1 November 1995.
15 Frances Driscoll (née Hardy), interview with PA, Elanora Heights, NSW, 13 October 1995.
16 Pauline B. Burren, *Mentone: The Place For A School—A History of Mentone Girls' Grammar School from 1899*, p. 88.
17 Jim Hardy, interview with PA.
18 Hardy, *The Hard Way*, p. 33.
19 *Ibid.*, p. 288.
20 Camm, *Bacchus Marsh*, p. 287.
21 Colin Jory, *The Campion Society*, pp. 33–4.
22 *Advocate*, 14 January 1937, p. 21.
23 Jory, *The Campion Society*, p. 87.
24 *Advocate*, 19 August 1937, p. 7.
25 Margaret Love, compiled by, *St. Bernard's Church Bacchus Marsh—1874–1974*. Booklet courtesy of Margaret Love.
26 Camm, *Bacchus Marsh*, pp. 288–9.
27 Noone, *Disturbing the War*, p. 28.
28 *Advocate*, 25 March 1937, p. 17, and various newspapers in author's collection.
29 B. A. Santamaria, interview with PA, North Melbourne, 4 April 1995.
30 *Advocate*, 19 August 1937, p. 7.
31 Camm, *Bacchus Marsh*, p. 289.
32 *Ibid.*, p. 221.
33 *Ibid.*, p. 289.
34 *Mary*, pseudonym.
35 Gibson, *My Years*, p. 108.
36 *Ibid.*
37 Noone, *Disturbing the War*, p. 29.
38 Les Barnes, compiled by, *Annals of the ACP.* [Australian Communist Party, a name adopted by the CPA for some

of its life], no publisher, date or page numbers.
39 Interviews, Shirley Hardy-Rix, Alan Hardy and Frances Driscoll with PA, 1995.
40 Frances Driscoll, interview with PA, 13 October 1995. (An enquiry to the Registry of Births, Deaths and Marriages, Melbourne, revealed no record of the birth. In 1941 it was not required to register a stillborn infant.)
41 Soldier Career Management Agency, documents re Francis Joseph Hardy's service in Citizen Military Forces and 2nd Australian Imperial Force; permission for PA to access records, courtesy of Alan Hardy.
42 Beverley Symons, 'All-Out For The People's War: Communist Soldiers In The Australian Army In The Second World War', *Australian Historical Studies*, Vol. 26, No. 105, October 1995, p. 596.
43 *Ibid.*, p. 597.
44 Frank Hardy, *The Four-Legged Lottery*, p. 150.
45 Symons, 'All-Out For The People's War', p. 598.
46 *Ibid.*, pp. 598–9.
47 Hardy, *The Hard Way*, p. 33.
48 Jim Hardy, interview with PA.
49 Hardy, *The Four-Legged Lottery*, p. 150.
50 *Mid-day Times*, 6 June 1942.
51 Jim Hardy, interview with PA, 1996.
52 Soldier Career Management Agency, Service and Casualty Form.
53 Malcolm Good, telephone interview with PA, 8 June 1994.
54 Bruce Armstrong, interview with PA, Chadstone, 20 June 1995.
55 *Mid-day Times*, Vol. 10., No. 25, Saturday, 19 June 1943, p. 1.
56 Malcolm Good, telephone interview with PA, 8 June 1994.
57 Hardy, *The Hard Way*, p. 39. Death certificate of Thomas Hardy, Registration No. 5668, Registry of Births, Deaths and Marriages, Melbourne, 5 December 1994, and the Fawkner Crematorium & Memorial Park burial records.
58 Mary Agatha O'Leary, 'Till The Shades Lengthen'—*Caritas Christi Hospice, Kew. 1938–1988*, p. 12.
59 James Griffin, *Australian Dictionary of Biography*, Vol. 12: 1891–1939, p. 582. Griffin discussion with PA.
60 Soldier Career Management Agency, Service and Casualty Form.
61 *Troppo Tribune*, News Mouthpiece of 8 A.A.O.D. Mataranka, Northern

Territory, Vol. 5., No. 5 (Number 45), Monday, 25 October 1943, shows the new editor as Pte F. J. Hardy, and the cost of the publication as 'priceless'.

62 *Australasian Post*, September 14, 1991, p. 38. and Hardy, *The Hard Way*, p. 33.

63 *Troppo Tribune*, p. 1.

64 Hardy, *The Hard Way*, p. 35.

65 Dulcie Mortier, interview with PA, Canberra, over period 27 September to 3 October 1992.

66 Symons, 'All-Out For The People's War', p. 604.

67 William H. Wilde, Joy Hooton and Barry Andrews (eds), *The Oxford Companion to Australian Literature*, p. 234.

68 Symons, 'All-Out For The People's War', p. 611.

69 Hume Dow, interview with PA, Kew, 25 June 1994.

70 Maclaren Gordon, interview with PA, South Yarra, 27 June 1994.

71 Ian Turner, 'My Long March', *Overland*, No. 54, Spring 1974, p. 29.

72 Symons, 'All-Out For The People's War', p. 610.

73 Vane Lindesay, 'Kismet Hardy', *Australian Book Review*, No. 78, February–March 1986, pp. 14–15.

74 Vane Lindesay, interview with PA, Ripponlea, 10 March 1992.

75 *Ibid.*

76 Wendy Lowenstein, telephone interview with PA, 6 June 1996. Harry

77 Hardy, *The Hard Way*, p. 36.

78 Author's recollections.

79 Hardy, *The Hard Way*, p. 41.

80 Bernard Smith, *Noel Counihan*, pp. 104–5.

81 Les Barnes, interview with PA, Brunswick, 18 June 1992.

82 Bruce Armstrong, interview with PA, December 1995.

83 Turner, *My Long March*, p. 31.

84 Les Barnes, interview with PA, Brunswick, 18 June 1992.

85 *Guardian*, 5 October 1945, p. 4.

86 University of Melbourne, Student Record No. 451514, Francis Joseph Hardy, Entry Arts 1945, Single Subject Modern English, courtesy of Gerry Barretto, Student Administration.

87 Hardy, *The Hard Way*, p. 154.

88 Hardy, *The Four-Legged Lottery*, pp. 152–3.

89 Eva Jago, interview with PA, McMahons Point, NSW, 11 October 1995, and *The Four-Legged Lottery*, pp. 95–9.

90 Rose Stone, interview with PA., Balaclava, 27 June 1995.

Drysdale Bett's premises at 300 King Street, Melbourne, were close to the Flagstaff Gardens; they had been commandeered by the US Army as an ordnance store. The newspaper staff were obliged to move down to the basement where the printing presses operated.

3 The Genesis of Power Without Glory

1 James Griffin, discussions with PA 1998–99; Niall Brennan, *John Wren: Gambler*, pp. 6–7.

2 James Griffin, *Australian Dictionary of Biography*, Vol. 12: 1891–1939, p. 580.

3 Brennan, *John Wren*, pp. 17–18.

4 *Ibid.*, pp. 15–16, 19.

5 *Ibid.*, p. 26.

6 *Ibid.*, p. 33.

7 *Victorian Parliamentary Debates 1898*, Vol. 90, pp. 3941–55.

8 Brennan, *John Wren*, p. 108.

9 Griffin, *ADB*, p. 581.

10 Ibid., p. 582.

11 Deirdre Moore (née Cable), interview with PA, Hawthorn East, 1 March 1995.

12 Cedric Ralph, letter to PA, 9 August 1995.

13 Cedric Ralph, interview with PA, Balook, Victoria, 13 September 1995.

14 *Ibid.*

15 Niall Brennan, *The Politics of Catholics*, p. 3., and B. A. Santamaria, *Santamaria A Memoir*, p. 32.

16 Santamaria, *Santamaria*, p. 66.

17 *Catholic Action at Work*, no author, no date, *c.* 1945; Santamaria, *Santamaria, A Memoir*, pp. 73–4.

18 Gerard Henderson, 'If ASIO comes clean, should Frank Hardy be far behind?', *Sydney Morning Herald*, 7 April 1992, p. 11.

19 Santamaria, *Santamaria*, p. 74.

20 *Catholic Action at Work*, p. 21.

21 Robin Gollan, *Revolutionaries and Reformists*, pp. 170–2.

22 *Guardian*, 10 November 1944, p. 1.

23 Les Barnes, interview with PA, Brunswick, 18 June 1992.

24 *Ibid.*

25 Cedric Ralph, letter to PA, 21 May 1996.

26 *Ibid.*

27 J. Sendy, 'What Democratic Centralism Is', *Communist Review*, No. 183, March 1957, p. 92.
28 Bernie Taft, *Crossing the Party Line*, p. 49.
29 Les Barnes, interview with PA, 18 June 1992.
30 *Ibid.*
31 *Ibid.*
32 Frank Hardy, *The Hard Way*, front flap of dust-jacket.
33 *Ibid.*, pp. 38–40.
34 Vane Lindesay, 'Kismet Hardy', *Australian Book Review*, No. 78, February–March 1986, p. 15.
35 Mungo MacCallum, *Plankton's Luck: A life in retrospect*, p. 35.
36 Deirdre Moore, interview with PA, 1 March 1995.
37 *Ibid.*
38 Bernie Taft, interview with PA, Clifton Hill, 9 August 1995.
39 *Ibid.*
40 Taft, *Crossing the Party Line*, colophon.
41 Bernie Taft, interview with PA, 9 August 1995.
42 Beryl Boag (née Thompson), interview with PA, Heidelberg, 5 April 1993.
43 Alex Boag, interview with PA, Heidelberg, 5 April 1993.
44 Les Barnes, interview with PA, 18 June 1992.
45 Deirdre Moore, interview with PA, 1 March 1995.
46 *Ibid.*
47 Cedric Ralph, interview with PA, Balook, 13 September 1995.
48 Deirdre Moore, interview with PA, 1 March 1995.
49 *Ibid.*
50 *Ibid.*
51 Hardy, *The Hard Way*, p. 46.
52 Nancy Wills, *Shades of Red*, pp. 127–9.
53 Walter Kaufmann, telephone interview with PA (Sydney/ Melbourne), 10 September 1994.
54 Hardy, *The Hard Way*, p. 40.
55 *Ibid.*, pp. 41–2.
56 *Ibid.*, p. 53.
57 Bernie Taft, interview with PA, 9 August 1995.
58 Bill Smith, interview with PA, Middle Park, 19 February 1992.
59 Hardy, *The Hard Way*, pp. 43–4.
60 *Ibid.*, p. 43.
61 *Ibid.*, p. 44.
62 Dot Thompson, interview with PA, Brunswick, 5 March 1995.
63 *Ibid.*
64 Ralph Gibson, *The Fight Goes On*, p. 51. The quotation is from Palme Dutte's article 'For a Lasting Peace and People's Democracy', in *Cominform Journal*, early 1952. Permission to quote from this publication courtesy of Hugh Anderson.
65 Hardy, *The Hard Way*, p. 48.
66 *Ibid.*
67 Amirah Inglis, *The Hammer & Sickle and the Washing Up*, p. 62.
68 *Mary*, pseudonym, letter to PA, 5 January 1999.
69 Les Barnes, telephone interview with PA, 24 June 1992.
70 Jack Blake, letter to PA, 28 September 1995.
71 Frances Driscoll (née Hardy), interview with PA, 13 October 1995.
72 Taft, *Crossing the Party Line*, p. 141.
73 *Ibid.*, p. 139.

4 The Gestation of Power Without Glory

1 Soldier Career Management Agency, Proceedings for Discharge and Determination of Demobilization Priority Forms.
2 Frank Hardy, *The Hard Way*.
3 Amirah Inglis, *The Hammer & Sickle and the Washing Up*, p. 55.
4 Les Barnes, interview with PA, 18 June 1992.
5 *Ibid.*
6 *Ibid.*
7 *Ibid.*
8 Hardy, *The Hard Way*, p. 91.
9 *Ibid.*, pp. 46–7, and interview Jim Hardy with PA, Dandenong, 25 January 1996.
10 Frank Hardy, 'Fella Slave', *Australian Literary Quarterly 3*, October 3–4, 1987, p. 3.
11 Hardy, *The Hard Way*, pp. 50–2.
12 *Ibid.*, pp. 44–5.
13 Ted Seedsman, telephone interview with PA, 2 August 1995, in response to her 'Help Needed' notice in the *Age*, 31 July 1995, page 12, seeking information about Frank Hardy. By coincidence, Ted Seedsman was well-known to PA since the 1950s, but she was unaware of his connections with John Wren.
14 *Ibid.*
15 Hardy, *The Hard Way*, pp. 49–50.

16 Ibid., p. 46.
17 Ibid., p. 59.
18 Ibid., p. 47.
19 Frank Hardy, *Who Shot George Kirkland?*, p. 4.
20 Hardy, *The Hard Way*, p. 47.
21 John McLaren, *Writing in Hope and Fear*, p. 7. (Note 17 in Prologue, p. 211. Interview, John McLaren with Ted Hill, Melbourne, August 1986.)
22 Ibid., p. 7.
23 Hardy, *The Hard Way*, p. 48.
24 Ibid., pp. 53–4.
25 Ibid., p. 57.
26 *Richmond Guardian*, 9 May 1925; *Richmond Chronicle*, 10 June 1942.
27 Vic Little, interview with PA, 23 March 1992. 'Squizzy' Taylor was a criminal who died in a shoot-out in 1927.
28 Ibid.
29 Hardy, *The Hard Way*, p. 49.
30 Frances Driscoll (née Hardy), interview with PA, Elanora Heights, NSW, 13 October 1995.
31 Dorothy Hewett, *Wild Card*, p. 180.
32 Dorothy Hewett, interview with PA, Faulconbridge, NSW, 27 August 1992.
33 Bill Smith, interview with PA, 19 February 1992.
34 Frank Hardy, *The Four-Legged Lottery*, p. 187.
35 Frances Driscoll (née Hardy), interview with PA, 13 October 1995.
36 June Stephens, interview with PA, Elwood, 16 November 1996.
37 Niall Brennan, audio-cassette of Council of Adult Education seminar held at Monash University in December 1976 on 'The historical significance of *Power Without Glory*'.
38 June Hearn, audio-cassette of Council of Adult Education seminar held at Monash University in December 1976 on 'The historical significance of *Power Without Glory*'.
39 Ibid.
40 Tom O'Lincoln, *Into The Mainstream—The Decline of Australian Communism*, p. 57.

5 *The Writing of* Power Without Glory

1 Frank Hardy, *The Hard Way*, p. 60, pp. 109–10.
2 Ibid., p. 111.
3 Ibid., p. 112.
4 Ibid., p. 113.
5 Carlo Canteri, interview with PA, Chadstone, May 1998.
6 Hardy, *The Hard Way*, p. 115.
7 Vane Lindesay, 'Kismet Hardy', *Australian Book Review*, Number 78, February–March 1986, pp. 14–15.
8 Margaret Hutton, Autobiography and History—A study of the Autobiographies of Australian Communists and Ex-Communists, unpublished BA Hons thesis, La Trobe University, October 1992, p. 2.
9 W. B. Yeats, *Autobiographies*, p. 3.
10 Hardy, *The Hard Way*, p. 115.
11 John Sendy, *Comrades Come Rally!*, p. 23.
12 A. Davidson, *The Communist Party of Australia*, p. 83.
13 Bruce Armstrong, interview with PA, Chadstone.
14 Hutton, Autobiography and History, p. 34.
15 Ibid., p. 35.
16 Hardy, *The Hard Way*, pp. 122–3.
17 Zoë O'Leary, *The Desolate Market—A Biography of Eric Lambert*, p. 36.
18 Ibid., pp. 37–8, 39.
19 Eric Stark, telephone interview with PA, 3 December 1996. J. B. Miles, Lance Sharkey and Jack Blake were members of the National Committee of the CPA.
20 Wendy Lowenstein, telephone interview with PA, 30 November 1996.
21 Ron Neave, telephone interview with PA, 23 November 1996.
22 Hardy, *The Hard Way*, p. 125.
23 Ibid., pp. 126–7.
24 Hume Dow, interview with PA, Kew, 25 June 1994.

6 *Printing, Binding and Publishing*

1 Frank Hardy, 'The Fella Slave', *Australian Literary Quarterly* 3, 3–4 October 1987.
2 Frank Hardy, *The Hard Way*, p. 130.
3 Vic Little, interview with PA, 23 March 1992.

4 Hardy, *The Hard Way*, pp. 128–9.
5 Les Barnes, interview with PA, 18 June 1992.
6 Bill Barnes, interview with PA, West Brunswick, 14 February 1996.
7 Vic Little, interview with PA, 23 March 1992.
8 Hardy, *The Hard Way*, p. 129.
9 *Ibid.*, p. 130.
10 Vic Little, interview with PA, 23 March 1992.
11 Les Barnes, interview with PA, 18 June 1992.
12 Vic Little, interview with PA, 23 March 1992.
13 Hardy, *The Hard Way*, p. 130.
14 Vic Little.
15 Vic Little.
16 Hardy, *The Hard Way*, p. 129.
17 *Ibid.*, pp. 130–1.
18 Vic Little, interview with PA, 23 March 1992.
19 *Ibid.*
20 *Ibid.*, and Hardy, *The Hard Way*, p. 131.
21 Hardy, *The Hard Way*, p. 131.
22 Vic Little, interview with PA, 23 March 1992, and several telephone discussions during 1995 and 1996.
23 Les Barnes, interview with PA, 18 June 1992.
24 Vic Little, telephone discussions during 1996.
25 Les Barnes, interview with PA, 18 June 1992.
26 *Ibid.*
27 *Ibid.*
28 Ralph Gibson, *The Fight Goes On*, p. 51.
29 *Ibid.*, p. 47.
30 Sue Camm, granddaughter of Jack Alexander Ross and niece of Phyl Dyson, telephone discussion with PA, 16 December 1996. Camm understood that her grandfather qualified as a solicitor at a later age than usual; she had heard that he became the head of the Titles Office. His politics were apparently conservative; Phyl Dyson's involvement with left-wing politics was of concern to her parents. It is of interest that, despite his misgivings, her father had agreed to make legal comments on the contents of *Power Without Glory*. Sue Camm's mother had informed her of the sequence of events.
31 Sharon Nicholson (née Keen), telephone interviews with PA, 12 and 18 June 1994. Nicholson is one of the children from Phyl Dyson's second marriage. She tendered the information that her half-sister, Janie Dyson, had their grandfather Ross's statement advising Hardy and Dyson which sections of *Power Without Glory* were possibly libellous.
32 Hardy, 'The Fella Slave'.
33 Nancy and Bill Irving, telephone interview with PA, 16 December 1996.
34 Frances Driscoll (née Hardy), interview with PA, 13 October 1995.
35 Joseph Waters, interview with PA, South Yarra, 12 August 1991.
36 Hardy, *The Hard Way*, p. 131.
37 Fred Farrall, interview with PA, the Alexandra Private Nursing Home, South Caulfield, 1991. The Reverend Victor James mentioned in the text was, at that time, the incumbent of the Unitarian Church, East Melbourne. He was also known as one of the 'Peace Parsons' during the Cold War years.
38 John Lamp (son of Marie Kaiser), telephone discussion with PA, 4 July 1998.
39 Vic Little, interview with PA, 23 March 1992.
40 Nick Pagonis, discussion with PA at Chadstone Shopping Centre and subsequent telephone interview on 5 August 1998.
41 Hardy, The Hard Way, pp. 134–5.
42 Bruce Armstrong, interview with PA, 16 December 1996.
43 Hardy, *Power Without Glory* (Melbourne: The Realist Printing and Publishing Co., April 1950), colophon. Author's collection.
44 John Sendy, *Melbourne's Radical Bookshops*, p. 118. Sendy is considered an authoritative source as to how the 'under the counter' sales of the first edition of *Power Without Glory* were handled. He was a prominent CPA functionary for many years '. . . his experience of radical bookshops in Melbourne has spanned his entire career'.
45 John Fraser, interview with PA, Doncaster, 23 November 1995. After comparing the April 1950 first edition and the copy in Fraser's possession, it was noted that there were slight differences. Cedric King of Dudley King & Sons, Typesetters, interview with PA, Vermont, 12 January 1996. King recalled that Frank Hardy used to come to their premises and talk to his father about the typesetting for *Power Without Glory*, but as he was not involved in the discussions, he could not recall whether it was late in 1949 or 1950. He said that his father, Dudley King, was paid for the work. Fraser &

46 Jenkinson, Printers, were on the floor below.
46 Hardy, *The Hard Way*, p. 139.
47 *Sun*, 3 August 1950, p. 2.
48 *Tribune*, 16 August 1950, p. 4; *Courier Mail*, 21 August 1950, p. 3; *West Australian*, 26 August 1950, p. 19; *Smith's Weekly*, 9 September 1950, p. 3.
49 *Argus*, 12 September 1950, p. 6.
50 *Australasian Post*, 14 September 1950, p. 37; *Guardian*, 15 September 1950, p. 3; *Smith's Weekly*, 23 September 1950, p. 3; *Bulletin*, 27 September 1950, p. 2, p. 35; *Meanjin*, Vol. 9, No. 3, Spring 1950, pp. 222–5.
51 Ian Mair, interview with PA, South Yarra, 25 March 1992.
52 *Ibid*.

7 Criminal Libel

1 Joseph Waters, interview with PA, South Yarra, 12 August 1991.
2 Frank Hardy, *The Hard Way*, p. 138.
3 Len Gale, discussion with PA, Trades Hall, Melbourne 1998.
4 *Age*, 30 September 1950, p. 2.
5 *Guardian*, 17 January 1947, p. 6, and 18 April 1947, p. 3.
6 James Griffin, *Australian Dictionary of Biography*, Vol. 12: 1891–1939, p. 580.
7 James Griffin, discussions with PA, 1998–99.
8 B. A. Santamaria, interview with PA, North Melbourne, 4 April 1995.
9 *Ibid*.
10 Frank Scully, telephone interview with PA, January 1999.
11 Geoff Browne, *Biographical Register of the Victorian Parliament 1900–84*, p. 13.
12 Frank Hardy, *Power Without Glory*, pp. 633–41, First edition, April 1950, in author's collection.
13 Joseph Waters, interview with PA, 12 August 1991.
14 Hardy, *The Hard Way*, pp. 168–71.
15 *Age*, 25 October 1950, p. 1.
16 *Bulletin*, 27 November 1976, p. 11.
17 Hardy, *The Hard Way*, p. 172.
18 Albie Heintz, interview with PA, Richmond, 22 January 1996.
19 Hardy, *The Hard Way*, pp. 133–4. Vic Little, telephone interview with PA, December 1996.
20 Eric Stark, interview with PA, Chadstone, 11 January 1997.
21 Hardy, *The Hard Way*, p. 72.
22 Cedric Ralph, telephone discussion with PA, November 1998.
23 Frank Hardy, 'The Fella Slave', *Australian Literary Quarterly* 3, 3–4 October 1987, p. 3.
24 Albie Heintz, interview with PA, 22 January 1996.
25 *Argus*, 24 October 1950, p. 1.
26 John Ross, *Chronicle of the 20th Century*, p. 712.
27 Hardy, *The Hard Way*, p. 168.
28 *Ibid*., p. 171.
29 *Argus*, 24 October 1950, and Stop Press, p. 1.
30 Hardy, *The Hard Way*, pp. 170–1.
31 *Ibid*., pp. 172–3.
32 *Ibid*., pp. 173–4.
33 Cedric Ralph, interview with PA, Balook, Victoria, 13 September 1995.
34 *Argus*, 26 October 1950, p. 1.
35 *Age*, 26 October 1950, p. 1.
36 *Argus*, 27 October 1950, p. 1.
37 *Ibid*.
38 Cedric Ralph, interview with PA, 13 September 1995.
39 *Argus*, 26 October 1950, p. 1.
40 *Ibid*.
41 *Argus*, 27 October 1950, p. 1.
42 *Guardian*, 23 November 1950.
43 'Why is Frank Hardy author of "Power Without Glory" Branded Guilty *Before Trial*?'—Leaflet printed by Realist Printing and Publishing Co., Melb. No publisher or date cited. Photocopy in author's collection.
44 *Guardian*, 23 November 1950.
45 *The Concise Oxford Dictionary*, p. 1036.
46 'Why is Frank Hardy . . .' leaflet.

8 The Frank Hardy Defence Committee

1 'Why is Frank Hardy . . .' leaflet.
2 Nancy Wills, *Shades of Red*, p. 86.
3 Alvie Booth, interview with PA, Essendon, 6 May 1993.
4 Wills, *Shades of Red*, p. 84.
5 *Ibid*., pp. 84–85.
6 Frank Hardy, *The Hard Way*, p. 55; Vic Williams, interview with PA, Sunshine, 15 September 1993.
7 Hardy, *The Hard Way*, p. 135.
8 Shirley Andrews, telephone interview with PA, July 1993.
9 Nadine Dalgarno, telephone interview with PA, 1995.

10 *Argus*, 28 November 1950, p. 5.
11 Jon Faine, *Taken On Oath—A Generation of Lawyers*, p. 44.
12 Review of the *Power Without Glory* Trial, ABC Radio National program 'The Law Report'; Jon Faine interviews Mr Frank Hardy and Sir John Starke, 8 December 1992.
13 Cedric Ralph, extract from his unpublished memoir, 'Political Struggles', p. 9. Copy in author's collection.
14 *Argus*, 28 November 1950, p. 5. The four Melbourne daily newspapers published comprehensive reports of Frank Hardy's arrest, committal proceedings and trial. After a study of the newspapers, the author decided to focus on the legal proceedings as reported by the *Argus*, as it was considered to be representative of the press coverage.
15 Faine, *Taken on Oath*, p. 45.
16 *Argus*, 28 November 1950, p. 5.
17 *Ibid.*, p. 6.
18 *Ibid.*, 29 November 1950, p. 5.
19 *Ibid.*
20 *Ibid.*
21 *Ibid.*
22 *Ibid.*, 28 November 1950, p. 6.
23 Hardy, *The Hard Way*, p. 146.
24 *Ibid.*, pp. 67–73, 75, 86.
25 Vance Marshall, *The World Of The Living Dead & Jail From Within*, pp. 7–11. This edition was published by the Federal Council of the Miscellaneous Workers' Union as a tribute to their first Organiser, [James] Vance Marshall. The first edition of *Jail From Within* was published under the auspices of The Social Democratic League, Sydney, by The Workers' Trade Union Press, St. Andrews Place, in May, 1918, price one shilling. The second edition was printed clandestinely. The first edition of *The World Of The Living Dead* was published by the working class press and the Trade Union Movement in Sydney, on 5 November 1918. A copy of the first edition of *Jail From Within*, and a copy of the combined 1969 edition of *The World Of The Living Dead & Jail From Within* can be located in the State Library of Victoria.
26 *Ibid.*
27 *Ibid.*, p. 7.
28 *Ibid.*, Preface, pp. 79–81.
29 Hardy, *The Hard Way*, pp. 77–78.
30 Marshall, *The World Of The Living Dead*, p. 21.
31 Hardy, *The Hard Way*, p. 86.
32 Marshall, *The World Of The Living Dead*, p. 19.
33 Hardy, *The Hard Way*, pp. 67–97 in particular, and others.
34 *Ibid.*, p. 81.
35 *Ibid.*, p. 95.
36 Paul Adams, *The Stranger from Melbourne—A Literary Biography 1945–1975*, p. 76.
37 Hardy, *The Hard Way*, pp. 95–7.
38 *Argus*, 29 November 1950, p. 1.
39 *Ibid.*, 30 November 1950.
40 *Ibid.*, 1 December 1950, p. 6.
41 *Ibid.*, 8 December 1950.
42 Hardy, *The Hard Way*, p. 98.
43 Fred Farrall, interview with PA, 1991, the Alexandra Private Nursing Home, South Caulfield, and earlier discussions.
44 Zelda D'Aprano, interview with PA, Camp Eureka, Yarra Junction, 26 January 1997. Telephone interview with PA, 22 July 1997.
45 Ted Thompson, interview with PA, Northcote, 5 March 1995.
46 Author's recollections of the events of the meeting and the aftermath, early Winter 1951.
47 Graham Pitts, telephone interview with PA, December 1996.
48 Sam Goldbloom, telephone interview with PA, 28 October 1992. Joseph Waters, interview with PA, 12 August 1991.
49 Philip Mendes, 'When left was right', *Age* Extra Arts & Books, 17 May 1997, p. 8.
50 John [Jack] Arrowsmith, telephone interview with PA, December 1993. Arrowsmith's recollections of the meeting and disturbance at Newport corroborates Hardy's written account in *The Hard Way*.
51 Don Tonkin, Adelaide, SA, letter and statement to PA, 31 March 1992.
52 Chris Wallace-Crabbe, discussion with PA, December 1998.
53 John McLaren, *Writing in Hope and Fear*, Prologue, p. 7.
54 Hardy, *The Hard Way*, p. 157.
55 *Ibid.*, p. 156.
56 *Ibid.*, p. 68, p. 156.
57 *Ibid.*, p. 156.

9 Concluding the Preliminary Hearing

1 *Argus*, 16 January 1951, p. 4.
2 *Ibid.*
3 *Ibid.*
4 *Ibid.*

5   *Ibid.*
6   *Ibid.*
7   *Ibid.*
8   *Ibid.*, pp. 4–5.
9   *Ibid.*, p. 4.
10 *Ibid.*
11 *Ibid.*, 20 January 1951, p. 6.
12 Frances Driscoll (née Hardy), interview with PA, Elanora, NSW, 13 October 1995; Alan Hardy, interview with PA, Hawthorn East, 8 November 1995.
13 *Argus*, 17 January 1951, p. 4.
14 Paul Adams, *The Stranger from Melbourne, Frank Hardy—A Literary Biography 1945–1975*, p. 76.
15 *Argus*, 17 January 1951, p. 4.
16 *Ibid.*
17 *Ibid.*
18 *Ibid.*
19 *Ibid.*, pp. 4–5.
20 *Ibid.*, p. 5.
21 *Ibid.*
22 *Ibid.*, p. 4.
23 *Ibid.*, pp. 4–5.
24 *Ibid.*, p. 1.
25 *Ibid.*, pp. 1, 4, 5.
26 *Ibid.*, p. 5.
27 *Ibid.*
28 *Ibid.*
29 *Ibid.*
30 *Ibid.*, 19 January 1951, p. 4.
31 *Ibid.*, p. 5.
32 *Ibid.*, p. 4.
33 *Ibid.*
34 *Ibid.*, pp. 4–5.
35 *Ibid.*, p. 5.
36 *Ibid.*
37 *Ibid.*
38 *Ibid.*
39 *Ibid.*
40 *Ibid.*

41 *Ibid.*
42 *Ibid.*
43 *Ibid.*
44 *Ibid.*, 20 January 1951, pp. 1, 5.
45 *Ibid.*
46 *Ibid.*, p. 5.
47 *Ibid.*
48 *Ibid.*
49 *Ibid.*
50 *Ibid.*, pp. 5–6.
51 *Ibid.*, p. 6.
52 *Ibid.*, 20 January 1951, pp. 1, 5.
53 *Ibid.*, pp. 1, 5, 6.
54 *Ibid.*, 26 January 1951, p. 4.
55 *Ibid.*
56 *Ibid.*
57 *Ibid.*
58 *Ibid.*
59 *Ibid.*
60 *Ibid.*
61 *Ibid.*
62 *Ibid.*
63 *Ibid.*
64 *Ibid.*
65 *Ibid.*
66 *Ibid.*, pp. 4, 9.
67 *Ibid.*, p. 9.
68 *Ibid.*
69 *Ibid.*
70 *Ibid.*
71 *Ibid.*
72 *Ibid.*
73 *Ibid.*
74 *Ibid.*
75 *Ibid.*
76 *Ibid.*
77 *Ibid.*, 27 January 1951, p. 5.
78 *Ibid.*
79 *Ibid.*
80 *Ibid.*
81 *Ibid.*, p. 1.

10   The Trial

1   *Guardian*, 1 February 1951, p. 8, *Tribune*, 25 January 1951, p. 7.
2   *Tribune*, 8 February 1951, p. 7.
3   *Ibid.*
4   *Guardian*, 22 February 1951, p. 3.
5   *Ibid.* (Hardy stated in *The Hard Way*, p. 157, that 15 000 copies of *The Man From Clinkapella* were sold. Copies are occasionally to be found in second-hand bookshops.)
6   *Guardian*, 8 March 1951, p. 6.
7   *Ibid.*
8   Jon Faine, *Taken On Oath: A Generation of Lawyers*, p. 44.
9   Frank Hardy, 'The Fella Slave', *Australian* Literary Quarterly 3, 3–4 October 1987.
10 Discussions with the late Peter Miller, a member of the Realist Artists and former CPA member, other CPA members and sympathisers, and the author's own experience, confirmed that this was Gibson's mode.
11 John Sendy, *Ralph Gibson—An Extraordinary Communist*, p. 1.
12 Cedric Ralph, letter to PA, 9 August 1995.
13 *Guardian*, 21 March 1951, p. 7.
14 *Ibid.*
15 *Ibid.*, 15 February 1951, p. 3.

16 *Ibid.*
17 *Ibid.*, 21 March 1951, p. 7.
18 *Ibid.*
19 *Ibid.*, 29 March 1951, p. 7.
20 *Ibid.*
21 *Ibid.*
22 John Arrowsmith, telephone interview with PA, December 1993.
23 Shirley Pinnell, telephone interview with PA, 30 June 1998.
24 Bill Smith, interview with PA, Middle Park, 19 February 1992.
25 Joseph Waters, interview with PA, South Yarra, 12 August 1991.
26 Bernie Taft, *Crossing the Party Line*, p. 68.
27 *Argus*, 13 June 1951, p. 11.
28 John McLaren, *Writing in Hope and Fear*, p. 2.
29 *Ibid.*
30 *Ibid.*
31 Jon Faine, 'The Law Report', ABC Radio National, 8 December 1992. Jon Faine interviews Frank Hardy and former Justice, Sir John Starke, on the *Power Without Glory* trial of June 1951, when Starke acted as junior counsel for Hardy.
32 Frank Hardy, *The Hard Way*, p. 183.
33 *Ibid.*, pp. 178–9.
34 *Argus*, 13 June 1951, p. 7.
35 *Ibid.*
36 *Ibid.*, p. 10.
37 *Ibid.*, p. 11.
38 *Ibid.*
39 *Ibid.*
40 *Ibid.*
41 *Ibid.*, 14 June 1951, pp. 1, 7, 18.
42 *Ibid.*, p. 7.
43 *Ibid.*
44 *Ibid.*
45 *Ibid.*, 15 June 1951, p. 7.
46 *Ibid.*
47 *Ibid.*
48 *Ibid.*, 16 June 1951, p. 7.
49 *Ibid.*
50 *Ibid.*, 19 June 1951, p. 7.
51 *Ibid.*, 16 June 1951, p. 7.
52 *Ibid.*
53 *Ibid.*
54 *Ibid.*, 19 June 1951, p. 7.
55 *Ibid.*
56 Hardy, *The Hard Way*, p. 236.
57 Jon Faine, 'The Law Report', ABC Radio National, 8 December 1992.
58 Hardy, *The Hard Way*, p. 240.
59 *Argus*, 19 June 1951, p. 1.
60 Les Barnes, interview with PA, 18 June 1992.
61 Tony Stephens, 'New claims add spice to a hardy tale of power', *Sydney Morning Herald*, 8 December 1992.
62 *Argus*, 19 June 1951, p. 1.
63 *Ibid.*
64 Dawn Anderson, discussion with PA, Fitzroy, 18 July 1997. Hugh Anderson, discussion and letter, 6 November 1998.

11 Aftermath

1 *Argus*, 20 June 1951, p. 7.
2 *Ibid.*, 22 June 1951, p. 1.
3 *Ibid.*, 5 July 1951, p. 5.
4 Alvie Booth, interview with PA, 6 May 1993.
5 *Argus*, 14 July 1951, p. 7.
6 Alvie Booth, interview with PA, 6 May 1993.
7 Peter Coleman, 'The Red Page', *Bulletin*, 30 September 1961, p. 34.
8 Unsigned, 'A Committed Australian', *Times Literary Supplement*, London, 11 August 1961, p. 494.
9 Ted Thompson, interview with PA, Northcote, 5 March 1995.
10 *Argus*, 20 June 1951, p. 7, and Joseph Waters, interview with PA, South Yarra, 12 August 1991.
11 Joseph Waters, interview with PA, 12 August 1991.
12 Bruce Armstrong, interview with PA, Chadstone, 15 December 1996.
13 Julia Carlson, edited for Article 19, *Banned in Ireland: Censorship and the Irish Writer*, p. 67.
14 Frank Hardy Defence Committee Receipt No. J18, Collection List No. 824, dated 18 October 1951, issued to G. Armstrong for the sum of twelve shillings. Courtesy of the late Gough Armstrong; now in the author's collection.
15 Gallacher Papers, CP/IND/GALL/04/03, Labour History Archive and Research Centre, Manchester, UK. Courtesy of Phillip Deery, Victoria University of Technology, Footscray.
16 Joseph Waters, interview with PA, 12 August 1991.
17 Frank Hardy, 'Fella Slave', *Australian Literary Quarterly* 3, October 3–4, 1987, p. 3.
18 Frank Hardy, 'Slanski's Wife', *Bulletin*, 25 January 1969, p. 40.

[19] Statement regarding Frank Hardy and W. G. Smith's visit to James Loughnan in 1979. One signed copy was given to Frank Hardy at his request; this is in Box 149, the Hardy Papers, NLA. One signed copy was retained by W. G. Smith. This copy is now in the author's collection, courtesy of W. G. Smith.

[20] State Parliamentary Records. Information obtained from the Librarian, Victorian State Parliament.

[21] *Guardian*, 12 July 1951, p. 8.

[22] *Ibid.*

[23] Joseph Waters, interview with PA, 12 August 1991.

[24] *Guardian*, 20 September 1951, p. 2.

[25] *Ibid.*, 11 October 1951, p. 2.

[26] Frank Hardy, *Journey Into The Future*, pp. 314, 317.

[27] *Elizabeth*, pseudonym, telephone interviews with PA, 23 April 1997 and January 1998.

[28] Bernard Smith, *Noel Counihan: Artist and Revolutionary*, p. 277.

[29] Hardy, *Journey Into The Future*, p. 319.

[30] Joseph Waters, interview with PA, 12 August 1991. Waters registered the ABS from his office in Collins House. He said that George Seelaf, Bill Wannan, Wilfred Burchett's brother, a trade union official, whose name he could not recall [Clive Burchett was an organiser for the Building Workers' Industrial Union], and a young woman [Marjorie Roe] from Cheshire's Bookshop whose name he also could not remember, were present. Anzac Day had been chosen as the one on which all interested parties could attend. This meeting was held prior to the *Power Without Glory* trial. Frank Hardy, Joseph Waters and George Seelaf were certainly prominent in the ABS's conception. The meeting in February 1952 coincides with Hardy's return from abroad. John McLaren, *Writing in Hope and Fear*, pp. 35–36 and p. 214. The confusion over the first meeting of the ABS possibly stems from the fact that the idea was discussed over a long period.

[31] Audrey Blake, 'Notes on the Development of the Eureka Youth League and Its Predecessors', p. 155, unpublished manuscript, EYL Papers, University of Melbourne Archives.

[32] Zoë O'Leary, *The Desolate Market: A Biography of Eric Lambert*, p. 14.

[33] *Ibid.*, pp. 14–15.

[34] Joseph Waters, interview with PA, 12 August 1991.

[35] *Ibid.*

[36] Ralph de Boissière, discussion and statement dated 5 November 1998.

[37] Frank Hardy, 'Fella Slave', *Australian Literary Quarterly*.

[38] Joseph Waters, interview with PA, 12 August 1991.

[39] Eileen Capocchi, telephone interview with PA, 5 June 1997.

[40] Alvie Booth, interview with PA, 6 May 1993.

[41] Ian Syson, 'Out From The Shadows: The Realist Writers' Movement, 1944–1970, and Communist Cultural Discourse', *Australian Literary Studies*, Volume 15, Number 4, 1992, p. 335.

[42] Seamen's Union of Australia official records of Frank Hardy's service on coastal ships. Courtesy of retired seaman A. W. Oliver, who obtained these records on author's behalf.

[43] *Ibid.*

[44] John Morrison, *The Realist Writer*, No. 9, March–April 1954, pp. 11–12.

[45] David Carter, *A Career in Writing*; John McLaren, *Writing in Hope and Fear*; Ian Syson, Tracing the Making of Australian Working Class Literature, unpublished PhD, University of Queensland, 1993; Syson, 'Out From The Shadows'; Ian Syson, 'Working Class Literature Without Class', *Social Alternatives*, Vol. 12, No. 3, October 1993, pp. 25–9.

[46] Carter, *A Career in Writing*, p. 112.

[47] Les Barnes, interview with PA, Brunswick, 18 June 1992.

[48] A. A. Zhdanov, *On Literature, Music and Philosophy*, p. 15.

[49] Patricia Blake and Max Hayward (eds), *Dissonant Voices in Soviet Literature*, p. xxi.

[50] Zhdanov, *On Literature, Music and Philosophy*, p. 13.

[51] Carter, *A Career in Writing*, p. 76.

[52] A. A. Zhdanov, 'On the Errors of Soviet Literary Journals', *Communist Review*, No. 66, February 1947, pp. 421–30; Bernard Smith, 'Reds, and Other Colors', *Age* Monthly Review, Vol. 1, No. 6, October 1981, p. 7.

[53] Frank Hardy, 'Make Literature a Mass Question', *Communist Review*, No. 132, December 1952, pp. 376–7, 379.

[54] McLaren, *Writing in Hope and Fear*, p. 49.

[55] Hardy, 'Fella Slave', *Australian* Literary Quarterly.

[56] Frances Driscoll (née Hardy), interview with PA, Elanora, NSW, 13 October 1995.

57 Ted Bull, telephone interview with PA, 21 November 1995.
58 Amirah Inglis, *The Hammer & Sickle and the Washing Up*, p. 133.
59 Alan Hardy, interview with PA, East Hawthorn, 8 November 1995.
60 Vic Little, interview with PA, Brunswick, 23 March 1992.
61 The late Mervyn Feehan, CPA member, Australian Railways Union activist and tours organiser for the Australia China Society, in a series of discussions with PA during 1960s and 1970s.
62 Vera Deacon, reply to questionnaire, 19–22 January 1996.
63 Fiona Capp, *Writers Defiled*, pp. 82–3.
64 W. H. Wilde and T. Inglis Moore (eds) *Letters of Mary Gilmore*, p. 309.
65 Frances Driscoll (née Hardy), interview with PA, 13 October 1995.
66 Alan Hardy, interview with PA, 8 November 1995.
67 Death certificate of Winifred Mary Hardy, Registration Number 11524, Registry of Births, Deaths and Marriages, Melbourne.
68 Alan Hardy, interview with PA, 8 November 1995.
69 *Ibid.*
70 Vic Little, interview with PA, 23 March 1992.
71 Frances Driscoll (née Hardy), interview with PA, 13 October 1995.
72 Vic Little, interview with PA, 23 March 1992.
73 Joan Hendry, statement typed on her behalf by Betty Collins, Marrickville, NSW. Statement given to PA during interview with Collins, Marrickville, 12 October 1995.
74 Frank Hardy, 'Make Literature a Mass Question', *Communist Review*, No. 132, December 1952, pp. 374–9; Frank Hardy, 'On The Cultural Front', *Communist Review*, No. 153, September 1954, pp. 272–5; Frank Hardy. (abridged) 'Congress Speech—Problems of Literature and Art', *Communist Review*, No. 163, July 1955, pp. 201–5; Frank Hardy, 'Greetings to Katharine Susannah Prichard', *Communist Review*, No. 168, December 1955, pp. 381–2; Frank Hardy, 'Some Ideological Problems of Communist Writers', *Communist Review*, No. 174, June 1956, pp. 182–7; Frank Hardy, 'Forty Years Of Art For The People', *Communist Review*, No. 191, November 1957, pp. 379–80.
75 Dorothy Hewett, *Wild Card*, p. 250.
76 O'Leary, *The Desolate Market*, p. 90.
77 Alan Hardy, interview with PA, 8 November 1995.
78 *Ibid.*
79 Michael Cannon, *That disreputable firm . . . the inside story of Slater & Gordon*, pp. 80–1; [16] ibid., item 213, Report No. 5427; AA a6119/22, item 344, folio 53; [17] AA A6119/79, item 780, folio 78; [18] ibid., item 781, folio 11; [19] ibid., item 783, folio 8.
80 *Ibid.*

12 The Turbulent Sixties

1 Fred Wells, 'The Hardy Episode', *Quadrant*, May–June, 1969, No. 58, Vol. XIII, No. 2, p. 60. [This issue was incorrectly numbered as XIV, see *Australian Literary Studies*, 1969, p. 267.]
2 Frank Hardy, *The Four-Legged Lottery*, pp. 48–54. Frank Hardy, *Legends from Benson's Valley*, pp. 133–40.
3 Wells, 'The Hardy Episode', p. 59.
4 Alan Hardy, interview with PA, East Hawthorn, 8 November 1995; Frances Driscoll (née Hardy), interview with PA, Elanora NSW, 13 October 1995.
5 Vera Deacon, telephone interview with PA, 9 February 2000.
6 Bruce Armstrong, interview with PA, Chadstone, December 1996.
7 Seamen's Union of Australia official records of Frank Hardy's service on coastal ships. Courtesy of retired seaman, A. W. Oliver, who obtained these records on author's behalf.
8 Anonymous, 'A Committed Australian', London *Times Literary Supplement*, 11 August 1961, p. 494; Robert Burns, 'He Who Hurts A Little Wren', *Nation*, 7 October 1961, pp. 21–2; Carl Harrison-Ford, 'Libel the Hardy Way', *Australian*, 27 February, 1972, p. 25; John McLaren, 'Missed Opportunities', *Overland*, No. 22, Summer 1961–62, p. 49; Rex Mortimer, 'The Story of "The Hard Way"', *The Realist Writer*, No. 7, October, 1961, pp. 18–20.
9 *Tribune*, 16 August 1961, p. 3.
10 Clement Semmler, *Pictures on the Margin: Memoirs*, p. 295.
11 *Ibid.*, pp. 296–7.

12 Dulcie Mortier, interview with PA, Canberra, 27 September to 3 October 1992.

13 Frank Hardy, 'As a Prime Minister, Bonnie Bob Makes a Great Punter', *People*, 23 August 1988, p. 29.

14 Semmler, *Pictures on the Margin*, p. 299.

15 *Ibid.*, p. 301.

16 *Ibid.*

17 Clem Christesen, interview with PA, Eltham, 28 March 1992; John Morrison, interview with PA, St Kilda, 1 August 1994.

18 AUSTLIT, CD-ROM, Guide to Frank Hardy Papers.

19 Ali Verrills, interview with PA, 1 February 1995.

20 Alan Hardy, interview with PA, 8 November 1995.

21 Nancy Cato, 'New Fiction', *Australian Book Review*, Vol. 1, No. 8, June 1963, p. 127.

22 David Forrest, 'Poles Apart', *Overland*, No. 29, Autumn 1964, p. 61.

23 *National Times*, 2–7 October, 1972, p. 23.

24 Damien Murphy, 'Reds Dead but not buried', *Bulletin*, 28 September 1993, p. 26.

25 Bernie Taft, *Crossing the Party Line*, p. 130.

26 Rupert Lockwood, 'One night in the life of Frank Hardy', *Nation Review*, 17–23 October 1975, p. 24.

27 Semmler, *Pictures on the Margin*, p. 302.

28 Walter Kaufmann, telephone interview with PA, Sydney to Melbourne, 10 September 1994.

29 Bill Wannan, interview with PA, North Caulfield, 21 August 1999.

30 Frank Hardy, 'Stalin's Heirs', *Bulletin*, 11 January 1969, p. 29.

31 Frank Hardy, *The Unlucky Australians*, outside back cover and pp. 17–18.

32 Fred Thompson, interview with PA, Townsville, Qld, 5 February 1994.

33 *Age*, 5 August, 1991, p. 5; 20 January 1973, p. 18.

34 Telephone discussion with Ann Godden, December 1998.

35 Pat Rappolt, 'The Cry of the Dispossessed', *Adelaide Advertiser*, 8 June 1968, p. 14.

36 Roger Garaudy, *From Anathema to Dialogue: The Challenge of Marxist-Christian Cooperation*, Collins, London, 1967.

37 Wells, 'The Hardy Episode', p. 58.

38 B. A. Santamaria, *Santamaria: A Memoir*, p. 60. Reproduced by permission of Oxford University Press Australia from *Santamaria: A Memoir* by B. A. Santamaria, OUP, 1996 © Oxford University Press.

39 Fred Hollows and Peter Corris, *Fred Hollows An Autobiography*, pp. 87–8.

40 Roland Perry, 'Comrades', *Australian Magazine*, 24–5 October 1992, p. 20.

41 Frances Driscoll (née Hardy), interview with PA, 13 October 1995.

42 John Docker, 'A Study in Context: And the Dead are Many', *Arena*, No. 41, 1976, pp. 57–8.

43 Dulcie Mortier, interview with PA, 27 September to 3 October 1992.

44 Frances Driscoll (née Hardy), interview with PA, 13 October 1995.

45 Alan Hardy, interview with PA, 8 November 1995.

46 Shirley Hardy-Rix, interview with PA, Doncaster East, 1 November 1995.

47 Dulcie Mortier, telephone interview with PA, 3 August 1997. In the early 1980s, Adrian Deamer had told Mortier that in 1968 Hardy had been engaged in negotiations with the *Australian* to write a series of articles about the events in Prague. The management was surprised to learn that the London *Times* had published 'Stalin's Heirs'.

48 Frank Hardy, 'Stalin's Heirs', *Bulletin*, 11 January 1969, pp. 27–30.

49 Frank Hardy, 'History Invited Us', *Bulletin*, 18 January 1969, p. 31, and Hardy, 'Stalin's Heirs', *Bulletin*, 11 January 1969, p. 28.

50 Hardy, 'Stalin's Heirs', *Bulletin*, 11 January 1969, p. 28.

51 Frank Hardy, 'Yevtushenko and the Oxford Election', *Bulletin*, 4 January 1969, pp. 57–8.

52 Sydney *Daily Mirror*, 'Author leads protest for Aboriginals', 15 November 1968, no page number. The incident was also mentioned in the *Age*, 16 November 1968.

53 Frank Hardy, 'Yevtushenko and the Oxford Election', p. 57.

54 Alan Hardy, interview with PA, 8 November 1995.

55 'Soviet News Bulletin', No. 2/174, 23 January 1969, published by the Press Office of the USSR Embassy in Australia, Griffith, Canberra, ACT. This was a reprint of an article from 'Literaturnaya Gazeta Answers The Australian Author', *Literaturnaya Gazeta*, No. 52, of 25 December 1968.

56 Sam Lipski, 'Why the party is split over Moscow', *Australian*, 25 February 1969, p. 9.
57 Wells, 'The Hardy Episode', p. 61.
58 *Age*, 22 January 1969, p. 1, and 29 January 1969, p. 22.
59 Wells, 'The Hardy Episode', pp. 60–1.
60 Frank Hardy, 'Slanski's Wife', *Bulletin*, 25 January 1969, p. 40.
61 Audrey Blake, *A Proletarian Life*, pp. 22–4.
62 Stuart Macintyre, *The Reds*, p. 376.
63 *Australian*, 5 March 1969, p. 1.
64 *Ibid*.
65 *Ibid*., 23 August 1969, p. 18.

13 Betrayals

1 Eva Jago, interview with PA, McMahon's Point, NSW, 11 October 1995.
2 *Ibid*.
3 Frances Driscoll (née Hardy), interview with PA, Elanora, NSW, 13 October 1995.
4 Eva Jago, interview with PA, 11 October 1995.
5 *Ibid*.
6 *Ibid*.
7 *Ibid*.
8 Brian Kiernan, 'A scatological romp with the garbo set', *Australian*, 11 September 1971, p. 19.
9 Robert Drewe, '"The Outcasts" await the final verdict', *Australian*, 17 September 1971, p. 9.
10 Max Beattie, 'Frank Hardy's "treason" amuses the upper crust', *Age*, 11 December 1971, p. 2.
11 Eva Jago, interview with PA, 11 October 1995.
12 Thomas Shapcott, *The Literature Board: A Brief History*, p. 86.
13 Eva Jago, interview with PA, 11 October 1995.
14 *Ibid*.
15 *Ibid*.
16 *Ibid*.
17 Logie Award for best TV drama, *Daybreak Killers*, 1972.
18 Eva Jago, interview with PA, 11 October 1995.
19 *Ibid*.
20 Clement Semmler, *Pictures on the Margin: Memoirs*, pp. 311–2.
21 Dave Nadel, 'Special Liftout', *The Battler*, 4 August 1976, courtesy of Lyle Allan, copy in author's collection.
22 Dulcie Mortier, interview with PA, Canberra, 27 September to 3 October 1992. Dulcie Mortier, 'Did Anne Hathaway Write Shakespeare?' courtesy of Dulcie Mortier, copy in author's collection. Nikki Mortier, telephone interview with PA, July 1997.
23 Hardy's inscription, courtesy of Dulcie Mortier, copy in author's collection.
24 Letter to Dulcie Mortier from Stephen, Jaques & Stephen, Attorneys, Solicitors and Notaries, signed A. Deamer, 27 May 1981. Adrian Deamer was a specialist in defamation and the former editor of the *Australian*. Courtesy of Dulcie Mortier, copy in author's collection.
25 Letter, Paul Mortier to Frank Hardy in Moscow, 6 February 1963, in the Frank Hardy Papers, National Library of Australia, Canberra. Dulcie Mortier has granted permission to reproduce this letter.
26 John McLaren, 'The Word Battle', Melbourne *Herald*, 10 April 1979, p. 28. (See also: John McLaren, 'Failing to cast much light on Stalin's shadow . . . "Frank Hardy's *But The Dead Are Many* is an intellectually and emotionally honest attempt to understand the attractions of Soviet communism, and provides a more convincing account of the surrender to them and subsequent disillusion than either Arthur Koestler or Victor Serge—both read at least as much on the left as on the right"', Letters to Editor, *Age*, 1 September 1994, p. 14.)
27 Michael McNay, 'Writers Assessed', *Australian*, 9 August 1975.
28 Max Harris, 'Browsing', *Australian*, 6 September 1975, p. 31.
29 John Docker, 'A Study in Context: And the Dead are Many', *Arena* No. 41, 1976, pp. 54–5, pp. 60–1.
30 SBS television 'Masterpiece' programme, Andrea Stretton talks to Frank Hardy, 6 February 1994. SBS television 'Book Show', Dinny O'Hearn talks to Frank Hardy, 4 February 1992. These programmes were shown posthumously.

14 The Ghosts of Power Without Glory

1 Eva Jago, interview with PA, McMahon's Point, NSW, 11 October 1995.
2 Paul Adams, *The Stranger from Melbourne*, p. 76.
3 Kevin Childs, *A month of lunches*, p. 74.
4 Eva Jago, interview with PA, 11 October 1995.
5 Alan Hardy, interview with PA, East Hawthorn, 8 November 1995.
6 Phillip Adams, interview with PA, Paddington, NSW, 10 October 1995.
7 *Ibid.*, and Phillip Adams, 'Too many laurels for our Hardy', *Australian* Weekend Review, 12–13 February 1994, p. 2.
8 Eva Jago, interview with PA, 11 October 1995.
9 Frank Hardy, *Who Shot George Kirkland?*, p. 35. The condition *pseudologia fantastica* is described in the work of Horace B. English and Ava C. English, *Comprehensive Dictionary of Psychological and Psychoanalytical Terms*, p. 415, 'Pseudologia fantastica, pathological and habitual lying'.
10 Ken Brass, *Australian Women's Weekly*, 3 December 1980, pp. 6–7.
11 Information obtained from the Registry of Births, Deaths and Marriages.
12 Information regarding Thomas George Hall's police service obtained from the Victoria Police Historical Unit.
13 Information obtained from the Registry of Births, Deaths and Marriages.
14 Information obtained from the Registry of Births, Deaths and Marriages.
15 Information regarding William Frederick John Egan's police service obtained from the Victoria Police Historical Unit.
16 *Ibid.*
17 Information obtained from the electoral rolls.
18 Hardy, *Who Shot George Kirkland?*, colophon and Chapter 4.
19 Hardy, *Who Shot George Kirkland?*, p. 34.
20 Close relative of Robert Allan Hall who does not wish to be identified.
21 Enquiries revealed that there is no record of Robert Allan Hall ever having been a member of the Victoria, Commonwealth or Federal Police.
22 Victoria Police Historical Unit records.
23 Hardy, *Who Shot George Kirkland?*, p. 12.
24 *Argus*, 1 January 1919, p. 7.
25 *Argus*, 20 February 1919, p. 7.
26 Hardy, *Who Shot George Kirkland?*, p. 7.
27 *Police Gazette*, 26 July 1924, and the *Brunswick & Leader* newspaper.
28 Victoria Police Historical Unit.
29 Information obtained from the Registry of Births Deaths and Marriages.
30 Copy of death certificate of William Frederick John Egan. Registration No. 10228, Registry of Births, Deaths and Marriages, Melbourne, 10 November 1998, author's collection. Information re Lucinda Evelyn Hall's death obtained from Registry of Births, Deaths and Marriages.
31 Review of *Power Without Glory* trial, ABC Radio National programme 'The Law Report'; Jon Faine interviews Mr Frank Hardy and Sir John Starke, 8 December 1992.
32 John Frow, 'Who Shot Frank Hardy? Intertextuality and Textual Politics', *Southern Review*, Volume 15, Number 1, March 1982, p. 25. See also Tim Rowse, 'Jack Beasley's *Red Letter Days*', *New Literature Review*, No. 6, 1979, pp. 40–4; Peter Williams, 'Plagiarism and Rewriting: The Case of Frank Hardy', *New Literature Review*, No. 10, 1982, pp. 45–53.
33 Chris Wallace-Crabbe, *Falling Into Language*, p. 29.
34 Garry Kinnane, *George Johnston—A Biography*, p. 84.
35 *Ibid.*, p. 70.
36 *Ibid.*, p. 216, p. 219.
37 Helen Thomson, 'Whose tribute is it anyway?', *Australian*, 12 June 1992, p. 14.
38 Kinnane, *George Johnston*, p. 242.
39 *Ibid.*, p. 107.
40 Eva Jago, interview with PA, 11 October 1995. Frank Hardy depicted his father in a most favourable light, both in his writing and during interviews. It seems clear that, in at least some aspects of his own life, he used his father as a role model.
41 Thomas Shapcott, *The Literature Board*, p. 25, p. 86.
42 Max Harris, 'Taking the Oz Literature Board for granted', *Australian* Weekend Magazine, 24–5 November 1979, p. 4.
43 *Sydney Morning Herald*, 26 October 1982, p. 2.
44 Paul Gray, 'Frank Hardy: how the Left creates its myths', *News-Weekly*, 26 February 1994, p. 14.

45 Max Harris, *Australian*, 6 September 1975, p. 20

46 Information supplied to PA by a librarian at the Carringbush Regional Library, July 1997. Following the amalgamation of the Collingwood, Fitzroy and Richmond Councils, the Carringbush City Library was renamed the Carringbush Regional Library. [In 1999 the telephone directory listed the Carringbush Adult Education Centre, the Carringbush Computer Services, the Carringbush Fine Foods, the Carringbush Florist, and the Carringbush Hotel.]

47 Carmel Shute, interview with PA, Ross House, Flinders Lane, Melbourne, 23 July 1997.

48 Frances Driscoll (née Hardy), interview with PA, 13 October 1995.

49 Vera Deacon, letter to PA, 19–22 January 1996, p. 8.

50 SBS television 'Masterpiece' programme, 4 February 1992.

51 Bruce Pascoe, 'Memories of my mate Frank Hardy', Sunday *Age*, 30 January 1994, p. 8.

52 Graham Pitts, telephone interview with PA. December 1996.

53 Vera Deacon, letter to PA, 19–22 January 1996, p. 8.

54 Walter Kaufmann, telephone interview with PA, Melbourne to Sydney, 10 September 1994.

55 Isobel Montgomery, 'Bukharin's widow a fighter to the end', *Age*, 13 March 1996, p. 14.

56 Rupert Lockwood, 'One night in the life of Frank Hardy', *Nation Review*, 17–23 October 1975, p. 24.

57 Walter Kaufmann, telephone interview with PA, 10 September 1994.

58 *Ibid.*

59 Frank Hardy, *The Obsession of Oscar Oswald*, pp. 88–90, pp. 93–4.

60 Walter Kaufmann, telephone interview with PA, 10 September 1994.

61 Vane Lindesay, interview with PA, Ripponlea, Victoria, 10 March 1992.

62 Frank Hardy, 'Grey bombers' unfair cop', *Australasian Post*, 23 November 1986, p. 42.

63 *Hollywood Ten—Melbourne One*, Swinburne Film School, 16 mm film, 30 minutes, 1986, written and directed by Daryl Dellora. Frank Hardy/Ross Franklyn appeared in the film. It was shown at the 1986 Melbourne Film Festival. Copy of the film is in the Baillieu Library, University of Melbourne.

64 Frank Hardy, 'The Most Australian Australian—Frank Hardy', *People*, weekly column, 1 January 1985 to 13 April 1987. The weekly column then appeared under 'Hardyarns', 20 April 1987 and concluded with the issue of 11 October 1988. The final issue overlapped, by three days, *Australasian Post's* first edition. Information obtained from National Library Australia, *People Collection*.

65 Frank Hardy, 'The Most Australian Australian', *Australasian Post*, weekly column, commenced 8 October 1988 and concluded with the issue of 30 January 1993. Information obtained from National Library Australia, *Australasian Post Collection*.

66 Fiona Capp, *Writers Defiled*, pp. 79–88.

67 Frank Hardy, 'How ASIO Spied On Me', *Age* Agenda 5, 22 March 1992. See also *Sydney Morning Herald*, 'Spectrum', 21 March 1992, p. 41. see pp. 79–88.

68 Capp, *Writers Defiled*, p. 81.

69 *Ibid.*

70 *Ibid.*

71 Author's recollections during the 1940s and 1950s in Melbourne.

72 Capp, *Writers Defiled*, p. 83.

73 John Larkin, Sunday *Age*, Agenda 8, 14 June 1992; Leonard Radic, *Age*, 12 June 1992, p. 14; Helen Thomson, 'Whose tribute is it anyway?', *Australian*, 12 June 1992, p. 14.

74 *Age*, 12 March 1993, p. 10.

75 SBS Television News, 6.30 pm., 29 January 1994.

76 Damien Murphy, 'Reds Dead but not buried', *Bulletin*, 28 September 1993, p. 25.

77 *Write On*, journal of the Victorian Writers' Centre, Vol. 4, No. 101, November 1993, p. 3.

78 Information supplied by the Literature Board of the Australia Council, July 1997.

79 *Herald-Sun*, 29 January 1994, p. 1, p. 3.

80 *Land Rights News*, Vol. 2, No. 32, April 1994, p. 17; Anonymous, 'Glory without power for our most treasured red', *Sydney Morning Herald*, 29 January 1994, p. 11; Anonymous, London *Daily Telegraph*, 31 January 1994, no page number, courtesy of the late Lloyd Edmonds.

81 SBS Television News, 6.30 p.m., 29 January 1994. Shirley Hardy-Rix was shown being interviewed outside her late father's Carlton home.

82 Phillip Adams, 'Too many laurels for our Hardy', *Australian* Weekend Review, 12–13 February 1994, p. 2.
83 *Age*, 5 February 1994, p. 1.
84 Programme, 'Celebration of the life of Frank Hardy', 5 February 1994, Collingwood.
85 *Age*, 5 February 1994, p. 1.
86 Programme, 'Celebration of the life of Frank Hardy', 13 March 1994, Sydney.

    Courtesy of Vera Deacon.
87 Information supplied to PA courtesy of the Fawkner Crematorium & Memorial Park, Fawkner, on 31 March 1994. The Hardy grave was inspected by PA. It was noted that the headstone on the grave showed Thomas Hardy's date of death as 11 June 1945; this is incorrect, as he died on 11 June 1943.
88 *Age*, Extra Books p. 7, 31 July 1999.

Epilogue

1 SBS 'Masterpiece' programme, 6 February 1994. Andrea Stretton talks to Frank Hardy. This was Hardy's last recorded television interview.
2 B. A. Santamaria, interview with PA, North Melbourne, 4 April 1995.
3 Jim Cairns, telephone discussion with PA, December 1998.
4 Frank Hardy, *Power Without Glory*, pp. 632–41.
5 Jim Cairns, telephone interview with PA, December 1998.
6 *News-Weekly*, 26 February 1994, cover and pp. 12–14.
7 Les Barnes, *Brunswick Sentinel*, 21 February 1994, p. 8.
8 Frank Hardy, *The Unlucky Australians*, p. 18.
9 John Morrison, informal discussion with PA, 1994.
10 Carmel Shea, interview with PA, Bacchus Marsh, 23 July 1998. Jim Hardy, interview with PA, Dandenong, 25 January 1996. Permission to copy photographs of Frank and Jim Hardy at the celebrations, courtesy of the late Laurie Wheelahan, curator, the Mary McKillop Convent Museum, Bacchus Marsh.

BIBLIOGRAPHY

Works of Frank Hardy

ARCHIVES
Frank Hardy Papers, National Library of Australia, MS4887.
National Library of Australia Oral History Collection includes twenty-five audio-cassettes, many of Hardy dictating.
Frank Hardy Collection, University College, The University of New South Wales, Australian Defence Force Academy, ADFA Library Manuscript Collection No. BRN 229155 Cons. 2 G300.
Australian Defence Force Academy Collection includes video-recording made by the ADFA on 28 February 1992—'Frank Hardy talks about his life and works'.

FOREIGN-LANGUAGE EDITIONS
It has been impossible to determine Hardy's foreign language publications from 1951 until 1968. In addition to his novels, short story collections, non-fiction, plays and essays, he wrote many articles for the Soviet Union and Eastern European countries' newspapers and journals. He participated in writers' conferences, and frequently his addresses were widely published. The most comprehensive records are probably available in his archival collections.

LITERARY FELLOWSHIPS AND GRANTS
1969—New South Wales Advisory Committee on Cultural Grants, Literary Fellowship, six months.
1973—The Literature Board of the Australia Council Fellowship, six months.
1985—The Literature Board of the Australia Council Writer's Assistance Grant.
1993—The Literature Board of the Australia Council Fellowship, four years.

BOOKS
Editions of the works of Frank Hardy referred to in the text.

Novels
Power Without Glory. Melbourne: The Realist Printing and Publishing Co., Melbourne, 1950.
The Four-Legged Lottery. London: T. Werner Laurie Ltd., 1958. Published in Australia by arrangement with the Australasian Book Society.
The Outcasts of Foolgarah. Allara Publishing Pty. Ltd., Melbourne, 1971.
But The Dead Are Many. The Bodley Head Ltd, London, 1975.

Who Shot George Kirkland? Pan Books (Australia) Pty Limited, Sydney, 1981. First published 1980. Co-winner of the Australian Natives' Association Literature Award.
The Obsession of Oscar Oswald. Pascoe Publishing, Carlton, Victoria, 1983.
Warrant of Distress. Pascoe Publishing, Carlton, Victoria, 1983. Companion Volume to *The Obsession of Oscar Oswald.* More properly described as a booklet, 40 pages.

Non-fiction
Journey Into The Future. Australasian Book Society, Melbourne, 1952.
The Hard Way. T. Werner Laurie Ltd, London, 1961. Published in Australia by arrangement with the Australasian Book Society.
The Unlucky Australians. Pan Books Ltd, London, 1978. First published 1968.

Short story collections
The Man from Clinkapella. Capricorn Printing Co., Auburn, Victoria, n.d. This was published during 1951 while Hardy was on bail awaiting trial.
Legends From Benson's Valley. T. Werner Laurie Ltd, London, 1963.
The Yarns of Billy Borker. A. H. L. & W. A. Reed, Auckland, 1965.
Billy Borker Yarns Again. Thomas Nelson (Australia) Limited, Melbourne, 1967.
The Great Australian Lover. Thomas Nelson (Australia), Melbourne, 1972. First published 1967.
It's Moments Like These. Gold Star Publications (Aust.) Pty Ltd, Melbourne, 1972.
The Needy And The Greedy. Frank Hardy and Athol Mulley. Libra Books, Canberra, 1976. First published 1975.
You Nearly Had Him That Time. Frank Hardy and Fred Trueman. Stanley Paul & Co. Ltd, London, 1978.
A Frank Hardy Swag. Edited with an Introduction by Clement Semmler. Harper & Row Australasia Pty Ltd, Adelaide, 1982. This short story collection also contains extracts from *Power Without Glory, But The Dead Are Many, The Hard Way, The Unlucky Australians, The Outcasts of Foolgarah,* adaptations from Hardy's *Stalin's Heirs* articles in the *Bulletin* and Hardy as literary critic and essayist.
The Loser now will be later to win. Pascoe Publishing Pty Ltd, Carlton, Victoria, 1986. First published 1985.
Hardy's People. Fairfield, Australia: Pascoe Publishing Pty Ltd, Fairfield, 1986.
Great Australian Legends. Century Hutchinson Australia Pty Ltd, Surry Hills, Australia, 1989. First published 1988.
Retreat Australia Fair. Hutchinson Australia, Milson's Point, Australia, 1990.

Competitions
In 1944 Hardy won the School of Modern Writers Short Story Competition with his story *A Stranger in the Camp.* In October 1945 he won the *Guardian* Short Story Competition for *The Man From Clinkapella* written under the pseudonym of Ross Franklyn. In 1962 he gained equal second with Merv Lilley in the Dame Mary Gilmore Awards for his short story *The New Policeman.*

FILMS
Three in One, producer Cecil Holmes, 1957, includes adaptations of Frank Hardy and Henry Lawson stories with a contemporary segment. The Cinematheque and the National Film and Sound Archive showed a 'Cecil Holmes Retrospective' at the State Film Centre, Melbourne, on 15 September 1995. *Three in One* was shown on that occasion.

Hollywood Ten—Melbourne One, 1986, producer, Daryl Delora, Swinburne Film School. Frank Hardy/Ross Franklyn appeared in this film. Shown at the 1986 Melbourne Film Festival. Copy in the Baillieu Library, University of Melbourne.

PLAYS

Stage and TV
The Nail on the Wall (1951, New Theatre, Melbourne).
Black Diamonds (1958. Produced on Czech television *c*. 1962).
The Ringbolter (1967. Dame Mary Gilmore Award Best Stage Play).
Daybreak Killers (1972. Logie Award best TV drama, 1972).
Who Was Harry Larsen? (1985).
Faces in the Street. Westgate, NSW 2038: Stained Wattle Press, 1990.
(First performed at the Everest Theatre, Seymour Centre, Sydney as part of the Sydney Drama Festival, 16 January 1988).
Mary Lives! Paddington, NSW: Currency Press Pty Ltd, 1992.
(First performed at the Malthouse, Melbourne, 1992).

Radio
Written under the pseudonym of Ross Franklyn.
Jacky-Jacky gentleman, bushranger and penal reformer. Australian Broadcasting Commission, 1946.
Usual Women. Australian Broadcasting Commission, 1946.
To Arms! To Arms! Australian Broadcasting Commission, July 1946.

UNPUBLISHED MANUSCRIPTS
The Red Fox Who Learned to Love Chickens. (Children)
Voices Off. (Autobiography)
The Woman Who Was Always Looking for Sex—and Other Stories about the Female of the Species. (Short Stories)
These three titles were supplied by Jennie Barrington, letter to PA dated 17 October 1991. All other unpublished manuscripts etc. are presumably located in the National Library of Australia and Australian Defence Force Academy, Canberra.

JOURNALISM

Weekly Columns in Magazines
People Magazine, 1 January 1985 to 13 April 1987, under the title 'The Most Australian Australian'. The column then appeared under 'Hardyarns' from 20 April 1987 and concluded with the issue of 11 October 1988.
Australasian Post Magazine, 8 October 1988, concluding with the issue of 30 January 1993.

Articles, short stories and letters published in journals and newspapers
'The Strange Genius of J. M. Synge', *New Theatre Review*, *c*. 1946.
'Communists Have Helped Literature', *Tribune*, 7 June 1951, p. 9.
'Make Literature a Mass Question', *Communist Review*, No. 132, December 1952, pp. 374–9.
'The Load of Wood', short story published in *The Tracks we Travel: Australian Short Stories*, edited by Stephen Murray-Smith, Melbourne, 1953, pp. 74–85.
'On The Cultural Front', *Communist Review*, No. 153, September 1954, pp. 272–5.

(Abridged) 'Congress Speech—Problems of Literature and Art', *Communist Review*, No. 163, July 1955, pp. 201–5.

'Edward Harrington', *Overland*, No. 3, Autumn, 1955, pp. 3–5.

'Frank Hardy Replies to Criticism', *Tribune*, 23 November 1955, p. 8. Article relates to earlier criticism in *Tribune*, 21 September 1955, p. 8, of Hardy's short story 'Death of a Unionist' in *Overland* No. 4, June, 1955, pp. 15–18.

'Greetings to Katharine Susannah Prichard', *Communist Review*, No. 168, December 1955, pp. 381–2.

'Some Ideological Problems of Communist Writers', *Communist Review*, June 1956, No. 174, pp. 182–7.

'The Only Fair Dinkum Raffle Ever Run in Australia', short story in *Overland*, No. 10, Spring, 1957, pp. 7–8.

'Forty Years Of Art For The People', *Communist Review*, No. 191, November 1957, pp. 379–80.

'The Crookest Raffle Ever Run' by Frank Hardy, as told by *Billy Borker* in the Redfern Hotel, *Overland*, No. 11, Summer, January 1958, pp. 7–9.

'In Crooks National Store: Waiting for the verdict on *Power Without Glory*', *Nation*, 30 January 1960, pp. 12–13.

'Where's Tommy?', short story, *Realist Writer*, Vol. 2, 1960, pp. 21–6.

'It's Moments Like These', short story, *Realist Writer*, Vol. 3, 1960, pp. 20–37.

'Two Fair Dinkum People—Welcome to Soviet Writers', editorial, *Realist Writer*, Vol. 1, August 1960, pp. 3–5.

'The Grim Reality Behind Unemployment Statistics', *Tribune*, 19 July 1961, pp. 6–7.

'Address Delivered at Archer Crawford's Funeral', *Realist Writer*, No. 5, 1961, pp. 19–21.

'Frank Hardy and Morris West on Television', interviewed by Bob Sanders, reported in *Realist Writer*, No. 13, 1963, pp. 20–2.

'The Genius of Henry Lawson: Time, Place and Circumstances', Part 1, *Realist Writer*, No. 13, 1963, pp. 10–14.

'The Genius of Henry Lawson: Time, Place and Circumstances', Part 2, *The Realist*, No. 14, 1964, pp. 8–13.

'The Mosquitoes are Big in the Territory', short story, *The Realist*, Vol. 15, 1964, pp. 26–7. As told by *Billy Borker* in the First and Last Hotel, Sydney.

'Not Like Here in Woolloomooloo', short story, *The Realist*, No. 19, 1965, pp. 31–2.

'Environment and Ideology in Australian Literature: A Personal View, Literary Australia': [Papers from Seminar of Literature in Australia, University of New England, January 1965] edited by Clement Semmler and Derek Whitelock, Melbourne, 1966, pp. 69–80.

'Stalin's Heirs', *Sunday Times* (London), published over a four-week period, commencing early November 1968.

'Stalin's Heirs', reprinted in the *Bulletin*, published over a four-week period, first article 11 January 1969.

'Page from a Diary', *Australian Left Review*, No. 6, 1969, pp. 34–5; *Australian Author*, Vol. 2, No. 3, 1970, pp. 40–2.

'The life and hard times of John Wren revisited', *The Review*, 20–6 November 1971, pp. 186–7.

'Researching *Power Without Glory*', *The Review*, 27 November–3 December 1971, p. 218. (Excerpts from *The Hard Way*.)

'Patrick White Needs No Mates', *Bulletin*, 3 April 1976, pp. 80–1.

'Relevance', *Australian Author*, Vol. 8, No. 3, 1976, pp. 8–9.

'Series Made Against the Stream', letter, *Australian*, 16 May 1977, p. 6.

'Authors' Statements—Frank Hardy', *Australian Literary Studies*, Vol. 10, No. 2, October 1981, pp. 201–3.

'Self-Portraits', *Australian Book Review*, No. 51, 1983, pp. 13–14.

'The Prophet Without Glory', *Sydney Morning Herald*, 21 July 1984, p. 38.
'Lawson v. Kramer: No contest', letter, *Sydney Morning Herald*, 24 April 1985, p. 10.
'In fear of a town called Welfare', *Bulletin*, 24 September 1985, pp. 64–74.
'Fella Slave', *Australian* Literary Quarterly 3, 3–4 October 1987.
'As a Prime Minister, Bonnie Bob Makes a Great Printer', *People*, 23 August 1988, p. 29.
'Mary Returns', Melbourne *Herald-Sun*, 2 April 1991, p. 91.
'My Old Mate', Melbourne *Herald-Sun*, 2 June 1991.
'ASIO and I', *Sydney Morning Herald*, 21 March 1992, p. 41; 'How ASIO Spied on Me', *Age* Agenda 5, 22 March 1992.
'ASIO Unlikely to Get Extension to 30-Year Access Rule on Files', *Sydney Morning Herald*, 30 March 1992, p. 15.
'Nellie West's Adultery: Truth or Police Plot?', *Sydney Morning Herald*, 17 April 1992, p. 9.
'Frank Hardy unveils the haunting "Nellie"', *West Australian* Big Weekend Features 5, 9 May 1992.
'Mary, My Mary', *Australian* Magazine, 23–4 May 1992, pp. 8–12.
'Frank Hardy's Last Blast in Defence of Truth', *Age*, 3 February 1994, p. 14.

Statement re the preceding items
Frank Hardy was a member of the editorial committee of the Realist Writers' Group, Sydney, from 1958 until 1966. His editorial comments have not been documented in the above listing, with the exception of 'Two Fair Dinkum People—Welcome to Soviet Writers, *Realist Writer*, Vol. 1, August 1960, pp. 3–5. Note that the *Realist Writer* underwent a name change; it became *The Realist* in March 1964, No. 14.

Frank Hardy contributed to the CPA weekly *Guardian* from the mid 1940s under the pseudonym of Ross Franklyn, and later under the name of Frank Hardy. He also wrote the racing column under one or two pseudonyms. Unattributed articles written by Hardy were published in the *Guardian* during the 1940s and 1950s; these have not been documented. From the 1950s he contributed articles to the CPA national weekly *Tribune*, and these have also not been documented.

From the mid-1940s until *c.* 1950–51, Frank Hardy wrote for and produced the trotting paper the *Beam*.

It is not purported that the articles, short stories and letters published in journals and newspapers above are a complete listing of Hardy's prolific output in these and other publications. Without access to Hardy's papers in the NLA and the ADFA, efforts have been made to locate those which were considered to be most significant.

Troppo Tribune
Photo-copies in author's collection. Supplied by NLA from Box 105, Hardy Papers.
Priceless—Pte F. J. Hardy, *The Troppo Tribune*, Vol. 5, No. 5 (Number 45), Monday, 25 October 1943. The editorial introduces and is signed by the new editor, 'Judge Hardy' (Frank Hardy); two foolscap pages.
Editor: Cpl Hardy, F. J., Priceless. *The Troppo Tribune*, New Series Number 1. Monday, 19 June 1944. Date amended in handwriting to 26 June 1944; two foolscap pages.

Salt
During his army service Frank Hardy worked as an illustrator on *Salt*, the Australian Army Education Service journal, from November 1944 until his discharge in February 1946. Many of the drawings in *Salt* were not identified.

Vane Lindesay and Ambrose Dyson were the principal artists; Hardy's main contribution was to draw the dinkuses.

Centre-fold cartoon strip 'Salt Artist is Back in the Big Smoke', pp. 32–3, signed Hardy, n.d. Photo-copy in author's collection.

Salt, Vol. 11, No. 6, 19 November 1945. Article on test cricket attributed to *Salt* Sports Reporter—possibly Frank Hardy. The sketch at the top of the article (pp. 16–17) is signed 'F. Hardy'. Article on p. 7 has an illustration (pen drawing) of Victoria Cross winner Captain C. H. Upham, signed 'Hardy'. Some of the dinkuses in this issue appear to be Hardy's work. Drawings by Ambrose Dyson appear throughout this issue. The dinkuses on pp. 6 and 8 are signed 'L' (probably Vane Lindesay). Original journal in author's collection.

CD–ROM Austlit as at January 1997
The CD–ROM *Austlit* records 297 items which relate to Frank Hardy. Included in this list are 123 short stories written by Hardy. Hardy stated, in an interview with Andrea Stretton on SBS television 'Masterpiece' program, 6 February 1994 (broadcast after his death), that he had written 600 short stories. It is assumed that many of these have not been published. Most of the short stories listed in the CD–ROM appear in Hardy's short story collections as identified in the relevant bibliography entry.

SONGS
'Hannah's Song' lyrics.
'Sydney Town' lyrics. This song reached the hit parade; frequently sung by performers Gary Shearston and Rolf Harris.

TELEVISION

Television panellist
Would you believe it? television series, 1970–74. Hardy was one of the panellists.

Television adaptations of Hardy's work
ABV2—*The Yarns of Billy Borker* (First of series commenced 14 September 1964—refer *TV Times* of 9 September 1964. A second series commenced 20 October 1965—refer *TV Times* of 13 October 1965.)
ABV2—Thirteen-part drama of *Power Without Glory* (1976).

CARTOONS
October 1937, Caricatures of the Committee of the Bacchus Marsh Branch, Returned Services League. Photo-copy in the author's possession.
Bacchus Marsh Express published Hardy's early cartoons and sketches, but he rarely received payment. Copies of the newspapers are held by the Bacchus Marsh Historical Society in the Bacchus Marsh Library.

Radio Times and Mid-day Times
Radio Times and *Mid-day Times* were published during the 1930s and 1940s by Harry Drysdale Bett. Bett waged an ongoing struggle for access to newsprint supplies which were controlled by a consortium dominated by Sir Keith Murdoch, owner of the *Herald & Weekly Times Ltd*. Bett maintained a long struggle to have his newspapers sold through normal outlets.

Photocopies of Frank Hardy's cartoons and sketches in the *Radio Times* are in the author's collection. Source: *Radio Times Collection*, Arts Library and La Trobe Newspaper Collection, State Library of Victoria.

Permission to copy the Frank Hardy cartoons and sketches in the *Mid-Day Times* was refused as the newspapers were in a fragile condition. The collection was incomplete. La Trobe Newspaper Collection, State Library of Victoria.

Works by other writers

BOOKS

Aarons, Eric. *What's Left?* Penguin Books Australia Ltd, Ringwood, Victoria, 1993.

Adams, Paul. *The Stranger from Melbourne, Frank Hardy—A Literary Biography 1945–1975*, University of Western Australia, Nedlands, Western Australia, p. 76.

Arena Publication, *Essays on Socialist Realism and the British Cultural Tradition*. Fore Publications Ltd, London, n.d.

Anderson, Don. *Real Opinions*. Mcphee Gribble, Penguin Books Australia Ltd, Ringwood, Victoria, 1986.

——. *Hot Copy. Reading and Writing Now*. Penguin Books Australia Ltd, Ringwood, Victoria, 1986.

Atkinson, Anne, general editor. *What Went Wrong?* The Fairfax Library, Annandale, NSW, 1987.

Beasley, Jack. *Red Letter Days*. Australasian Book Society, Sydney, 1979.

——. *Journal of an Era*. With introduction by John Docker. Wedgetail Press, Earlwood, NSW, 1988.

Becker, George J. *Documents of Modern Literary Realism*. Princeton University Press, Princeton, New Jersey, 1965. Contains item on Socialist Realism by Maxim Gorky and others.

Blake, Audrey. *A Proletarian Life*. Kibble Books, Malmsbury, Victoria, n.d., published *c*. 1973.

Blake, Patricia, and Hayward, Max (eds). *Dissonant Voices in Soviet Literature*. George Allen and Unwin Ltd, London, 1964.

Bottom, Bob, with Silvester, John. *Inside Victoria*. Pan Macmillan Publishers Australia, Chippendale, NSW, 1991.

Brennan, Niall. *John Wren, Gambler: His Life and Times*. Hill of Content Publishing Co. Pty Ltd, Melbourne, 1971.

——. *The Politics of Catholics*, Hill publishing, Melbourne, 1972.

Broome, Richard. *Tracing Past Lives*. The History Institute, Victoria Inc., Carlton, Victoria, 1993.

Browne, Geoff. *Biographical Register of the Victorian Parliament 1900–84*. F. D. Atkinson, Government Printer, Melbourne, 1985.

Brown, W. J. *The Communist Movement and Australia*. Australian Labor Movement History Publications, Haymarket, NSW, 1986.

Buggy, Hugh. *The Real John Wren*. Widescope International Publishers Pty Ltd, Camberwell, Victoria, 1977.

Burren, Pauline B. *Mentone—The Place For A School—A History of Mentone Girls' Grammar School from 1899*. Hyland House Publishing Pty Limited, South Yarra, Victoria, 1984.

Calwell, A. A. *Be Just and Fear Not*. Lloyd O'Neil Pty Ltd, Hawthorn, Australia, 1972. Mention is made of Dr Mannix and *Power Without Glory*, see pp. 152–3.

Camm, Geoffrey (comp.). *Bacchus Marsh by Bacchus Marsh. An Anecdotal History*. Hargreen Publishing Company, North Melbourne, Victoria, 1986.

Cannon, Michael. *The Human Face of the Great Depression*. Self-published, Mornington, Victoria, 1996.

——. *That disreputable firm . . . the inside story of Slater & Gordon*. Melbourne University Press, Carlton South, Victoria, 1998.

Capp, Fiona. *Writers Defiled*. Mcphee Gribble, Penguin Books Australia Ltd, Ringwood, Victoria, 1993.

Carlson, Julia, edited for *Article 19*. *Banned in Ireland—Censorship & the Irish Writer*. Routledge, London, 1990.

Carter, David. *A Career in Writing. Judah Waten and the Cultural Politics of a Literary Career.* Association for the Study of Australian Literature, Toowoomba, Queensland, 1997.

Childs, Kevin. *A Month of Lunches.* Oxford University Press, Melbourne, 1984.

Close, Robert L. *Love Me Sailor.* White Lion Publishers Limited, London, 1972. First published, W. H. Allen, London, 1948.

——. *Of Salt and Earth, an autobiography.* Thomas Nelson (Australia) Limited, West Melbourne, Victoria, 1977.

Cook, Peter. *Red Barrister: A Biography of Ted Laurie.* La Trobe University Press, Bundoora, Victoria, 1994.

Curthoys, Ann, and Merritt, John. *Australia's First Cold War Vol.1. Society, Communism and Culture.* George Allen & Unwin Australia Pty Ltd, North Sydney, NSW, 1984.

Daniel, Helen (comp.). *The Good Reading Guide.* McPhee Gribble Publishers, Melbourne, 1989. This publication contains reviews by various contributors of a number of Frank Hardy's books.

D'Aprano, Zelda. *Zelda.* Spinifex Press Pty Ltd, North Melbourne, Victoria, 1995. First published by Zelda D'Aprano, 1977.

Davidson, A. *The Communist Party of Australia.* Hoover Institution Press, Stanford, US, 1969.

Davidson, Jim. *Lyrebird Rising.* Melbourne University Press, Carlton, Victoria, 1994.

Davies, Lloyd. *In Defence Of My Family.* Pepper Gully Press, Peppermint Grove, WA, 1987. Davies is the former husband of writer Dorothy Hewett.

Devanny, Jean (ed. Carole Ferrier). *Point of Departure.* University of Queensland Press, Queensland, 1986.

Dutton, Geoffrey. *The Australian Collection—Australia's Greatest Books.* Angus & Robertson Publishers, North Ryde, NSW, 1992.

——. *The Literature of Australia.* Penguin Books, Ringwood, Victoria, 1964.

——. *The Literature of Australia.* Penguin Books, Ringwood, Victoria, 1982.

Duwell, Martin, and Hergenhan, Laurie (eds). *The ALS Guide to Australian Writers.* University of Queensland Press, St Lucia, Queensland, 1992.

Encyclopaedia Britannica, Vol. 11, Encyclopaedia Britannica Ltd, London, 1959.

English, Horace B., and English, Ava C. *Comprehensive Dictionary of Psychological and Psychoanalytical Terms.* David McKay Inc., New York, 1962.

Ewers, John K. *Creative Writing in Australia.* Georgian House Pty Ltd, Melbourne, 1966.

Faine, Jon. *Taken On Oath: A Generation of Lawyers.* The Federation Press, Leichardt, NSW, 1992.

Fast, Howard. *Literature and Reality.* Current Book Distributors, Sydney, 1952. First published in New York, 1950.

Ferrier, Carole (ed.). *Gender, Politics and Fiction: Twentieth Century Australian Women's Novels.* University of Queensland Press, St Lucia, Queensland, 1985.

——. *Jean Devanny Romantic Revolutionary.* Melbourne University Press, Carlton South, Victoria, 1999.

Fox, Len. *Broad Left, Narrow Left.* Len Fox, Chippendale, NSW, 1982.

Frow, John. *Marxism and Literary History.* Harvard University Press, Cambridge, Massachusetts, 1986.

Garaudy, Roger. *From Anathema to Dialogue: The Challenge of Marxist–Christian Cooperation,* Collins, London, 1967.

Gibson, Ralph. *My Years In The Communist Party.* International Bookshop, Melbourne, 1966.

——. *One woman's life: A memoir of Dorothy Gibson.* Hale & Iremonger Pty Limited, Sydney, 1980.

——. *The People Stand Up*. Red Rooster Press, Ascot Vale, Victoria, 1983.

——. *The Fight Goes On*. Red Rooster Press, Ascot Vale, Victoria, 1987.

Gollan, Robin. *Revolutionaries and Reformists*. Australian National University Press, Canberra, 1975.

Green, Clif. *The Four Scripts*. Hyland House Publishing Pty Ltd, Melbourne, 1978. Green wrote the script for the *Power Without Glory* television series.

Green, H. M. *A History of Australian Literature*, Volume II, 1923–1950. Angus & Robertson, Sydney, 1961.

Griffin, James. *Australian Dictionary of Biography*, Vol. 12: 1891–1939. Melbourne University Press, Carlton, Victoria, 1990.

Hamilton, Ian. *Keepers of The Flame—Literary Estates and the Rise of Biography*. Random House UK Ltd, London, 1992.

Hamilton, K. G. (ed.). *Studies in the Recent Australian Novel*. University of Queensland Press, St Lucia, Queensland, 1978.

Hardy, Frank J. See Works of Frank Hardy in this bibliography.

Hergenhan, Laurie. *The Penguin New Literary History of Australia*. Penguin Books, Ringwood, Victoria, 1988.

Hetherington, John. *Forty-Two Faces*. F. W. Cheshire Pty Ltd, Melbourne, 1962.

Hewett, Dorothy. *Wild Card*. McPhee Gribble, Ringwood, Victoria, 1991.

Hollows, Fred, with Corris, Peter. *Fred Hollows: An Autobiography*. Kerr Publishing Pty Ltd, Balmain, NSW, 1992.

——. *Fred Hollows—the updated autobiography*. Kerr Publishing Pty Ltd, Balmain, NSW, 1992.

Howells, A. F. *Against the Stream*. Hyland House Publishing Pty Ltd, South Yarra, Victoria, 1983.

Huelin, Frank. *Keep Moving*. Penguin Books Australia Limited, Ringwood, Victoria, 1983.

Inglis, Amirah. *Amirah: An un-Australian Childhood*. William Heinemann Australia, Richmond, Victoria, 1983.

——. *The Hammer & Sickle and the Washing Up*. Hyland House Publishing Pty Limited, South Melbourne, 1995.

Inglis, K. S., assisted by Brazier, Jan. *This is the A.B.C.—Australian Broadcasting Commission 1932–1983*. Melbourne University Press, Carlton, Victoria, 1983.

Inglis Moore, T. *Social Patterns in Australian Literature*. Angus & Robertson (Publishers) Pty Ltd, Sydney, 1971.

Johnston, George. *My Brother Jack*. Collins, London and Sydney, 1964.

Jones, Joseph, and Jones, Johanna. *Australian Fiction*. Twayne Publishers, Boston, Mass., 1983.

Jory, Colin. *The Campion Society*. Harphan Pty Limited, Kogarah, NSW, 1986.

Jupp, James. *Australian Party Politics*. Melbourne University Press, Carlton, Victoria, 1968.

Kinnane, Garry. *George Johnston A Biography*. Nelson Publishers, Melbourne, Victoria, 1986.

Koestler, A., et al. *The God that Failed: Six Studies in Communism*. Hamish Hamilton, London, 1950.

Kramer, Leonie (ed.). *The Oxford History of Australian Literature*. Oxford University Press, Melbourne, 1981.

Lindsay, Jack. *Decay and Renewal—Critical Essays on Twentieth Century Writing*. Wild & Woolley Limited, Glebe, NSW, and London, 1976.

——. *Life Rarely Tells*. Penguin Books Australia Limited, Ringwood, Victoria, 1982.

MacCallum, Mungo. *Planckton's Luck: A life in retrospect*, Century Australia Pty Ltd, Hawthorn, Victoria, 1986.

McCalman, Janet. *Struggletown.* Penguin Books Australia Ltd, Ringwood, Victoria, 1988. [First edition 1984, revised edition 1988.]

Macintyre, Stuart. *The Reds.* Allen & Unwin, St Leonards, NSW, 1998.

McKenzie, John A. *Challenging Faith.* Fremantle Arts Centre Press, South Fremantle, WA, 1993.

McKernan, Susan. *A Question of Commitment.* Allen & Unwin Australia Pty Ltd, North Sydney, NSW, 1989.

McLaren, John. *Writing in Hope and Fear.* Cambridge University Press, Oakleigh, Victoria, 1996.

Marshall, Vance (James). *The World of the Living Dead* and *Jail From Within.* Wentworth Press, Sydney, 1969. *The World of the Living Dead* first published in Sydney in 1919.

——. *Jail From Within.* The Workers' Trade Union Print, St Andrew's Place, Sydney, 1918.

Martin, David. *My Strange Friend.* Pan Macmillan Publishers Australia, Chippendale, NSW, 1991.

Matthews, Brian. *Louisa.* McPhee Gribble/Penguin, Fitzroy, Victoria, 1988.

Merewether, Charles. *Art & Social Commitment: An end to the city of dreams 1931–1948.* Art Gallery of New South Wales, Sydney, n.d., c. 1984.

Modjeska, Drusilla. *Exiles At Home.* Angus & Robertson Publishers, Sydney, 1981.

Morrison, Elizabeth, and Talbot, Michael (eds). *Books, Libraries & Readers in Colonial Australia.* Graduate School of Librarianship, Monash University, Clayton, Victoria, 1985.

Niall, Brenda. *Martin Boyd: a Life.* Melbourne University Press, Carlton, Victoria, 1989. First published 1988.

——. *Georgiana.* Melbourne University Press, Carlton, Victoria, 1995. First published 1994.

Noone, Val. *Disturbing The War—Melbourne Catholics and Vietnam.* Spectrum Publications, Richmond, Victoria, 1993.

O'Farrell, Patrick. *The Irish in Australia.* New South Wales University Press, Kensington, NSW, 1988. First published 1986.

O'Leary, Zoë. *The Desolate Market: A Biography of Eric Lambert.* Edwards & Shaw Pty Ltd, Sydney, 1974.

O'Lincoln, Tom. *Into the Mainstream—The Decline of Australian Communism.* Stained Wattle Press, Westgate, NSW, 1985.

Ross, John (Editor-in-Chief). *Chronicle of the 20th Century.* Chronicle Australia Pty Ltd, Ringwood, Victoria, 1990.

Rowse, Tim. *Australian Liberalism and National Character.* Kibble Books, Malmsbury, Victoria, 1978.

Santamaria, B. A. *Against the Tide.* Oxford University Press, Melbourne, 1981.

——. *Santamaria A Memoir.* Oxford University Press, South Melbourne, Victoria, 1997.

Searle, N. E. (publishing director). *Notable Australians, The Pictorial Who's Who.* Prestige Publishing Division, Paul Hamlyn, Sydney, 1978.

Semmler, Clement. *The Art of Brian James and Other Essays on Australian Literature.* University of Queensland Press, St Lucia, Queensland, 1972.

——. *Pictures on the Margin: Memoirs.* University of Queensland Press, St Lucia, Queensland, 1991.

Semmler, Clement, and Whitelock, Derek (eds.). *Literary Australia.* F. W. Cheshire Pty Ltd, Melbourne, 1966.

Sendy, John, *Ralph Gibson. An Extraordinary Communist.* Ralph Gibson Biography Committee, Melbourne, 1988.

——. *Melbourne's Radical Bookshops.* International Bookshop Pty Ltd, Brunswick, Victoria, 1983.

——. *Comrades Come Rally*. Thomas Nelson Australia Pty Ltd, West Melbourne, Victoria, 1978.

Shapcott, Thomas. *The Literature Board: A Brief History*. University of Queensland Press, St Lucia, Queensland, 1988.

Shelston, Alan. *Biography*. Methuen, London and New York, 1977.

Smith, Bernard. *Noel Counihan, Artist and Revolutionary*. Oxford University Press Australia, South Melbourne, Victoria, 1993.

Stivens, Dal. *Coast to Coast, Australian Stories of Today*. Halstead Press, Sydney, 1958.

Symons, Beverley, with Wells, Andrew, and Macintyre, Stuart. *Communism in Australia*. National Library of Australia, Canberra, ACT, 1994.

Taft, Bernie. *Crossing the Party Line*. Scribe Publications, Newham, Victoria, 1994.

Torre, Stephen. *The Australian Short Story 1940–1980, A Bibliography*. Hale & Iremonger Pty Limited, Sydney, 1984.

Uren, Tom. *Straight Left*. Random House Australia Pty Ltd, Milson's Point, NSW, 1994.

Wallace-Crabbe, Chris. *Falling into Language*. Oxford University Press, Melbourne, Victoria, 1990.

Wilde, William H., Hooton, Joy, and Andrews, Barry. *The Oxford Companion to Australian Literature*. Oxford University Press, Melbourne, 1986.

Wilde, W. H., and T. Inglis Moore (eds). *Letters of Mary Gilmore*. Melbourne University Press, Carlton, Victoria, 1980.

Wills, Nancy. *Shades of Red*. Communist Arts Group, Lota, Queensland, 1980.

Yeats, W. B. *Autobiographies*. Macmillan and Company, London, 1966.

JOURNAL ARTICLES AND REVIEWS

Carter, David. 'Re-Viewing Communism: *Communist Review* (Sydney), 1934–1966: A Checklist of Literary Material', *Australian Literary Studies*, Vol. 12, No. 1: May 1985, pp. 93–105.

Cato, Nancy. 'New Fiction', *Australian Book Review*, Vol. 1, No. 8, June 1963, p. 127.

Docker, John. 'A Study in Context: *And the Dead are Many*', *Arena*, No. 41, 1976, pp. 48–61.

Ellis, M. H. 'The Writing of Australian Biographies', *Australian Historical Studies*, Vol. 6, No. 124, May 1955, pp. 432–46.

Forrest, David. 'Poles Apart', *Overland*, No. 29, Autumn 1964, p. 1.

Frow, John. 'Who Shot Frank Hardy? Intertextuality and Textual Politics', *Southern Review*, Vol. 15, No. 1, March 1982, pp. 22–39.

Lindesay, Vane. 'Kismet Hardy', *Australian Book Review*, No. 78, February–March 1986, pp. 14–15.

McLaren, John. 'Comment', *Overland*, No. 135, Winter 1994, pp. 61–2.

——. 'Missed Opportunities', *Overland*, No. 22, Summer 1961–62, p. 49.

Mortimer, Rex. 'The Story of *The Hard Way*', The Realist Writer, No. 7, October 1971, pp. 18–20.

Rowse, Tim. 'Jack Beasley's *Red Letter Days*', *New Literature Review*, No. 6, 1979, pp. 40–4.

Semmler, Clement. 'Record of a Life', *Australian Author*, Summer issue, January 1971, pp. 5–10.

Sendy, John. 'What Democratic Centralism Is', *Communist Review*, No. 183, March 1957, pp. 92–5.

Symons, Beverley. 'All-Out For The People's War: Communist Soldiers in The Australian Army In The Second World War', *Australian Historical Studies*, Vol. 26, No. 105, October 1995, pp. 596–614.

Syson, Ian. 'Out From The Shadows: The Realist Writers' Movement 1944–1970, and Communist Cultural Discourse', *Australian Literary Studies*, Vol. 15, No. 4, October 1992, pp. 333–51.

Turner, Ian. 'My Long March', *Overland*, No. 59, Spring 1974, pp. 23–40.

Wilding, Michael. '*Journal of an Era: Notes from the Red Letter Days* by Jack Beasley', *Australian Literary Studies*, Vol. 14, No. 2, October 1989, pp. 264–5.

Williams, Peter. 'Plagiarism and Rewriting: The Case of Frank Hardy', *New Literature Review*, No. 10, 1982, pp. 45–53.

JOURNALS

Arena
Australian Author
Australian Book Review
Australian Historical Studies
Australian Left Review
Australian Literary Studies
Communist Review
Eureka Street
Labour History
Linq
Meanjin
New Literature Review
New Theatre Review
Overland
Quadrant
Realist Writer (Victoria)
Realist Writer (NSW)
The Realist (NSW)
Social Alternatives
Southerly
Southern Review
World News and Views (UK)
Write On

LEAFLETS AND MISCELLANEOUS PAPERS

Australasian Book Society—'SENSATIONAL BOOK NEWS'. A three-page newsletter outlines that this was the first serious attempt to bring the books that people want to the people that want them. An Enrolment Form addressed to: The Australasian Book Society, Room 90, Third Floor, Collins House, 360 Collins Street, Melbourne, Vic., was issued with the leaflet, *c.* 1952. There was no joining fee and subscribers were required to pay fifty shillings to cover the estimated cost of six books. The address shown on the form was that of Joseph Waters, book distributor. Photo-copy in author's collection.

Australasian Book Society News Bulletin announces that Ralph de Boissière's *Crown Jewel* and Frank Hardy's *Journey Into The Future* were ready. It is also announced that Peter Pinney's *Road In The Wilderness* was to be available in the October–November Selection. Page two of the News Bulletin listed other books available at a reduced price for members: Eric Lambert, *Twenty Thousand Thieves*, 12/6d.; Zaharia Stancu, *Barefoot*, 10/6d.; David Martin, *Stones of Bombay*, 7/6d.; John A. Lee, *Children of the Poor*, 10/-d.; Judah Waten, *Alien Son*, 11/6d.; Wilfred Burchett, *Peoples' Democracies*, 5/-d.; Wilfred Burchett, *Cold War in Germany*, 5/-d. The *ABS* announced that it was a non-profit-making venture, and that it was hoped that the membership would reach 5000 members in the first twelve months. This leaflet was printed by the CPA's

Coronation Press Pty Ltd, 1952. Photo-copy in author's collection. (Imperial Currency: 12d (12 pence) = one shilling; 20 shillings = 1 pound (£1). In 1966 decimal currency was introduced in Australia—£1 then became $2.)

Australasian Book Society Enrolment Form leaflet. The photograph on the front page shows 'Popular writer Frank Hardy addressing a factory gate meeting on the Australasian Book Society', c. 1952–53. Photo-copy of double-sided leaflet in author's collection.

A later Australasian Book Society leaflet shows subscribers were entitled to four books and four issues of *Overland* for the sum of fifty shillings, or twelve shillings and sixpence for each book, c. 1954. The books listed on this leaflet show No. 15, Judah Waten, *Shares in Murder*; No. 16, Henry Lawson, *The Men Who Made Australia*; No. 17, A. A. Phillips, *The Australian Tradition*; No. 18, F. B. Vickers, *Though Poppies Grow*. Photo-copy in author's collection.

Frank Hardy Defence Committee Receipt No. J.18, Collection List No. 824, dated 18 October 1951, issued to Mr. G. Armstrong for the sum of twelve shillings, dated 18 October 1951, and signed by Jack Coffey for the Frank Hardy Defence Committee. The collection of donations continued after Hardy's acquittal in June 1951. At the time this receipt was issued, Frank and Rosslyn Hardy had gone to London and Europe. Original receipt in author's collection, courtesy of the late Gough Armstrong.

'WE DEFEND *FRANK HARDY*—AUTHOR OF "POWER WITHOUT GLORY".' Issued by The Frank Hardy Defence Committee and printed by the Capricorn Printing Co., 106 Liddiard Street, Auburn. Photo-copy of double-sided leaflet in author's collection.

'WHY IS . . . FRANK HARDY Author of "POWER WITHOUT GLORY" *BRANDED* GUILTY *BEFORE* TRIAL?' Issued by The Frank Hardy Defence Committee and printed by The Realist Printing and Publishing Co., Melbourne. Original double-sided leaflet in author's collection.

Tourist Brochure, Koroit Hotel, Koroit, proprietor Mick Bourke (cousin to Frank Hardy). Original in author's collection.

MAGAZINES, PERIODICALS AND NEWSLETTERS

Australasian Post
Australian Women's Weekly
Beacon (Journal of the Unitarian Church, Melbourne)
Bulletin
Nation
New Idea
People
Prime Time (Over 50s Magazine)
The Battler (Trotskyist publication)
The Hummer (Newsletter of the Sydney Branch, Australian Society for the Study of Labour History)
The Recorder (Newsletter of the Melbourne Branch of the Australian Society for the Study of Labour History Inc.)
News Weekly
The Troppo Tribune
TV Times
Soviet News Bulletin, Soviet Embassy, Canberra, ACT

NEWSPAPERS

Adelaide Advertiser
Advocate (Melbourne)
Age (Melbourne)

Argus (Melbourne)
Australian
Australian Financial Review
Bacchus Marsh Express
Telegraph (Bacchus Marsh)
Courier Mail (Brisbane)
Sentinel (Brunswick)
Canberra Times
Daily Mirror (Sydney)
Daily Telegraph (London)
Farrago (University of Melbourne SRC)
Footscray Mail
Guardian (CPA Melbourne Weekly)
Guardian Weekly (UK)
Herald (Melbourne)
Herald-Sun (Melbourne)
Independent Australian
Land Rights News (Northern Territory)
Leader (early Brunswick and Coburg paper)
Melbourne Times which incorporates Melbourne Review
Mid-day Times (Melbourne)
Nation Review
National Times
Newswit (Media Students', NSW Institute of Technology)
Radio Times (Melbourne)
Review (Melbourne)
Smith's Weekly (National)
Southern Cross (Prahran and District)
Sun (Melbourne)
Sunday Mail (Adelaide)
Sun-Herald (Sydney)
Sydney Morning Herald
Times (London)
Townsville Bulletin
Tribune (CPA National Weekly)
Truth (Melbourne Weekly)
Vanguard (CPA Marxist-Leninist Party Newspaper)
Waverley Gazette
West Australian
Western Independent (Melton/Bacchus Marsh Edition)
Western Times (Footscray/Williamstown District)

OFFICIAL SOURCES

Allansford State School
Anglican Parish of Kilmore
Australian Broadcasting Commission Archives, Sydney
Bacchus Marsh Historical Society
Fawkner Crematorium and Memorial Park
Infant Jesus Catholic Church, Koroit
Mentone Girls' Grammar School
Registry of Births, Deaths and Marriages, Melbourne
St Brendan's Catholic Church, Kilmore
Seamen's Union Employment Records
Soldier Career Management Agency

St Joseph's Catholic Church, Warrnambool
St Joseph's Convent, Bacchus Marsh
Treacy Centre, Christian Brothers College, Parkville
University of Melbourne, Student Records

PAMPHLETS AND BOOKLETS

Australian Society for the Study of Labour History, Melbourne, 1988. *Celebration of Fred Farrall's 90th Birthday.*

Barnes, Les. *Annals of the ACP* [Australian Communist Party, a name adopted by the CPA for some of its life], no publisher, date or page numbers. 1944?

Communist Party of Australia (?). *Catholic Action at Work.* International Bookshop Pty Ltd, n.d. [*c.* 1945–46]

Gorky, Maxim. *Creative Labour and Culture.* Current Book Distributors, Sydney, 1945.

Gould, L. Harry. *Art, Science and Communism.* Current Book Distributors, Sydney, 1946.

Love, Margaret. *A History of St. Bernard's Church, Bacchus Marsh,* 1874–1974. Bacchus Marsh Parish Council, Bacchus Marsh, 1974.

Mortier, Paul. *Danger NCC At Work.* Current Book Distributors, Sydney, 1962.

Nicolls, Yvonne. *Not Slaves, Not Citizens.* Australian Council for Civil Liberties, Melbourne, 1952.

O'Leary, Mary Agatha. *'Till The Shades Lengthen'—Caritas Christi Hospice, Kew. 1938–1988.* Publisher unnamed.

Wheelahan, L. F. *A Century of Dedicated Service in Bacchus Marsh.* Bacchus Marsh, Victoria: L. F. Wheelahan for St Bernard's Parish, Bacchus Marsh, 1990.

Zhdanov, A. A. *On Literature, Music and Philosophy.* Lawrence & Wishart Ltd, London, 1950.

PROGRAMMES OF SERVICES IN CELEBRATION OF THE LIFE OF FRANK HARDY

Order of Service for Frank Hardy's funeral and celebration of his life, held at the Collingwood Town Hall, 4 February 1994. Original in author's collection.

Order of Service for 'Celebration of the life of Frank Hardy' held in Sydney, 13 March 1994. Original in author's collection, courtesy of Vera Deacon.

UNPUBLISHED WORKS

Unpublished documents

Gallacher Papers, CP/IND/GALL/04/03, Labour History and Research Centre, Manchester, UK. Courtesy of Phillip Deery.

W. G. Smith: signed statement regarding the events surrounding his visit with Frank Hardy to Jim Loughnan, Richmond, when they discussed the events associated with the publication of *Power Without Glory.* W. G. Smith gave one signed copy to Frank Hardy; this is now in his papers at NLA. The other signed copy is in author's collection, courtesy of W. G. Smith.

List of names of characters in *Power Without Glory* identifying them with real-life people. These lists were printed by wax stencil duplicating machine onto foolscap paper; a copy is in author's collection. Others were typed with carbon copy duplicates; a copy is also in author's collection. These were sold and distributed clandestinely. Frank Hardy has always asserted that he had nothing to do with the production or the sale of the lists.

Unpublished memoirs
Blake, Audrey, 'Notes on the Development of the Eureka Youth League and Its Predecessors', unpublished manuscript, EYL Papers, University of Melbourne Archives. Copy in the author's collection.
Ralph, Cedric, 'Political Struggles', Vol. 2, Chapter 2. Copy in the author's collection.

Unpublished theses
Adams, Paul, The Author as Producer: Frank Hardy and Socialist Realism, MA, Monash University, 1988.
Adams, Paul, The Stranger From Melbourne Crisis and Modernism in the Writings of Frank Hardy: A Literary Biography 1944–1975, PhD, Monash University, 1997.
Armstrong, Pauline, A Critical Biography of Frank Hardy, PhD, University of Melbourne, 1997.
Cavenagh, R. H., The fiction of Frank Hardy, B.Litt., University of New England, 1972.
Hutton, Margaret, Autobiography and History: A Study of the Autobiographies of Communists and Ex-Communists, BA Hons, La Trobe University, 1992.
Kinnane, Garry, A Critical Biography of George Johnson, PhD, University Melbourne, 1988. (Kinnane had previously published *George Johnston A Biography*, Nelson Publishers, Melbourne, Victoria, 1986.)
Symons, Beverley, All-out for the People's War: 'Red Diggers' in the Armed Forces and the Communist Party of Australia's policies in the Second World War, BA Hons, University of Wollongong, 1993.
Syson, Ian, Tracing the Making of Australian Working Class Literature, PhD, University of Queensland, 1993.

AUDIO-VISUAL MATERIAL

Audio cassettes
1976: Council of Adult Education 1976 Seminar (Monash University) *Power Without Glory*: Its historical significance.
Speakers: Niall Brennan, Frank Hardy, Dr June Hearn, Dr Lloyd Robson. (Copies of CAE cassettes—total of three.) Edited version. Class No. A899-63. HAR: COU 1976. Accession No. TC 3007.
Undated: Frank Hardy interview with Geoffrey Camm for *Bacchus Marsh by Bacchus Marsh*, Hargreen Publishing Company, North Melbourne, Victoria, 1986. Audio-tape courtesy of Geoffrey Camm.
8 December 1992: Radio National Law Report. Jon Faine interviews Frank Hardy and former Justice Sir John Starke.
15 July 1993: Doug Aiton interviews Frank Hardy on Radio 3LO programme, 'Personality of the week'.
9 November 1993: Fiona Capp interviewed by Terry Lane on Radio 3LO on *Writers Defiled*, published 1993.
29 January 1994: Radio National. The Daily Bread of Betrayal. Tom Morton talks to a number of writers about the moral difficulties of judging collaborators who informed on them to the Stasi (the East German secret police) in the old East Germany. He asks why some who were persecuted by the Stasi believe there should be retribution for those who informed on them.
4 February 1994: Radio 3LO from Collingwood Town Hall. Celebration of the life of Frank Hardy. Master of Ceremonies: Jon Faine. Speakers included: Jennie Barrington, Bob Brown (former Federal Labor Minister), Alan Hardy, Shirley Hardy-Rix, Gabi Hollows, Gough Whitlam and two representatives of the Gurindji people.

10 May 1994: Seminar, Victoria University of Technology, St Albans Campus. PhD candidate, Paul Adams: 'The Early Writings of Frank Hardy'.

16 April 1995: Radio National. Books and Writing: Ramona Koval interviews Helen Garner and Cassandra Pybus on the problems of writing biographical material where the people concerned are unwilling to co-operate.

Video cassettes

19 May 1968, Frank Hardy and Morris West were interviewed by Bob Sanders on the 'People' television series. The discussion centred on how the Communist and Catholic beliefs of the authors influenced their work. See report in the *Realist Writer*, No. 13, November 1963, pp. 20–2.

4 February 1992: Television Channel SBS 'Bookshow' program. Dinny O'Hearn talks to Frank Hardy.

29 January 1994: SBS Television News, 6.30 p.m. Report on Frank Hardy's death; shows Hardy and Barrington in a hall prior to the Federal elections of 13 March 1993.

4 February 1994: Television Channel ABV2 7 p.m. News. Celebration of Frank Hardy's Life, Collingwood Town Hall, includes Hardy family, Gabi Hollows, Gough Whitlam, and two Gurindji representatives from the Northern Territory. Program concludes with the singing of 'The Internationale'.

6 February 1994: Television Channel SBS 'Masterpiece' programme. Andrea Stretton talks to Frank Hardy. This was Hardy's last interview which had been recorded some time before his death. This documentary was written, produced and directed by Frank Heiman, as part of the Film Australia's series, Australian Biography. Executive Producer Sharon Connolly wrote, 'a TV series which takes a closer look at people who shaped 20th century Australian life'. (Film Australia, Vol. 8, Issue 2, May 1994, p. 1).

21 April 1994: Television Channel ABV2—'Bons Bons and Roses for Dorothy'. Frank Hardy appears in this profile of Dorothy Hewett.

3 May 1994: Television Channel Ten 5 p.m. News. Paul Gray, news commentator, claimed that Frank Hardy was not the sole author of *Power Without Glory*. This elicited an angry response from the Hardy family.

Transcript of television interview

Transcript of television channel ABV2 'Spectrum' series—Tony Morphett interviews 'Frank Hardy on Commitment', 28 September 1966. A copy in author's collection, courtesy of Geoff Harris, ABC Document Archives, Sydney.

INDEX